D1625973

Magicians of the Gods

GRAHAM HANCOCK

Magicians of the Gods

The forgotten wisdom of earth's lost civilisation

CORONET

First published in Great Britain in 2015 by Coronet
An imprint of Hodder & Stoughton
An Hachette UK company

1

A CIP catalogue record for this book is available from the British Library.

Hardback ISBN 978 1 444 77967 7
Trade Paperback ISBN 978 1 444 77968 4
Ebook ISBN 978 1 444 77969 1

Typeset in Minion Pro 10/13pt by
Palimpsest Book Production Limited, Falkirk, Stirlingshire

Printed and bound by Clays Ltd, St Ives plc

Hodder & Stoughton policy is to use papers that are natural, renewable
and recyclable products and made from wood grown in sustainable forests.
The logging and manufacturing processes are expected to conform to the
environmental regulations of the country of origin.

Hodder & Stoughton Ltd
Carmelite House
50 Victoria Embankment,
London EC4Y 0DZ

www.hodder.co.uk

For Santha, my soul mate.

Photo and Graphics Credits:

Photo credits:

All photos by **Santha Faiia** except:
Plates 1 and 62, **Nico Becker**, German Archaeological Institute, Orient Department.
Plate 7, **Klaus Schmidt**, German Archaeological Institute, Orient Department.
Plate 41: **Daniel Lohmann** who was also the excavator of the column drum. The astronomical interpretations of Pillar 43 at Gobekli Tepe, Plates 50 and 51, were rendered in graphic form by **Luke Hancock**.

Graphics credits:

Camron Wiltshire (www.sacredgeometryinternational.com): Figure numbers 1, 2, 3, 7, 10, 11, 12, 13, 14, 15, 16, 17, 18, 19 (with Randall Carlson), 20, 21, 22, 23, 24, 25, 26, 27, 32, 33, 34, 35, 36, 40, 41, 42, 43, 44, 45, 47, 48, 49, 51, 53 through 56 (with Afua Richardson), 57, 58, 59, 60, 61, 62, 63, 64, 65, 68, 69, 70, 71, 72.

Afua Richardson: Figure numbers 4, 8 (top row), 46 (with Luke Hancock), 50 (with Luke Hancock), 52, 53 through 56 (with Camron Wiltshire), 66 (with Luke Hancock).

Luke Hancock: Figure numbers 37, 38, 46 (with Afua Richardson), 50 (with Afua Richardson), 66 (with Afua Richardson), 67, 73.

Michael Mauldin: Figure numbers 6, 8 (lower row, right), 28, 29, 30.

Samuel Parker: Figure numbers 5, 8 (lower row, left)

Pon S. Purajatnika: Figure number 9.

Contents

Acknowledgements

First and foremost my love and appreciation to the photographer Santha Faiia, who honoured me twenty years ago by becoming my wife. She had her own successful career long before she met me, but she kindly agreed to work with me. Santha took the majority of the photographs in this book, as in so many of my previous books, and has travelled with me every step of the way on the long journey from *Fingerprints of the Gods* to *Magicians of the Gods*. Thank you! Thanks also to our children Sean, Shanti, Ravi, Leila, Luke and Gabrielle. While I was writing *Magicians* our first grandchild, Nyla, was born and it is a delight to welcome her to our big, boisterous family. Thanks too to my mum Muriel Hancock, and to my uncle James Macaulay, and I keep in my heart fond memories of my dad, Donald Hancock, who taught me so much and who passed away in 2003 after years of unstinting support for my work.

My brilliant literary agent Sonia Land has worked wonders and is everything a great agent should be. My UK editor Mark Booth and my US editor Peter Wolverton have both played hugely positive roles in nurturing *Magicians of the Gods* and putting it before the public in just the right way at just the right time.

The graphics team who created the maps, charts, drawings and diagrams for this book were Camron Wiltshire and Afua Richardson, with backup from Michael Maudlin and Samuel Parker. My son Luke Hancock also provided a number of diagrams. Each artist is acknowledged individually in the graphics credits but I want to thank them all collectively here for their dedication, talent, intelligence and hard work.

The late Professor Klaus Schmidt of the German Archaeological Institute went far above and beyond the call of duty when he showed me around Gobekli Tepe in Turkey in 2013. As the discoverer and excavator, Klaus possessed unique knowledge of this very special site that he generously shared with me during three days of visits and on-the-spot interviews. I regret his passing but trust that his name will be remembered by history.

I made a research visit to Lebanon in 2014. My work there was greatly facilitated by the kindness, good will and logistical support on the ground given by my friends Ramzi Najjar and Samir and Sandra Jarmakani. Subsequent to the trip I benefitted enormously from extensive correspondence concerning Baalbek with archaeologist and architect Daniel Lohmann. He was patient and persuasive in his valiant efforts to persuade me of the merits of the mainstream analysis.

In Indonesia special thanks go to Danny Hilman Natawidjaja, the excavator of the extraordinarily ancient pyramid site of Gunung Padang. Thanks also to his colleagues Wisnu Ariestika and Bambang Widoyko Suwargadi who joined us on an extensive field trip in Java, Sumatra, Flores and Sulawesi.

In the United States I am particularly grateful to Randall Carlson for his deep insights into catastrophist geology and for the knowledge he shared with me during our journey by road from Portland, Oregon, to Minneapolis, Minnesota, to study the effects on the land of the cataclysmic floods that afflicted this entire region at the end of the Ice Age. Thanks, too, to Bradley Young who accompanied us on the journey and did all the driving – a heroic effort!

I am grateful to Allen West, corresponding author amongst the large group of scientists investigating the Younger Dryas comet impact. I tell the story of their work at length in Chapters 3 through 6, and Allen was very helpful in ensuring that I got the facts right and in offering me further insights into the implications of the cataclysm.

Thanks also to Richard Takkou and Raymond Wiley for their sterling efforts as my research assistants at different stages of the project.

Many, many thanks to our dear friends Chris and Cathy Foyle for their solidarity and wise advice.

And last but not least, thanks to my loyal and supportive readers all around the world who have stuck with me for more than twenty years as I've pursued my quest for the lost civilization. *Magicians of the Gods* is the latest destination on that journey and while it is a new work I have inevitably, at a few points, had to revisit ground that I first explored in *Fingerprints of the Gods* and in my other books in order to place the new evidence I present here in its proper context.

Graham Hancock
Bath, England, September 2015

Introduction
Sand

A house raised on sand will always be in danger of collapse.

The evidence is mounting, though most of the later construction is of high quality, that the edifice of our past built by historians and archaeologists stands on defective and dangerously unsound foundations. An extinction-level cataclysm occurred on our planet between 12,800 and 11,600 years ago. This event was global in its consequences and it affected mankind profoundly. Because the scientific evidence that proves it happened has only emerged since 2007, and because its implications have not yet been taken into account at all by historians and archaeologists, we are obliged to contemplate the possibility that everything we have been taught about the origins of civilization could be wrong.

In particular it must be considered as a reasonable hypothesis that worldwide myths of a golden age brought to an end by flood and fire are true, and that an entire episode of the human story was rubbed out in those 1,200 cataclysmic years between 12,800 and 11,600 years ago – an episode not of unsophisticated hunter-gatherers but of advanced civilization.

Did that civilization, if it existed at all, leave any traces that we might still be able to identify today, despite the passage of so much time? And, if so, does its loss have any real significance for us?

This book is an attempt to answer those questions.

Part I

Anomalies

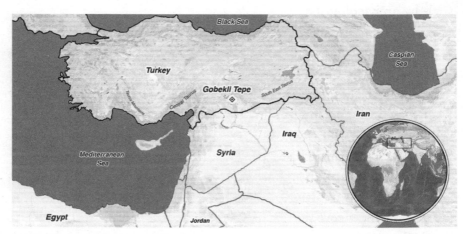
Figure 1: Location of Gobekli Tepe and its regional setting

Chapter 1
'There is so much mystery here . . .'

———◆———

Göbekli Tepe is the oldest work of monumental architecture so far found anywhere in the world, or at any rate the oldest accepted as such by archaeologists.

And it's *massive*.

Awesome, magnificent, numinous and overpowering are amongst the adjectives that dismally fail to do it justice. For the last couple of hours I've been wandering round the site with its excavator, Professor Klaus Schmidt, and my mind is frankly boggled.

'How does it feel,' I ask him, 'to be the man who discovered the temple that's rewriting history?'

A rubicund German archaeologist with a barrel chest and a grizzled beard, Schmidt is wearing faded jeans, a blue denim shirt with a streak of mud on the sleeve, and scuffed sandals on his bare, dirty feet. It's September 2013, three months before his sixtieth birthday and although neither of us know it yet, he'll be dead in less than a year.

As he ponders my question he wipes a bead of sweat from the glistening dome of his forehead. It's not yet mid-morning but the sun is high here in Turkey's Southeastern Anatolia region, the sky is cloudless and the ridge of the Taurus mountains on which we stand is baking hot. There's no breeze, not even a hint or a breath of air, nor is there any shade to be had. In 2014 a roof will be erected to cover and protect the site but in 2013 only its foundations are in place so we're standing exposed on a makeshift wooden walkway. Down below us in a series of semi-subterranean, more or less circular, walled enclosures are the dozens of giant T-shaped megalithic pillars that Schmidt and his team from the German Archaeological Institute have brought to light here. Before they began their work the place had the appearance of a rounded hill – in fact 'Göbekli Tepe' means 'Hill of the Navel'[1] sometimes also translated as 'Potbelly Hill'[2] – but the excavations have removed most of that original profile.

'Of course we cannot say that Göbekli Tepe is a temple exactly,' Schmidt answers eventually, obviously choosing his words with care. 'Let us call it a hill sanctuary. And I do not claim that it is rewriting history. Rather I would say that it is adding an important chapter to existing history. We thought that the transition from hunter-gatherers to farmers was a slow, step-by-step process, but now we realise that it was a period when exciting monuments that we didn't expect were made.'[3]

'And not just monuments,' I prompt. 'At the beginning the local people were hunter-gatherers and there was no sign of agriculture.'

'No,' Schmidt concedes, 'none.' He gestures expansively at the circles

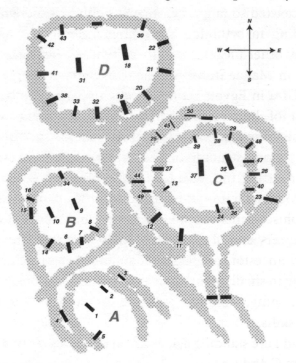

Figure 2: The central group of excavated enclosures – A, B, C and D – at Gobekli Tepe. All the pillars have been numbered, for ease of reference, by the German Archaeological Institute.

6

of pillars. 'But the people who came to Göbekli Tepe, and who did all this work, *invented* agriculture! So we see a connection between what happened here and the later emergence of Neolithic societies dependent on farming.'

My ears prick up at that word 'invented'. I want to be sure I'm getting this right. 'So,' I emphasise, 'you go so far as to say that the people who made Göbekli Tepe actually *invented* agriculture?'

'Yes. Yes.'

'Could you elaborate on that?'

'Because in this region we have the early domesticates, both animals and plants. It's done in this region. So they are the same people.'

'And as far as you are concerned this is the first – the oldest – agriculture in the world?'

'The first in the world. Yes.'

I sense that Schmidt is becoming impatient at the way I'm probing this point, but I have my reasons. The areas of Göbekli Tepe that have been excavated so far are close to 12,000 years old which makes them (according to orthodox chronology) more than 6,000 years older than any other megalithic sites anywhere – sites like Gigantiga and Mnajdra in Malta, Stonehenge and Avebury in England, or the Pyramids of Giza in Egypt. Yet those sites all belong to that phase of the evolution of human civilization that archaeologists call the 'Neolithic' (the 'New Stone Age') when agriculture and the organiza-tion of society along structured, hierarchical lines were already well advanced, permitting the emergence of skilled specialists who had no need to produce their own food because they could be supported from the surpluses generated by farmers. Göbekli Tepe, by contrast, belongs to the very end of the 'Upper Paleolithic', the late 'Old Stone Age' when our ancestors are supposed to have been nomadic hunter-gatherers living in small, mobile bands and incapable of tasks requiring long-term planning, complex division of labour and high-level management skills.

Schmidt and I are standing at a point on the walkway that overlooks both Enclosure C and Enclosure D, where I've learned from my back-ground research of an intriguing image carved on one of the pillars. I intend to ask the archaeologist's permission to climb down into

Enclosure D so that I can take a closer look at this image, but I want to get his views about the origins of agriculture, and its relationship to the megalithic architecture, completely clear first. Enclosure C, the largest of the four main pits so far excavated, is dominated by two huge central pillars, both of which are broken. In their original state they would each have been more than 6 metres (20 feet) high and weighed around 20 tons. Inset into the wall around them stand a dozen other pillars. They're slightly smaller but still prodigious. The same goes for Enclosure D – again a ring of smaller pillars surrounding two towering central pillars, in this case both intact. Their T-shaped tops, angled slightly down to the front, have no features but are none-theless eerily reminiscent of giant human heads – an impression that is reinforced by the faint outlines of arms, crooked at the elbow, running down the flanks of the pillars and terminating in carefully carved human hands with long fingers.

'All this,' I say, 'the megaliths, the iconography, the general concep-tion and layout of the site . . . to be honest it looks to be as big a project as a place like Stonehenge in England, yet Stonehenge is much younger. So how does what you've found at Göbekli Tepe fit in with your notion of a hunter-gatherer society?'

'It's much more organised than we expected,' Schmidt allows. 'What we can see here are hunter-gatherers who obviously had a division of labour because the work on the megaliths is specialist work, not for everybody. They were also able to transport these heavy stones and erect them, which means they must have had some engineering know-how, and again we didn't expect that for hunter-gatherers. It's the first architecture really, and it's architecture on a monumental scale.'

'So if I understand you correctly, Professor Schmidt, you are saying that we are standing at the place where both monumental architecture and agriculture were invented.'

'Yes, that's right.'

'And yet you don't see anything really revolutionary in this? You see it as a process which you can fit comfortably into the existing frame of history?'

'Yes. Into existing history. But this process is much more exciting than we expected. Especially since what we have here at Göbekli Tepe belongs more to the world of the hunter-gatherers than to the farming societies. It's towards the end of the hunter-gatherers but not yet the beginning of the Neolithic.'

'It's a time of transition then. A cusp moment. And maybe more than that? What I'm getting from our conversation, and from what you've showed me of the site this morning, is the notion that Göbekli Tepe was a kind of prehistoric think-tank or a centre of innovation, perhaps under the control of some sort of resident elite. Are you okay with that?'

'Yes, yes. It was a place where people came together. People were gathering here and it was undoubtedly a platform for the distribution of knowledge and innovation.'

'Including knowledge of large-scale stone working and knowledge of agriculture. Would you dare to describe those who controlled the site and disseminated these ideas as a sort of priesthood?'

'Whoever they were, they certainly were not practicing simple shamanism. They were a bit more like an institution. So, yes, they were on the road to becoming a priesthood.'

'And since Göbekli Tepe was in unbroken use for well over a thousand years, would this be one continuous culture with its own institutions, with the same ideas and the same "priesthood" who continued to manage the site throughout that whole period?'

'Yes. But the strange thing is that there was a clear collapse in the effort that was made as the centuries went by. The truly monumental structures are in the older layers; in the younger layers they get smaller and there is a significant decline in quality.'

'So the oldest is the best?'

'Yes, the oldest is the best.'

'And you don't find that puzzling?'

Klaus Schmidt looks almost apologetic. 'Well, we hope that eventually we will discover even older layers and that there we will see the small beginnings that we expect but haven't yet found. Then we have this monumental phase, and later a decline again.'

It occurs to me that 'hope' is the operative word in what Professor Schmidt has just said. We are used to things starting out small and simple and then progressing – *evolving* – to become ever more complex and sophisticated, so this is naturally what we expect to find on archaeological sites. It upsets our carefully structured ideas of how civilizations should behave, how they should mature and develop, when we are confronted by a case like Göbekli Tepe that starts out perfect at the beginning and then slowly *devolves* until it is just a pale shadow of its former self.

Nor is it so much the process of devolution that we object to. We know that civilizations can decay. Just look at the Roman Empire, or the British Empire for that matter.

No, the problem at Göbekli Tepe is the pristine, sudden appearance, like Athena springing full-grown and fully armed from the brow of Zeus, of what appears to be an already seasoned civilization so accomplished that it 'invents' both agriculture *and* monumental architecture at the apparent moment of its birth.

Archaeology can no more explain that than it can explain why the earliest monuments, art, sculptures, hieroglyphs, mathematics, medicine, astronomy and architecture of Ancient Egypt are perfect at the beginning without any traces of evolution from simple to sophisticated. And we might well ask of Göbekli Tepe, as my friend John Anthony West asks of Ancient Egypt:

> How does a complex civilization spring full-blown into being. Look at a 1905 automobile and compare it to a modern one. There is no mistaking the process of 'development'. But in Egypt there are no parallels. Everything is right there at the start.
>
> The answer to the mystery is of course obvious but, because it is repellent to the prevailing cast of modern thinking, it is seldom considered. Egyptian civilization was not a 'development', it was a legacy.[4]

Could this be the case, also, at Göbekli Tepe?

Klaus Schmidt has no time for ideas of a lost civilization that was the progenitor of all later known civilizations, so when I press him he reiterates his point that most of Göbekli Tepe remains unexcavated. 'As I said,' he growls, somewhat testily, 'I expect when we get to the earlier levels we will find evidence of evolution.'

He could be right. One of the stunning things about Göbekli Tepi, which had already been the subject of *eighteen years* of continuous excavation when Klaus Schmidt showed me round the site in 2013, is that so much of it still remains under the ground.

But how much?

'It's hard to say,' Schmidt tells me. 'We've done a geophysical survey – ground-penetrating radar – and from this we can see that at least sixteen further large enclosures remain to be excavated.'

'Large enclosures?' I ask. I point at the towering megaliths of Enclosure D. 'Like this one?'

'Yes, like this one. And sixteen is the minimum. In some areas our geophysical mapping did not give us complete results and we cannot really see inside, but we expect there are many more than sixteen. Maybe in reality it will turn out to be double that number. Maybe even as many as fifty.'

'Fifty!'

'Yes – fifty of the big enclosures, each enclosure with fourteen or more pillars. But, you know, it's not our target to excavate everything. Just a little part, because excavation is destruction. We want to keep most of the site untouched.'

It dilates the imagination to reflect on the scale of the enterprise undertaken at Göbekli Tepe by the ancients. Not only are the circles of megalithic pillars already excavated here at least 6,000 years *older* than any other known megalithic sites anywhere in the world, but also, I now realise, Göbekli Tepe is *huge* – occupying an area that might eventually prove to be as much as thirty times larger than the fullest extent of a big site like Stonehenge, for example.

We are confronted, in other words, by vast, inexplicable antiquity, immense scale, and unknown purpose – and all of it seeming to unfold out of nowhere, with no obvious background or preparation, shrouded utterly in mystery.

Enclosures of the giants

I'm used to archaeologists making the sign of the evil eye and turning their backs on me when I show up at their excavations. But Professor

Schmidt is refreshingly different. Although he knows very well who I am, he permits me and my wife, the photographer Santha Faiia, to climb down into Enclosure D and explore it. All four of the main enclosures so far excavated at Göbekli Tepe are strictly off limits to the public and under the eye of watchful guards, but there's an image on one of the pillars in Enclosure D that I need to take a much closer look at than the walkway affords – indeed I can't even see it from the walkway – so Schmidt's generosity of spirit is welcome.

We enter the enclosure along a plank which leads to an as yet

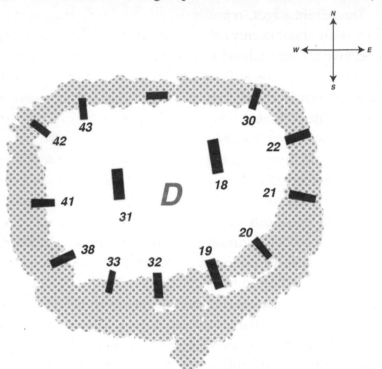

Figure 3: Layout of the pillars in Enclosure D at Gobekli Tepe. Pillar 43 is of the greatest interest.

unexcavated two-metre high partition of rubble and earth separating the two main central pillars, one to the east and the other to the west. Quarried from the very hard crystalline limestone of the region, and polished to a flawlessly smooth finish, these colossal pillars glow mellow gold in the sun. I know from Professor Schmidt that they are about 5.5 metres (18 feet) tall and that each of them weighs more than 15 tons.[5] Scrambling down onto the floor of the enclosure I note that they stand on stone plinths each about 20 centimetres (8 inches) high that have been carved directly out of the living bedrock. In a row along the front edge of the plinth under the eastern pillar, squatting back on their tails with no wings evident, seven seemingly flightless birds have been sculpted in high relief.

With their stylised anthropomorphic appearance enhanced by their angled T-shaped 'heads' the central pillars loom over me like twin giants. Though they are not my primary target, I seize the opportunity to examine them closely.

Their front edges, representing their chests and bellies, are quite slim – only about twenty centimetres wide – while their flanks measure a bit over a metre (about 4 feet) from front to back. Both figures, as I'd noticed from the walkway, have arms carved in low-relief at their sides, crooked at the elbows and terminating in hands with long, thin fingers. These fingers wrap round the fronts of the pillars, almost meeting over their 'bellies'.

Above the hands, covering their 'chests' are hints of an open-fronted garment. Just below the hands, both figures also wear a broad belt – again carved in low relief – decorated with a distinctive buckle. In both cases what appears to be part of an animal skin – thought by Schmidt to represent the hind legs and tail of a fox pelt[6] – is shown hanging suspended from the buckle so that it covers the genital region.

Both figures also wear necklaces. In the case of the eastern figure the necklace is decorated with a crescent and disc motif and in the case of the western figure with a bull's head.

In addition both pillars stand on their pedestals in exactly the same peculiar way – not securely fixed but resting precariously in slots just 10 centimetres (4 inches) deep. Klaus Schmidt and his team have stabilised them with wooden props and I can only imagine that they must also have been held upright in a similar way in antiquity – unless, perhaps, there was a frame over the enclosure into which the heads of the figures were somehow fixed. Since the builders of Göbekli Tepe were clearly masters of fashioning, moving and positioning large megaliths, it is mysterious that they chose not to cut deeper slots in which the pillars could have been securely mounted. There must have been some purpose to this, but I cannot fathom it.

So much for the similarities between the two central pillars, but there are also differences. For example, the eastern figure has an almost life-sized depiction of a fox carved in high relief on its right flank so that it appears to be leaping forward from the crook of its elbow. And whereas the belt of the western pillar is undecorated other than by its buckle, the belt of the eastern pillar bears a number of intriguing adornments including a series of glyphs like the Roman letter 'C' and others like the Roman letter 'H'. As I study them I reflect that we cannot possibly know what these symbols meant to the people of Göbekli Tepi, from whom we are separated by a vast span of more than eleven thousand years. It is far-fetched to imagine that they had any kind of writing – let alone writing in the alphabet we use today! Nonetheless there is something strangely modern and purposive about the way these pictograms are used and displayed and it seems to me that they are more than merely decorative. Nothing else like them exists anywhere in the world of Upper Palaeolithic art, and the same is true of the animal and bird figures. At this early period, such a combination of megaliths and sophisticated sculptures is utterly unique and unprecedented.

I move on to examine the dozen pillars disposed around the edges of the Enclosure D, which forms more of an ellipse than a strict circle, measuring approximately 20 metres (65 feet) from west to east and just over 14 metres (46 feet) from north to south. The surrounding pillars are generally about half the height of the central pair and for the most part are not free-standing but rather are embedded into the enclosure wall. Most, though not all, are T-shaped and most are richly decorated with images of birds, insects and animals as though the cargo of Noah's Ark has been turned to stone: foxes, gazelles, wild boars, numerous species of birds including several cranes with serpents at their feet, many more serpents both individually and in groups, a spider, a wild ass, wild cattle, a lion with its tail curving forward over its spine – and many more.

Making the most of our *laissez-passer*, I take my time but eventually, on the north-western side of the enclosure I come to the pillar I particularly want to see. For ease of reference Schmidt and his colleagues have numbered all the pillars at Göbekli Tepe and this is 'Pillar No. 43'. I know from my prior research that it has a large depiction of a scorpion carved in relief on its base; some have suggested it might be an image of the zodiacal constellation that we call Scorpio today.[7] However, to my great disappointment the figure is no longer visible. The archaeologists have covered it with rubble – to protect it from damage, Schmidt claims. I tell him of my interest in a possible astronomical connection but he scoffs at this – 'There are no astronomical figures here; the zodiac constellations were not recognised until Babylonian times, nine thousand years after Göbekli Tepe' – and he refuses point-blank to allow me to clear the heaped-up rubble away.

I'm about to get into an argument with him – there is in fact excellent evidence that the zodiac was codified long before Göbekli Tepe[8] – when I notice a group of other figures higher up the same pillar that have not been covered with rubble. These include a prominent depiction of a vulture with its wing outstretched in the manner of a human arm and with a solid disc poised over that arm-like wing as though being upheld or cradled by it. Another human characteristic of the vulture, quite dissimilar to any examples of this bird that I have ever seen in nature, is that it is portrayed with its 'knees' bent forward and with strangely elongated flat feet – a bit like some of the cartoon representations of the 'Penguin' character in the old Batman comics. It is, in other words, a therianthrope (from the Greek *therion*, meaning wild beast, and *anthropos*, meaning man), a hybrid creature – part human and part vulture.[9]

Above it are more of the H-shaped pictograms arranged in a row between a series of upright and inverted 'V' shapes. Again there is a sense of some message, some communication here, that is impossible to interpret. Finally, at the top of the pillar, are depictions of what appear to be three large handbags – rectangular containers, at any rate, with curved handles. Separating them, positioned over the front of the handles in each case, are three figures – at the left a bird with long, human-like legs that mark it out almost certainly as another therianthrope, a quadruped with its tail arched forward over its body, and a salamander.

Figure 4: Pillar 43 in Enclosure D. The lower part of the pillar was covered by rubble at the time of my visit, but has been reconstructed here from earlier photographs (see Plate 7).

There is something hauntingly familiar about the whole ensemble, and I feel certain that I have seen it – or something very like it – somewhere before. The only problem is I can't remember where or what! I ask Santha to take detailed photographs of the pillar and when she is done Schmidt suggests that we accompany him to a different part of the site a few hundred metres to the north-west on the other side of the ridge where he and his team have an active excavation underway. It's just one of the dozens of buried enclosures with large pillars that they have identified with ground-penetrating radar, and the first of these that they are investigating.

Paradigms

As we walk I ask the Professor how and when he became involved with Göbekli Tepe. Ironically, given his firm views on the evolution of architecture, it turns out that he got his big break because other archaeologists also had firm views on the same subject! In 1964 a joint team from the University of Chicago and the University of Istanbul visited the area with a specific brief to search out and discover Stone Age sites. However when they saw the top of a large T-shaped pillar sticking out of the ground, and the remains of other broken limestone pillars that had been ploughed up by local farmers lying nearby, they dismissed Göbekli Tepe as irrelevant to their interests and moved on elsewhere.

The reason?

The American and Turkish team had judged the workmanship on the pillars to be too fine – too advanced, too sophisticated – to have been produced by Stone Age hunter-gatherers. In their opinion, despite the presence of worked flints lying alongside the limestone fragments, Göbekli Tepe was nothing more than an abandoned medieval cemetery and therefore of no prehistoric interest whatsoever.

Their loss was to be Schmidt's gain. At the end of the 1980s and the beginning of the 1990s he had been involved in another project in Turkey – the excavation of an early Neolithic site called Nevali Cori which was soon to be flooded by the waters of the Ataturk Dam. There he and a team of archaeologists from the University of Heidelberg

17

discovered, and rescued from the advancing floodwaters, a number of finely-worked T-shaped limestone pillars that were conclusively dated to between 8,000 and 9,000 years of age. Some had arms and hands carved in relief along their sides. 'So we recognised that this region had something about it that was different from other sites known from this period. Nevali Cori was our first hint of the existence of large-scale limestone sculptures during the transition from hunter-gatherer societies to early village farming communities.'

A little later, in 1994, Schmidt came across the report of the Turkish-American survey done thirty years earlier and stumbled upon a single paragraph that mentioned the presence of worked flints alongside fragments of limestone pillars lying on the surface at Göbekli Tepe. 'I was a young archaeologist,' he explains, 'I was looking for my own project, and I immediately realised that there could be something of significance here, perhaps even another site as important as Nevali Cori.'

'Which your predecessors had missed, because flints and architectural pillars are not normally associated in the minds of archaeologists?'

I'm hoping he'll get my hint that he, too, might be missing something at Göbekli Tepe because of the established paradigm, but he seems oblivious and replies, 'Yes, exactly.'

I glance ahead. For the past few moments, as we've been walking and talking, we've approached a scene of intense activity. I hadn't been aware of it from the four main enclosures because it had been concealed from us by the summit of the ridge, but now we've hiked north over the ridge line and are making our way down the other side into the new excavation, nominated as Enclosure H, that Schmidt has opened at Göbekli Tepe.[10] Here five or six German archaeologists are busily at work, some scraping away layers of soil with trowels or pouring buckets of earth and stones through sieves, others directing the efforts of a team of thirty Turkish labourers. The focus is on a large rectangular cavity. Perhaps half the size of a football pitch, it's internally subdivided by knee-high walls of earth into a dozen or so smaller segments. From the floor of these, at several points, hulking limestone pillars protrude. Most are T-shaped but my eye is drawn to one that has a smooth curved top, marred only by a small broken segment, and upon which is carved a particularly fine figure of a male lion. Like the lions in Enclosure D, its long tail sweeps forward over its spine but the workmanship of this piece is of a higher order than anything I've seen so far today.

'That's a very substantial pillar,' I say to Schmidt. 'Can we take a look at it?'

He agrees and we pick our way through the excavations until we're just a couple of metres from the lion pillar. It's leaning at an angle against a remnant of the rubble of cobble-sized stones and earth that had clearly filled the entire enclosure before the archaeologists began work here. Right at the edge of this segment of the dig, the head of another pillar can be seen, while in the middle of the segment a deeper trench has been cut – to expose what I guess is the top third of the lion pillar – and this trench, too, is lined by the same rubble of cobbles and earth.

I ask Schmidt about the rubble. 'All those cobbles,' I say. 'How did they get there? They don't look like the result of natural sedimentation.'

'They're not,' he replies. He's looking, I think, a little smug. 'They were put there deliberately.'

'Deliberately?'

'Yes, by the makers of Göbekli Tepe. After the megaliths were put in place, and used for a period of unknown duration, every one of the enclosures was deliberately and rapidly buried. For example Enclosure C is the oldest we have found so far. It appears that it was closed, filled in from top to bottom so that all the pillars were completely covered, before 'D', the next enclosure in the sequence, was made. This practice of deliberate infilling has been a great advantage to archaeology because it effectively sealed each of the enclosures and prevented the intrusion of later organic material thus allowing us to be absolutely certain about the dating.'

I'm thinking rapidly as Schmidt talks. The point he makes about dating is interesting, for at least three reasons.

First, the implication is that at megalithic sites around the world where this 'sealing' process *didn't* happen, the dates archaeologists have arrived at could be falsely young as a result of the intrusion of later organic materials (which, by the way, is the only kind of material that is subject to carbon dating; because of course you can't carbon date inorganic materials like stone). Theoretically this could mean that famous megalithic sites that were not deliberately buried by their builders (the temples of Malta, for example, or the *taulas* of Menorca, or the stone circles of Avebury and Stonehenge in England) could turn out to be much older than we are presently taught.

Secondly, if the bulk of the dates at Göbekli Tepe are derived from organic materials in the fill – a fact that I'm later able to confirm from Schmidt's published papers[11] – then this tells us only about the age of the fill; the megalithic pillars themselves must be at least that old, but they could be older since they stood in place before being buried, for 'a period of unknown duration'.

Thirdly, and perhaps most important, *why* was the site infilled? What could possibly be the motive for going to all this trouble to create a series of spectacular megalithic circles only to end up deliberately burying them so thoroughly and so efficiently that more than 10,000 years would pass before they were found again?

The first thought that comes to my mind is . . . time capsule – that Göbekli Tepe was created to transmit a message of some kind to the future and buried so that its message could be kept intact and hidden for millennia. It's a thought that will return to haunt me many times as I continue my investigation, but another full year will pass before it comes to fruition, as we'll see in later chapters. Meanwhile, when I put the question to Klaus Schmidt he offers a completely different explanation for the deliberate burial of the circles of pillars.

'In my opinion this was their programme,' he says. 'They made the enclosures to be buried.'

'Made to be buried?' I'm intrigued. I'm waiting for him to say 'as a time capsule' but instead he replies, 'Like, for example, the megalithic cemeteries in Western Europe – huge constructions and then a mound on top.'

'But then they're for burial of bodies. Is there any evidence of burial of bodies here?'

'We don't have burials yet. We have some fragments of human bones mixed in with animal bones within the filling material but no burials at the moment. We expect we will find some soon.'

'So you believe Göbekli Tepe was a necropolis?'

'It still has to be proved. But that's my hypothesis, yes.'

'And those fragments of human bones you've found mixed with animal bones in infill. What do you make of those? Sacrifice? Cannibalism?'

'I don't think so. My guess is that those bones are evidence of some special treatment of the human body after death – perhaps deliberate excarnation. Such rites were practiced at a number of other known sites in this region that are of about the same age. For me the presence of human bones in the filling material strengthens the hypothesis that we will find primary burials somewhere at Göbekli Tepe, burials that were opened after some time for a continuation of very specific rituals performed with the dead.'[12]

'What, then, was the function of the pillars?'

'The T-shaped pillars are certainly anthropomorphic, yet often with animals depicted on them, perhaps telling us stories connected with the T-shaped beings. We cannot be sure, of course, but I think they represent divine beings.'

'And even when they're not T-shaped?' I point to the lion pillar. 'Like this one? It too has an animal depicted upon it.'

Schmidt shrugs. 'We cannot know for sure. Perhaps we will never know. There is so much mystery here. We could excavate for fifty years and still not find all the answers. We are just at the beginning.'

'But even so you do have some answers. You clearly have some ideas. This lion pillar, for example. Are you at least able to say how old it is?'

'Honestly we don't know. When we excavate beneath it we will hopefully find some organic material that we can carbon date. But until we do we can't be sure.'

'But what's your impression from the style?'

Schmidt shrugs again before conceding, a little begrudgingly, 'It looks similar to some of the pillars in Enclosure C.'

'Which are the oldest?'

'Yes – so something of that age.'

'And that would be what exactly?'

'Exactly 9600 BC, calibrated, is the earliest date we have.'

Radiocarbon years and calendar years drift further and further apart as time goes by because the amount of the radioactive isotope carbon-14 in the atmosphere and in all living, *organic*, things varies from epoch to epoch. Fortunately scientists have found ways – too complicated to go into at this point – to correct for such fluctuations. The process is called calibration so when Schmidt says '9600 BC calibrated' he is giving me calendar years. What '9600 BC calibrated' means in 2013 when I'm talking to him is therefore 9600 years plus the 2013 years that have elapsed since the time of Christ – i.e. 11,613 years ago. I am writing this sentence in December 2014 and you might not read it until 2016, by which time that oldest date that Schmidt is referring to will work out at 11,616 years before the present.

You get the idea.

In other words, put simply, and in round numbers, the oldest parts of Göbekli Tepe to have been excavated so far are a little over 11,600 years old. And, despite all the cautions and qualifications he has expressed, what Schmidt is telling me is that in his informed opinion, on stylistic grounds, the lion-pillar we are looking at is likely to be at least as old as anything hitherto excavated at Göbekli Tepe.

Indeed, although he hasn't said so much – there's very little evidence one way or the other – the possibility has to be considered that it might even be *older*. After all, he's already admitted that the best work at Göbekli Tepe is the oldest. It's troubling, therefore, despite the hope he's expressed that further excavation will reveal 'the small beginnings that we expect but haven't yet found', that this first piece of further excavation has in fact uncovered no such 'small beginnings'. On the contrary what it has brought to light is a massive, superbly executed megalithic pillar, with a lion rampant carved upon it in exquisite high relief, that appears, at least on stylistic grounds, to be extremely old.

Perhaps, rather than Schmidt's hoped-for 'small beginnings', further excavations will only uncover more of the same?

'We know the end,' the Professor tells me firmly. 'The youngest layers at Göbekli Tepe date to 8200 BC. That's when the site is abandoned forever. But we don't know the beginning yet.'

'Except that date of 9600 BC, 11,600 years ago, that you have from

Enclosure C. That's the beginning – at least as far as you've been able to establish it up to now?'

'The beginning of the monumental phase, yes.' There's a glint in the Professor's eye. 'And you know, 9600 BC is an *important* date. It isn't just a number. It's the end of the Ice Age. It's a global phenomenon. So since this goes in parallel—'

The date Schmidt is putting such emphasis on rings a sudden bell in my mind, relating to other research I've been doing, and I feel compelled to interrupt.

'9600 BC! That's not just the end of the Ice Age. It's the end of the Younger Dryas cold spell that starts in, what – 10,800 BC?'

'And ends in 9620 BC,' Schmidt continues, 'according to the ice cores from Greenland. So how likely is it to be an accident that the monumental phase at Göbekli Tepe starts in 9600 BC when the climate of the whole world has taken a sudden turn for the better and there's an explosion in nature and in possibilities?'

I can only agree. It doesn't seem likely that it's an accident at all. On the contrary, I feel certain there must be a connection. We'll explore that connection, and the mysterious cataclysmic period that geologists call the Younger Dryas – and what those Greenland ice cores tell us – in Part II.

Meanwhile, back in 2013, I close my interview with Klaus Schmidt with some praise. And in December 2014, as I sit at my desk going through the transcript of the recording I made at Göbekli Tepe, and knowing that Klaus died of a massive, unexpected heart attack on 20 July 2014, I'm glad I did so. 'You're a very humble man,' I say. 'But the fact is you've discovered a site that has caused us all to rethink our ideas of the past. This is a remarkable thing and I believe that your name, as well as the name of Göbekli Tepe, will go down in history.'

The bringers of civilization

After leaving Göbekli Tepe in mid-September 2013, I make an extensive journey throughout the length and breadth of Turkey before I finally return home.

The lion pillar sticks in my mind, but what particularly haunts me is the scene on Pillar No. 43 in Enclosure D – the scene showing the vulture with its bent human-like knees, and its wing that so much resembles an arm, holding up a solid disc.

I download Santha's photographs onto my computer and call up that scene. It has many remarkable elements as well as the disc. Both wings of the vulture are shown, I now realise, the other stretched out behind its body. To the right of the vulture is a serpent. It has a large triangular head, as do all serpents depicted at Göbekli Tepe, and its body is coiled into a curve with its tail extending down towards an 'H'-shaped pictogram. The serpent is nestled close to another large bird – not a vulture but something more like an Ibis with a long, sickle-shaped beak. Between it and the vulture is yet another bird, again with a hooked beak, but smaller, with the look of a chick.

I turn my attention to the disc. I don't know what to make of it, but the obvious guess from its shape is that it's meant to represent the sun.

There's something else that interests me more, however, if I can just put my finger on what it is – something evocative, something hauntingly familiar, about the imagery on this ancient pillar from Göbekli Tepe. Santha has shot hundreds of frames of it, from every possible angle, and obsessively I keep going through them, hoping for some clue. The vulture . . . the disc . . . and in the next register above the vulture, that weird row of bags, with their curved handles . . .

Bags.

Handbags.

Suddenly I get it. I go to the shelf in my library where I keep reference copies of my own books, pull out *Fingerprints of the Gods*, and start leafing through the photo sections. The first section deals with South America and what I'm looking for isn't there. But the second section is devoted to Mexico and, on the fifth page, I find it. It's image number 33 with the caption: 'Man in Serpent sculpture from the Olmec site of La Venta'. It's Santha's photograph, taken way back in 1992 or 1993, of an impressive relief carved on a slab of solid granite measuring about 1.2 metres (4 feet) wide and 1.5 metres (5 feet) high. The relief features what is believed to be the earliest representation of the Central American deity whom the Maya (a later civilization than the Olmecs)

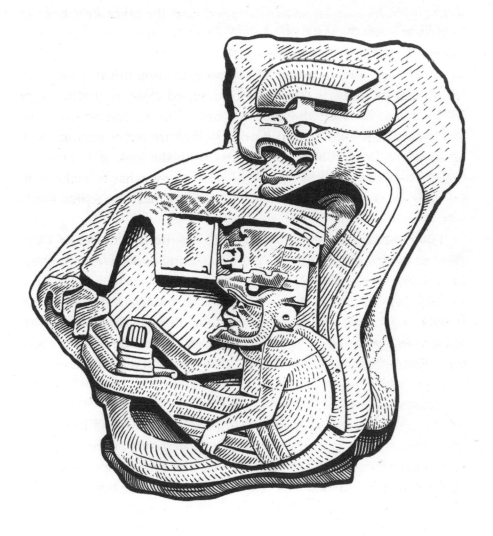

Figure 5: 'Man in Serpent' sculpture – the earliest surviving representation of the Central American deity later known as Quetzalcoatl.

would call *Kukulkan* or *Gucumatz*, and who was known by the even later Aztecs as *Quetzalcoatl*.¹³ All three names mean 'Feathered Serpent' (sometimes translated as 'Plumed Serpent') and it is such a serpent, decorated with a prominent feathered crest on its head, that we see here. Its powerful body coils sinuously around the outer edge of the relief, cradling the figure of a man who is depicted in a seated position as though he is reaching for pedals with his feet. In his right hand he is holding what I described at the time as 'a small, bucket-shaped object'.¹⁴

I return to Santha's images from Enclosure D at Göbekli Tepe and am immediately able to confirm what I suspected. The three bags on the pillar closely resemble the 'bucket-shaped' object from La Venta in Mexico. The same curved handle is there in both cases and the profile of the 'bags' and of the 'bucket' – slightly wider at the bottom than at the top – is also very similar.

If that were all there was to it, this would surely be a coincidence. The 'Man in Serpent' relief from La Venta is thought by archaeologists to date to the period between the tenth and the sixth centuries BC¹⁵ – about nine thousand years younger than the imagery from Göbekli Tepe – so how could there possibly be a connection?

That's when I remember a second curious image I reproduced in *Fingerprints of the Gods*. I check the index for the name Oannes, turn to Chapter Eleven, and find another figure of a man carrying a bag or bucket. I hadn't noticed the resemblance between it and 'Man in Serpent' before but it's obvious to me now. Although not absolutely identical, both bags have the same curved handle that is also depicted on the Göbekli Tepe pillar. Quickly I scan through the report I wrote twenty years earlier. Oannes was a civilizing hero revered by all the ancient cultures of Mesopotamia. He was said to have appeared there in the remotest antiquity and to have taught the inhabitants:

the skills necessary for writing and for doing mathematics and for all sorts of knowledge: how to build cities, found temples . . . make laws . . . determine borders and divide land, also how to plant seeds and then to harvest their fruits and vegetables. In short [he] taught men all those things conducive to a civilised life. ¹⁶

Figure 6: Oannes, a civilizing hero from before the flood, revered by all the ancient cultures of Mesopotamia. The reasons for his strange clothing or costume – he is often referred to as a 'fish-garbed figure' – are given in Chapter 8.

The fullest account we have of Oannes is found in surviving fragments of the works of a Babylonian priest called Berossos who wrote in the third century BC. Fortunately I have a translation of all the Berossos fragments in one volume in my library so I dig it out along with a few other sources on ancient Mesopotamian myths and traditions. It doesn't take me long to discover that Oannes did not do his work alone but was supposedly the leader of a group of beings known as the *Seven Apkallu* – the 'Seven Sages' – who were said to have lived 'before the flood' (a cataclysmic global deluge features prominently in many Mesopotamian traditions, including those of Sumer, Akkad, Assyria and Babylon). Alongside Oannes, these sages are portrayed as bringers of civilization who, in the most ancient past, gave humanity a moral code, arts, crafts and agriculture and taught them architectural, building and engineering skills. [17]

That's a list, I can't help thinking, that includes all the skills supposedly 'invented' at Göbekli Tepe!

I call up a map on my computer screen and see that not only does southeastern Turkey adjoin Mesopotamia geographically but also that the two areas are linked in an even more intimate and direct way. Largely occupied today by the modern state of Iraq, the ancient name *Mesopotamia* means, literally, '[land] between rivers' – the rivers in question being the Tigris and the Euphrates, which reach the sea in the Persian Gulf, but which both have their headwaters in the same

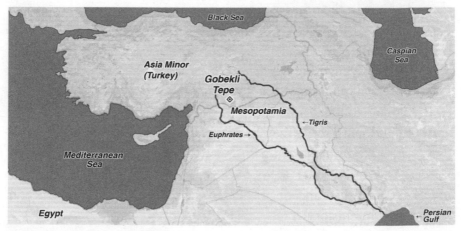

Figure 7: Location of Gobekli Tepe in relation to the headwaters of the Tigris and Euphrates rivers of Mesopotamia

28

Taurus mountain range of southeastern Turkey where Göbekli Tepe is situated.

While I'm online I run some searches for images of the Seven Sages. I don't get many hits at first, but the moment I change the search terms to 'Apkallu' and 'Seven Apkallu' I open a colossal archive of images from all over the internet, many of them reliefs from Assyria, a culture that thrived in Mesopotamia from approximately 2500 BC to about 600 BC. I add 'Assyrian Apkallu' to the search parameters and even more images flood my screen. Often they show bearded men holding bags or buckets which closely resemble those depicted on the Göbekli Tepe pillar and the one held by the Mexican 'Man in Serpent' figure. It's not just the curved handles of these containers, or their shape – where the resemblance is much closer than on the original Oannes relief I reproduced in *Fingerprints of the Gods*. Even more striking is the peculiar and distinctive way that the figures from both Mesopotamia and Mexico hold these containers with the fingers of the hands turned inwards and the thumb crooked forward over the handle.

There's something else as well. A good number of the images show not a man but a therianthrope – a birdman with a hooked beak exactly like the hooked beak of the therianthrope on the Göbekli Tepe pillar. What makes the resemblance even closer is that in the Mesopotamian reliefs the birdman is holding the container in one hand and a cone-shaped object in the other. The shape is a little different but a comparison with the disc cradled above the wing of the Göbekli Tepe birdman is hard to resist.

I can't prove anything yet. It could, of course, all be coincidence, or I could be imagining links that aren't there. But my curiosity is aroused by the similar containers on different continents and in different epochs and so I jot down a series of questions that can form the frame of a loose hypothesis for future testing. For instance, could these containers (whether they are bags or buckets) be the symbols of office of an initiatic brotherhood – far travelled and deeply ancient, with roots reaching back into the remotest prehistory? I feel that this possibility, extraordinary though it may seem on the face of things, is worth looking into and is strengthened by the distinctive hand postures. Might these not have served the

Figure 8: Representations of Oannes and the Apkallu in Mesopotamian art and sculpture where they are frequently depicted as composite fish-man or bird-man figures.

same sort of function as Masonic handshakes today – providing an instant means of identifying who is an 'insider' and who is not?

And what might have been the purpose of such a brotherhood?

Curiously enough, in both Mexico and Mesopotamia where myths and traditions have survived in connection with the imagery and symbolism, we are left in no doubt as to what the purpose was. Stated simply it was to teach, to guide and to spread the benefits of civilization.

This, after all, was the explicit function of Oannes and the Apkallu sages who taught the inhabitants of Mesopotamia 'how to plant seeds and then to harvest their fruits and vegetables' – agriculture in other words – and who also taught them architectural and engineering skills, notably the building of temples. If they needed to be taught these things then they must have had no knowledge of them before the arrival of the sages. They must, in other words, have been nomadic hunter-gatherers just as the inhabitants of southeastern Turkey were until the sudden and surprising entry onto the world stage of Göbekli Tepe.

The same, it transpires, was believed to be the case with the ancient inhabitants of Mexico before the arrival of Quetzalcoatl, the Feathered Serpent, who came to teach them the benefits of settled agriculture and the skills necessary to build temples. Although this deity is frequently depicted as a serpent, he is more often shown in human form – the serpent being his symbol and his alter ego – and is usually described as 'a tall bearded white man'[18] . . . 'a mysterious person . . . a white man with a strong formation of body, broad forehead, large eyes and a flowing beard'.[19] Indeed, as Sylvanus Griswold Morley, the doyen of Mayan studies, concluded, the attributes and life history of Quetzalcoatl:

are so human that it is not improbable that he may have been an actual historical character . . . the memory of whose benefactions lingered after his death, and whose personality was eventually deified.[20]

The same could very well be said of Oannes – and just like Oannes at the head of the Apkallu (likewise depicted as prominently bearded) it seems that Quetzalcoatl travelled with his own brotherhood of sages and magicians. We learn that they arrived in Mexico 'from across the sea in a boat that moved by itself without paddles',[21] and that Quetzalcoatl was regarded as having been 'the founder of cities, the framer of laws and the teacher of the calendar'.[22] The sixteenth century Spanish chronicler, Bernardino de Sahagun, who was fluent in the language of the Aztecs and took great care to record their ancient traditions accurately, tells us further that:

> Quetzalcoatl was a great civilizing agent who entered Mexico at the head of a band of strangers. He imported the arts into the country and especially fostered agriculture . . . He built spacious and elegant houses, and inculcated a type of religion which fostered peace.[23]

So, in summary, as well as a complex pattern of shared symbols and iconography, Quetzalcoatl and Oannes shared the same civilizing mission, which they delivered in widely separated regions of the world in an epoch that is always described as being very far back in time – remote, antediluvian and hoary with age.

Could it have been as far back as 9600 BC – the epoch of Göbekli Tepe where many of the same symbols are found and where, although we have no surviving legends, the signs of a civilizing mission in the form of the sudden appearance of agriculture and monumental architecture are everywhere to be seen?

The implications, should I ever be able to prove this hypothesis, are stunning. At the very least it would mean that some as yet unknown and unidentified people somewhere in the world, had already mastered all the arts and attributes of a high civilization more than twelve thousand years ago in the depths of the last Ice Age and had sent out emissaries around the world to spread the benefits of their knowledge. Who might these shadowy emissaries have been, these sages, these 'Magicians of the Gods' as I was already beginning to think of them? And why was there this insistent connection to the date of 9600 BC?

For as Klaus Schmidt rightly pointed out as he showed me round Göbekli Tepe under the baking sun of the Taurus Mountains, 9600 BC is indeed 'an important date' – important not only because it marks the end of the Ice Age but for another, rather surprising reason as well.

The Greek lawmaker Solon visited Egypt in 600 BC and there he was told a very extraordinary story by the priests at the Temple of Sais in the Nile Delta – a story that was eventually handed down to his more famous descendant Plato, who in due course shared it with the world in his Dialogues of Timaeus and Critias.

It is, of course, the story of the great lost civilization called Atlantis swallowed up by flood and earthquake in a single terrible day and night nine thousand years before the time of Solon.[24]

Or, in our calendar, in 9600 BC.

Chapter 2
The Mountain of Light

❖

'Everything we've been taught about the origins of civilization may be wrong,' says Danny Hilman Natawidjaja, PhD, senior geologist with the Research Centre for Geotechnology at the Indonesian Institute of Sciences. 'Old stories about Atlantis and other great lost civilizations of prehistory, long dismissed as myths by archaeologists, look set to be proved true.'

It's December 2013. We're in Cianjur Regency, about 900 metres

Figure 9: Artist's impression of ancient Gunung Padang. (Courtesy of Pon S. Purajatnika)

(2,950 feet) above sea level and 70 kilometres (43 miles) west of the city of Bandung on the island of Java, Indonesia. I'm climbing with Dr Natawidjaja up the steep slope of a 110 metre (360 feet) high step-pyramid set amidst a magical landscape of volcanoes, mountains and jungles interspersed with paddy fields and tea plantations.

In 1914, lying scattered amongst the dense trees and undergrowth that then covered the summit of the pyramid, ancient man-made structures formed from blocks of columnar basalt were first shown to archaeologists. Local people held the site to be sacred and called it Gunung Padang, the name it still goes by today, often mistranslated as 'Mountain Field' by those unaware that the language of this area is not Indonesian but Sundanese – in which Gunung Padang means 'Mountain of Light', or 'Mountain of Enlightenment'. The structures were found to be arranged across five terraces with a combined area of about 150 metres (492 feet) long by 40 metres (131 feet) wide. The visiting archaeologists were told that the terraces had been used as a place of meditation and retreat since time immemorial – and again this remains true today.

However, neither the archaeologists, nor apparently the locals realised the pyramid was a pyramid. It was believed to be a natural hill, somewhat modified by human activity, until Natawidjaja and his team began a geophysical survey here in 2011 using ground-penetrating radar, electrical resistivity and seismic tomography. By then the summit had long since been cleared and the structures on the terraces recognised as works of megalithic architecture. But no radiocarbon dating had yet been done and the age attributed to the site – about 1000 BC – was based on guesswork rather than on excavations.

The first scientific radiocarbon dating was done by Natawidjaja himself on organic materials in soils underlying the megaliths at or near the surface. The dates produced – around 500 to 1500 BC – were close enough to the archaeological guesswork to cause no controversy. But a surprise was in store as Natawidjaja and his team extended their investigation using tubular drills that brought up cores of earth and stone from much deeper levels.

First, the drill cores contained evidence – fragments of worked columnar basalt – that more man-made megalithic structures lay far beneath the surface. Secondly, the organic materials brought up in the drill cores began to yield older and older dates – 3000 BC to 5000 BC, then 9600 BC as the drills bit deeper, then around 11,000 BC, then 15,000 BC and finally, at depths of 27.5 metres (90 feet) and more, an astonishing sequence of dates of 20,000 BC to 22,000 BC and earlier.

'This was not at all what my colleagues in the world of archaeology expected or wanted to hear,' says Natawidjaja, a world-renowned expert in the geology of megathrust earthquakes who earned his PhD at Cal Tech in the United States and who, it becomes apparent, regards archaeology as a thoroughly unscientific discipline.

A truly cataclysmic period . . .

The problem is that those dates going back before 9600 BC take us deep into the last Ice Age, when Indonesia was not a series of islands as it is today but was part of a vast antediluvian Southeast Asian continent dubbed 'Sundaland' by geologists.

Sea level was 122 metres (400 feet) lower then. Huge ice caps 3.2 kilometres (2 miles) deep covered most of Europe and North America until the ice caps began to melt. Then all the water stored

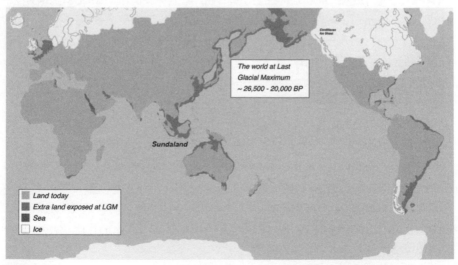

Figure 10

in them returned to the oceans and sea-level rose, submerging many parts of the world where humans had previously lived. Thus Britain was joined to Europe during the Ice Age (there was no English Channel or North Sea). Likewise there was no Red Sea, no Persian Gulf, Sri Lanka was joined to southern India, Siberia was joined to Alaska, Australia was joined to New Guinea – and so on and so forth. It was during this epoch of sea-level rise, sometimes slow and continuous, sometimes rapid and cataclysmic, that the Ice Age continent of Sundaland was submerged with only the Malaysian Peninsula and the Indonesian islands as we know them today high enough to remain above water.

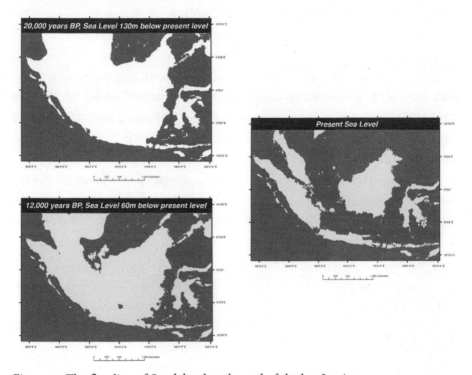

Figure 11: The flooding of Sundaland at the end of the last Ice Age.

As we saw in the last chapter, the established archaeological view of the state of human civilization until the end of the last Ice Age is that our ancestors were primitive hunter-gatherers, ignorant of agriculture and incapable of any architectural feats bigger than wigwams and bivouacs.

This is why Göbekli Tepe in southeastern Turkey is so significant

– because it breaks that paradigm wide open and cries out for serious consideration of a possibility, previously relegated to the lunatic fringe, that civilization might be much older and more mysterious than we thought.[1] With the date of its foundation presently set at 9600 BC ('*exactly* 9600 BC' as Klaus Schmidt was at pains to point out to me), Göbekli Tepe also requires us to reopen the cold case of Atlantis which archaeologists have long ridiculed, pouring scorn and derision on anyone daring to utter the much reviled 'A' word. As noted at the end of the last chapter, the Greek philosopher Plato, whose dialogues *Timaeus and Critias* contain the earliest surviving mention of the fabled sunken kingdom, sets the catastrophic destruction and submergence of Atlantis by floods and earthquakes at 9,000 years before the time of Solon[2] – i.e. at *exactly* 9600 BC. The Greeks could not have known of Göbekli Tepe (let alone that it was mysteriously founded at the very moment Atlantis was said to have died). Moreover they had no access to the Greenland ice cores dating the end of the Ice Age to 9620 BC, just twenty years before the foundation of Göbekli Tepe, nor to modern scientific knowledge about the rapidly rising sea levels (often accompanied by cataclysmic earthquakes as the weight of the melting ice caps was removed from the continental landmasses) that occurred in this period. With all this in mind, therefore, the date Plato gives is, to say the least, an uncanny coincidence.

In Danny Natawidjaja's view, however, it is no coincidence at all. His research at Gunung Padang has convinced him that Plato was right about the existence of a high civilization in the depths of the last Ice Age – a civilization that was indeed brought to a cataclysmic end involving floods and earthquakes in an epoch of great global instability between 10,800 BC and 9600 BC.

This epoch, which geologists call the 'Younger Dryas' has long been recognised as mysterious and tumultuous. In 10,800 BC, when it began, the earth had been emerging from the Ice Age for roughly 10,000 years, global temperatures were rising steadily and the ice caps were melting. Then there was a sudden dramatic return to colder conditions – nearly as cold as at the peak of the Ice Age 21,000 years ago. This short, sharp deep freeze lasted for 1,200 years until 9600 BC when the warming trend resumed, global temperatures shot up again and

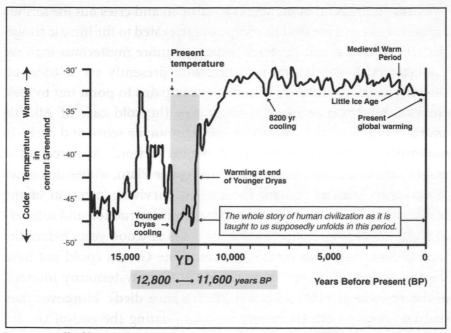

Figure 12: All of human history as it is presently taught to us follows the Younger Dryas – the mysterious cataclysmic period between 10,800 BC (around 12,800 years ago) and 9,600 BC (around 11,600 years ago).

the remaining ice caps melted very suddenly, dumping all the water they contained into the oceans.

'It is difficult,' Natawidjaja says, 'for us to imagine what life on earth must have been like during the Younger Dryas. It was a truly cataclysmic period of immense climate instability and terrible, indeed terrifying, global conditions. It's not surprising that many large animal species, such as the mammoths, went extinct during this precise time and of course it had huge effects on our ancestors – not just those 'primitive' hunter-gatherers the archaeologists speak of but also, I believe, a high civilization that was wiped from the historical record by the upheavals of the Younger Dryas.'

A controversial pyramid

What has brought Natawidjaja to this radical view is the evidence he and his team have uncovered at Gunung Padang. When their drill cores began to yield very ancient carbon dates from organic materials embedded in clays filling the gaps between worked stones, they expanded their investigation using geophysical equipment – ground-penetrating radar, seismic tomography and electrical resistivity – to get a picture of what lay under the ground. The results were stunning, showing layers of massive construction using the same megalithic elements of columnar basalt that are found on the surface but with courses of huge basaltic rocks beneath them extending down to thirty metres (100 feet) and more beneath the surface. At those depths the carbon dates indicate that the megaliths were put in place more than 12,000 years ago and in some cases as far back as 24,000 years ago.

Columnar basalt does form naturally – the famous Giant's Causeway in Northern Ireland is an example – but at Gunung Padang it has been used as a building material and is laid out in a form never found in nature.

'The geophysical evidence is unambiguous,' Natawidjaja says. 'Gunung Padang is not a natural hill but a man-made pyramid and the origins of construction here go back long before the end of the last Ice Age. Since the work is massive even at the deepest levels, and bears witness to the kinds of sophisticated construction skills that were deployed to build the pyramids of Egypt, or the largest megalithic sites of Europe, I can only conclude that we're looking at the work of a lost civilization and a fairly advanced one.'

'The archaeologists won't like that,' I point out.

'They don't!' Natawidjaja agrees with a rueful smile. 'I've already got myself into a lot of hot water with this. My case is a solid one, based on good scientific evidence, but it's not an easy one. I'm up against deeply entrenched beliefs.'

The next step will be a full-scale archaeological excavation. 'We have to excavate in order to interrogate our remote sensing data and our carbon dating sequences and either confirm or deny what we believe we've found here,' says Natawidjaja, 'but unfortunately there's a lot of obstacles in our way.'

When I ask what he means by obstacles he replies that some senior Indonesian archaeologists are lobbying the government in Jakarta to prevent him from doing any further work at Gunung Padang on the grounds that they 'know' the site is less than three thousand years old and see no justification for disturbing it.

'I don't deny that the megaliths at the surface are less than three thousand years old,' Natawidjaja hastens to add, 'but I suggest they were put here because Gunung Padang has been recognised as a sacred place since time immemorial. It's the deepest layers of the structure at between 12,000 and more than 20,000 years old that are the most important. They have potentially revolutionary implications for our understanding of history and I think it's vital that we be allowed to investigate them properly.'

Atlantis

Happily, there was a decisive Presidential intervention during 2014 and I can now report that Danny (I'll use his first name henceforth as we have become friends) was given *carte blanche* to excavate the site. He and his team began work in August 2014, completing a short season there between August and October, but as the experience at Göbekli Tepe shows, painstaking, detailed archaeology is a slow process and they do not expect to reach the deepest layers until 2017 or 2018. As the first season neared its end, however, Danny emailed me an update:

> The research progress has been great. We have excavated three more spots right on top of the megalithic site in the past couple of weeks, which give more evidence and details about the buried structures. We have uncovered lots more stone artefacts from the excavations. The existence of the pyramid-like structure beneath the megalithic site is now loud and clear; even for non-specialists, it is not too difficult to understand if they come and see for themselves. We have found some kind of open hall buried by soil five to seven metres thick; however we have not yet got into the main chamber. We are now drilling to the suspected location of the chamber (based on subsurface geophysic) in the middle of the megalithic site.[3]

Buried structures? Chambers? Ah, yes, I forgot to mention those. We'll go into the implications of all this in more detail in a later chapter, but in brief, the geophysical survey work that Danny and his team did between 2011 and 2013, deploying the latest technologies in electrical resistivity, seismic tomography, ground-penetrating radar and core drilling, revealed not only deeply buried massive constructions and very ancient carbon dates at Gunung Padang but also the presence of three further hidden and as yet unexcavated chambers, so rectilinear in form that they are most unlikely to be natural. The largest of these lies at a depth of between 21.3 and 27.4 metres (70 to 90 feet) and measures approximately 5.5 metres (18 feet) high, 13.7 metres (45 feet) long and 9.1 metres (30 feet) wide.

Could it be the fabled 'Hall of Records' of Atlantis? Danny has put his impeccable scientific credentials on the line with the controversial claim that it might be. Not only does he refuse to scoff at the idea of Atlantis but also he's written a book arguing that Indonesia – or rather the huge areas of ancient 'Sundaland' that were drowned by rising sea levels at the end of the Ice Age – might actually *be* Atlantis.[4]

Danny and I made an extensive research trip around the whole of the Indonesian archipelago in June 2014 searching out megalithic sites off the beaten track that have never been properly studied by archaeologists. In Chapter Eighteen I'll describe our findings, and how they relate to the Gunung Padang mystery, but meanwhile I want to report here on the opinion of Dr Robert Schoch, Professor of Geology at Boston University, who was with me in December 2013 when I first met Danny at Gunung Padang.[5]

The view of Professor Robert Schoch

Schoch is a renowned figure, indeed notorious, for the case he's made, based on strict geological evidence, that the Great Sphinx of Giza bears the unmistakable erosion patterns of thousands of years of heavy rainfall.[6] This means it has to be much older than 2500 BC (the orthodox date, when Egypt received no more rain than it does today) and must originally have been carved around the end of the Ice Age when the Nile valley was subjected to a long period of intense precipitation.

A tall, rangy, scholarly man with a full beard and a mop of unruly hair, Schoch was in his element at Gunung Padang carefully interrogating the results of the geophysical scans with Danny, collecting samples and minutely examining the site. Afterwards, when he'd returned to the US and had time to analyse the data, he wrote:

The first important observation is that . . . Gunung Padang goes back to before the end of the last Ice Age, circa 9700 BC. Based on the evidence, I believe that human use of the site began by circa 14,700 BC. Possibly the earliest use of the site goes back to 22,000 BC, or even earlier.

In my assessment, Layer Three, some 4 to 10 metres (13.1 to 32.8 feet) or so below the surface, includes the period of the very end of the last Ice Age, circa 10,000 to 9500 BC, when major climatic changes took place, with dramatic global warming, rising sea levels, torrential rains, increased earthquake and volcanic activity, widespread wildfires . . . and other catastrophes occurring across the surface of earth . . . There is evidence of collapsed structures in Layer Three, possibly the result of the tumultuous conditions at that time.

Visiting Gunung Padang, pondering the dates and evidence of collapse and rebuilding that may have occurred here, I could not help but think about another major site – representing very ancient civilization – that spans the end of the last Ice Age, namely Göbekli Tepe in southeastern Turkey . . . I also think of Egypt and my own work on re-dating the Great Sphinx. The extreme weathering and erosion seen on the proto-Sphinx (the head was re-carved and the monument reused during dynastic times), caused by torrential rains, could have been a result of the extreme climatic changes at the end of the last Ice Age.

Putting together the evidence of Gunung Padang with that derived from Göbekli Tepe, the Sphinx of Egypt, and other sites and lines of data from around the world, I believe we are coming closer to understanding the cataclysmic times and events at the end of the last Ice Age. Genuine civilizations of a sophisticated nature existed prior to circa 9700 BCE, which were devastated by the events that brought the last Ice Age to a close.[7]

Looking for the smoking gun . . .

At six thousand or more years older than the stone circles of Stonehenge, the megaliths of Göbekli Tepe, like the deeply buried megaliths of Gunung Padang, mean that the timeline of history taught in our schools and universities for the best part of the last hundred years can no longer stand. It is beginning to look as though civilization, as I argued in my controversial 1995 bestseller *Fingerprints of the Gods*, is indeed much older and much more mysterious than we thought.

In essence what I proposed in that book was that an advanced civilization had been wiped out and lost to history in a global cataclysm at the end of the last Ice Age. I suggested there were survivors who settled at various locations around the world and attempted to pass on their superior knowledge, including knowledge of agriculture and architecture, to hunter-gatherer peoples who had also survived the cataclysm. Indeed even today we have populations of hunter-gatherers, in the Kalahari Desert, for instance, and in the Amazon jungle, who co-exist with our advanced technological culture – so we should not be surprised that equally disparate levels of civilization might have co-existed in the past.

What I could not do when I wrote *Fingerprints*, because the data was not then available, was identify the exact nature of the cataclysm that had wiped out my hypothetical lost civilization. Instead I speculated on a number of possible causes, notably the radical 'earth crust displacement' theory of Professor Charles Hapgood which, though endorsed by Albert Einstein,[8] has since found little favour amongst geologists. This absence of a credible 'smoking gun' was one of the many aspects of my argument that was heavily criticised by archaeologists. Since 2007, however, a cascade of scientific evidence has come to light that has identified the smoking gun for me. It's all the more intriguing because it's the work of a large group of impressively credentialled mainstream scientists, and because it does not rule out, indeed it in some ways reinforces, the case for massive crustal instability that I made in *Fingerprints of the Gods*.

We'll explore this new evidence, and its stunning implications, in the following chapters.

Part II
Comet

Chapter 3
A Wall of Green Water Destroying Everything in its Path . . .

—◆—

Could certain ancient myths and traditions, judged to be of no historic value by scholars, in fact encode accurate recollections of an epoch when humanity experienced a crisis so devastating, so cataclysmic and so dislocating that we lost our memory of our true past? Consider this account from the Ojibwa, a Native American people:

> The star with the long, wide tail is going to destroy the world some day when it comes low again. That's the comet called Long-Tailed Heavenly Climbing Star. It came down here once, thousands of years ago. Just like the sun. It had radiation and burning heat in its tail.
>
> The comet burnt everything to the ground. There wasn't a thing left. Indian people were here before that happened, living on the earth. But things were wrong; a lot of people had abandoned the spiritual path. The holy spirit warned them a long time before the comet came. Medicine men told everyone to prepare. Things were wrong with nature on the earth . . . Then that comet went through here. It had a long, wide tail and it burnt up everything. It flew so low the tail scorched the earth . . . The comet made a different world. After that survival was hard work. The weather was colder than before . . .[1]

There are other interesting details in the various versions of this myth told amongst the Ojibwa and recorded by anthropologist Thor Conway. For example there is a reference to the comet killing off 'giant animals

. . . You can find their bones today in the earth. It is said that the comet came down and spread his tail for miles and miles'.[2] At the time of this event, usually referred to as 'the first burning of the earth', we're told that the Ojibwa 'lived near the edge of the Frozen Lands'.[3] It is also recorded that soon after the comet disaster 'the first flooding of the earth' occurred.[4]

Just as the Ojibwa tradition laments that 'things were wrong . . . people had abandoned the spiritual path', thus implicating human behaviour in the disaster that followed so, too, the Brule, one of the tribes of the Lakota Nation tell of a time, 'in the world before this one', when 'the People and animals turned to evil and forgot their connection to the Creator'. In response, the Creator resolved 'to destroy the world and start over'. He first warned a few good people to flee to the highest mountaintops, then sent down 'fierce Thunderbirds to wage a great battle against the other humans and the giant animals' (again, as in the Ojibwa myth, the Brule account speaks of animals of extraordinary size).[5]

> Finally, at the height of the battle, the Thunderbirds suddenly threw down their most powerful thunderbolts all at once. The fiery blast shook the entire world. Toppling mountain ranges and setting forests and prairies ablaze. The flames leapt up to the sky in all directions, sparing only the few People on the highest peaks . . . Even the rocks glowed red hot, and the giant animals and evil people burned up where they stood.

Now the Creator began to make the world anew:

> As the Creator chanted the song of creation it began to rain. The Creator sang louder and it rained harder until the rivers overflowed their banks and surged across the landscape. Finally the Creator stamped the Earth, and with a great quake the Earth split open, sending great torrents across the entire world until only a few mountain peaks stood above the flood, sheltering the few People who had survived . . . [After the flood subsided], as the People went out over the land they found the bleached bones

of the giant animals buried in rock and mud . . . People still find them today in the Dakota Badlands.[6]

Of particular note, when we remember that a species of giant beaver became extinct in North America at the end of the Ice Age,[7] is a myth of the Passamaquoddy, Micmac and Malisee that speaks of a being called Glooscap, described as 'a spirit, a medicine man and a sorcerer', who created the first animals, amongst them the first beaver – a creature so large that when it built a dam it 'flooded the country from horizon to horizon'. Glooscap tapped the beaver on its back and it shrank to its present size.[8]

The reference to a flood in this story is one amongst hundreds in the myths of the Native Americans. Many of them contain intriguing details of great relevance to new scientific information about events in North America at the end of the Ice Age that we will explore in the following pages. For example, the Cowichan of British Columbia recall a time in the remote past when their seers became greatly troubled on account of strange dreams which foretold destruction. One man said: 'I have dreamed a strange thing. I dreamed that such rain fell that we were all drowned.' Another said, 'I dreamed that the river rose and flooded the place, and we were all destroyed.' 'So did I,' chimed another. 'And I too.'[9]

The seers were disbelieved by their people but nonetheless resolved to build a huge raft of many canoes joined together. Not long after they were done the rain commenced. The drops were as large as hailstones and so heavy that they killed the little babies. The river rose and all the valleys were covered. The seers, and those few of their friends who had believed them:

> took their families and placed them on the raft and took food and waited. By and by the raft rose with the water . . . At length the rain stopped, and they felt the waters going down, and their raft rested on the top of Cowichan Mountain . . . Then they saw the land, but what desolation met their eyes! How their hearts were wrung with anguish. It was indescribable.[10]

Unusually large hailstones feature in a Quillayute cataclysm myth:

> For days and days great storms blew. Rain and hail and then sleet and snow came down upon the land. The hailstones were so large that many of the people were killed . . . [The survivors] grew thin and weak from hunger. The hailstones had beaten down the ferns and the camas and the berries. Ice locked the rivers so that the men could not fish.[11]

The Pima, or 'River People', presently live in Arizona whence they migrated in remote antiquity from much further north. As is the case with the Cowichan, a seer features in their cataclysm traditions – in this case a seer who was warned by a great eagle that a flood was coming. The eagle visited the seer four times and each time he ignored its warnings. 'You'd better believe what I'm telling you,' said the eagle. 'The whole valley will be flooded. Everything will be destroyed.' 'You're a liar,' said the seer. 'And you're a seer who sees nothing,' said the eagle:

> The bird flew away, and hardly had he gone when a tremendous thunderclap was heard, the loudest there has ever been . . . The sun remained hidden behind dark clouds, and there was only twilight, gray and misty. Then the earth trembled, and there came a great roar of something immense moving. The people saw a sheer green wall advancing toward them, filling the valley from one side to the other. At first they did not know what it was, and then they realised that it was a wall of green water. Destroying everything in its path, it came like a huge beast, a green monster, rushing upon them, foaming, hissing, in a cloud of spray. It engulfed the seer's house and carried it away with the seer, who was never seen again. Then the water fell upon the villages, sweeping away homes, people, fields and trees. The flood swept the valley clean as with a broom. Then it rushed on beyond the valley to wreak havoc elsewhere.[12]

The Inuit of Alaska preserve a tradition of an earthquake, accompanied by a terrible flood that swept so rapidly over the earth that only a few people managed to escape in their canoes, or take refuge on the tops of the highest mountains.[13] The Luiseno of California also remember a flood that covered the mountains and destroyed most of mankind. Only those few who fled to the highest peaks were spared when all the rest of the world was inundated.[14] Similar flood myths were recorded amongst the Hurons.[15] And the Montagnais, who belong to the Algonquin family, relate how the god Michabo reconstructed the world after a great flood:

> Michabo was hunting with his pack of trained wolves one day when he saw the strangest sight: the wolves entered a lake and disappeared. He followed them into the water to fetch them, and as he did so the entire world flooded. Michabo then sent forth a raven to find some soil with which to make a new earth, but the bird returned unsuccessful in its quest. Then Michabo sent an otter to do the same thing, but again to no avail. Finally he sent the muskrat and she brought him back enough earth to begin the reconstruction of the world.[16]

Lynd's *History of the Dakotas*, written in the nineteenth century, preserves many indigenous traditions that would otherwise have been lost. These include an Iroquois myth that 'the sea and the waters had at one time infringed upon the land so that all human life was destroyed'. The Chickasaws asserted that the world had been destroyed by water, 'but that one family was saved and two animals of every kind'. The Lakota (Dakotas) also spoke of a time when there was no dry land and when all men disappeared from existence.[17]

Myths speaking to science

For years an often acrimonious debate has been underway amongst scholars regarding the peopling of the Americas. Who are the Native Americans, exactly? When did they first arrive in the New World? And by what route?

Whenever a resolution has begun to look possible, whenever some kind of consensus has been about to emerge, new information has been presented, by one side or the other, that calls for a rethink. What has never been in dispute, however, is that the ancestors of today's Native Americans were already in North America 12,800 years ago, when the mysterious cold event that geologists call the Younger Dryas began, and that they witnessed and hunted the megafauna that flourished during the Ice Age including the gigantic Columbia Mammoth, the somewhat smaller Wooly Mammoth, the giant beaver, short-faced bears, giant sloths, two species of tapirs, several species of peccaries and the fearsome American lion.

It's thought likely, therefore, that the references to very large animals in the myths cited above are not mere fantasies but preserve eye-witness accounts of some of the many genera of mega-mammals that were present in North America before the Younger Dryas began, but had passed into extinction by the time it ended 1,200 years later. The same goes for the floods that the myths describe,[18] for geologists agree that North America was indeed subjected to episodes of cataclysmic flooding in the final millennia of the last Ice Age. What new research has called into question in the past decade, however, is whether the scale, extent and, most importantly, the *causes* of those floods have been properly understood. The mainstream view is copiously represented, and endlessly repeated in books and journals published since the 1960s, but in order to get to grips with a powerful alternative view that now poses a serious challenge to established theories, I made an extensive field trip across North America in September and October 2014 with catastrophist researcher Randall Carlson.[19]

Randall cannot be a reincarnation of J Harlen Bretz, because J Harlen Bretz (whose first name was J and who hated it when proof-readers tried to treat it like an initial) passed away on 3 February 1981, by which time Randall was already thirty years old. However in his passion for real fieldwork, for walking the walk rather than just reading the literature, and in his dogged advocacy of a radical geological hypothesis concerning the cataclysmic floods that tore North America apart at the end of the Ice Age, Randall is in every meaningful sense the new J Harlen Bretz.

I will describe my travels with Randall, and the compelling evidence he presented me with, in the chapters that follow, but first, you may well be wondering, who was J Harlen Bretz?

Meet J Harlen Bretz

Here is Bretz, writing in 1928 after one of his field trips across Washington State in the Pacific Northwest of the US:

No one with an eye for landforms can cross eastern Washington in daylight without encountering and being impressed by the 'scabland'. Like great scars marring the otherwise fair face of the plateau are these elongated tracts of bare, or nearly bare, black rock carved into mazes of buttes and canyons. Everybody on the plateau knows scabland. It interrupts the wheat lands, parcelling them out into hill tracts less than 40 acres to more than 40 square miles in extent. One can neither reach them nor depart from them without crossing some part of the ramifying scabland. Aside from affording a scanty pasturage, scabland is almost without value. The popular name is an expressive metaphor. The Scablands are wounds only partially healed – great wounds in the epidermis of soil with which Nature protects the underlying rock.

With eyes only a few feet above the ground the observer today must travel back and forth repeatedly and must record his observations mentally, photographically, by sketch and by map before he can form anything approaching a complete picture. Yet long before the paper bearing these words has yellowed, the average observer, looking down from the air as he crosses the region, will see almost at a glance the picture here drawn by piecing together the ground-level observations of months of work. The region is unique: let the observer take the wings of the morning to the uttermost parts of the earth: he will nowhere find its likeness.[20]

By 1928 Bretz was an experienced and highly credentialled field geologist. Born in 1882, he'd started his career as a high school biology teacher in Seattle but spent most of his spare time exploring the geology of Puget Sound. Although he didn't have a geology degree at the time, he succeeded in getting several articles on his findings published in scientific journals.[21] In 1911 he enrolled at the University of Chicago to pursue a doctorate in geology. He graduated *summa cum laude* in

1913 and immediately thereafter returned to Seattle where he accepted a position as assistant professor of geology at the University of Washington.[22] He had difficulties with the attitudes of other teaching staff there (he later described them as 'stick-in-the-muds'[23]) and by 1914 he was back at the University of Chicago, initially as an instructor but soon afterward as an assistant professor.[24]

The first field trip Bretz made to the Scablands of eastern Washington was in 1922. By this point, as a result of his earlier work, he was fully informed about the Ice Age in all its dimensions and more aware than most other geologists that immense ice sheets up

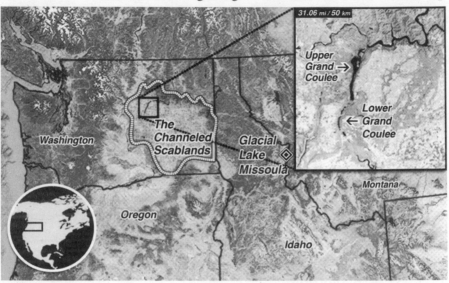

Figure 13

to two miles deep, had covered North America for the best part of 100,000 years until the ice melted dramatically somewhere between 15,000 and 11,000 years ago. Thus when he saw huge numbers of erratics – giant boulders that didn't belong naturally in the area but had clearly been brought in from elsewhere – he was inclined to assume that they might have travelled here in icebergs carried on some great glacial flood. This impression was strengthened when he explored Grand Coulee and Moses Coulee – gigantic channels gouged deeply in the earth – and visited the Quincy Basin at the southern end of Grand Coulee where he found the whole 600-square-mile depression filled up to a depth of 400 feet with small particles of basalt debris. He couldn't help but wonder, 'where had all the debris come from, and when?'[25] Again the answer that presented itself to him was a flood.

Bretz was back in the Scablands in 1923 for three months of exploration and it seems to have been during this field trip that his later views – namely that 'some spectacular hydrological event . . . had begun in this region, then abruptly stopped', really began to take shape.[26]

In the November–December 1923 issue of the *Journal of Geology* Bretz published a paper summarizing his findings. To understand the somewhat defensive tone of the paper it is important to keep in mind the prevailing geological doctrine of the time, the principle known as 'uniformitarianism'. This is the assumption that existing processes, *acting as at present*, are sufficient to account for all geological changes. Integral to it is the parallel assumption of gradualism, namely that 'the present is the key to the past' and that the rate of change observable today is an accurate guide to rates of change that prevailed in the past.

Such ideas, which had acquired the status of an unchallengeable truth by Bretz's day, had themselves arisen from the necessary – indeed essential – overthrow of the old religious belief in creationism and the notion that God whimsically intervened in the earth's history by ordaining cataclysms such as the Biblical Flood. In righteous opposition to these thoughts of supernatural creation and destruction, uniformitarianism seemed a profoundly rational response that saw only the forces of nature at work upon the earth over periods of millions, or indeed billions of years.

> Mountains had not been built overnight, but had risen slowly, imperceptibly over time. Likewise had fantastic geological features such as the Grand Canyon been eroded by the flow of rivers over many millions of years.[27]

Bretz was an eminently rational man, and certainly no religious dogmatist, yet, as his biographer John Soennichsen notes, 'while hiking through the hot, dry, ragged world of the Scablands, everything he had seen pointed not to a slow, uniform change over time but to a catastrophe, a sudden release of colossal quantities of water that had quickly washed away the loessial topsoil and then carved deeply into the basalt rock beneath.'[28]

The problem was – where had all this water come from? It was well understood that at the margin of the north American ice sheets there must have been some melting – as one indeed sees at the edges of all glaciers today. But such melting could hardly explain the magnitude of the erosive changes that were visible in the field. As Bretz noted in his 1923 paper:

The writer confesses that during ten weeks of study of the region, each newly examined scabland tract reawakened a feeling of amazement that such huge streams could take origin from such small marginal tracts of an ice sheet, or that such an enormous amount of erosion, despite high gradients, could have resulted in the very brief times these streams existed. Not River Warren, nor the Chicago outlet, not the Mowhawk channel, nor even Niagara Falls and Gorge itself approach the proportions of some of these scabland tracts and their canyons. From one of these canyons alone [Upper Grand Coulee] 10 cubic miles of basalt was eroded by its glacial stream.[29]

Concluding the paper, and moving towards the profoundly heretical and anti-uniformitarian idea that would soon get him into a great deal of trouble, namely that *a single cataclysmic flood* unleashed in a very short period had been responsible for all the devastation he had witnessed, Bretz wrote:

Fully 3,000 square miles of the Columbia plateau were swept by the glacial flood, and the loess and silt cover removed. More than 2,000 square miles of this area were left as bare, eroded, rock-cut channel floors, now the Scablands, and nearly 1,000 square miles carry gravel deposits derived from the eroded basalt. It *was* a debacle which swept the Columbia Plateau.[30]

In other words, as Bretz's biographer summarises, the geologist now believed that the features he had documented 'could only have been created by a flood of unimaginable proportions, possibly the largest flood in the history of the world'.[31]

The reaction of the geological establishment was one of stunned, embarrassed silence. To have strayed so far from the doctrine of uniformitarianism could only mean that Bretz must have gone mad. David Alt, Professor Emeritus of Geology at the University of Montana, describes one of the lectures that Bretz gave in which he expounded on the ideas in his 1923 paper:

> The geologists . . . were aghast in the same way that a roomful of physicists would be upon hearing a colleague explain how he had made a perpetual motion machine out of old popsicle sticks. Physicists had all learned very early of the futility of perpetual motion machines, and no properly educated geologist was supposed to traffic in catastrophes of any sort.[32]

Alt describes an old professor of his own undergraduate days who had been a student sitting in the audience when Bretz read his 1923 paper. It seems the professor did a hilarious impersonation of Bretz 'pounding on the podium with both fists and stomping on the floor as he used vivid language and gestures to convey his idea of a catastrophic flood to his horrified audience'.[33]

Quite apart from the theatricals, the geologists were shocked to hear Bretz invoke:

> a sudden catastrophe to explain the Scablands of eastern Washington. In their view this was a reversion to the unscientific thinking of some 125 years before. To this day, most geologists consider it nothing less than heresy to invoke a catastrophic explanation for a geologic event. So Bretz stepped off the edge of a very long limb when he suggested that a great flood had eroded the Scablands . . . [It made] him a pariah among geologists, an outcast from the politer precincts of society.[34]

The outcast did not give up, however. On the contrary, he doggedly continued with his research, bringing down ever more controversy on his head in the process but believing that facts, ultimately, would vindicate him.

The crunch came on 12 January 1927 when Bretz was ambushed by a lynch mob of his colleagues at a lecture he'd been invited to give to the Geological Society of Washington in the Cosmos Club, Washington DC. Bretz was by now calling 'his' flood the 'Spokane Flood' (after the town of Spokane) and liked to refer to the ice sheet from which it had emerged as the 'Spokane ice sheet' (neither term is used today but Bretz's Spokane ice sheet was, effectively the southern part of that great late Pleistocene ice sheet now known as the 'Cordilleran'). He believed that large parts of it must have melted with extraordinary rapidity, because 'the volume of water was very great, almost incredibly great . . . In spite of high gradients to draw it off, the pre-existing valleys first entered were inadequate to carry it all,

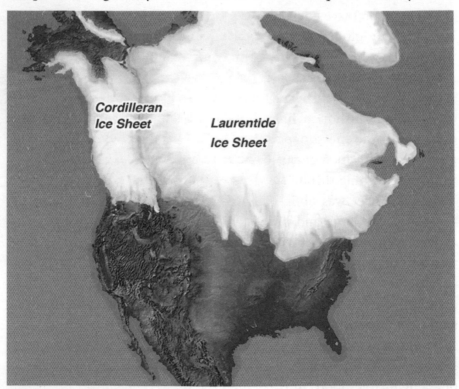

Figure 14: North America during the Ice Age.

and the flood spread widely in a complicated group of anastomosing routes.'[35]

W.C. Alden, then the Chief of Pleistocene Geology with the profoundly conservative US Geological Survey, objected to 'the idea that all the channels must have been developed simultaneously in a very short time' and took great offence at 'the tremendous amount of water' postulated by Bretz.[36] 'It seems to me impossible,' Alden protested, 'that such part of the great ice fields as would have drained across the Columbia Plateau could, under any conditions, have yielded so much water as is called for in so short a time.'[37] He admitted that he had never visited the Scablands himself but felt sure that a uniformitarian explanation was what was required: 'The problem would be easier if longer time and repeated floods could be allotted to do the work.'[38]

James Gilluly, well known as an apostle of geologic gradualism, dismissed the notion of a single cataclysmic flood with words like 'preposterous', 'incompetent', and 'wholly inadequate'.[39] He found nothing in Bretz's evidence to exclude his own preferred solution, namely that multiple smaller floods had been involved and that these would have been 'of the order of magnitude of the present Columbia's, or at most a few times as large'.[40]

Likewise G.R. Mansfield doubted that 'so much work could be done on basalt in so short a time . . . The Scablands seem to me better explained as the effects of persistent ponding and overflow of marginal glacial waters, which changed their position or their places of outlet from time to time through a somewhat protracted period.'[41]

O.E. Meinzer was obliged to confess that 'the erosion features of the region are large and bizarre' but he, too, preferred a gradualist explanation: 'Before a theory that requires a seemingly impossible quantity of water is fully accepted, every effort should be made to account for the existing features without employing so violent an assumption . . . I believe the existing features can be explained by assuming normal stream work of the ancient Columbia River . . .'[42]

In summary, not a single voice was raised in support of Bretz and there was much patronizing dismissal of his 'outrageous hypothesis' of a single large flood. In particular, the massed geologists homed in on what they clearly believed was the fatal flaw in the case for a sudden and overwhelming cataclysm – namely that Bretz had failed to identify a convincing source for his floodwaters.

Bretz replied that he saw no logic in this, since lack of a documented source for the flood did not prove that there had been no flood. 'I believe that my interpretation of Channeled Scabland should stand or fail on the scabland phenomena themselves,' he argued.[43] He was, he said, as sensitive as anyone else to adverse criticism, and had 'no desire to invite attention simply by advocating extremely novel views.' Moreover, he himself had repeatedly been driven to doubt 'the verity of the Spokane Flood',[44] only to be forced 'by reconsideration of the field evidence, to use again the conception of enormous volume . . . These remarkable records of running water on the Columbia Plateau, and in the valleys of the Snake and Columbia Rivers, cannot be interpreted in terms of ordinary river action and ordinary valley development . . . Enormous volume, existing for a very short time, alone will account for their existence.'[45]

It was this accumulation of compelling field evidence that Bretz asked to be considered – not by emotion, not by intuition, not by reference to received wisdom, but only by 'the established principles of the scientific method'.[46] 'Ideas without precedent,' he was to write later:

are generally looked on with disfavour and men are shocked if their conceptions of an orderly world are challenged. A hypothesis earnestly defended begets emotional reaction which may cloud the protagonist's view, but if such hypotheses outrage prevailing modes of thought the view of antagonists may also become fogged.

On the other hand, geology is plagued with extravagant ideas which spring from faulty observation and misinterpretation. They are worse than 'outrageous hypotheses', for they lead nowhere. The writer's Spokane Flood hypothesis may belong to the latter class, but it cannot be placed there unless errors of observation and direct inference are demonstrated.[47]

And this was the problem with all the criticisms of Bretz both before and after the Washington meeting. The geological establishment did not like what he had to say, it flew in the face of their gradualist reference frame, and they regarded it as a 'heresy that must be gently but firmly stamped out'.[48] In the final analysis, however, they could not disprove his science, only disapprove of it, which is a very different thing.

The heart of the matter remained Bretz's assertion that the ice cap had melted precipitously and his inability to propose a mechanism that could have brought about such melting. He himself, as noted, did not regard this as a significant stumbling block, but his critics did. Over the years, therefore, in attempts to appease them, he several times reluctantly, proposed two possible solutions. These were some sort of radical, short-lived climate change, on the one hand or, on the other, an episode of volcanic activity beneath the ice cap. He admitted of the former, however, that 'no such climatic change is recorded else-where, and the rapidity demanded seems impossible', while of the latter, he observed that 'nothing has been found in the literature to suggest Pleistocene volcanism in the area which was drained across the Columbia Plateau.'[49]

Interestingly, by the time Bretz faced his hostile peers in Washington he was *already* aware of – but had dismissed – the very explanation for cataclysmic flooding that would much later be taken up by the geological establishment and open the door to the universal acceptance of his evidence that prevails today. In his outline for his January 1927 presentation he wrote: 'Both Mr Alden and Mr Pardee have suggested that I consider the sudden draining of a glacial lake to account for the flood . . . Mr Pardee [in a 1925 letter to Bretz] specifies Lake Missoula, which is the only one of any magnitude known in the region that might have functioned.'[50]

Eventually, in the 1940s, Bretz would indeed embrace a sudden draining of Glacial Lake Missoula as the source for his flood but the reason why he did *not* do so in 1927 is important and, as we shall see, of the greatest relevance to the evolving debate about what exactly happened in North America at the end of the Ice Age. In brief Bretz's view in 1927, as his biographer explains, was that the volume of Lake Missoula 'might not have been adequate to form the Scablands. "Twould run the flood for only 2 weeks," reads a handwritten comment by Bretz in this section of his outline.'[51]

In March 1930, Bretz published a brief abstract in the *Bulletin of the Geological Society of America*. The abstract was titled 'Lake Missoula and the Spokane Flood'. In it Bretz wrote that this lake had first been named and described by the geologist J.T. Pardee (whose letter on the subject he'd received in 1925), that it stood more than 4,000 feet above sea level and that it was at least 2,100 feet deep. Without going into any detail he noted that the lake had been held in place by an ice dam and that 'seventy miles to the south-west, along the western arm of Purcell Trench and Spokane Valley, are the easternmost heads of the scabland channels. If a bursting of the dam occurred, water could escape only along this seventy-mile stretch.'[52]

By 1932 Bretz had warmed further to the idea that Lake Missoula could be the culprit behind his flood, although he felt that issues concerning the hypothetical ice dam and its proposed cataclysmic failure remained to be worked out.[53] At this point in his life, however, he seemed ready to move on and was to devote most of the next decade to other, completely different, geological puzzles. Then, in 1940, he was invited to speak on his Scablands theory at a meeting of the American Association for the Advancement of Science being held in Seattle. He declined the invitation, saying that his views and evidence

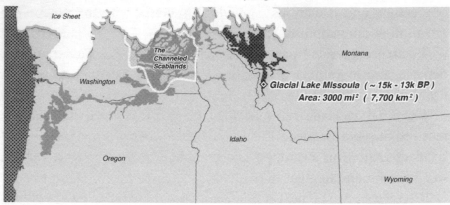

Figure 15

were already in print, but the event turned out to be a seminal one. J.T. Pardee was there and presented a paper on his work on Glacial Lake Missoula, making public for the first time his long-held conclusion that there had been a failure of an ice dam and that 'the entire lake had drained catastrophically and, most likely, quite dramatically'.[54]

Curiously Pardee did not connect his Missoula findings to Bretz's own long-standing and well-known case about the creation of the Channeled Scablands by a catastrophic flood, but much later, Bretz would write: 'He never said, at least in print, anything about the final deposition of this vigorous discharge. I do believe, however, that he was generously leaving that to me.'[55]

In the process of making the most of what had been left to him, Bretz abandoned his single cataclysmic flood model in favour of one more palatable to his opponents. 'There were several floods,' he was eventually to write (in 1959). 'The theory is elastic enough to take care of that.' [56] In the same year, Bretz was presented with the Neil Milner Award in honour of his exceptional contributions to Earth Sciences.[57]

A few years later, in 1965, Bretz's transformation from pariah to poster boy seemed complete. The International Union for Quaternary Research organised a field trip to the Columbia Plateau for many former critics of the catastrophic flood theory. The group traversed the full length of Grand Coulee, part of the Quincy Basin, and much of the Palouse-Snake scabland divide. At the end of the trip the participants, humbled by what they had seen, and satisfied as to the source of the flood-damage in Glacial Lake Missoula, sent Bretz a telegram of greetings and salutations. The telegram closed with the words: 'We are all now catastrophists.'[58]

'Be assured,' wrote Bretz, 'that after 30 years, and 30 papers in self-defence, and more than 30 people who vigorously denied my theory, it did my heart good like medicine.'[59]

The final accolade came in 1979 when Bretz, by then aged 96, received the Penrose Medal, the Geological Society of America's highest accolade. After this award, he told his son: 'All my enemies are dead, so I have no one to gloat over.'[60]

Bretz went on to his next great adventure, aged 98 years, on 3 February 1981.

Gradualism draws the teeth of Bretz's cataclysm

So . . . all seemed well. The evidence of a land scoured by cataclysmic deluge could not be denied. The timing had been set – perhaps not precisely, but at any rate somewhere in the last millennia of the Ice Age between 15,000 and 11,000 years ago. The source of the deluge had been tracked down to Glacial Lake Missoula. And the crunch-point of whether there had been just one gigantic flood – which Bretz's honed instincts as a field geologist had originally suggested – or multiple floods as his gradualist colleagues preferred, had been conceded with reference to the elasticity of his theory and an allowance of 'several' floods.

It becomes clear in later papers published by Bretz that he was willing to accept that up to eight floods had occurred.[61] This was, undoubtedly, a concession to gradualism – eight smaller floods politely spread out over a period of some thousands of years being more palatable to those of a uniformitarian persuasion (i.e. to most geologists, then and now) than a single humungous event of great violence that occurred suddenly, did massive damage, and was over and done with in about three months. Nonetheless Bretz remained a catastrophist at heart. Victor R. Baker of the Department of Hydrology and Water Resources at the University of Arizona notes in his study, *The Spokane Flood Debates*, that while Bretz did indeed extensively modify his original hypothesis,

> there was a lingering suspicion that one was dealing with an unusual exception to a general rule. Bretz himself had claimed: 'The unique assemblage of forms . . . described . . . as the Channeled Scabland . . . records a unique episode in Pleistocene history . . . Special causes seem clearly indicated.'[62]

In other words, regardless of any concessions, what is referred to here are causes that were still unique and special enough to be described as catastrophic and that did not undermine the conclusion that 'it *was* a debacle which swept the Columbia plateau'.[63] It is surely significant that in his last published work, a note he wrote to the Geological Society of America in 1979 accepting its highest accolade, the Penrose Medal, that Bretz took the opportunity to drive this point home. 'Perhaps,' he wrote:

I can be credited with reviving and demystifying legendary catastrophism and challenging a too rigorous uniformitarianism.[64]

What Bretz the catastrophist and challenger of uniformitarianism could not have known, however was that once he had invited the vampire of gradualism through the door it would not be satisfied with the compromise that he had tried to strike, but would keep on remorselessly sucking the blood out of any notion that what had happened in the Channeled Scablands had been any sort of 'debacle' at all.

Thus, as the years have gone by and new generations of gradualist scholars have taken their places at universities around the world, the eight floods that were first allowed to modify Bretz's single cataclysm have steadily increased in number – to a dozen, then to more than twenty, then to thirty-five, then to 'about forty', and finally, in recent papers, to as many as ninety or more![65] 'The most current opinion,' summarises Vic Baker, 'is that there were about eighty floods that all occurred within a period of 2,500 years [roughly between 15,000 years ago and 12,000 years ago], possibly at regular intervals.'[66]

Eighty floods in 2,500 years works out at one flood approximately every thirty-one years – thus doing away with any need for a single exceptional cataclysm and accounting for the horrendous mess of the Channeled Scablands by the accumulated effects of a rather regular, predictable, essentially gradualist series of events. Better still, from the uniformitarian point of view, outburst floods from ice-dammed glacial lakes still occur today. They happen regularly in Iceland, for example, where they are called *jökulhlaups*, the term that has been adopted for them worldwide, and that I will continue to use here. Other locations where they are common include the Himalayas, Antarctica, Northern Sweden, and North America. As Geology Professor David Alt points out, several glacially dammed lakes in Alaska and northern British Columbia are prone to episodes of very fast drainage. These events usually occur 'in summer when a fast snowmelt rapidly raises the level of the lake. The ice dam that held

Glacial Lake Missoula probably floated and broke during the summer for the same reason.'[67]

In this way the uniformitarian doctrine that 'the present is the key to the past', and that the rate of change observable today is an accurate guide to rates of change that prevailed in the past, has quietly reasserted itself and Bretz's disturbing flood evidence has been explained away as nothing very much to worry about after all. The scholars have also rather cleverly contrived to have their cake and eat it: on the one hand giving Bretz a medal and proclaiming that they are 'all catastrophists now'; on the other quietly transmuting Bretz's catastrophe into the sort of thing that one sees every summer in Alaska and British Columbia.

This is all very reassuring, of course, but suppose that Bretz's original insight was right and that what happened in North America at the end of the Ice Age really was a sudden, cataclysmic flood, something unprecedented and unmatched since?

Suppose it really was a debacle?

Back to Bretz

Randall Carlson is quite certain that it was indeed a debacle – one that unfolded on an almost unbelievable scale – and has spent the last twenty years trekking back and forth across the Channeled Scablands asking local geologists difficult questions that no one else seems to have considered and building a formidable case.

The sort of case, I suspect, that Bretz would be making if he were still with us and at the height of his powers.

I first met Randall in 2006. The North American Ice Age floods were amongst the subjects we discussed and I was startled to discover that he didn't accept the ice dam theory *at all*, and regarded Glacial Lake Missoula as a huge diversion – an easy solution that panders to uniformitarian prejudices and has led geologists away from the truth. In the years that followed we corresponded from time to time and occasionally bumped into each other at conferences where we were both speaking. I was enormously impressed by his depth of knowledge, by his field experience and by the intriguing new insights his research seemed to offer into the mysterious events that brought the Ice Age to an end. I found we shared a particular and growing interest in the Younger Dryas – that return to full glacial conditions that began suddenly 12,800 years ago, just when the world seemed to be warming up, and that ended equally suddenly 1,200 years later.

During this peculiar episode certain Stone Age hunter-gatherer peoples such as the 'Clovis' culture of North America vanished from the archaeological record and there were mass extinctions of animal species – so clearly something unusual was going on – yet no uniformitarian or gradualist explanations have ever been offered. Moreover, although I didn't investigate it in my 1995 book *Fingerprints of the Gods*, I realised afterwards that the span of the Younger Dryas, from 12,800 years ago to 11,600 years ago, coincided exactly with the 'window' during which I had argued that an advanced civilization of prehistoric antiquity was obliterated from the face of the earth and lost from human memory.

Accordingly in my book *Underworld*, published in 2002, I was more attentive to the Younger Dryas problem. 'At around 13,000 years ago,' I noted:

the long period of uninterrupted warming that the world had just passed through (and that had greatly intensified, according to some studies, between 15,000 years ago and 13,000 years ago[68]) was instantly brought to a halt – all at once, everywhere – by a global cold event known to palaeoclimatologists as the 'Younger Dryas' . . .[69] In many ways mysterious and unexplained, this was an almost unbelievably fast climatic reversion – from conditions that are calculated to have been warmer and wetter than today's 13,000 years ago,[70] to conditions that were colder and drier than those at the last glacial maximum just a few hundred years later.[71]

From that moment, around 12,800 years ago, it was as though an enchantment of ice had gripped the earth. In many areas that had been approaching terminal meltdown full glacial conditions were restored with breathtaking rapidity and all the gains that had been made since the LGM [Last Glacial Maximum – around

21,000 years ago] were simply stripped away: 'Temperatures . . . fell back on the order of 8-15 degrees centigrade . . . with half this brutal decline possibly occurring within decades. The Polar Front in the North Atlantic redescended to the level of Cabo Finisterre in northwest Spain and glaciers readvanced in the high mountain chains. With respect to temperature the setback to full glacial conditions was nearly complete . . .'[72]

For human populations at the time, in many except the most accidentally favoured parts of the world, the sudden and inexplicable plunge into severe cold and aridity must have been devastating.[73]

The sense of mystery – and mortal danger to mankind – that clung about the Younger Dryas continued to intrigue me, encouraging me to read up on it and try to understand it better. I recall a number of conversations and email exchanges with Randall after 2006 that focused on the subject and it became increasingly obvious to me that the Younger Dryas had been a global cataclysm in every meaningful sense of the term. It wasn't until 2013, however, when Randall made the case to me that North America, and particularly the Channeled Scablands, had stood at the epicentre of that cataclysm, that I decided it was time to see the evidence on the ground. On impulse I invited him to join me on a field trip. It took more than a year to find a time that worked for both our schedules but finally, in September 2014 I met Randall in Portland, Oregon, and we took off east and north into neighbouring Washington State to explore the Scablands in the big, red four-wheel drive we'd hired.

Chapter 4
Journey Through the Scablands

—◆—

We're on a 2,500 mile (4,000 kilometre) road trip from Portland, Oregon to Minneapolis, Minnesota. The journey would be shorter if we took the direct route. But we're stopping and diverting into coulees and river valleys and around buttes and up the sides of mountains and across the Channeled Scablands immediately south of the vast Cordilleran and Laurentide ice caps that once covered much of North America. The objective is for me to get as full an understanding as possible of what happened here and by the fourth day, when we reach Dry Falls in the middle of the extraordinary scar on the landscape called Grand Coulee, the picture is beginning to become clear.

The ground under our feet is ancient black basalt covered with a thin layer of topsoil. The basalt, extruded by volcanic eruptions between seventeen million and six million years ago, covers much of the Columbia Plateau and in some places is 2,000 metres (6,600 feet) thick.[1]

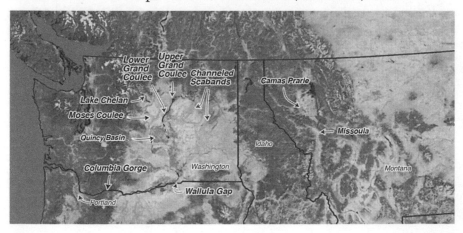

Figure 16

Not in Grand Coulee, though, because here it's as if some capricious force, perhaps even the hand of God himself, has seized a giant chisel with a blade miles wide, plunged it violently into the earth and gouged out a sheer-sided gash hundreds of feet deep and almost 60 miles (96 kilometres) long. The 'chisel', however, was not made of steel but of immense quantities of rushing, turbulent, debris-laden water that flowed for a few weeks only – the water of Bretz's flood. 'Grand Coulee,' he wrote, affords:

> the greatest example of canyon-cutting by glacial streams not alone for the Columbia Plateau, but for the world . . . A glacial river three miles in minimum width spilled southward here over the divide and down a steep monoclinal slope . . . The stream descended nearly 1,000 feet on a grade of approximately 10 degrees . . . Such a situation is unparalleled, even in this region of huge, suddenly initiated, high-gradient rivers . . . At least 10 cubic miles of basalt were excavated and removed.[2]

Bretz refers here only to the northern or Upper part of Grand Coulee.[3] But the same amount of basalt again was also excavated from Lower Grand Coulee as 'the stream' rushed on. Making our way here today we paused in the Ephrata Erratics Fan, south of the southern end of Lower Grand Coulee to see where all that basalt excavated by the waters was dumped. It was a chaotic, jumbled, disturbing sight – disturbing because as far as the eye could see in all directions across the prairie lay scattered countless thousands – more likely millions – of jagged, broken basalt boulders, some about the size of a family car, some smaller – down to the size of a football – and many larger.

'Everything was reduced to rubble,' Randall Carlson explained to me, as we stood there in the midst of the Fan, 'and that's what you're seeing. This rubble was part of the former world.'

'The former world?'

'Yes. The antediluvian world. And what's lying here on the surface is just a fraction of what the flood flushed out of Grand Coulee. The rubble goes down deep. Hundreds of feet deep.'

From the Ephrata Fan we drove north on Washington State Route 17 into Lower Grand Coulee, it's sheer, forbidding basalt cliffs rearing up on either side of us, the grey rainclouds above reflected darkly in the chain of alkaline lakes – Soap Lake, Lenore Lake, Blue Lake and Park Lake – that lie ponded in its floor. Now we've reached Dry Falls at the head of Lower Grand Coulee and as we get out of the truck Randall reminds my wife Santha to bring her camera. 'You're going to see something cataclysmic here,' he announces with a mischievous grin.

Meet Randall Carlson

You may be too young to remember the 1977 TV series called *The Life and Times of Grizzly Adams*, but you can always Google it if you weren't here.

The eponymous hero, a tough woodsman played by actor Dan Haggerty, was a big, bluff, bearded sort of fellow and Randall Carlson, by virtue of his enormous beard, his general appearance and his rough, gruff personal style, reminds me of him a lot. Randall lives in Atlanta, Georgia, now, but he spent most of his youth in rural Minnesota and his voice still carries the quirky undertones of Scandinavian and German that make the Minnesota accent so recognizable.

He grew up on the shores of Schmidt Lake, one of tens of thousands of small meltwater lakes spread across Minnesota and Wisconsin, and he used to go fishing there as a boy, perched on a huge boulder that he afterwards understood to be a glacial erratic – 'a boulder quarried from bedrock and carried by an advancing glacier perhaps many hundreds of miles from its source to be deposited in a location far removed from its origin'.[4]

Today, half a century on from his boyhood, he says that the Midwestern landscapes of his youth have left an indelible imprint on his psyche:

From these early experiences I entered into a sort of dialogue with the earth which continues unabated to this day. This dialogue has involved thousands of hours spent in the field, traversing

71

and studying a wide variety of landscapes, along with thousands of hours in the study of various sciences related in one way or another to the goal of understanding this extraordinary planet upon which we are engaged in this ongoing human experience . . . It is a fearsomely dynamic planet, one that has undergone profound changes on a scale far exceeding anything within recent times. In fact I now realise that what we think of as history is merely the record of human events that have transpired since the last, great planetary catastrophe. I also understand that the imprint of these catastrophes is to be found all around us, in virtually every environment, and we are just beginning to be able to perceive and decipher the evidence.[5]

Randall makes his living as an architect and builder but his passion is geology.

Catastrophist geology.

And as those who have attended one of his lectures will attest, he knows more about it than pretty much anyone else you are ever likely to meet. He has gleaned his knowledge from a vast reading of the scientific literature and, as he says above, from thousands of hours of fieldwork. To me this sort of in-depth on the ground learning, the miles walked through the wilderness, the years of dedicated library research, mean far more than any university degree. Randall is not a geologist and does not claim to be a geologist but his grasp of the subject is worth a dozen PhDs.

And right now we're standing on a sort of concrete pier with waist-high fencing, suspended out over the plunging horseshoe amphitheatre of Dry Falls. There's a chill wind blowing this late September day and Randall is about to give me a geology lesson . . .

Dry Falls

'Ever been to Niagara Falls?' Randall asks.[6]

I confess that I have not.

'But you've seen photographs? You have a sense of the place?'

'I suppose, so, yes . . .'

'OK, so just a guess . . . Which is bigger?' He indicates the vista that confronts us. 'Dry Falls? Or Niagara?'

I'm thinking it's a trick question. Randall being a Minnesotan, is of course compelled to ask trick questions. I look out at the natural amphitheatre. It's a long way down. And a long way across. A couple of circular lakes of pooled rainwater, overgrown with reeds, decorate the base of the towering horseshoe of sheer cliffs confronting me – over which, it is absolutely obvious, huge quantities of water must once have flowed. I haven't been to the Niagara Falls, which are 51 metres high, but I did spend a day of amazement at Victoria Falls in southern Africa, and they're 108 metres high. The classic horseshoe shape of Niagara that you see in all the pictures is repeated at Victoria Falls. And here's the same horseshoe shape in Washington State in the US, preserved in the dry fossil of an ancient cataract.

'Dry Falls is bigger than Niagara,' I say, sounding more confident than I feel.

'Okay, good so far, but how *much* bigger?'

'Twice as big,' I hazard a guess.

'Not bad,' Randall says. 'But actually Dry Falls is close to three times as high as Niagara and more than six times as wide.' He points. 'See how the cliffs are scalloped there?'

I do. The Dry Falls horseshoe is in fact two horseshoes side by side, one to the east, one to the west.

'Well, Niagara would fit easily into just half of the eastern horseshoe and its rim would be almost two hundred and fifty feet beneath the rim of Dry Falls. Also – look there . . .' Randall draws my attention to the eastern side of the horseshoe where there's a gap and then a high, narrow fin of cliffs running south. 'That's Umatilla Rock,' he says, indicating the fin. It would have been a kind of island at the peak of the flood. An underwater island.'

'Underwater?'

'Yes. When the flood came through here, the water was more than five hundred feet deep. It would have overtopped Umatilla Rock, and the Falls themselves, and right here where we're standing, by, oh, a hundred, maybe a hundred and fifty feet.'

'So if I'd been able to stand here then . . .'

'Which you wouldn't have . . .'

'I know. I'd have been swept away, but just for the sake of argument, if I had been able to stand here, I take it I *wouldn't* have seen a sheer sheet of water bursting over the lip of the falls and crashing down hundreds of feet?'

'No, because that was happening far beneath the surface. What you would have seen at this point would have looked more like a whirling, churning slope in the torrent with some kind of abrupt bump or gradient in it than an actual waterfall, but all the work that a waterfall does on rock was still going on, under the surface . . .'

'What do you mean by work on the rock?'

'The water is coming through here in enormous quantities and horribly fast, running at up to seventy miles an hour according to some estimates, and you've got to realise that it isn't just water. It's more like a slurry of thick mud, and there's whole forests torn up by their roots that are roiling around in it, and fleets of icebergs jostling on the surface, and down at the bottom there's a huge rumbling rubble of rocky debris, boulders like the ones we saw dumped all over the Ephrata Fan, and this whole mess is rushing and tumbling and plucking as it passes . . .'

'Plucking?'

'Yes, that's the best way to describe it. Like giant fingers plucking out blocks of the basalt bedrock, ripping them out, dragging them into the torrent and sweeping them downstream – that's how the erosive work is done.' Randall gestures again at the scalloped, horseshoe cliffs. 'But what we see from here is less than half the picture. If we were up in an airplane looking down we'd see another set of horseshoes even bigger than these ones off to the east, wrapping round beyond Umatilla Rock . . .'

'So with all that taken into account, what's the total extent of Dry Falls?'

'About three and a half miles . . . That was where it had got to when the flood stopped. God only knows what it would have ended up looking like, or where it would have been today, if the flood had continued even for another couple of weeks . . .'

'I don't understand.'

'The indications are that the flood only lasted a matter of weeks, and throughout that time the falls were constantly migrating northwards . . .'

'Migrating?'

'Yes, all falls migrate, at different rates depending on the amount and force of the water flowing over them. They pluck at the bedrock and constantly eat it away upstream. Take Niagara, for example. It's retreated seven miles in the last twelve thousand years,[7] but that's puny compared with what happened here, where the retreat was about thirty miles – the whole length of Lower Grand Coulee – in less than a month.'

'So the rate of erosion was incredibly fast?'

'Yes! Thousands of times faster than Niagara, because of the incredible amount and force of the water here. Dry Falls was the greatest waterfall that's ever existed on planet earth.'

'And all that water's supposed to have come out of Glacial Lake Missoula?'

'Well,' says Randall. His beard juts out stubbornly. 'That's the theory.'

Erratic hunting

Randall doesn't buy the gradualist theory that multiple emptyings of Lake Missoula through multiple breakings and remakings and breaking again of its ice-dam can account for the evidence on the ground. He doesn't dispute that the glacial lake existed, or that there were outburst floods from it, but he's convinced it was never anywhere near big enough to account for all the cataclysmic features of the Channeled Scablands. Like J Harlen Bretz in the 1920s, he believes that one sudden, short-lived, totally exceptional flood of truly immense proportions was the real culprit.

On another day Randall takes me 'erratic hunting' to explain why. We pull off Interstate 97 onto the Waterville Plateau and drive across rugged, rolling country where occasional green and yellow fields intermingle with wilder moorland too poor ever to be farmed. Pretty soon we start seeing huge clusters, flocks, packs, crowds, of giant boulders all of ominous black basalt, all alien to this landscape and I know enough, now, to recognise them for what they are. As ice caps move and spread they snatch up, enchain and transport huge rocks that then remain locked within them until the ice melts and drops it load. What happened here – the place is actually called 'Boulder Park' and is recognised as a National Natural Landmark – was a different aspect of the same process. 'When the Ice Age flood came pouring down over the Waterville Plateau,' Randall explains:

> it was carrying thousands of icebergs with it – icebergs as big as oil-tankers with house-sized boulders frozen inside them. When they bumped up against hillsides [he points to a distant ridge with ranks of colossal boulders strewn across it] the icebergs grounded and stuck there. Eventually, after the flood had subsided, they melted out leaving the boulders where they sit to this day strewn all over the top of the plateau beyond the ridge and carpeting the hillside for twenty miles going north.'

'But that ridge must be what, eight hundred, maybe nine hundred feet above us,' I observe.

'Exactly! Which tells us that the water was at least that deep here. Or rather, not simply water but a sludge slurry, and as the flood starts to subside the slurry just gets thicker and thicker with sediment until it finally leaves the whole valley floor covered in sediment hundreds of feet thick and filled with embedded boulders. I mean, again, we are looking at the ruins and wreckage of a former world.'

We get back onto Interstate 97 heading south along the west bank of the majestic Columbia river and divert west on Alternate 97 towards Lake Chelan. Fifty miles long and never more than a mile and a half wide, lying in the bottom of a forested, steep-sided valley overshadowed by lofty mountains, Chelan has the look and feel of a grand Scottish

Figure 17

loch. It is appropriate, therefore, that it also has traditions of a lake monster – a dragon, according to Native American legends – that ate up all the game, leaving the people starving. The Great Spirit was angered and decided to intervene. He descended from the sky:

> and struck the earth with his huge stone knife. All the world shook from his blow. A great cloud appeared over the plain. When the cloud went away, people saw that the land had changed. Huge mountain peaks rose on all sides of them. Among the mountains were canyons. Extending from the north-west to the south-east for a two days' journey was a very deep canyon. The Great Spirit threw the monster's body into this deep and long gorge. Then he poured much water into it and so formed the lake. Long afterward, Indians called it Chelan.[8]

Chelan means 'Deep Water' in the local Salish Indian language, and Lake Chelan is indeed 1,468 feet (453 metres) deep, making it the third deepest lake in the US and the twenty-sixth deepest in the world.[9] Some aspects of the myth, I note in passing, are evocative of earth changes at the end of the Ice Age. Mountains that had been hidden beneath the ice cap, and that therefore no one had seen before, did indeed appear when the ice melted. Canyons were indeed carved through the whole of the Columbia Plateau by the rushing waters of Bretz's flood. And as we will see in the next chapter there may also be more than meets the eye to the huge stone knife from the sky striking the ground so hard that 'the world shook', and to that ominous cloud that appeared over the land. Likewise, the presence of an immense iceberg-rafted erratic above the town of Manson on Chelan's north shore,[10] suggests that the notion of 'much water' being poured into the lake, in other words of a flood passing through here, may also be rooted in memories of real events.

After passing more erratics scattered around the southern end of Lake Chelan,[11] we head back to Interstate 97, cross to the east bank of the Columbia River at Beebe Bridge, then go north to the mouth of McNeil Canyon where yet more boulder-strewn moorland awaits us. Numbering in their thousands, the erratics here are known locally as 'haystack boulders' because of their distinctive appearance, but the rounded profile they show from a distance gives way, close up, to a mass of jagged and splintered black basalt. Many of them are thought to weigh more than 10,000 tons, and as Randall and I examine them, I'm daunted by their great height and mass, and amazed at the power and energy of the floodwaters that brought them here.

We get back on Interstate 97 again and drive the forty miles south to the confluence of the Wenatchee and Columbia Rivers near the eastern foothills of the Cascade Mountains. Here Randall has a last giant erratic to show me, this one weighing, he estimates, 18,000 tons. It stands high up on the side of a long, wide valley, looming over a modern housing development, hundreds of feet above the confluence of the rivers and the town of Wenatchee.

We scramble to the top of the erratic so we can look down on the rivers glistening far below. 'Obviously,' Randall explains, 'the flood waters must have filled the whole valley from bottom to top so when the iceberg floated in it stranded right here then melted away and left this sitting on the ridge.'

'And the flood itself? Where did it go next?'

'The water coming down through here met the water coming out of Grand Coulee and Moses Coulee and many other scabland channels, and then it all together flowed down to Pasco Basin and Wallula Gap . . .'

Black rain

The next day finds us on top of a high bluff overlooking Wallula Gap. 'So the water here rose up to roughly 1,200 feet above sea level,' Randall says.[12] He consults his GPS, 'and where we're standing now is 1,150 feet above sea level, so the flood would have been fifty feet over our heads.'

'And the water came from which direction?'

Randall points north: 'It came roaring out of the Channeled Scablands. A mass of different flows converged here, and then passed on through, down the Columbia. So this was the gathering of the waters. Here's where all of these great flood streams came together.'

I look out over the scene below, a drama of earth, and sky . . . and water.

The sky is grey, thunderous and filled with rain as it has been throughout our trip. The earth element begins with a very thick, powdery layer of soft dun-coloured dust called loess that lies everywhere under our feet on the top of the bluff. But then the bluff plunges away in a steep tumbling fall down to the Columbia – which forms the water element – below. Across the stream, more than a mile wide here, the terrain rises again towards the east, not so sheer as on the west side where we're standing, still covered by that same thick layer of powdery loess and marked in addition by distinctive scabland topography, with cliffs plunging into valleys and a series of outcrops carved by the ancient floods – most prominently the two isolated basalt pillars known as the 'Twin Sisters' that stand directly opposite us.

'Those Twin Sisters,' Randall explains, 'are a remnant . . . Look there, immediately to the left of the Sisters you can see a shelf. That would have all been continuous . . . I believe that was the pre-flood valley floor . . . When the flood hit, it ripped through here and lowered the valley floor by about two hundred feet, based on the present depth of the river and the height of the Twin Sisters. Had the flood continued

for a week longer the Twins would have been washed away as well
. . . They would have been about eight hundred feet underwater. And
really, if you look across – there, way above the level of the Sisters –
you'll see that uppermost outcrop of basalt, roughly at our level. That
would have been the high water mark and everything below that was
underwater at the peak of the flood – so what you're seeing over there
in the scabland around the Sisters is that spectacular erosion of the
basalt by the water, just ripping through here at sixty or seventy miles
an hour because the back pressure would have been so great.'

'Fearsome and ferocious flows,' I hazard.

'Oh, my God, yes! Like an inland sea, except that it's moving . . .'

'And it's turbulent and it's angry . . .'

'And the turbulence is increasing massively as it comes up to this
constriction at Wallula Gap. But when you look at the capacity of this
valley, it would have had to have been a hell of a lot of water pouring
in from the north to backflood to the extent that it did. The valley
out of Lake Missoula is no bigger than this one and it's two hundred
miles north of here. So how could that water have spilled out of Lake
Missoula, travelled two hundred miles to here, and not have attenuated
to the degree that it would just pass through without ponding above
the gap? But it did pond, massively and deeply as we can tell from the
high water mark. And that, to me, is just incontrovertible evidence
that there was more water pouring into this than could ever have been
pouring out of Lake Missoula.'

'So,' I summarise, 'we have water twelve hundred feet deep which
flows through here turbulently . . .'

'Very turbulently . . .'

'And then how long does it stay that deep?'

'The estimates are that it's probably one to three weeks, and then it
begins to ebb away. Because . . . they call this hydraulic ponding. This
was effectively a hydraulic dam in the sense that the water itself, forced
through a constriction like Wallula Gap, becomes a kind of dam – and
especially so since the water here was filled with massive icebergs. All
throughout the flood pathway are erratics that were carried by icebergs
– all the way down into Eugene, Oregon . . . You gotta picture it. You've
got a moving sea choked with thousands of icebergs . . .'

I'm getting the picture all right. 'Wild scene,' I say.

'Wild scene,' Randall agrees. 'All of these icebergs are jostling up against each other and getting jammed in the gap. And what that's going to do is cause the water level to rise still further until the pressure increases enough to push the whole mass down through the gap – then the water level drops until the next jam occurs. So I think what we're seeing is a pulsating hydrograph that every time it rises, it backfloods further up the valley, and then the water level drops and then it rises again.'

The next point I put to Randall, closely connected to the vision of the flooded hellworld that he's just conjured up, relates to the central enigma I wish to explore in the rest of this section, but which I have not yet placed before the reader. It concerns the growing body of evidence that 12,800 years ago a giant comet travelling on an orbit that took it through the inner solar system broke up into multiple fragments, and that many of these fragments, some more than a mile (2.4 kilometres) in diameter, hit the earth. It is believed that North America was the epicentre of the resulting cataclysm with several of the largest impacts on the North American ice cap causing floods and tidal waves and throwing a vast cloud of dust into the upper atmosphere that enshrouded the earth, preventing the sun's rays from reaching the surface and thus initiating the sudden, mysterious global deep freeze that geologists call the Younger Dryas. We will go into the evidence for all this, and how it relates to 'Bretz's flood' – which might not, after all, have emerged from Lake Missoula – in the chapters that follow. But for now, please bear with me as I play out the rest of my conversation with Randall at Wallula Gap.

'And there's been a comet impact,' I say, 'so we're expecting that the sky is going to be bad too . . .'

'Oh, it's got to be . . .'

'Dark . . .' I think about it, then add: 'Lots of *stuff* wafted up there by the impact.'

'Stuff!' Randall kicks a furrow in the soft dust with the toe of his hiking boot. 'That's what I think this six-foot layer of loess is. All over the flood areas you see this six, seven, eight-foot thick layer of loess – and clearly it rained down out of the atmosphere.'

'Like the legends of Kon-Tiki Viracocha.' I name the South American civilizing hero, white-skinned and bearded like Quetzalcoatl and the Apkallu sages described in Chapter One, who was said to have come to the Andes during a terrifying period, thousands of years in the past, 'when the earth had been inundated by a great flood and plunged into darkness by the disappearance of the sun'.[13] (Exactly like Quetzalcoatl in Mexico, and the Apkallu sages in Mesopotamia, Viracocha's civilizing mission in the Andes had been to bring laws and a moral code to the survivors of the disaster, and to teach them the skills of agriculture, architecture and engineering.)

'Ah yes,' Randall muses. 'The legends of Viracocha. Wasn't there something there about a black rain?'

'There was, absolutely. A thick, black rain. It's pretty much universal to the flood myths I've studied . . .'

Randall kicks the loess again. 'This stuff is puzzling you know. It has a kind of vertical structure. Most theories suggest that it's wind-borne, but the vertical structure is inconsistent with that. I'm developing an idea that it's actually both water and windborne, because I think that the final rainout after the comet hit the ice cap was essentially a rainout of mud. There would have been a huge injection of superheated water into the stratosphere – filthy, particle-laden water – which would have then spread rather like the debris cloud of a nuclear explosion and the end result would undoubtedly have been a very intense, and prolonged rainout.'

But did a comet hit the earth 12,800 years ago?

As we'll see in the next chapter, the evidence assembled by an international team of highly credentialled scientists is taking the comfortable world of gradualist, uniformitarian geology by storm.

Chapter 5
Nanodiamonds Are Forever

Continuing our journey east through the northern states of the US, after leaving Washington and driving across the Idaho panhandle, Randall made a point of showing me some of the spectacular features of Camas Prairie in western Montana. There, what look to the unpractised eye like a series of colossal dunes march in serried ranks across the flat yellow floor of an elliptical basin, twelve miles long and ten miles wide, in the midst of the Rocky Mountains. But the 'dunes', it turns out, are not dunes at all. Instead they are giant current ripples, some more than fifty feet high and three hundred feet long, formed at the end of the Ice Age when Camas Prairie was part of the bed of Glacial Lake Missoula and lay under about 1,400 feet of water.[1] Geologists are agreed that the ripples were shaped by powerful currents set in motion when the lake drained catastrophically.[2]

'And I don't dispute it,' Randall says, as we stand on a vantage point above the prairie. A largely deserted highway runs through

Figure 18

the floor of the ancient basin, but now as a vehicle appears, providing scale, I see that it's dwarfed to matchbox size by the ripples.

'So,' I ask, 'you have nothing against the existence of Lake Missoula as such? Or the notion that it did drain catastrophically?'

'No, nothing at all. I have no doubt there were dozens of *jökulhlaups* out of Lake Missoula. Some were even pretty big. My point, though, is that none of them were of sufficient size to cause the spectacular flood damage that we've seen in the Channeled Scablands. That was done by an event orders of magnitude bigger than anything Lake Missoula could provide. So yes, the lake was dammed by ice in the Clark Fork valley, just as the gradualists maintain, and yes, that ice dam did break frequently over a period of a few thousand years, say from 15,000 years ago down to about 13,000 years ago. But the amount of water released in these periodic floods was minuscule, just a drop in the bucket compared to the final event – in which Lake Missoula was also involved, of course, but definitely not as the main culprit.'

'And that final event had to do with the impact of our comet?' (I've started calling it 'ours', but it's usually referred to in the scientific literature as the 'Clovis comet' or the 'Younger Dryas Comet'.)

'You bet,' Randall replies. 'But not just one impact. Multiple impacts. I'm guessing as many as four of the fragments – each of them maybe half a mile across, maybe bigger – hit the Cordilleran and Laurentide ice caps in a sort of scatter gun effect and caused just a *massive* amount of instantaneous melting. The meltwater was everywhere, in enormous quantities. Naturally some of it cascaded into Lake Missoula, filling it up suddenly and causing it to burst its ice dam, thus adding its contents to the much bigger floods that were already sweeping down from the north.'

'So Lake Missoula was more of an innocent bystander, really, than the culprit.'

Randall chuckles. 'Yes, that's right. The lake was the innocent bystander that was in the way and that later got accused of the crime. But the comet was the culprit.'

Laurentide and Cordilleran Ice Sheet
Meltwater Discharge Routes
Courtesy of Randall Carlson

Figure 19

Conspiracy corner

I'm no conspiracy theorist but I have a sneaking feeling – nothing more – that something a bit like a conspiracy is at work in science to prevent the proper consideration and wide public uptake of catastrophist ideas. I gave the example of J Harlen Bretz in Chapter Three. The frosty and deeply unpleasant reception initially given to his findings, the years that he spent in academic limbo afterwards, the repeated, persistent efforts made by a host of scholars to dismiss his evidence entirely, or, failing that, to account for it by gradualist means, and then at last, years later, when all that had failed and the notion of outburst floods from Glacial Lake Missoula had offered itself as a solution, the realization that he had been right all along. But *not* right, *not* right under any circumstances, *not* right in any imaginable universe, on the issue of the single cataclysmic 'debacle' that his instincts had originally led him to! If J Harlen Bretz was to be *right*, then it was necessary that he should be right in a politically correct way – in other words, in a way that could be redacted by skilled uniformitarian spin-meisters to edit out any hint of lurking cosmic disaster!

Indeed, within the fantasy of such a conspiracy (I sincerely hope it is a fantasy!) the *jökulhlaups* idea is an exceptionally useful one. First of all, it provides what purports to be a wholesomely rational, sober and above all 'scientific' account of the tortured geological features witnessed by Bretz in the Scablands. Secondly, *jökulhlaups* happen every year in various parts of the world today, and thus do not violate the commandment that existing processes, *acting as at present*, must be held sufficient to account for all geological changes. Thirdly, present relevance can be assigned. The Ice Age floods need not be simply of scholarly interest; since *jökulhlaups* still occur in the twenty-first century, science can be brought to bear to anticipate and ameliorate their effects.

All of this might start to look like a very effective diversion from the truth, if the truth is that a cataclysm, a single, prodigious cataclysm, did occur at the end of the Ice Age . . .

And might furthermore recur.

What, in other words, if the Ojibwa prophecy is true?

What if the star with the long, wide tail is, indeed, 'going to destroy the world some day when it comes low again'?

Would those who know this benefit from sharing their knowledge with others? Or might they think it served their interests better to keep quiet about the whole thing?

We'll return to this in Chapter Nineteen. By comparison, the question we have to ask and answer first is much simpler.

Was the Younger Dryas cold event that began so suddenly and so mysteriously 12,800 years ago brought on by the effects of a large comet hitting the earth?

The evidence for the comet

'The Younger Dryas (YD) impact hypothesis,' as its proponents restated it in a keynote paper in *The Journal of Geology* in September 2014,

1. Overview of Gobekli Tepe with Enclosure D in the foreground.

2. Enclosure D with the enigmatic Pillar 43 at left.

3. The author with Professor Klaus Schmidt at Gobekli Tepe in 2013. Professor Schmidt (at left of picture) passed away in 2014.

4. Eastern central pillar, Enclosure D.

5. Pillar plinth.

6. Detail from west side of pillar figure's belt.

7. Pillar 43 in Enclosure D at Gobekli Tepe. This early photograph was taken by the excavator, Klaus Schmidt. Subsequently the lower part of the pillar showing the scorpion was reburied.

8. Enclosure B Gobekli Tepe.

9. The author with unfinished T-shaped pillar abandoned in the quarry at Gobekli Tepe.

10. The author with geologists Robert Schoch of Boston University (left) and Danny Natawidjaja (ccntre) at Gunung Padang, Indonesia, studying scans of the interior of the pyramid.

11. The author with Danny Natawidjaja at Gunung Padang.

12, 13. Overview of the principal terraces at Gunung Padang. In this form the site has been know to archaeology for a century. But only when geophysical survey work began in 2011 was it realize that there are hidden structures and much earlier layers of construction beneath the terraces.

14. The author with Randall Carlson at Dry Falls.

15. Wallula Gap, 'the gathering of the waters', scabland and the 'Twin Sisters' in the background.

16. The giant current ripples of Camas Prairie, some more than 50 feet high.

17. 'Boulder Park', Washington State. Huge boulders of 10,000 tons and more were carried here in icebergs by the cataclysmic floods at the end of the Ice Age.

'proposes that a major cosmic impact event occurred at the Younger Dryas Boundary (YDB) 12,800 years ago.'[3] The paper, as we will see, presented a mass of new evidence in support of the hypothesis – in particular confirming and greatly extending earlier evidence of the copious presence of nanodiamonds in samples from the Younger Dryas Boundary layer taken in many different countries. Nanodiamonds are microscopic diamonds that form under rare conditions of great shock, pressure and heat, and are recognised as being amongst the characteristic fingerprints – 'proxies' in scientific language – of powerful impacts by comets or asteroids.[4]

By 2014 when the *Journal of Geology* paper was published, debate over whether or not a comet impact was involved in setting off the Younger Dryas had been raging for seven years. The first headline that caught my eye was in *New Scientist* magazine of 22 May 2007 and asked provocatively:

DID A COMET WIPE OUT PREHISTORIC AMERICANS?

At that time, 2007, I was taking a break from the lost civilization mystery that had absorbed my energies, and been the subject of so many of my books, for so long. The *New Scientist* article tweaked my curiosity, however, because it referred to the exact epoch that I had focused on in my books. The article didn't speak of a lost civilization, but began with a reference to the so-called 'Clovis' culture of North America which, as we saw in Chapter Three, vanished from the archaeological record during the Younger Dryas between 12,800 and 11,600 years ago. 'The Clovis people,' the article observed:

flourishing some 13,000 years ago, had a mastery of stone weaponry that stood them in good stead against the constant threat of large carnivores, such as American lions and giant short-faced bears. It's unlikely, however, that they thought death would come from the sky.

According to results presented by a team of 25 researchers this week at the American Geophysical Union meeting in Acapulco, Mexico, that's where the Clovis people's doom came from. Citing several lines of evidence, the team suggests that a wayward comet hurtled into earth's atmosphere around 12,900 years ago [N.B. that date would later be revised downwards by a hundred years to 12,800 years ago], fractured into pieces and exploded in giant fireballs. Debris seems to have settled as far afield as Europe.[5]

As I read on, I learned that the team the article was referring to was composed of highly credentialled and eminently respectable mainstream scientists:

> Jim Kennett, an oceanographer at the University of California, Santa Barbara, and one of the team's three principal investigators, claims immense wildfires scorched North America in the aftermath, killing large populations of mammals and bringing an abrupt end to the Clovis culture. 'The entire continent was on fire,' he says.
>
> Lead team member Richard Firestone, a nuclear analytical chemist at the Lawrence Berkeley National Laboratory in California, says the evidence lies in a narrow 12,900-year-old carbon-rich layer of sediment found at eight well-dated Clovis-era sites and a peppering of sediment cores across North America, as well as one site in Belgium.[6]

Probed as to why no crater had yet been identified with this hypothetical impact 12,900 years ago, a third team member, Arizona-based geophysicist Allen West, suggested that smaller, low-density parts of the comet would have exploded in the atmosphere, while larger fragments might have crashed into the two-mile deep ice cap that covered North America at that time. 'Such craters,' West observed, 'would have been ice-walled and basically melted away at the end of the last ice age,' leaving few traces.[7]

The article went on to explain that the sediment samples the team's evidence focused on contained several different types of debris that could only have come from an extraterrestrial source, such as a comet or an asteroid. As well as nanodiamonds, the debris included tiny carbon spherules that form when molten droplets cool rapidly in air, and carbon molecules containing the rare isotope helium-3, far more abundant in the cosmos than on earth.[8]

> 'You might find some other explanation for these individually,' says Firestone, 'but taken together, it's pretty clear that there was an impact.' The team says the agent of destruction was probably a comet, since the key sediment layer lacks both the high nickel and iridium levels characteristic of asteroid impacts.[9]

Last but not least, the *New Scientist* article confirmed, all the evidence pointed to North America as the epicentre of the disaster:

> Levels of the apparent extraterrestrial debris, for example, are highest at the Gainey archaeological site in Michigan, just beyond the southern reach of North America's primary ice sheet 12,900 years ago. Moreover, levels decrease the further you go from Gainey, suggesting that the comet blew up largely over Canada . . .[10]

In other words, largely over the ice cap that covered the northern half of North America during the Ice Age – the source of all the meltwater that scarred and hacked the Scablands of Washington State in 'Bretz's flood' (whether or not that meltwater came exclusively from Lake Missoula or gushed forth in far larger quantities than Lake Missoula, alone, could ever have held). Bretz himself, as we've seen, was forced to abandon his own strong intuition that there had been a single, massive meltwater flood in favour of multiple flushings of limited amounts of meltwater out of Lake Missoula again and again over thousands of years.

The primary reason he embraced this theory, however, was not that he had become a convert to gradualism, but because he was never able to explain how a large enough area of the ice-cap to supply all the vast amounts of water needed for his flood could simply have melted all at once. He had proposed two possibilities – dramatic overnight global warming on the one hand, or volcanic activity under the ice cap on the other – but, as the reader will recall, he very quickly conceded there was no evidence for either. What Bretz did not consider, and *could not* consider – because the supporting evidence only began to come in a quarter of a century after his death – was the possibility that the ice cap could have undergone cataclysmic melting as a result of a comet impact.

If only Bretz had known . . .

A few months after the article appeared in *New Scientist*, the 'Clovis comet' team published a detailed paper on their findings. It appeared in the prestigious *Proceedings of the National Academy of Sciences* (*PNAS*) on 9 October 2007. Despite the sober setting, the headline was dramatic:

EVIDENCE FOR AN EXTRATERRESTRIAL IMPACT 12,900
YEARS AGO
THAT CONTRIBUTED TO THE MEGAFAUNAL
EXTINCTIONS
AND THE YOUNGER DRYAS COOLING

A carbon-rich layer, summarised the team:

> dating to around 12,900 years ago, has been previously identified at Clovis-age sites across North America and appears contemporaneous with the abrupt onset of the Younger Dryas (YD) cooling. The *in situ* bones of extinct Pleistocene megafauna, along with Clovis tool assemblages, occur below this black layer but not within or above it. Causes for the extinctions, YD cooling, and termination of Clovis culture have long been controversial. In this paper, we provide evidence for an extraterrestrial (ET) impact event close to 12,900 years ago, which we hypothesise caused abrupt environmental changes that contributed to YD cooling, major ecological reorganization, broad-scale extinctions, and rapid human behavioural shifts at the end of the Clovis Period. Clovis-age sites in North America are overlain by a thin, discrete layer with varying peak abundances of (i) magnetic

grains with iridium, (ii) magnetic microspherules, (iii) charcoal, (iv) soot, (v) carbon spherules, (vi) glass-like carbon containing nanodiamonds, and (vii) fullerenes with ET helium, all of which are evidence for an ET impact and associated biomass burning circa 12,900 years ago . . . We propose that one or more large, low-density ET objects exploded over northern North America, partially destabilizing the Laurentide Ice Sheet and triggering YD cooling. The shock wave, thermal pulse, and event-related environmental effects (e.g., extensive biomass burning and food limitations) contributed to megafaunal extinctions . . .[11]

Nor were the mammoths, mastodons, ground sloths, horses, camels, giant beaver and other megafauna alone. In total, it is particularly striking that no less than thirty-five *genera* of mammals (with each genus consisting of several species) became extinct in North America between 12,900 and 11,600 years ago, i.e. precisely during the mysterious Younger Dryas cold event.[12] What was now emerging, therefore, was an explanation both for the sudden onset of the Younger Dryas itself and for the accompanying extinctions, and perhaps for much else besides – including the cataclysmic flooding that left its marks on the Channeled Scablands of Washington State.

This seemed all the more plausible when I learned that Firestone, Kennett and West's proposal for their comet was that it was a conglomeration of impactors including one that might have been as much as 4 kilometres (2.5 miles) in diameter.[13] Furthermore, that 4-kilometre object would itself have been just one amongst multiple fragments resulting from the earlier disintegration – while still in orbit – of a giant comet up to 100 kilometres or more in diameter.[14] Many of the fragments of the parent comet (including some of great size as we'll see in Chapter Nineteen) remained in orbit. Those that hit the earth at the onset of the Younger Dryas underwent further explosive fragmentation (accompanied by powerful airbursts that would themselves have had cataclysmic effects), as they entered the atmosphere over Canada.

Nonetheless, the authors thought it likely that a number of large impactors, *up to 2 kilometres in diameter*, would have remained intact to collide with the ice-cap.[15] There, as West had earlier told *New Scientist*, any craters would have been transient, leaving few permanent traces on the ground after the ice had melted. 'Lasting evidence,' the *PNAS* paper added, 'may have been limited to enigmatic depressions or disturbances in the Canadian Shield, e.g. under the Great Lakes, or Hudson Bay.'[16]

Summarizing the damage, the authors envisaged:

a devastating, high-temperature shock wave with extreme over-pressure, followed by underpressure, resulting in intense winds travelling across North America at hundreds of kilometres an hour, accompanied by powerful, impact-generated vortices. In addition, whether single or multiple objects collided with the earth, a hot fireball would have immersed the region near the impacts . . . At greater distances the re-entry of high-speed, super-heated ejecta would have induced extreme wildfires which would have decimated forests and grasslands, destroying the food supplies of herbivores and producing charcoal, soot, toxic fumes and ash.[17]

And how might all this have caused the dramatic cooling of the Younger Dryas? The authors offered many mechanisms operating together, amongst the most prominent of these being the huge plume of water vapour from the melted ice cap that would have been cast into the upper atmosphere, combined with immense quantities of dust and debris 'composed of the impactor, ice-sheet detritus, and the underlying crust' as well as the smoke and soot from continent-wide wildfires.[18] Taken in sum, it's quite easy to understand how so much lofted debris could, as the authors propose, 'have led to cooling by blockage of sunlight'; meanwhile the water vapour, smoke, soot and ice would have promoted the growth of 'persistent cloudiness and noctilucent clouds, leading to reduced sunlight and surface cooling . . . [thus reducing] the solar insolation at high latitudes, increasing snow accumulation and causing further cooling in the feedback loop.'[19]

Severe and devastating enough in themselves, these factors none-theless pale into insignificance when compared with the consequences of the hypothesised impacts on the ice cap:

The largest potential effect would have been impact-related partial destabilization and/or melting of the ice sheet. In the short term this would have suddenly released meltwater and rafts of ice into the North Atlantic and Arctic Oceans, lowering ocean salinity with consequent surface cooling. The longer-term cooling effects would have resulted largely from the consequent weakening of thermohaline circulation in the northern Atlantic, sustaining YD cooling for [more than] 1,000 years until the feedback mechanisms restored ocean circulation.[20]

Impact-related partial destabilization and/or melting of the ice sheet! And on a scale capable of disrupting the circulation of the world's oceans for more than a thousand years! This matter of thermohaline circulation is an important one that requires explanation. We will return to it. But what most struck me in the paragraph quoted above was that the authors had only considered the consequences of the huge quantities of icebergs and meltwater dumped into the oceans north and east of the epicentre of their proposed comet impacts. They did not consider the effects of that gigantic icy flood on the lands lying immediately *south* of the ice cap – which most certainly would not have been spared.

Once again I found myself wondering how J Harlen Bretz might have reacted if information about a possible comet impact had been at his disposal during his lifetime. I cannot prove it, of course, but I think he would have been much less likely to be seduced by Lake Missoula gradualism and much more likely – now that a credible heat source had been provided – to stick to his catastrophist guns. A single, cataclysmic meltwater flood on a truly gigantic scale coming directly off the ice cap to scour the Scablands begins to look very feasible indeed in the light of the case made by Firestone, West, Kennett and the large team of scientists working with them.

Meanwhile my own hypothesis of an advanced civilization of prehistoric antiquity obliterated from the face of the earth during the Younger Dryas 'window', is also strengthened by their work. For if their calculations are correct the explosive power of the Younger Dryas comet would have been of the order of *ten million megatons*.[21] That makes it two million times greater in its effects than the former USSR's *Tsar Bomba*, the largest nuclear weapon ever tested,[22] and a thousand times greater than the estimated explosive power (10,000 megatons) of all nuclear devices stockpiled in the world today.[23] A global disaster of such magnitude at exactly the time I suggested in *Fingerprints of the Gods* does not prove the existence of a lost civilization of the Ice Age but does at least provide us with a mechanism large enough – if such a civilization did exist – to have obliterated it almost entirely from human memory.

The evidence continues to mount

Because it has such important ramifications for almost everything we think we know about the safety and security of the earth's cosmic environment, and about our own past, it is reasonable to ask how solid the Younger Dryas comet impact theory really is. Since 2007, when it was first proposed, how has it stood up to scientific scrutiny and what new evidence has been brought forward in support of it?

The answer is that it has stood the test of time well and benefitted from a steady accumulation of new evidence set out in the proper way in the scientific literature and subject to rigorous peer review. There is neither space nor need, here, to explore this extensive literature in depth, but to give the general picture I will list the dates and titles of a few of the more important papers, with brief summaries of the conclusions and full references in the footnotes:

2008: *Wildfire and abrupt ecosystem disruption on California's Northern Channel Islands at the Allerod-Younger Dryas Boundary.* Evidence for ecosystem disruption at 13,000 to 12,900 years ago on these offshore islands is consistent with the Younger Dryas Boundary cosmic impact hypothesis.[24]

2009: *Shock-synthesised hexagonal diamonds in Younger Dryas Boundary sediments.* The presence of shock-synthesised hexagonal and other nanometre-sized diamonds in YDB sediments in association with soot and other wildfire indicators is consistent with a cosmic impact at 12,900 years ago, and the hypothesis that the earth crossed paths with a swarm of comets or carbonaceous chondrites producing airshocks and/or surface impacts that contributed to abrupt ecosystem disruption and megafaunal extinctions in North America.[25]

2010: *Discovery of a nanodiamond-rich layer in the Greenland ice sheet.* The presence of rounded nanodiamonds and lonsdaleite in Greenland ice suggests that a large cosmic impact occurred . . . The existence of this layer . . . appears consistent with the occurrence of a major impact event that correlates with the nanodiamond-rich YDB in North America at 12,900 years ago.[26]

2010: *Palaeolithic extinctions and the Taurid Complex.* Intersection with the debris of a large (50-100 km) short-period comet during the Upper Palaeolithic provides a satisfactory explanation for the catastrophe of celestial origin which has been postulated to have occurred around 12,900 years ago and which presaged a return to Ice Age conditions of about 1,300 years duration. The Taurid Complex appears to be the debris of this erstwhile comet; it includes about 19 of the brightest near-earth objects.[27] [N.B. The implications of this important paper by astronomer Bill Napier of the Centre for Astrobiology at the University of Cardiff, Wales, UK, will be considered in greater detail in Chapter Nineteen.]

2010: *Evidence for a Cosmogenic Origin of fired glaciofluvial beds in the Northwestern Andes: Correlation with Experimentally Heated Quartz and Feldspar.* Fired sediment, considered equivalent to the 'Black Mat' impact of 12,900 years ago has been located and analyzed in the Andes of Northwestern Venezuela. The 'Black Mat' refers to possible fallout from the Encke Comet airburst presumed to have occurred over the Laurentide Ice Sheet, the impact spreading ejecta over large portions of North America and Europe, making it an interhemispheric event of considerable magnitude . . . The presence of copious monazite in the carbonaceous coatings is considered part of the incoming ejecta, as it is not a common indicator mineral in the local lithology . . . The intergrowth of carbonaceous 'black mat' material with thermally disrupted and fragmented quartz and feldspar, a 'welded' patina of 100–400nm thickness, could only occur with temperatures in excess of 900 degrees Centigrade, the event here interpreted to be of cosmogenic origin.[28]

2011: *Framboidal iron oxide: Chondrite-like material from the black mat, Murray Springs, Arizona.* At the end of the Pleistocene a Younger Dryas 'black mat' was deposited on top of the Pleistocene sediments in many parts of North America. A study of the magnetic fraction from the basal section of the black mat at Murray Springs, AZ, revealed the presence of amorphous iron-oxide framboids in a glassy iron-silica matrix. [Our] data suggest that the observed textures are . . . due . . . to a shock event that fractured and largely amorphised the grains . . . Therefore, we argue that these particles are the product of a hypervelocity impact event.[29]

2012: *Evidence from central Mexico supporting the Younger Dryas extraterrestrial impact hypothesis.* We report the discovery in Lake Cuitzeo in central Mexico of a black, carbon-rich lacustrine layer, containing nanodiamonds, microspherules, and other unusual materials that date to the early Younger Dryas . . . We . . . find the evidence cannot be explained by any known terrestrial mechanism. It is, however, consistent with the Younger Dryas boundary impact hypothesis postulating a major extraterrestrial impact involving multiple airbursts and/or ground impacts at 12,900 years ago.[30]

2012: *Very high-temperature impact melt products as evidence for cosmic airbursts and impacts 12,900 years ago.* We examined sediment sequences from 18 dated Younger Dryas boundary (YDB) sites across three continents . . . All sites display abundant microspherules in the YDB with none or few above and below. In addition, three sites . . . display vesicular, high-temperature siliceous scoria-like objects, or SLO's, that match the spherules geochemically . . . Our observations indicate that YDB objects are similar to material produced in nuclear airbursts, impact crater plumes and cosmic airbursts, and strongly support the hypothesis of multiple cosmic airbursts/impacts at 12,900 years ago. Data presented here require that thermal radiation from air shocks was sufficient to melt surface sediments at temperatures up to or greater than the boiling point of quartz (2,200 degrees centigrade).[31]

2013: *Large Pt anomaly in the Greenland ice core points to a cataclysm at the onset of Younger Dryas.* One explanation of the abrupt cooling episode known as the Younger Dryas (YD) is a cosmic impact or airburst at the YD boundary that triggered cooling and resulted in other calamities. We tested the YD impact hypothesis by analyzing ice samples from the Greenland Ice Sheet Project 2 (GISP2) ice core across the Bolling-Allerod/YD boundary for major and trace elements. We found a large platinum (Pt) anomaly at the YDB . . . Circumstantial evidence hints at an extraterrestrial source . . . [perhaps] a metal impactor with an unusual composition . . .[32]

2013: *New Evidence from a Black Mat Site in the Northern Andes Supporting a Cosmic Impact 12,800 years ago.* The spherules from Venezuela are morphologically and compositionally identical to YDB spherules documented elsewhere . . . on three continents, North America, Europe and Asia, confirming the YDB magnetic spherule results of previous researchers. Their microstructural texturing indicates they formed from melting and rapid quenching . . . Thus the most likely origin of the spherules seems to be by cosmic impact/airburst 12,800 years ago with interhemispheric consequences. The site in Venezuela, along with one in Peru, are the two southernmost sites currently known to display evidence for the YDB impact event, and these sites represent the first evidence that the effects of the impact event extended into South America, even into the Southern Hemisphere.[33]

2014: *Nanodiamond-Rich Layer across Three Continents Consistent with Major Cosmic Impact at 12,800 Cal BP.* A major cosmic-impact event has been proposed at the onset of the Younger Dryas cooling episode at 12,800 years (plus or minus 150 years) before the present, forming the Younger Dryas Boundary (YDB) Layer distributed across up to 50 million square kilometres on four continents. In 24 dated stratigraphic sections in 10 countries of the Northern Hemisphere, the YDB layer contains a clearly-defined abundance peak in nanodiamonds (NDs), a major cosmic impact proxy . . . The large body of evidence now obtained about YDB NDs is strongly consistent with an origin by cosmic impact around 12,800 years ago and is inconsistent with formation of YDB ND by natural terrestrial processes, including wildfires, anthropogenesis, and/or influx of cosmic dust.[34] [NB. This paper and its important implications will be discussed in more detail later in this chapter.]

Taking on the dogmatic uniformitarians

One would have thought, with such an impressive accumulation of evidence, that the Younger Dryas impact theory would, by now, be fully accepted and that researchers would have moved on to a broader consideration of the *implications* of such a recent and hitherto unsus-pected global cataclysm for our understanding of the history of the earth and of our own species. However, we've already seen from the example of J Harlen Bretz how scientists wedded to the uniformitarian and gradualist reference frame react with extreme negative force to catastrophist theories.

Nor was Bretz an exception. Alfred Wegener, who first proposed the notion of continental drift – plate tectonics – was similarly pillo-ried, as, subsequently, were Luis and Walter Alvarez (the Chicxulub, 'K-T' impact), Steven J. Gould (punctuated equilibrium), Victor Clube and Bill Napier (coherent catastrophism), and James Lovelock, Sherwood Rowland, Mario Molina and Lynn Margulis for their contri-butions to geophysiology and the Gaia theory. It should come as no surprise, therefore, that Richard Firestone, Allen West, James Kennett and others who have followed the evidence and stuck their necks out to suggest that a comet impact caused the Younger Dryas, have also come under sustained and bitter attack.

Indeed the triumphant crowing of critics who clearly believe they have done away, once and for all, with the heretical catastrophism of Firestone, West and Kennett, has filled the academic air several times in the past few years. On each occasion you can almost hear the collective sigh of relief as if to say 'thank God; we finally got those bastards'; but then a few months later comes the devastating and absolutely convincing refutation that forces the critics back to the drawing board. This is why eight years of sustained attacks have only served to prove – again and again – that the science behind the theory of the Younger Dryas comet is good.

It's quite noticeable, reviewing the literature, that academics form themselves into gangs. The ringleaders in the 'anti-YD-comet' camp, whose names appear frequently at the top of critical articles, include Mark Boslough, a physicist on the technical staff of Sandia National Laboratories and Nicholas Pinter, a geology professor at Southern Illinois University. In 2012 they teamed up with half a dozen other scientists to publish a paper entitled 'Arguments and Evidence Against a Younger Dryas Impact Event'.[35] And a year earlier Pinter and some of the authors of the 2012 attack had joined forces to write a paper hubristically entitled 'The Younger Dryas Impact Hypothesis: A Requiem'.[36]

To paraphrase Mark Twain, reports of the death of the comet theory had been greatly exaggerated.

For example one of the key critiques made by Boslough et al in their 2012 article was that:

Magnetic microspherule abundance results published by the impact proponents have not been reproducible by other workers. Analyses of the same YD site stratigraphy by Surovell et al [2009] could not replicate observations for two of the impact markers published by Firestone et al [2007]. The study by Surovell et al [2009] found no peaks of abundance unique to the YD time interval.[37]

But the impact proponents were later able to show that Boslough and his co-authors 'neglected to cite nine independent spherule studies on two continents that reported finding significant YDB [Younger Dryas Boundary] spherule abundances.'[38] More damning, though, was the fact that when other scientists repeated the analysis of Surovell et al, their findings did indeed support an impact. The scientists concluded that:

> the inability of Surovell et al to find YDB spherule peaks resulted from not adhering to the prescribed extraction protocol. For example, Surovell et al did not conduct any analyses using scanning electron microscopy, a necessary procedure clearly specified by Firestone et al.[39]

A separate independent study by Malcolm A. Le Compte et al noted that Surovell et al 'collected and analysed samples from seven YDB sites, purportedly using the same protocol as Firestone et al, but did not find a single spherule in YDB sediments at two previously reported sites.'[40] LeCompte et al set out to examine this discrepancy. After a thorough investigation of all the evidence their results cast the work of Surovell et al into an even deeper shadow:

> We conducted an independent blind investigation of two sites common to both studies, and a third site investigated only by Surovell et al. We found abundant YDB microspherules at all three widely separated sites consistent with the results of Firestone et al and conclude that the analytical protocol employed by Surovell et al deviated significantly from that of Firestone et al. Morphological and geochemical analysis of YDB spherules suggest they . . . formed from abrupt melting and quenching of terrestrial materials and . . . are consistent with . . . a previously proposed cosmic impact 12,900 years ago . . .[41]

Unsurprisingly, after all this, Pinter's 'requiem' for the Younger Dryas impact hypothesis turned out to have been premature:

Pinter et al. claimed to have sampled the YDB layer at a location 'identical or nearly identical' with the location reported by Kennett et al, as part of three studies that reported finding no YDB spherules or nanodiamonds. However, the published Universal Transverse Mercator coordinates reveal that their purported continuous sequence is actually four discontinuous sections. These locations range in distance from the site investigated by Kennett et al by 7,000 m, 1,600 m, 165 m, and 30 m, clearly showing that they did not sample the YDB site of Kennett et al. Furthermore, this sampling strategy raises questions about whether Pinter et al sampled the YDB at all, and may explain why they were unable to find peaks in YDB magnetic spherules, carbon spherules, or nanodiamonds.[42]

In 2012–13, in an effort to limit the scope for poor or misleading scholarship to be cited as though it discredits their work – when in fact it does no such thing – Jim Kennett, Richard Firestone, Allen West and a formidable group of pro-impact scientists launched 'one of the most comprehensive investigations of spherules ever undertaken'.[43] The investigation focused on eighteen sites across North America, Europe and the Middle East (the latter represented by Abu Hureyra in Syria), and conducted more than 700 analyses on spherules using energy dispersive X-ray spectroscopy for chemical analysis and scanning electron microscopy for surface microstructural characterization.

The results, published in *PNAS* on 4 June 2013, took advantage of recent advances in radiocarbon technology to refine the date of the Younger Dryas impact from 12,900 to 12,800 years ago[44] and enabled a much more detailed map of the YDB field to be drawn up, covering close to 50 million square kilometres of North, Central and South America, a large segment of the Atlantic Ocean, and most of Europe, North Africa and the Middle East. Calculations indicate that the impact deposited around *ten million tonnes of spherules* across this vast strewnfield.[45] Nor, was there any doubt in the researchers' minds that an impact had been at the heart of the matter:

The analyses of 771 YDB objects presented in this paper strongly support a major cosmic impact at 12,800 years ago . . . Spherules . . . are (i) widespread at 18 sites on four continents; (ii) display large abundance peaks only at the YD onset at around 12,800 years ago; (iii) are rarely found above or below the YDB, indicating a rare event; and (iv) amount to an estimated 10 million tonnes of materials distributed across around 50 million square kilometres of several continents, thus precluding a small, local event.[46]

Despite the annoying ability of the Younger Dryas comet to keep on proving itself, and of its proponents to keep on refuting all attacks, Nicholas Pinter, lead author of the 2011 'Requiem' paper, felt moved in an interview with NBC News in September 2013 once again to attempt to cast the hypothesis into scientific limbo. 'My only comment,' he said, 'is that the pro-impact literature is, at this point, fringe science being promoted by a single journal.'[47]

A number of observers with no particular axe of their own to grind were puzzled by this remark. First of all, as *National Geographic* correspondent Robert Kunzig noted, it smacked a little of wishful thinking, even desperation, on Pinter's part. 'Some opponents of the hypothesis,' wrote Kunzig, 'want so badly for it to go away that they have attempted to declare it dead.'[48] Secondly, the journal that Pinter accused of promoting fringe science was none other than the revered, utterly mainstream, and extensively peer-reviewed *Proceedings of the National Academy of Sciences (PNAS)*.[49] Thirdly, although a number of articles by Kennett, West, Firestone and their team have appeared in *PNAS*, it is simply not true to suggest that *PNAS* is promoting their cause. On the contrary, at the time Pinter blurted out his protest to NBC the critics of the YD comet hypothesis had published ten times in *PNAS*, whereas the proponents of the hypothesis had published there only eight times. Likewise Pinter's claim that the hypothesis is only being presented in a single journal could hardly be more wrong. By September 2013, in addition to their eight papers in *PNAS*, proponents had published no less than fifteen papers in thirteen other journals.[50]

The scholarly fight over the Younger Dryas impact hypothesis is far from over. At the time of writing, the most recent salvo fired by critics of the hypothesis was entitled 'Anthropogenic origin of siliceous scoria droplets from Pleistocene and Holocene archaeological sites in northern Syria'. Authored by P. Thy, G. Willcox, G.H. Barfod and D.Q. Fuller, it was published online on 16 December 2014 and in print in January 2015 in the *Journal of Archaeological Science*.[51] The essence of the argument in this paper is that siliceous scoria droplets (composed mostly of glass matrix and bubbles together with partially melted mineral grains) from Abu Hureyra in Syria – cited by pro-impact scientists as evidence for their case – were nothing to do with the comet but were instead a product of ancient buildings destroyed by house fires:

> We therefore conclude that melting of building earth in ancient settlements can occur during fires reaching modest temperatures. There is no evidence to suggest that siliceous scoria droplets result from very high temperature melting of soil and are the result of a cosmic event.[52]

'For the Syria site the impact theory is out,' boasted lead author Peter Thy in a press interview headlined 'Study Casts Doubt on Mammoth-Killing Cosmic Impact'.[53] But once again it seems the bluster was premature. Allen West is listed as the corresponding author on the majority of scholarly papers published by the team of scientists working on the Younger Dryas impact, so I emailed him on 18 March 2015 to ask if he and his colleagues had any response to the critique by Thy et al. West replied as follows:

> We agree with Thy et al that hut fires can produce glass, but it does not follow, therefore, that *all* glass comes from hut fires, as they conclude. We have analysed natural glasses supplied by one of the authors of that study, and the 12,800-year-old glass from Syria is only superficially similar. Instead it matches known cosmic impact glass, as well as high-temperature atomic bomb glass.

Most importantly, those authors did not discuss or look for the evidence of abundant high-temperature minerals presented in our previous papers on three sites on two continents (Pennsylvania, South Carolina and Syria) where we found suessite that melts at around 2,300 degrees Centigrade and corundum at around 1,800 degrees Centigrade. Now we have even stronger evidence from the Syrian site and are working on a new paper to be published this year. The 12,800-year-old Syrian glass contains a range of minerals that melted at extraordinarily high temperatures. See the table below from our new paper:

Melted minerals	Formula	Est. melt T (°C)
Chromite	$(Fe)Cr_2O_4$	≈2265
Quartz	SiO_2	≈1720
Chert	impure SiO_2	≈1720
Magnetite	Fe_3O_4	≈1550
Native Fe	Fe	≈1530
Chlorapatite	$Ca_5(PO_4)_3Cl$	≈1530

Those temperatures are sufficient to melt steel. Furthermore the same glass-rich layer at the Syrian site contains large peaks in nanodiamonds, nickel and platinum. No building fire can duplicate that range of evidence – such fires can't produce nanodiamonds or platinum enrichments. All this evidence refutes the hypothesis of Thy et al that this glass was produced in low-temperature building fires.[54]

When the new paper by West and his colleagues is published later in 2015 (after this book has gone to press), I have no doubt that it will, effectively, refute the arguments of Thy et al – just as all previous attacks have been successfully refuted. But I also have no doubt that others, who for whatever reasons of their own are philosophically opposed to the notion of a cataclysm 12,800 years ago, will publish yet more so-called 'requiems' for the Younger Dryas impact hypothesis in the years ahead, even while the constant discovery of new evidence means that it continues to thrive and grow. As we've seen throughout this book, catastrophist ideas, no matter how thoroughly documented and persistently argued and presented they may be, are routinely and regularly brushed under the carpet by the uniformitarian establishment. Thus while he lacked nothing in persistence, or in the thoroughness of his documentation, J Harlen Bretz faced years of discouragement before his ideas were welcomed by the mainstream.

Jim Kennett, Richard Firestone, Allen West and their colleagues have argued the catastrophist case for the Younger Dryas comet impact with equally commendable persistence and with equal mastery of documentation and they, too, have faced rejection and hostility. Two things are different in their case, however. First, this is the twenty-first century and we have the internet, which allows the very rapid sharing and proliferation of ideas. That was not the case when Bretz began his lonely struggle. Secondly, Kennett, Firestone and West seem to have a better understanding of the politics of science than Bretz did and have greatly strengthened their own hand by mobilizing support for their work from many colleagues. It is one thing to shout down and silence a lone wolf like Bretz. It is quite another to shout down and silence a large team of highly credentialled scientists from multiple disciplines and universities.

And the team is growing. As I complete this chapter in March 2015, I have before me on my desk the latest paper published by Firestone, Kennett and West. The paper, entitled 'Nanodiamond-Rich Layer across Three Continents Consistent with Major Cosmic Impact 12,800 Years Ago', appears in the September 2014 issue of *The Journal of Geology*. The lead author is Carles R. Kinzie of the Department of Chemistry, DePaul University, Chicago. Firestone, Kennett, West and twenty-two other leading scientists from prestigious universities and research institutes around the world are co-authors.[55] The gravity of the paper, of its authors and of the journal in which it appears, together with the further detailed refutations it contains of prior critiques,[56] combine to make a laughing stock of Nicholas Pinter's claim that the Younger Dryas comet hypothesis is 'fringe science'.

Indeed, the contrary is true – what is clearly happening is that an extraordinary hypothesis has again and again met the demand for extraordinary evidence to support it and has begun to force its way through the staunchly-defended doors of the mainstream. It will not be an easy struggle; it never is. There will be setbacks as well as progress. But the 2013 paper on spherules and the 2014 paper on nanodiamonds contain a wealth of evidence that even the most hard-ened gradualists must find hard to dismiss entirely. As Wallace Broecker, a geochemist and climate scientist at Columbia University's Lamont-Doherty Earth Observatory recently begrudgingly admitted: 'Most people were trying to disprove this. Now they're going to have to realise there's some truth to it.'[57]

But there cannot be just 'some' truth to it. The Younger Dryas comet hypothesis is either right or wrong. My own assessment, having pored through more than seven years of research papers and having read every attack and refutation since the first public airing of the hypothesis in 2007, is that the case for the impact is a very strong one that grows stronger and more convincing every day. I could give many further examples of the successful efforts by the proponents of the hypothesis to defend their ideas over the years, but rather than doing so here, I refer the interested reader to the sources given in the foot-note.[58]

Meanwhile the September 2014 paper, summarizing the evidence presented, concludes:

> A cosmic impact event at the onset of the Younger Dryas cooling episode is the only hypothesis capable of explaining the simul-taneous deposition of peak abundances in nanodiamonds, magnetic and glassy spherules, melt-glass, platinum and/or other proxies across at least four continents (approaching 50 million square kilometres). The evidence strongly supports a cosmic impact 12,800 years ago.[59]

Of particular note, adds James Kennett, is the fact that the glassy and metallic materials in the YDB layers could only have formed at temperatures in excess of 2,200 degrees Celsius and therefore could not have resulted from any alternative scenario other than a massive comet impact.[60]

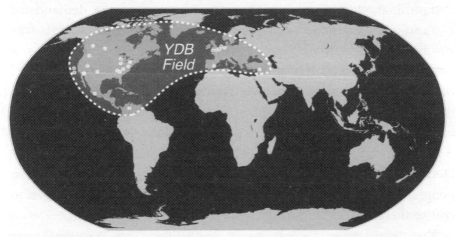

Figure 20: The Younger Dryas Boundary Strewnfield (after Wittke et. al., 2013 and Kinzie, Kennett et. al., 2014). The area enclosed by the dotted line defines the current known limits of the YDB field of cosmic-impact proxies spanning 50 million square kilometres.

The exact size of that impact remains to be resolved with further research. Until then, says Kennett, 'There is no known limit to the YDB strewnfield which currently covers more than 10 percent of the planet, indicating that the YDB event was a major cosmic impact . . . The nanodiamond datum recognised in this study gives scientists a snapshot of a moment in time called an isochron.'[61]

Worldwide, to this day, scientists know of only two layers of sediment 'broadly distributed across several continents that exhibit coeval abundance peaks in a comprehensive assemblage of cosmic impact markers, including nanodiamonds, high-temperature quenched spherules, high-temperature melt-glass, carbon spherules, iridium and aciniform carbon'.[62] These layers are found at the Younger Dryas Boundary 12,800 years ago, and at the Cretaceous-Tertiary boundary 65 million years ago, when it has long been agreed that a gigantic cosmic impact in the Gulf of Mexico (in that case the impactor is thought to have been an asteroid some ten kilometres in diameter) caused the mass extinction of the dinosaurs.[63]

'The evidence we present settles the debate about the existence of abundant YDB nanodiamonds,' Kennett says. 'Our hypothesis challenges some existing paradigms within several disciplines, including impact dynamics, archaeology, paleontology and paleoceanography/paleoclimatology, all affected by this relatively recent cosmic impact.'[64]

The point Kennett makes here has important implications for the study and understanding of our past. Archaeologists have been in the habit of regarding cosmic impacts, supposedly only occurring at multi-million year intervals, as largely irrelevant to the 200,000-year story of anatomically modern humans. When we believed that the last big impact had been the dinosaur-killing asteroid of 65 million years ago, there was obviously little point in trying to relate cosmic accidents on such an almost unimaginable scale in any way to the much shorter time-frame of 'history'. But the very real possibility confirmed by Kennett's study that a huge, earthshaking, extinction-level event occurred just 12,800 years ago, in our historical backyard, changes everything.

Chapter 6
Fingerprints of a Comet

———◆———

The evidence from deposits of nanodiamonds, microspherules, high-temperature melt-glass and other 'ET-impact proxies' at the Younger Dryas Boundary points strongly towards a cataclysmic encounter between the earth and a large comet around 12,800 years ago. The point of entry would have been somewhere over Canada, by which time the comet might already have broken up into multiple fragments on its journey through space (as was the case with Comet Shoemaker-Levy 9 when its 'freight-train' of large fragments hit Jupiter with spectacular effect in 1994). It is equally possible, however, that the break up of the Younger Dryas comet did not occur until after it had entered the earth's atmosphere. Either way, some of the fragments very soon exploded in the air, others, with diameters of up to two kilometres, smashed down at various points on the North American ice cap, yet others streaked on in a south-easterly direction across the Atlantic Ocean where further impacts followed on the European ice cap, and still others remained aloft until they reached the Middle East in the vicinity of Turkey, the Lebanon and Syria, where the final rain of impacts occurred.

Because the evidence for the comet is so new, and because the impact hypothesis is still disputed, almost no consideration has yet been given to the immediate effects of the multiple major impacts that are thought to have taken place on the North American ice cap. In all cases the ice itself, still more than two kilometres thick 12,800 years ago, would have absorbed most of the shock of the impact leaving very few lasting features on the ground. Even so, researchers have begun to home in on a number of possible craters.

One candidate is the so-called Charity Shoal feature in Lake Ontario. Consisting of a raised rim around a small circular basin approximately a kilometre in diameter and 19 metres deep, it was studied by a team of scientists led by Troy Holcombe, who concluded that it was likely to be of extraterrestrial impact origin and might have been created in the late Pleistocene around the time of the onset of the Younger Dryas.[1]

Similarly, the half-kilometre diameter, 10-metre deep, Bloody Creek Structure in southwestern Nova Scotia was identified as a possible impact crater by Ian Spooner, George Stevens and others in a 2009 paper in the journal *Meteoritics and Planetary Science*. They could not be confident as to its age, but noted that 'impact onto glacier ice during the waning stages of the Wisconsin Glaciation about 12,000 years ago may have resulted in dissipation of much impact energy into the ice, resulting in the present morphology of the Bloody Creek Structure.'[2]

A third candidate is the Corossol Crater in the Gulf of Saint Lawrence, Canada. Discovered by the Canadian Hydrographic Service during underwater mapping, Corossol is 4 kilometres in diameter, implying an impacting object with a diameter of up to half a kilometre. The crater presently lies in 40 to 185 metres of water and was originally thought to be very ancient, dating to some point after the middle Ordovician, about 470 million years ago.[3] Recent research, however, casts doubt on this chronology. For example, M.D. Higgins and his

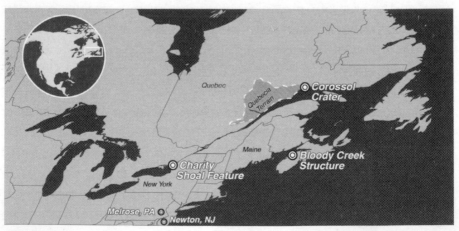

Figure 21

colleagues from the University of Quebec and the Geological Survey of Canada argued in a paper presented at the 42nd Lunar and Planetary Science Conference in March 2011 that:

> The paucity of sediments in the crater might be taken to indicate that it is young. The minimum age was established using data from a 7 metre core taken in the central trough. Calibrated carbon-14 ages of shells in the sediments can be extrapolated to give an estimate of the age of the base of the sedimentary sequence of around 12,900 years ago . . . This is taken to be the youngest possible age of the impact.[4]

That 'youngest possible' age of 12,900 years is comfortably within the margin of error of 12,800 years plus or minus 150 years that is presently accepted for the Younger Dryas Boundary.[5] In other words if the findings of Higgins and his team are confirmed, Corossol could well be one of the hitherto 'missing' impact craters left by the Younger Dryas comet. Firm identification of such a crater would be jam on the cake for Firestone, Kennett, West and other pro-impact scientists, but as they have made clear many times, they do not *need* craters to prove their hypothesis, since prominent craters are not to be expected either from airbursts or from impacts on ice caps.

Nonetheless Charity Shoal, Bloody Creek and Corossol do not stand alone. A fourth possible impact site has been identified somewhat to the west of Corossol in an area known to geologists as the Quebecia Terrain. High concentrations of YDB microspherules found near the towns of Melrose in Pennsylvania and Newtonville in New Jersey were analysed by Wu, Sharma, LeCompte, Demitroff and Landis in a paper published in September 2013 in the *Proceedings of the National Academy of Sciences*. Their conclusion was that an impact on the Laurentide ice sheet penetrated to the bedrock of the Quebecia Terrain throwing ejecta high into the atmosphere. The ejecta included spherules in the range of 2 to 5 millimetres in diameter that were spread by the winds and rained down hundreds of miles away in the Melrose–Newtonville area. Significantly the spherules turned out on analysis to contain:

minerals such as suessite that form at temperatures in excess of 2,000 degrees Centigrade. Gross texture, mineralogy, and age of the spherules appear consistent with their formation as ejecta from an impact 12,900 years ago . . . The rare earth element patterns and Sr and Nd isotopes of the spherules indicate that their source lies in the Quebecia Terrain.[6]

'We have provided evidence for an impact on top of the ice sheet,' concluded study co-author Mukul Sharma. 'We have for the first time narrowed down the region where a Younger Dryas impact did take place, even though we have not yet found its crater.'[7]

Judging from the apparent north-west to south-east trajectory of the Younger Dryas comet,[8] the Charity Shoal feature in Lake Ontario, ejecta from Quebecia Terrain, the Corossol crater in the Gulf of Saint Lawrence, and the Bloody Creek structure in Nova Scotia might mark the impacts of the last large fragments to hit North America. But the even larger fragments – in the range of two kilometres in diameter that Firestone, Kennett and West envisage – would inevitably have hit the ice cap *earlier* in the trajectory and thus at points lying further to the north and west. It is to these hypothetical impacts on the western fringes of the Laurentide Ice Cap, and on the Cordilleran Ice Cap, that we should look for the possible source of the meltwater for Bretz's flood.

Radical thinking

Although the notion of outburst floods from Glacial Lake Missoula has long been accepted by mainstream science as the source of the spectacular flood damage documented by Bretz, it is important to recognise that a number of senior, highly credentialled scientists continue to dissent from this view. Prominent amongst the dissenters is John Shaw, Professor of Earth Sciences at the University of Alberta in Canada. Shaw argues that the volume of water in Lake Missoula, estimated at around 2,000 cubic kilometres at its peak, is not sufficient to account for the field evidence. His own theory is that huge quantities of meltwater – of the order of 100,000 cubic kilometres – were impounded in a subglacial reservoir deep beneath the North American ice cap and he proposes that the flood damage was caused by a single, massive release from this reservoir.[9]

Japanese researchers Goro Komatsu, Hideyaki Miyamoto, Kazumasa Itoh and Hiroyuki Tosaka have carried out extensive computer simulations of large-scale cataclysmic floods across the Scablands and agree with Shaw that Glacial Lake Missoula was not, on its own, anywhere near large enough to account for the flood damage:

> Even the whole draining of Lake Missoula cannot explain the field evidence of high water marks . . . The subglacial flooding from the north proposed by Shaw may provide an explanation for the increased volume of water required to explain the high water-mark evidence in the Channeled Scabland.[10]

Likewise Victor Baker, Professor of Hydrology and Water Resources at the University of Arizona, and Jim O'Connor of the US Geological Survey's Water Science Center, have expressed concern about the 'case for periodic colossal *jökulhlaups*' out of Glacial Lake Missoula:

> In our view, anomalies still exist between some aspects of the field evidence and the conceptual models that have been advocated. The position that the 'scores-of-floods hypothesis completes Bretz's imaginative theory' (Waitt, 1985, p. 1286) may prematurely divert attention from some of the outstanding problems that remain in interpreting the spectacular features of the Channeled Scabland.[11]

In 1977 geologist C. Warren Hunt set out to conduct a detailed investigation into Bretz's flood. He did so because, like the scholars cited above, he was unconvinced by the theory – which had already assumed the status of unassailable fact by the mid-1970s – that all the water damage visible in the Scablands had been caused by outburst floods from Lake Missoula. Hunt's dissatisfaction stemmed from his own extensive knowledge of dams and how to design them to take best advantage of local geology. The bottom line, according to his calculations, was that the proposed ice dam on the Clark Fork River, behind which Lake Missoula is supposed to have backed up, would have been, quite literally, *impossible*.

Let us first of all consider the statistics. According to the US Geological Survey, Glacial Lake Missoula at its highest level – the level it is presumed to have reached before the Clark Fork ice dam broke – covered an area of about 3,000 square miles and contained an estimated 500 cubic miles (2,084 cubic kilometres) of water. Its surface would have been at 4,150 feet above sea level, but the bottom terrain varied in altitude from point to point so the USGS calculates that the lake would have been about 950 feet deep at present day Missoula, 260 feet deep at Darby and around 1,100 feet deep near Polson. At the ice dam itself, however, a gradient in the underlying terrain meant the glacial lake would have been more than 2,000 feet deep (its deepest point – more than twice the depth of modern Lake Superior).[12]

While broadly concurring with the US Geological Survey's figures, C. Warren Hunt emphatically rejected 'the suggestion that ice might have dammed Clark Fork so as to impound water to a depth of 2,100 ft (640 metres) . . . When one considers,' he wrote:

> that modern engineering employs bedrock grouting for securing the footings of 500-ft (150-m) dams, it must surely strike any reader as virtually frivolous to suggest that chance emplacement of glacial ice might have dammed Clark Fork across a 7-mile (11-km) span lacking in intermediate abutments, and then retained water at four times the pressure of modern engineered concrete dams![13]

Hunt's incredulity at the notion of an ice dam more than 2,000 feet high and 7 miles long receives support from studies which argue that 'at a lake depth of approximately 200 metres (656 feet), the hydrostatic pressure exerted on the damming ice is sufficient to begin to force a hole through the ice. Once formed this hole will enlarge by frictional melt-widening, enabling the drainage of ice-dammed lake water to occur.'[14]

At more than thrice 200 metres in height, therefore, the hypothetical Clark Fork ice dam does, indeed, begin to look 'impossible'.

Yet, as noted, Hunt accepted the USGS statistics. The surface of Lake Missoula certainly did at one point stand 4,150 feet above sea level and the lake therefore must indeed have reached around 2,100 feet deep in the Clark Fork Valley between the Bitteroot and Cabinet mountain ranges. That it did so is confirmed by an ancient strandline at that altitude, and other strandlines have been found at lower altitudes which clearly show many subsequent lower water levels after the high one.[15] Hunt's solution, however, since he continued to regard the Clark Fork dam as a geological impossibility, was to propose that *a gigantic flood, thousands of feet deep*, must have washed over the entire region at the end of the Ice Age, in the process filling the various basins of Glacial Lake Missoula up to the 4,150 foot level where the highest strandline is found and leaving the lower strandlines as it receded.[16]

As the source of his proposed region-wide flood, Hunt suggested that:

> tidal inundation brought on by some form of gravitational attraction from a celestial source, the nature of which is beyond the competence of the writer, must have resulted in a . . . tide . . . rising to 5,000 feet (1,600 metres) above present sea level . . . The waters were held there several weeks . . . during which there was much surging, partial floating of glaciers, and development of the highest beaches in 'Lake Missoula'. The tidal ebb and flood with successive lower beaches developing allowed sweeping of the canyons, removal of previous glacial deposits, fans and talus, scouring of the 'Scablands', ice-rafting, polishing of standing rock obstructions to tidal surge, aggradation of valley and 'by-pass' floors, and discharge of boulders into submarine deltas and fans. Lastly, a layer of silt was left in the wake of the tide, especially in the quieter waters of cul-de-sac estuaries.[17]

In other words, Hunt had very much gone 'back to Bretz' in proposing a single gigantic flood as the source of all the damage on the Columbia

Plateau. His 1977 notion that it was a tidal inundation of sea-water rushing up estuaries (and brought on by the gravitational attraction of some hypothetical celestial body)[18] is, however, untenable, and Hunt himself recognised this when he revisited the subject some years later in his 1990 book *Environment of Violence*. Conceding that 'the tidewater solution is weakened by the great distance to tidewater and the absence of a trail of evidence along the possible routes',[19] he sought out other possible sources of water in sufficiently vast quantities to inflict the damage to the landscape that he had observed in the field. In the process, he briefly considered John Shaw's theory of a subglacial reservoir of 100,000 cubic kilometres of meltwater, but asked some pertinent questions:

> How could such melting take place without a heat source such as the volcanic heat which precipitates Icelandic *jökulhlaups*? What climatic regimen would allow such melting in the first place? Why would the water not have lifted the periphery of the ice sheet and emerged without accumulating soon after it was produced by melting? What containment mechanism would allow accumulation of a great under-ice lake . . . beneath 3,000 metres of ice. And would not water beneath the maximum ice thickness tend to escape toward the lesser confining pressures under peripheral areas of the ice sheet? Is there any possible way such a huge under-ice chamber of water could accumulate?[20]

To cut a long story short, Hunt reasoned that there was not. Besides the 100,000 cubic kilometres that Shaw's theory offered was, in his opinion, insufficient. Almost ten times as much water would be needed to account for all the field evidence. With a tidal source, Glacial Lake Missoula and Shaw's under-ice reservoir all dismissed, therefore, Hunt found himself left with only one possible – though startlingly catastrophist – solution. Somehow, in some way, very rapid, cataclysmic melting of an immense area of the North American ice cap must have taken place. After doing the necessary calculations Hunt concluded that 840,000 cubic kilometres of ice, i.e. about ten per cent of the entire glaciated area, 'would have had to melt'.[21]

The reader will recall that Bretz originally envisaged something similar but was defeated by the inability of either radical global warming or sub-glacial volcanism (quite simply, neither happened) to account for the vast quantities of meltwater 'his' flood called for. In the end, as we saw, he settled for outburst floods from Glacial Lake Missoula as the answer. In 1990, Hunt faced the same dilemma – with the exception that he had already ruled out Lake Missoula – but showed himself to be an extraordinarily competent and prescient innovator when, without any preamble, he wrote:

> Earth heat cannot have melted continental ice to produce flood-waters in the volumes required . . . *A cometary heat source could have served the purpose.*[22] (Emphasis added).

To melt ten per cent of the North American ice cap, Hunt calculated that the kinetic energy of a half-kilometre diameter comet would be sufficient:

> A comet of the type that exploded above the Tunguska site in 1908 could have provided this heat. The great lake it might have created in the middle of the ice sheet would rapidly have tunnelled under the remaining glacier and emerged as catastrophic floods in many directions. *Cometary melting of the ice seems necessary to yield so much water in such a short time.*[23] (Emphasis added)

Anticipating the objection that no crater had been found, Hunt pointed out that the Tunguska event – an airburst – likewise left no crater or ejecta blanket. Furthermore, in the case of a hypothetical comet impact on the North American ice cap:

> all ejecta and cometary matter would likely have been swept away in the ensuing flood, coming to rest widely dispersed in the drift blanket far from its source. Thus diluted and mixed with other debris, direct evidence for either the exploded projectile or ejecta from the site could be difficult to recognise, if not lost to science permanently.[24]

Last but not least – and again the prescience is almost eerie! – Hunt noted that 'glass spherules if found in glacial debris could support the theory'.[25]

He could not have known then, writing a quarter of a century ago, that from 2007 onwards a team of leading scientists would champion the cause of comet impacts on the North American ice cap and, in the absence of obvious craters would derive much of their evidence from microspherules, fused glass and nanodiamonds.

How to change global climate in an instant

Hunt's suggestion was that a single relatively small half-kilometre diameter object would have packed sufficient kinetic energy to set off the melting of approximately one tenth of the North American ice cap, producing a cataclysmic flood. Twenty-five years on, the proponents of the Younger Dryas comet hypothesis, as we have seen, are proposing that 'multiple two-kilometre' objects may have impacted the ice cap.[26] If they are correct, the scale of the ensuing floods must have been almost unimaginably large. Nor would they have been confined only to the Channeled Scablands of the Columbia plateau. The comet hypothesis envisages a rain of impacts right across the ice sheet from the Pacific to the Atlantic coasts of North America, so we should find evidence of flooding everywhere.

We do. The Columbia plateau displays flood-ravaged scablands but so too does the state of New Jersey much further to the east. The Columbia plateau is notable for its fields and hillsides strewn with huge ice-rafted erratics but so, too, is the state of New York. Indeed, perched on the bare rock surfaces of Manhattan's Central Park are many imposing erratic boulders, including diabase from the Palisades Sill along the Hudson River and shist from even further afield. Interestingly, too, just as the Columbia plateau has its coulees, so New York State has its Finger Lakes. These latter were long thought to have been carved by glaciers but their geomorphology closely parallels that of the coulees and some researchers now believe they were cut by glacial meltwater at extreme pressures – a process linked by sediment evidence to 'the collapse of continental ice sheets'.[27]

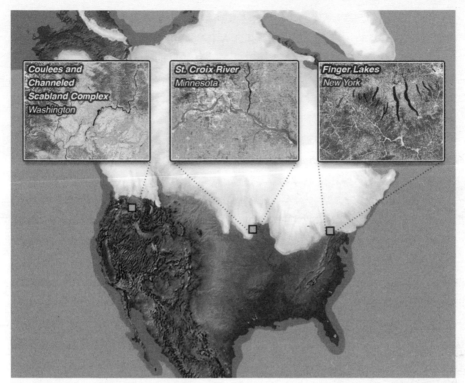

Figure 22

Likewise in Minnesota, on the Saint Croix River where Randall Carlson and I finished our long road trip across North America, there is a spectacular array of more than eighty giant glacial potholes. One is 10 feet wide and 60 feet deep, making it the deepest explored pothole in the world. Others, as yet unexcavated, are even wider, suggesting the probability that they may be deeper as well. And all of them, without exception, were carved out by turbulent floods at the end of the Ice Age – floods emanating, Randall believes, from the superior lobe of the Laurentide ice cap.

'You could spend a lifetime,' he tells me, 'travelling this land and still not see it all. The effects of mega scale flood flows have been extensively documented in the eastern foothills of the Rocky Mountains in both Canada and the US, across the prairie states, in the vicinity of the Great Lakes, in Pennsylvania and western New York, and in New England. All the Canadian provinces preserve large-scale evidence of gigantic water flows. All regions within or proximal to the area of the last great glaciation show the effects of intense, mega-scale floods.'

But the question that remains concerns the source of these floods.

Having been dragged kicking and screaming into conceding that flooding occurred at all, gradualist science, as we have seen, subsequently engaged in a love affair with Glacial Lake Missoula, elevating it and its epic *jökulhlaups* to serve as the sole explanation for all the astonishing diluvial features of the Channeled Scablands of the Columbia plateau. It is not surprising, therefore, that other Ice Age floods, wherever they are admitted to have occurred, are also attributed to *jökulhlaups* from glacial lakes.

More than that, it is the floodwaters from these glacial lakes – rather than anything so vulgarly catastrophist as a comet – that are presently regarded by mainstream science as the most likely cause of the Younger Dryas cold event. The giant Glacial Lake Agassiz, which lay across most of Manitoba, northwestern Ontario, northern Minnesota, eastern North Dakota and Saskatchewan is particularly implicated. Around 13,000 years ago – i.e. immediately before the onset of the Younger Dryas – Lake Agassiz is thought to have covered an area as great as 440,000 square kilometres (170,000 square miles) when an ice dam broke and allowed a substantial fraction of its contents, perhaps as much as 9,500 cubic kilometres, to spill out along a flood path running through the Mackenzie River system in the Canadian Arctic coastal plain, and thence into the Arctic Ocean.[28] There the anticyclonic circulation of a current known as the Beaufort Gyre would have gradually moved it onwards into the subpolar North Atlantic in the Transpolar Drift:

> The slow release of meltwater south through Fram Strait provides a mechanism unique to the Arctic that is capable of turning a short duration, high-magnitude meltwater discharge into a significantly longer, more moderated and sustained meltwater rerouting event to the North Atlantic.[29]

What made matters worse, however, was that *at the same time* huge quantities of icy meltwater were also being dumped into the North Atlantic from the other glacial lakes and directly off the Laurentide ice sheet itself.[30] The combined effect, so the theory goes, disrupted ocean circulation to such an extent that it radically affected global climate:

> A great gush of cold freshwater derived from the melting Laurentide ice sheet swept across the surface of the North Atlantic. It prevented warm, salty water from the southern ocean flowing deep beneath the surface (the Gulf Stream) from rising to the surface. The normal overturning of the ocean water stopped. As a consequence the atmosphere over the ocean, which would normally have been warmed, remained cold and so, in consequence, did the air over Europe and North America.[31]

These are highly technical matters, with which we do not need to concern ourselves at too great length here. In brief, though, the Atlantic meridional overturning circulation, also known as the thermohaline circulation, is the great ocean conveyer belt[32] that not only carries warm salty equatorial water to the surface and thence northwards where it eventually cools and sinks off the coasts of Greenland and Norway, but also carries the resultant cold North Atlantic deep water south, returning it slowly to the equator where it mixes with warmer water, rises again to the surface and thus continues the cycle:

> It transports large amounts of water, heat, salt, carbon, nutrients and other substances around the globe and connects the surface ocean and atmosphere with the huge reservoir of the deep sea. As such it is of critical importance to the global climate system.[33]

It was the shutting down of this delicately balanced, intricately interconnected, hugely complex, *critical* cycle, scientists agree, that caused the dramatic global cooling of the Younger Dryas. That the shutdown was the result of colossal meltwater floods out of glacial lakes, and directly off the Laurentide ice cap, is also agreed. A major puzzle, however, as S.J. Fiedel points out in a keynote paper in the journal *Quaternary International*, is why this should have happened 12,800 years ago, rather than say 800 or 1,000 years earlier at the height of the warm phase – known as the Bølling–Allerød interstadial – that immediately preceded the Younger Dryas.[34] Intuitively one feels the meltwater floods should have been at their peak during the warming phase. In reality however it was only at the Bølling–Allerød/Younger Dryas Boundary that the meltwater releases occurred.

The solution to the mystery seems transparently obvious to Richard Firestone, Allen West, Jim Kennett and other proponents of the Younger Dryas impact hypothesis. Quite simply, there is no mystery! In their reckoning, the huge meltwater floods that so radically affected global climate were caused by multiple large fragments of a comet ripping through the earth's atmosphere and smashing down into the ice cap – not just one fragment of half a kilometre or so as envisaged by C. Warren Hunt, but as many as eight fragments, and possibly more, including some that might have been as much as two kilometres in diameter.[35]

The colossal heat generated by such impacts, with a combined explosive power estimated as we have seen at ten million megatons, provides all the energy needed to set off a truly cataclysmic meltdown of huge sectors of the North American ice cap. The gigantic flood that would have followed, after scouring the land in its path, would indeed have entered the oceans as 'a great gush of freshwater' and provided the shock to the Atlantic meridional overturning circulation that kept global climate savagely cold for the next 1,200 years. The situation would have been worsened by the injection of dust and immense quantities of smoke into the upper atmosphere 'blocking sunlight for an extended period of time', which would, of course, have had the effect of lowering temperatures even further. Moreover:

> The impact event, followed by extensive fires and sudden climate change, likely contributed together to the rapid extinction of the megafauna and many other animals.[36]

The reader will recall that no less than thirty-five genera of North American mammals became extinct during the Younger Dryas.[37] We are therefore, by definition, looking for 'an extinction mechanism that is capable of wiping out up to thirty-five genera across a continent in a geologic instant'.[38] Nor is it just North America that we must consider – for most of the diverse megafauna of South America that had flourished before the Younger Dryas also suffered extinction by 12,000 years ago, i.e, before the Younger Dryas came to an end.[39]

Could it have been 'overkill' by human hunters? The question touches upon a contentious issue – namely when, in fact, and from where, did human beings first arrive in the Americas? Whatever the answer, it seems implausible that bands of nomadic hunter-gatherers would have been either motivated, or ruthlessly efficient enough, to wipe out so many animals, including giants like the Columbian mammoth, in so short a time across two continents. Moreover there is much to suggest that human beings in the Americas themselves entered a period of deep distress during the Younger Dryas that would have further reduced their motivation and efficiency. Archaeological evidence from South America is limited, but in North America, this was the time when the Clovis culture, with its sophisticated stone weapons technology, abruptly vanished from the record. Indeed, all available indicators point to 'a significant decline and/or reorganization in human population during the early centuries of the Younger Dryas'.[40]

Once again, therefore, the only explanation that makes complete sense of the evidence is the comet-impact hypothesis of Firestone, Kennett, West and their large group of colleagues and co-authors.

In the light of their findings, which we have reviewed extensively in the preceding chapters, I propose the following:

1. There was indeed cataclysmic flooding in North America at the end of the Ice Age.
2. It was not primarily caused by outburst floods from glacial lakes but rather by the rapid, almost instantaneous, meltdown of a large area of the ice cap.
3. The heat source needed to initiate this meltdown came from the kinetic energy of a series of impacts from fragments of a giant comet that entered the earth's atmosphere over North America 12,800 years ago and bombarded the North American ice cap.
4. North America, while being the epicentre of the disaster was by no means the only region hit. Other fragments of the disintegrating comet, including some particularly large objects, appear to have smashed into the European ice cap. In this

connection it may be of relevance that recent high-resolution sonar scans of the English Channel, the floor of which was above water during the Ice Age, have revealed evidence of cataclysmic flooding there in the form of a 400-kilometre-long network of submerged and partially infilled valleys carved into the bedrock. 'The data show a collection of landforms that, taken together, indicate a catastrophic flood origin,' state the authors of a study published in *Nature*. The study specifically likens these now submerged landforms to 'the Cheney–Palouse terrain of the Channeled Scabland of Washington, USA'. The authors state that they 'cannot resolve the absolute timing of the flooding events'. They do conclude, however, that their study 'provides the first direct evidence that a mega-flood event was responsible for carving the English Channel valley network. Our observations are consistent with erosion by high-magnitude flows, as in the Channeled Scabland'.[41]

5 Altogether more than 50 million square kilometres of the earth's surface were affected by impacts and airbursts of fragments of the Younger Dryas comet, some large, some smaller, but all devastating in their effects, extending from North America, right across the Atlantic Ocean and across Europe with the final rain of fragments falling as far afield as the Middle East.

6 The combined effect of these multiple impacts, particularly the immense freshwater floods into the Arctic and Atlantic Oceans that followed, set off the Younger Dryas cooling event, itself a cataclysm on a truly global scale that resulted in the extinction of huge numbers of animal species and pressed humanity very hard.

7 The human costs of the disaster might not have been confined to the complete destruction of hunter-gatherer cultures, such as the 'Clovis' people of North America. The possibility must be considered that an advanced civilization, now lost to history, might also have been obliterated.

Spring is coming

What is particularly striking is that the very radical climate changes at both the onset and the termination of the Younger Dryas were global and were accomplished within the span of a human generation.[42] Again the comet-impact hypothesis makes the best sense of this. The estimated combined explosive force of the impacts at ten million megatons would have lofted sufficient ejecta into the atmosphere 12,800 years ago to plunge the earth into a long, sustained twilight, akin to a nuclear winter – the 'time of darkness' that so many ancient myths speak of – capable of reducing solar radiation for more than 1,000 years. The dramatic warming that began 11,600 years ago would then be explained by the final dissipation of the ejecta cloud coupled with an end to the system-wide inertia that had beset thermohaline circulation in the North Atlantic.[43]

Another possibility, not necessarily mutually contradictory with any of the above mechanisms, is that 11,600 years ago the earth interacted again with the debris stream of the same fragmenting comet that had caused the Younger Dryas to start 12,800 years ago. On the second occasion, however, analysis suggests that the primary impacts were not on land or onto ice but into the world's oceans throwing up vast plumes of water vapour and creating a 'greenhouse effect' that caused global warming rather than global cooling.[44]

According to renowned British astronomer Sir Fred Hoyle:

> The difference between a warm ocean and a cold one amounts to a 10-year supply of sunlight. Thus the warm conditions produced by a strong water vapour greenhouse must be maintained for at least a decade in order to produce the required transformation of the ocean, and this is just about the time for which water, suddenly thrown into the stratosphere, might be expected to persist there. The needed amount of water is so vast, 100 million million tons, that only one kind of causative event seems possible, the infall of a comet-sized object into a major ocean.[45]

More research certainly needs to be done to establish the exact mechanisms, in all their complexity, that brought about the sudden end of the Younger Dryas, but the effects on global climate are already well understood. The Greenland ice cores, those invaluable windows into the past, tell us that:

> temperatures rose in less than a decade at the climate transition marking the end of the Younger Dryas cold interval and the beginning of the warmer Holocene epoch at 11,600 years before the present.[46] In less than 20 years, the climate in the North Atlantic region turned into a milder and less stormy regime, as a consequence of a rapid retreat of sea-ice cover. A warming of 7 degrees Centigrade was completed in about 50 years.[47]

In exactly the same interval, in the subalpine belt of Western Europe, tree species that had never been present before, including *Laris, Pinus cembra* and *Betula*, suddenly began to proliferate.[48]

In Northwestern Montana, in the USA, glacial ice in Marias Pass had receded upvalley from the canyon mouth and the Sun River Glacier had completely vanished by 11,200 years ago.[49]

A thousand other examples could be cited, but the message is the same everywhere – from Tasmania to the Andes, from Turkey to Japan, from North America to Australia, from Peru to Egypt, winter had ended and a great global spring had begun. 'Such is the rebirth of the Cosmos,' as the Hermetic Texts proclaim. 'It is a making again of all things good, a holy and awe-inspiring restoration of all nature . . .'[50]

A rebirth?

A making again?

A restoration?

But of what? Who went before? What exactly was to be reborn?

We will consider these questions in the following chapters.

Part III

Sages

Chapter 7
The Fire Next Time

———◆———

Three singularities occurred near the end of the last Ice Age, linked to the sudden onset and equally sudden termination of the mysterious epoch known as the Younger Dryas:

- Somewhere around 12,800 years ago, after more than two thousand years of uninterrupted global warming (and with a margin of error of plus or minus 150 years that is as close as the resolution of the data allows us to get to the actual moment), a flood of icy meltwater entered the North Atlantic so suddenly and in such quantities that it disrupted ocean circulation. The source of the flood was the North American ice cap. Since the previous two millennia had witnessed continuous sea-level rise, the resolution of the data means there is no way of knowing exactly how much coastal land was swallowed up by this singular event. With so much new water that had previously been locked in ice abruptly added, however, we may surmise that a dramatic and instantaneous rise in sea-level did occur.[1]

- In the same geological instant that the meltwater flood was unleashed, global temperatures plummeted and the world's climate underwent a reversal from that balmy two-thousand-year-long 'summer' that had begun about 15,000 years ago (by 13,000 years ago, conditions are thought to have improved to such an extent that they were warmer and wetter than they are today) to a savage and icy global winter. Again the resolution of the data does not allow us to say exactly how soon after the meltwater flood the deep-freeze began but, as we saw in the previous chapter, there is much to suggest that this radical reversal of temperatures was achieved within the span of a single human generation. In that same span the ice sheets that had everywhere been melting and in retreat began remorselessly to re-advance and sea-level rise ceased.

● Around 11,600 years ago, again with a margin of error of 150 years in either direction imposed by the data – but again apparently within a single generation – the freeze suddenly ended, global temperatures soared, and the remnant ice caps collapsed, shedding their residual water burden into the world's oceans which rose dramatically to close to today's level.

Our ancestors passed through these tumultuous changes and it is inconceivable that they would not have remarked upon them or sought to speak about their experiences to one another. Their stories and eyewitness accounts, would, in turn, have become part of revered oral traditions and as such would have been passed down from generation to generation until they became hoary with age. As the reader will recall from Chapter Three, certain Native American 'myths' do, absolutely, seem to speak of events at the end of the last Ice Age. The terrible floods that scoured and ravaged the land are described in detail. But of even greater interest are the traditions of the 'star with the long wide tail' that 'came down here once, thousands of years ago', that 'burnt up everything' and that 'made a different world' in which 'the weather was colder than before'.

These traditions appear to memorialise the devastating effects of the comet impact that we can now date conclusively, within the understood margins of error, to around 12,800 years ago. We've seen how scientists Richard Firestone, Allen West, Jim Kennett and others believe the comet broke into multiple fragments, perhaps eight of which – some with diameters approaching two kilometres – hit the North American ice cap generating huge amounts of heat and instantly transforming great masses of ice into the floods of meltwater that disrupted oceanic circulation and played a key role in bringing on the deep freeze of the Younger Dryas. The reader will also recall that other fragments of the giant comet are thought to have hit the Northern

European ice cap and to have gone on to rain down on even more distant lands as far away as the Middle East. Thus, though the epicentre was in North America, it is not surprising that the Younger Dryas was a global event that affected peoples and cultures all around the world.

What is surprising is the remarkable consistency with which traditions from every part of the globe speak not only of cataclysmic events but also of very specific warnings given to certain selected 'wise', or 'good' or 'pure' humans in *advance* of the impending cataclysm. We

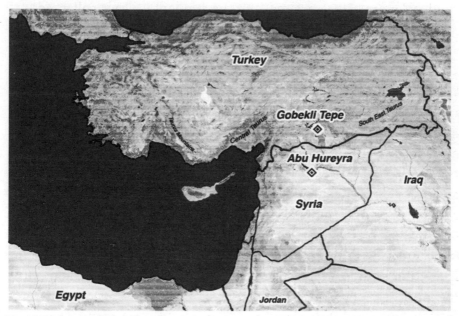

Figure 23

saw several examples of such warnings in the Native American traditions reviewed in Chapter Three, but if we travel oceans and continents away from the epicentre of the impacts we find similar accounts of warnings preserved in the Middle East at the furthest extent to which the effects of the comet have so far been documented. Note this does not mean that the 'strewnfield' of comet debris is confined to the 50 million square kilometres presently recognised. It simply means that samples of sediment from other regions have thus far not been assayed for nanodiamonds, magnetic and glassy spherules, melt-glass, platinum and other tell-tale proxies of impact.

Up to the limit of research so far done, however, the site furthest from North America that has produced firm evidence of the presence and effects of the Younger Dryas comet is an archaeological mound, or tell, called Abu Hureyra in Syria which was excavated in 1974 just before completion of the Taqba Dam on the Euphrates River caused it to disappear forever beneath the advancing waters of Lake Assad. Sediment samples from the archaeological trenching of Abu Hureyra were removed and preserved before the site was flooded and it was the Younger Dryas Boundary layer of one of these samples (from Trench E, and dated to 12,800 years ago) that Firestone, West, Kennett and their team assayed in 2012. As we saw in Chapter Five, they found nanodiamonds, abundant cosmic impact spherules and melt-glass that could only have formed at temperatures in excess of 2,200 degrees Celsius suggesting that the site was 'near the centre of a high-energy air-burst/impact'.[2]

Abu Hureyra cannot be subjected to further direct archaeological investigation since it now lies under Lake Assad, but Firestone, Kennett and West believe the effects of the comet on 'that settlement and its inhabitants would have been severe'.[3] Of note is the fact that the site lies close both to southeastern Turkey, where Göbekli Tepe is situated, and to the modern state of Iran – formerly Persia – where traditions of great antiquity have been preserved in the scriptures of Zoroastrianism, the pre-Islamic religion of ancient Persia.

'The fatal winters are going to fall . . .'

Exactly how old Zoroastrianism is has not yet been satisfactorily established by scholars, since even the lifetime of its prophet Zarathustra (more usually known as Zoroaster) is uncertain. Indeed, as Columbia University's authoritative *Encyclopedia Iranica* admits: 'Controversy over Zarathustra's date has been an embarrassment of long standing to Zoroastrian studies.'[4]

The Greek historians were amongst the first to address themselves to the matter. Plutarch, for example, tells us that Zoroaster 'lived 5,000 years before the Trojan War'[5] (itself a matter of uncertain historicity but generally put at around 1300 BC, thus 5,000 plus 1,300 = 6300 BC). A similar chronology is given by Diogenes Laertius who relates that

Zoroaster lived '6,000 years before Xerxes' Greek campaign'[6] (i.e. around 6480 BC). More recent scholars have proposed dates as far apart as 1750 BC and '258 years before Alexander'[7] (i.e. around 588 BC). Whatever the truth of the matter, it is agreed that Zoroaster himself borrowed from much earlier traditions and that Zoroastrianism, therefore, like many other religions, has roots that extend very far back into prehistory.

In the Zoroastrian scriptures known as the Zend Avesta certain verses in particular are recognised as drawing on these very ancient oral traditions.[8] The verses speak of a primordial father figure called Yima, the first man, the first king and the founder of civilization and appear in the opening section of the Zend Avesta known as the Vendidad. There we read how the god Ahura Mazda created the first land, 'Airyana Vaejo, by the good river Daitya',[9] as a paradise on earth and how 'the fair Yima, the great shepherd . . . was the first mortal' with whom Ahura Mazda chose to converse, instructing him to become a preacher.[10] Yima refused, at which the god set him a different task:

> Since thou wantest not to be the preacher and the bearer of my law, then make my world thrive, make my world increase; undertake thou to nourish, to rule and to watch over my world.[11]

To this Yima agreed at which the god presented him with a golden ring and a poniard – a long, tapered thrusting knife – inlaid with gold. Significantly, for we will see in Chapter Seventeen there are close parallels to this story as far away as the Andes mountains of South America, Yima then:

> pressed the earth with the golden ring and bored it with the poniard.[12]

By this act, we learn he 'made the earth grow larger by one third than it was before', a feat that over the course of thousands of years he repeated twice more – in the process eventually doubling the land area available for 'the flocks and herds with men and dogs and birds', who gathered unto him 'at his will and wish, as many as he wished'.[13]

Anatomically modern humans like ourselves have existed, so far as we know, for a little less than two hundred thousand years (the earliest anatomically modern human skeleton acknowledged by science is from Ethiopia and dates to 196,000 years ago).[14] Within this time-span there has been only one period when those parts of the earth that are useful to humans increased dramatically in size and that was during the last Ice Age between 100,000 and 11,600 years ago. Indeed, previously submerged lands totalling 27 million square kilometres – equivalent to the area of Europe and China added together – were exposed by lowered sea-levels at the last glacial maximum 21,000 years ago. While it is probably far-fetched to suppose that it is this very real increase of useful land – of which a great part was still above water at the beginning of the Younger Dryas 12,800 years ago – that is referred to in the Yima story, or that it has anything to do with the golden age that Yima's benign rule supposedly achieved in Airyana Vaejo,[15] it is interesting to note what happened next.

After another immense span of time, we read, Yima was summoned to 'a meeting place by the good river Daitya' where the god Ahura Mazda appeared to him bearing an ominous warning of sudden and catastrophic climate change:

O fair Yima, upon the material world the fatal winters are going to fall, that shall bring the fierce, foul frost; upon the material world the fatal winters are going to fall that shall make snowflakes fall thick, even on the highest tops of mountains . . .

Therefore make thee a Vara [a hypogeum, or underground enclosure] long as a riding ground on every side of the square, and thither bring the seeds of sheep and oxen, of men, of dogs, of birds, and of red blazing fires . . . Thither thou shalt bring the seeds of men and women of the greatest, best and finest kinds on this earth; thither shalt thou bring the seeds of every kind of cattle, of the greatest, best and finest kinds on this earth. Thither shalt thou bring the seeds of every kind of tree, of the greatest, best and finest kinds on this earth; thither shalt thou bring the seeds of every kind of fruit, the fullest of food and sweetest of odour. All those seeds shalt thou bring, two of every kind, to be kept inexhaustible there, so long as those men shall stay in the Vara. There shall be no humpbacked, none bulged forward there; no impotent, no lunatic . . . no leprous.[16]

So . . . you get the idea? This underground hideaway was to serve as a refuge from a terrible winter that was about to seize Airyana Vaejo a winter at the onset of which, as the Bundahish, another Zoroastrian text, informs us:

the evil spirit . . . sprang like a snake out of the sky down to the earth . . . He rushed in at noon, and thereby the sky was as shattered and frightened by him as a sheep by a wolf. He came onto the water which was arranged below the earth, and then the middle of this earth was pierced and entered by him . . . He rushed out upon the whole creation and he made the world quite as injured and dark at midday as though it were dark night.[17]

Studying these accounts I couldn't help but be reminded of the two millennia of warm, fine weather, which must indeed have seemed like a golden age, before the sudden lethal onset of the Younger Dryas 12,800 years ago. The Zoroastrian texts would not be far wrong in describing it as a 'fierce, foul frost' and as 'a fatal winter'. The 'evil spirit' to whom this affliction is attributed is Angra Mainyu, the agent of darkness, destruction, wickedness and chaos, who stands in opposition to and seeks to undermine and undo all the good works of Ahura Mazda – for Zoroastrianism is a profoundly dualistic religion in which human beings, and the choices we make for good or evil, are seen as the objects of an eternal competition, or contest, between the opposed forces of darkness and light.

And in this contest the darkness sometimes wins. Thus the Vendidad reminds us that although Airyana Vaejo was 'the first of the good lands and countries' created by Ahura Mazda, it could not resist the evil one:

Thereupon came Angra Mainyu, who is all death, and he counter-created by his witchcraft the serpent in the river, and winter, a

135

work of the demons . . . [Now] there are ten winter months there, two summer months, and these are cold for the waters, cold for the earth, cold for the trees. Winter falls there, with the worst of its plagues.[18]

In other translations the phrase 'the serpent in the river, and winter' is given as 'a great serpent and Winter' and, alternatively, as 'a mighty serpent and snow'.[19]

Again . . . you get the idea. The metaphor that is being repeatedly driven home here is that of the mighty serpent who springs from the sky down to the earth, who penetrates the earth, and who brings a prolonged winter upon the world so severe that it is 'dark' ('most turbid, opaque' according to some translations[20]) at midday, and even the fleeting summer months are too cold for human life. Once again, the whole scenario seems very accurately to describe the terrible conditions that would have afflicted the world after the Younger Dryas comet spread its trail of destruction across at least 50 million square kilometres, brought on 'a vehement destroying frost' and threw such quantities of dust into the upper atmosphere, together with smoke from the continent-wide wildfires sparked off by airbursts and super-heated ejecta, that a turbid, opaque darkness would indeed have filled the skies, reflecting back the sun's rays and perpetuating something very like a nuclear winter for centuries.

The Zoroastrian texts leave us in no doubt that these conditions posed a deadly threat to the future survival of civilization. It was for this reason that Ahura Mazda came to Yima with his warning and his instruction to build an underground shelter where some remnant of humanity could take refuge, keeping safe the seeds of all animals and plants, until the dire winter had passed and spring returned to the world. Moreover the account reveals very little that seems 'mythical', or that obviously derives from flights of religious fancy. Rather the whole thing has about it an atmosphere of hard-headed practical planning that adds a chilling note of veracity.

For example the admonition that deformed, impotent, lunatic and leprous people should be kept out of the Vara sounds a lot like eugenics, a distasteful policy to be sure, but one that might be implemented if the survival of the human race was at stake and there was limited space available in the refuge. For the same reasons it is not surprising that only the seeds of 'the greatest, best and finest' kinds of trees, fruits and vegetables, those that are 'fullest of food and sweetest of odour' are to be brought to the Vara. Why waste space on anything but the best?

Also although it is certain that a number of carefully selected people were to be admitted to the Vara, perhaps as caretakers and managers of the project, and as future breeding stock, the emphasis throughout is on seeds – which in the case of human beings would be sperm from the males and eggs from the females. So when we read that the Vara is to be constructed in three subterranean levels, each smaller than the one above, each with its own system of criss-crossing 'streets', it is legitimate to wonder whether some kind of storage system, perhaps with ranks of shelves arranged in criss-crossing aisles might not really be what is meant here:

> In the largest part of the place thou shalt make nine streets, six in the middle part, three in the smallest. To the streets of the largest part thou shalt bring a thousand seeds of men and women; to the streets of the middle part, six hundred; to the streets of the smallest part, three hundred.[21]

If it seems fanciful to imagine that we might, in an almost high-tech sense, be looking at the specifications of a seed bank here, then how are we to assess other 'technological' aspects of the Vara – for example its lighting system? As well as making a door to the place, and sealing it up with the golden ring already given to him by Ahura Mazda, Yima is also to fashion 'a window, self-shining within'.[22] When Yima asks for clarification as to the nature of this 'self-shining' window Ahura Mazda tells him cryptically 'there are uncreated lights and created lights'. The former are the stars, the moon and the sun, which will not be seen from within the confines of the Vara during the long winter, but the latter are 'artificial lights' which 'shine from below'.[23]

Yima did as he was instructed and completed the Vara which, thereafter, 'glowed with its own light'.[24] That accomplished, he then:

made waters flow in a bed a mile long; there he settled birds, by the evergreen banks that bear never-failing food. There he established dwelling places, consisting of a house with a balcony, a courtyard and a gallery . . .[25]

There, too, we are reminded, in accord with the commands of the god,

he brought the seeds of men and women . . . There he brought the seeds of every kind of tree [and] . . . every kind of fruit . . . All those seeds he brought, two of every kind, to be kept inexhaustible there, so long as those men shall stay in the Vara . . .[26]

Finally, we learn that:

every fortieth year, to every couple two are born, a male and a female. And thus it is for every sort of cattle. And the men in the Vara, which Yima made, live the happiest life.[27]

Interestingly the translator explains, in a footnote drawn from various ancient learned commentaries on the text, that the human inhabitants of the Vara 'live there for 150 years; some say they never die'.[28] Moreover, and particularly intriguing, the births of offspring to every couple do not result from sexual union but 'from the seeds deposited in the Vara'.[29]

Other hints of a mysterious lost technology connected to Yima include a miraculous cup in which he could see everything that was happening anywhere in the world and a jewelled glass throne (sometimes described as 'a glass chariot') that was capable of flight.[30]

Flood and rain

As well as a climate catastrophe in the form of an overnight reversion to peak Ice Age cold, we also know that the Younger Dryas involved extensive global flooding as a large fraction of the North American ice cap melted and poured into the world ocean. It is therefore noteworthy that the Zoroastrian texts speak not only of the 'vehement, destroying frost' of a global winter but also of an associated flood accompanied by heavy precipitation, in which:

> Every single drop of rain became as big as a bowl and the water stood the height of a man over the whole of this earth.[31]

On the other side of the world and much closer to the North American epicentre of the cataclysm, the *Popol Vuh*, an original document of the ancient Quiche Maya of Guatemala, based on pre-conquest sources, also speaks of a flood and associates it with 'much hail, black rain and mist, and indescribable cold'.[32] It says, in a remarkable echo of the Zoroastrian tradition, that this was a period when 'it was cloudy and twilight all over the world . . . The faces of the sun and the moon were covered'.[33] Other Maya sources confirm that these strange and terrible phenomena were experienced by mankind 'in the time of the ancients. The earth darkened . . . It happened that the sun was still bright and clear. Then, at midday, it got dark . . .'[34] Sunlight was not seen again 'until the twenty-sixth year after the flood'.[35]

Returning to the Middle East, the famous account of the Hebrew patriarch Noah and the great Ark in which he rides out the flood, commands attention. It is obvious that there are many parallels with the story of Yima and his Vara. The Vara, after all, is a means of surviving a terrible and devastating winter which will destroy every living creature by enchaining the earth in a freezing trap of ice and snow. The Ark, likewise, is a means of surviving a terrible and devastating flood which will destroy every living creature by drowning the world in water. In both cases a deity – Ahura Mazda in the case of the Zoroastrian tradition, the God Yahweh in the case of the Hebrew tradition – intervenes to give advance warning to a good and pure man to prepare for the coming cataclysm. In each case the essence of the project is to preserve the seeds, or the breeding pairs, of all life:

> And of every living thing of all flesh, two of every sort shalt thou bring into the Ark, to keep them alive with thee; they shall be male and female.

Of fowls after their kind, and of cattle after their kind, of every creeping thing of the earth after his kind, two of every sort shall come unto thee, to keep them alive.[36]

Easily missed, but noteworthy, is the fact that Noah's Ark, like Yima's Vara, is to have a 'window', is to be closed with a 'door' and is to consist of three levels:

A window shalt thou make to the Ark, and in a cubit shalt thou finish it above; and the door of the Ark shalt thou set in the side thereof; with lower, second, and third stories shalt thou make it.[37]

Last but not least, there are hints of a lost lighting technology in Noah's Ark that parallel the references to the 'artificial lights' in the Vara. In *The Legends of the Jews*, Louis Ginzberg's remarkable and comprehensive compilation of ancient stories and traditions connected to the Hebrew Bible, we read that the whole journey of the Ark, 'during the year of the flood', was conducted in darkness both by day and by night:

All the time it lasted, the sun and the moon shed no light . . .[38]

However just like the 'self-shining window' of the Vara:

The Ark was illuminated by a precious stone, the light of which was more brilliant by night than by day, so enabling Noah to distinguish between day and night.[39]

Underground cities

Noah's Ark, as is well known, is said to have ended its journey on the slopes of Mount Ararat, the symbolic heartland of ancient Armenia but now, as a result of wars in the early twentieth century, located within the modern state of Turkey. Turkey, in turn, shares a border with Iran – ancient Persia – from which the accounts of Yima's Vara come down to us.

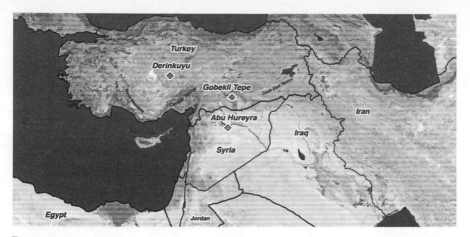

Figure 24

It is therefore intriguing that Turkey's Cappadocia region has a very large number of ancient underground structures hewn out of solid rock and usually, like the Vara, consisting of multiple levels stacked one above the other. These underground 'cities', as they are known, include the eerie and spectacular site of Derinkuyu, which I was able to visit in 2013. Lying beneath a modern town of the same name, eight of its levels are presently open to the public, although further levels remain closed off below and, astonishingly, a subterranean tunnel several kilometres in length connects it to another similar hypogeum at Kaymakli.

Entering Derinkuyu was like crossing some invisible barrier into an unexpected netherworld. One minute I was standing in bright sunshine; the next, after I had ducked into the cool, dank, dimly-lit system of tunnels and galleries (no self-shining windows now; only low wattage electric light), I felt I had been transported to a realm carved out by mythical dwarves at the dawn of time. In places the tunnels are low and narrow so that one must stoop and walk in single file between walls stained and blackened with ancient smoke and overgrown here and there with green mould. At regular intervals, slid back into deep recesses, I passed hulking megalithic doors, shaped like millstones, 5 to 6 feet (1.5 to 1.8 metres) in diameter and weighing close to half a ton. These were clearly designed to be rolled out to block access. Stairways and steep ramps led down from level to level and, although all the levels were interconnected, the rolling stone doors could be used to isolate them from one another when needed.

141

I noticed a remarkable system of plunging, sheer-sided ventilation shafts connecting the deepest levels with the surface – and doing so to such good effect that the gusts of fresh air were still palpable 80 metres (260 feet) or more beneath the ground. In some places the passageway I was following would debouch into a junction where tunnels branched off in several directions and more stairways led down to even lower levels. And here and there, now to one side of the passageway, now to the other, sometimes accessed by means of holes cut in the wall, sometimes through full-sized doorways, lay small low-ceilinged grottos in which even a few people sitting together would have felt cramped. But sometimes those doors would lead into inter-connected networks of chambers and passages and sometimes they would open out suddenly into lofty halls and spacious rooms with barrel-vault ceilings looming high overhead, supported on monolithic columns hewn from the living rock.

The whole place, in short, is a complex and cunning labyrinth on an immense scale – a work of astonishing architectural complexity that would be impressive if it had been built above ground, but that is utterly breathtaking when one considers that it all had to be mined, chiselled, hammered, cut and gouged out of the volcanic bedrock. Later, studying a plan, I realised that this vast hypogeum, looking in cross-section like a gigantic rabbit warren and extending over an area of more than 4 square kilometres,[40] lay underfoot wherever one went in the modern town of Derinkuyu, streets beneath streets, rooms beneath rooms, a secret antipodal city of unknown antiquity and of unknown purpose but certainly the product of immense ingenuity, determination and skill.

And Derinkuyu is just one of *two hundred* such subterranean complexes, each containing a minimum of two levels (with around forty containing three levels or more) that have been identified in Turkey in the area between Kayseri and Nevsehir.[41] Moreover, new discoveries are constantly being made. Derinkuyu itself was found in 1963 after builders renovating the cellar of a modern home broke through to an ancient passageway below. And most recently, in 2014, workers preparing the ground for a new housing project at Nevsehir, an hour's drive north of Derinkuyu, stumbled upon yet another unsuspected hypogeum. Archaeologists were called in and it was quickly realised that this one was bigger than any others so far known. As Hasan Unver, Mayor of Nevsehir put it, Derinkuyu and Kaymakli are little more than 'kitchens' when compared to the newly-explored site. 'It is not a known underground city', added Mehmet Ergun Turan, head of Turkey's Housing Development Administration. "Tunnel passages of seven kilometres are being discussed. Naturally, when the discovery was made, we stopped the construction we were planning to do in the area.'[42]

Several commentators immediately speculated that the newly discovered site might be '5,000 years old',[43] but there is no basis for this – or really for any date. All we can say for sure is that the earliest surviving historical mention of Turkey's underground cities is found in the *Anabapsis* of the Greek historian Xenophon written in the fourth century BC[44] – so they are older than that.

But the question is, how much older?

As the reader will recall from Chapter One, there is no objective way to date structures made entirely of rock. What archaeologists look for, therefore, are organic materials that can be carbon dated. To be useful, however, these organic materials must be excavated from locations – under a megalith that has never been moved, for example, or in the original mortar in a joint between two stone blocks – that allow reasonable deductions to be made about the date the associated structural elements were put in place.

This is why the mysterious decision by the builders of Göbekli Tepe to *bury* the megalithic enclosures there has been so helpful to archaeology. Once buried they stayed buried and organic materials in the fill can thus be used to make valuable inferences about their age. In many other sites, by contrast, there is the possibility that the intrusion of later organic materials will give a falsely young date, and in some – the underground cities of Turkey being a prime example – no reliable dating can be done. This is because the sites were used, reused and indeed repurposed, many times down the ages by many different peoples, with organic materials being introduced on every occasion, thus making it impossible to draw any inferences about the epoch of their original construction.

The general view of archaeologists is that the underground structures were originally developed in the seventh or eighth centuries BC by an Indo-European people called the Phrygians who lived in Cappadocia at the time. The theory is that the Phrygians began the project by widening and deepening natural caves and tunnels that already existed in the volcanic rock, making use of the spaces they created for storage and possibly as places of refuge from attackers.

By Roman times, with the Phrygians long gone, the inhabitants of the area were Greek-speaking Christians who further developed and expanded the underground caverns, rededicating some of the rooms as chapels and leaving inscriptions in Greek, some of which survive to this day. In the Byzantine era, from the eighth to the twelfth centuries AD, the Eastern Roman Empire was locked in wars with newly Islamicised Arabs and the underground cities became places of refuge again – a function they continued to serve during the Mongol invasions of the fourteenth century AD. Later still, Greek Christians used the cities to escape persecution at the hands of Turkish Muslim rulers, and this practice continued into the twentieth century when the structures finally fell into disuse after the truce and population exchange between Greece and Turkey in 1923.[45]

With such a chequered history it is easy to see why the underground cities cannot be dated using objective archaeological techniques. Moreover the vast effort that went into their excavation out of solid rock, and their sophisticated ventilation systems, speak of powerful long-term motives far beyond the limited and temporary need for shelter from attackers. With this in mind let us consider a scenario in which the Phrygians, favoured for no good reason by archaeologists as the first makers of the cities, were themselves just one of the many later cultures to make use of them. It is perfectly possible that this is the case and, if so, then it is also possible that these extraordinary underground structures might date back to a time long before the Phrygians – perhaps even as far back as the 'fatal winters' of the Younger Dryas that set in around 12,800 years ago.

There is no proof of this, of course. Nonetheless Turkish historian and archaeologist Omer Demir, author of *Cappadocia: Cradle of History*, is of the opinion that Derinkuyu does in fact date back to the

Palaeolithic.[46] His argument is based partly on the notion that it already existed in Phrygian times,[47] partly on stylistic differences between the upper (older) levels and the lower (younger) levels[48] and partly on the fact that marks of the implements used to cut the rock have worn completely away in the upper levels but are still visible in the lower levels:

> It is necessary for a long period of time to pass for the chisel marks to disappear. This means that there was quite a time difference between the years of construction of the first stories and the last stories.[49]

Demir also suggests that the huge quantities of rock excavated to make the underground city – which are nowhere in evidence in the vicinity today – were dumped into local streams and carried off.[50] In one of these streams, the Sognali, at a distance of 26 kilometres (16 miles) from Derinkuyu, hand-axes, rock-chips and other Palaeolithic artefacts were found.[51]

The evidence is suggestive at best. I would not want to bet my life or my reputation on it! Nonetheless the scenario that sees Derinkuyu and the other underground cities constructed in the Upper Palaeolithic around 12,800 years ago at the onset of the Younger Dryas has the great merit of no longer leaving us casting about for a motive commensurate with the huge effort involved. We are informed of that motive quite explicitly in the story of Yima. Stated simply, the cities are Varas, cut down into the depths of the earth as places of refuge from the horrors of the Younger Dryas, which were not limited to the 'vehement destroying frost' but – as we know from the cosmic impact spherules and melt-glass found in sediment samples at nearby Abu Hureyra – also included the terrifying threat of bombardment from the skies.

Like a snake out of the sky

It is close to certain, if our planet did indeed cross the path of a giant comet 12,800 years ago as Firestone, Kennett and West maintain, that the bombardment would *not* have been limited to the large fragments

145

that came down during the first event. The comet's debris stream would have remained on an earth-crossing orbit and would, very likely have resulted in decades, perhaps even centuries, of subsequent bombardments – not on the same scale of intensity as the initial encounter, but nonetheless able to cause catastrophic damage and to spread enough fear and dismay of the mighty 'serpent' lingering in the heavens to justify the construction of secure underground shelters.

Indeed, as we will see, the earth may *still* cross the debris stream of the giant Younger Dryas comet today and large, deadly objects, blacker than coal, invisible to our telescopes, may still be orbiting in that stream today. I'm reminded again of the Ojibwa prophecy reviewed in Chapter Three:

> The star with the long, wide tail is going to destroy the world some day when it comes low again. That's the comet called Long-Tailed Heavenly Climbing Star.

Is the Younger Dryas comet coming back? Could it be that it did not spend all its anger and destructive force with the fragments that hit the earth and caused the vehement destroying winter of the Younger Dryas 12,800 years ago?

Curiously the ancient Iranian traditions contain a prophecy also, for it is said that Yima will return, and will walk again amongst men, when:

> the signs foreshadowing the last of days appear. Of these the worst will be a winter more terrible than any the world has seen before when it will rain and snow and hail for three long years.[52]

The fiery descent of more fragments of the comet could bring about such a winter, just as happened 12,800 years ago. And just as happened then, it would do so in part because the skies would be darkened by debris and smoke from the wildfires caused by airbursts and by the superheated ejecta from the impacts on land. These are grave matters, and we will return to them in Chapter Nineteen. But first we must consider the story of Noah, the Hebrew counterpart of Yima, carried by the waters of the flood – so we are told – to the slopes of Mount Ararat, just a few days' walk from Göbekli Tepe. The Noah story also contains a prophecy which is made manifest in the New Testament, 2 Peter 3: 3-7:

> By water the world of that time was deluged and destroyed. By the same word the present heavens and earth are reserved for fire, being kept for the day of judgment and destruction of ungodly men.

Or as the old song has it:

> God gave Noah the rainbow sign: no more water, the fire next time.

Chapter 8
The Antediluvians

—◆—

The Biblical story of the Deluge is too familiar to require extensive repetition here. The essential elements can be summarised as follows:

- A life-destroying global flood, sent by God to punish human wickedness.[1]
- A man (Noah) selected by God and given advance warning of the coming cataclysm so that he can build a survival ship (the Ark).[2]
- The preservation in the Ark of the seeds, or breeding pairs, of all forms of life, with a particular emphasis on human life (Noah and his wife together with their sons and their wives) and animal life ('of fowls after their kind', as we saw in the last chapter, 'and of cattle after their kind, of every creeping thing of the earth after his kind, two of every sort shall come unto thee, to keep them alive').[3]
- The Ark rides out the flood until the waters subside.[4]
- The Ark comes to rest 'on the mountains of Ararat'.[5]
- When the waters have 'dried up from the earth' God instructs Noah to leave the Ark with his family and to 'bring out every kind of living creature that is with you – the birds, the animals, and all the creatures that move along the ground – so they can multiply on the earth and be fruitful and increase in number on it.'[6]
- Noah builds an altar on which he sacrifices some of the animals and birds that he has just saved from the flood. The smell of the burnt offerings is pleasing to God.[7]

- The surviving humans and animals go forth and multiply 'and fill the earth' as they have been commanded.[8]

Mount Ararat rises to 5,137 metres (16,853 feet) and geologists assure us, on the basis of excellent science, that no part of it has ever been covered by oceanic floodwaters since it began to take shape as a mountain near the end of the early Miocene some sixteen million years ago. The presence of anatomically modern humans in the world, as we saw in the last chapter, cannot be traced back further than two hundred thousand years, and even the last common ancestor with the chimpanzee – a creature that was very far from being in any sense 'human' – takes us back barely six million years, so the notion of a boat with humans on board being washed up on Mount Ararat is a chronological impossibility.

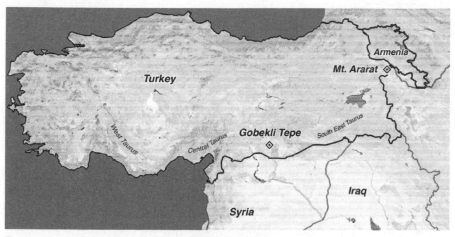

Figure 25

Nonetheless, it is intriguing that the story of the Deluge as given in the Old Testament makes specific and deliberate mention of 'the mountains of Ararat' (the 'Mount' does in fact have twin peaks) which, in Biblical times, were understood as being part of the 'Kingdom of Ararat',[9] the historic land of Urartu, conquered by the Assyrian King Shalmaneser in the late second millennium BC.[10] Due to the limited archaeology that has been undertaken in the region, historians confess that 'the origins of Urartu must remain obscure',[11] but the earliest known settlements and the beginnings of agriculture in the region have been traced back to 'approximately 10,000 to 9000 BC'[12] – in other words to the period of Göbekli Tepe.

Moreover, this whole area, Mount Ararat and Göbekli Tepe very much included, formed the heartland of historic Armenia, the direct descendant of the Biblical Kingdom of Ararat whose inhabitants saw – and still today see – themselves as 'the Peoples of Ararat'.[13] Written in the fifth century AD, Moses Khorenatsi's influential *History of the Armenians* attributed the founding of the nation to the patriarch Haik, who, it was said, was the great-great-great-grandson of Noah himself and thus in the close lineage of the flood survivors who emerged from the Ark.[14] Indeed it is because of Haik that even in the twenty-first century Armenians still refer to themselves as Hai, and to their land as Haiastan.[15] They see it simply as a tragedy of history that so much of this land, again including Göbekli Tepe and Mount Ararat, is now in the possession of the Republic of Turkey, following the Armenian genocide of 1915-23 in which more than one million ethnic Armenians are believed to have been killed by Turkish forces.[16]

Nationalistic feelings still run high in the communities of the Armenian diaspora scattered around the world and in the tiny rump of historic Armenia that forms the Armenian Republic today. These tensions have not left Göbekli Tepe untouched, and many Armenians are outraged that Turkey claims this uniquely important site as its own heritage as though the ancient Armenian connection did not even exist. A few minutes search on the internet using the keyword '*Portasar*', the former Armenian name of Göbekli Tepe, will confirm this. I'll give a single example here, a YouTube video entitled 'Turkey Presents Armenian Portasar as Turkish Göbekli Tepe'.[17] Amongst the comments, fairly typical of the remarks made by many viewers, we read:

This is the way I look at Portasar (Göbekli Tepe). These people deliberately buried a sacred temple. They did this in the antici-pation of having it discovered many years in the future. They believed in reincarnation. Those people who built Portasar

(Göbekli Tepe) are here among the Armenians. Their spirits have transcended into the Armenian people of today. When you pass on something in your family you want to make sure that it goes to only that family member and no one else. Portasar and those lands will be returned back to the Armenians in accordance with the laws of nature . . .[18]

In the same vein, though now entirely within the borders of Turkey, Mount Ararat remains a potent symbol of Armenian nationalism. A landscape of Mount Ararat, with the floodwaters receding and Noah's Ark at the summit, dominates the coat of arms of the Republic of Armenia while the mountain itself – so near and yet so far – looms over the Armenian capital city Yerevan, a haunting and ever present reminder that:

The past is never dead. It's not even past.[19]

Thus there are many ways in which the story of Noah and his Ark, and of a world made anew after a terrible global cataclysm, is still a living force in the region of Göbekli Tepe, that mysterious sanctuary in the Taurus mountains where the great stone circles began to be put in place in 9600 BC – a date that marks the exact end of the long 'fatal winter' of the Younger Dryas. As Klaus Schmidt asked me rhetorically when I interviewed him at the site (see Chapter One):

How likely is it to be an accident that the monumental phase at Göbekli Tepe starts in 9600 BC, when the climate of the whole world has taken a sudden turn for the better and there's an explosion in nature and in possibilities?

There's something else about that date too. Just as the beginning of the Younger Dryas in 10,800 BC was accompanied by huge global floods and an episode of rapidly rising sea levels, as icy meltwater from the North American ice cap poured suddenly into the Atlantic Ocean,[20] so too a second global flood occurred around 9600 BC as the remnant ice caps in North America and northern Europe collapsed simultaneously amidst worldwide global warming. The late Cesare Emiliani, Professor in the Department of Geological Sciences at the University of Miami, carried out isotopic analysis of deep-sea sediments[21] that produced striking evidence of cataclysmic global flooding 'between 12,000 and 11,000 years ago'.[22]

So although the floods at the end of the Ice Age could never have carried Noah and his Ark thousands of feet above present sea level to the slopes of Mount Ararat, they were indeed global in their extent and would have had devastating consequences for humans living at that time. Mountainous regions such as the Ararat range would have been natural places of refuge – natural places to bring 'the seeds of all life' and to start again. Therefore, while the Noah story cannot be literally true in every detail, we must consider the possibility that it is true in its essence, i.e. that it does record the construction of an 'Ark', in which seeds of useful plants and breeding pairs of animals were perhaps preserved by people who already knew agriculture and who possessed architectural skills, who survived the Flood, who migrated to the lands between Mount Ararat and Göbekli Tepe, and who subsequently disseminated agricultural and architectural knowledge to the indigenous hunter-gatherers of that region.

The sudden, and indeed completely unprecedented, appearance of giant stone circles at Göbekli Tepe, which surely could only have been conceived and implemented by people with extensive prior experience of megalithic architecture, and the simultaneous 'invention' of agriculture in the exact same locale, are, in my view, highly suggestive of this possibility. Then, too, there is the haunting sense that Göbekli Tepe itself constitutes a kind of 'Ark' frozen and memorialised in stone, for its iconography is not only all about animals but also – in a number of intriguing reliefs that show women with exposed genitalia[23] and males with erect penises[24] – about human fertility. Imagery of the latter sort, including a figure that Karl Luckert, Professor of the History of Religions at Missouri State University, interprets as a classic 'Earth Mother',[25] call to mind God's command to Moses and his family to 'be fruitful and multiply and replenish the earth'.[26]

Meanwhile, where else but in Noah's Ark can we find a menagerie as eclectic as the one portrayed on the megaliths of Göbekli Tepe – a menagerie, as we saw in Chapter One, that includes spiders, scorpions and snakes ('every creeping thing of the earth'), birds and cattle ('fowls after their kind, and cattle after their kind'), and foxes, felines, goats, sheep, gazelles, boars, bears, etc, etc (in short – as Genesis 6: 20 has it, 'every kind of animal and every kind of creature')?

A final touch. Noah sacrificed some of the animals and birds that he had just saved from the Flood as an offering to God. At Göbekli Tepe archaeologists have found the butchered bones of many of the animal species depicted on the megalithic pillars.[27]

Cities from before the Flood

It has long been recognised by scholars that the Biblical Flood narrative is not original to the Old Testament but was borrowed from a much earlier source, indeed a source dating back to the oldest true civilization so far acknowledged by archaeology – ancient Sumer in Mesopotamia, which arose in the fifth millennium BC, flourished during the fourth and third millennia BC, and survived into the second millennium BC.[28] The two earliest surviving written versions of this global flood 'myth' can be seen today at the University of Pennsylvania Museum of Archaeology and Anthropology,[29] and in the private Schøyen Collection in Norway.[30] Both are written in cuneiform characters in the Sumerian language and both have come down to us as fragments rather than complete texts.

Of the two, however, it is the University of Pennsylvania tablet, found during excavations of the Sumerian city of Nippur[31] (located on the Euphrates 200 kilometres south of the modern city of Baghdad) that is the most complete, consisting of the lower third of what was once a six-column tablet of baked clay[32] and dated to the seventeenth century BC.[33] The Schøyen tablet, though less of it survives, is a little older (dated to the nineteenth to eighteenth centuries BC[34]), repeats some of the lines of the Pennsylvania fragment and adds a few new details not found elsewhere.[35]

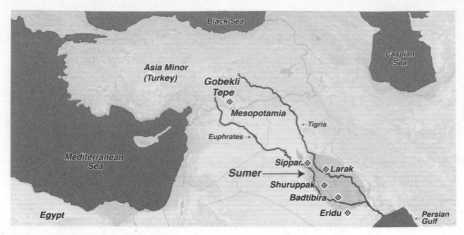

Figure 26: Map of Ancient Sumer showing the antediluvian cities

What rare and precious things these little broken slabs of baked mud are! And what a tale they have to tell. When I first read that tale I was instantly intrigued, because it contains explicit references to the existence of five antediluvian cities which, we are informed, were swallowed up by the waters of the Flood.

The first thirty-seven lines of the University of Pennsylvania tablet are missing so we do not know how the story begins, but at the point where we enter it the Flood is still far in the future.[36] We hear about the creation of human beings, animals and plants.[37] Then another break of thirty-seven lines occurs after which we find that we have jumped forward in time to an epoch of high civilization. We learn that in this epoch, before the Flood, 'kingship was lowered from heaven'.[38]

Then comes the reference to the foundation of Sumer's antediluvian cities by an unnamed ruler or a god:

After the lofty crown and the throne of kingship had been lowered from heaven,
He perfected the rites and the exalted divine laws . . .
Founded the five cities . . . in pure places,
Called their names, apportioned them as cult centres.

The first of these cities, Eridu . . .

154

The second Badtibira . . .
The third Larak . . .
The fourth Sippar . . .
The fifth Shuruppak . . .[39]

'The preserver of the seed of mankind . . .'

When we rejoin the narrative after a third thirty-seven-line lacuna, the scene has changed bewilderingly. Although the Flood is still in the future, the foundation of the five antediluvian cities is now far in the past. It is apparent from the context that in the intervening period the cities' inhabitants have behaved in such a way as to incur divine displeasure and that a convocation of the gods has been called to punish mankind with the terrible instrument of an earth-destroying flood. At the moment where we pick up the story again, a few of the gods are dissenting from this decision and expressing their unhappiness and dissatisfaction with it.[40]

Without preamble, a man called Zisudra is then introduced – the Sumerian archetype of the Biblical patriarch Noah. The text describes him as 'a pious, god-fearing king'[41] and allows us to understand that one of the gods has taken pity on him. The name of this god has not survived in the University of Pennsylvania tablet, but the Schøyen fragment gives us a clue when it reveals that Zisudra was not only a king but also a priest of the god Enki.[42] This god, of whom we will hear more later, tells Zisudra:

> Take my word, give ear to my instructions:
> A flood will sweep over the cult centres.
> To destroy the seed of mankind,
> Is the decision, the word of the assembly of gods.[43]

A text break of forty lines follows which scholars deduce, from the many later recensions of the same myth, 'must have continued with detailed instructions to Zisudra to build a giant boat and thus save himself from destruction'.[44]

When the story resumes, the cataclysm has already begun:

All the windstorms, exceedingly powerful, attacked as one,
At the same time the flood swept over the cult centres.
For seven days and seven nights the flood swept over the land,
And the huge boat was tossed about by the windstorms on the great
waters.[45]

Throughout the cataclysm the skies remain dark. Then, on the eighth day, the sun breaks through the clouds, and the rains and raging storms cease. Opening the 'window' of his survival ship, Zisudra looks out over a world that has changed forever and sacrifices an ox and a sheep to the gods.[46]

An infuriating lacuna of thirty-nine lines follows, presumably telling us about the place where Zisudra makes landfall and the steps that he takes thereafter. When we pick up the story again, near the end of the text, we find him in the presence of the high gods of the Sumerian pantheon, *Anu* and *Enlil*, who have repented of their earlier decision to wipe mankind entirely from the face of the earth and are now so grateful to Zisudra for building his ark and surviving the Flood that they decide to make him immortal:

Life like a god they gave him;
  Breath eternal like a god they brought down for him,
  . . . Zisudra the king,
  The preserver of the name of vegetation and of the seed of
  mankind.[47]

The final thirty-nine lines are missing.[48]

The Seven Sages

The late Professor Samuel Noah Kramer, one of the great authorities on ancient Sumer, observed that there are 'tantalizing obscurities and uncertainties' in this oldest surviving written version of the worldwide tradition of the Flood.[49] What there can be no doubt about at all, however, is that the tablet speaks of an urban civilization that existed before the Flood and provides us with the names of its sacred cities:

Eridu, Badtibira, Larak, Sippar, Shuruppak. These cities, we are told quite specifically, were swallowed up in the deluge. Moreover, long after Sumer itself had ceased to exist, rich traditions concerning the five cities, the antediluvian epoch, and the Flood survived in Mesopotamia, and were repeated by the cultures of Akkad, Assyria and Babylon that later rose to prominence, almost down to Christian times.[50] Indeed it is fair to say that the traditional history of this region, as it was told in antiquity, is very clearly divided into two different periods – before and after the Flood – and that both periods were regarded by the peoples of the region as absolutely factual and real.

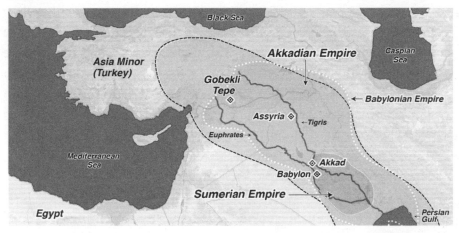

Figure 27: The ancient empires of Mesopotamia rose to prominence at different periods of history but all maintained traditions of a global Flood that had all-but destroyed mankind in remote antiquity.

We saw in Chapter One how the Mesopotamian traditions not only preserved memories of antediluvian cities, but also of an antediluvian civilizing hero called Oannes, and the brotherhood of Seven Sages, the 'Seven Apkallu' who are said to have supported his civilizing mission. As the reader will recall, these sages are often depicted in the surviving art of the region as bearded men holding a peculiar kind of bag or bucket, but sometimes they are also shown as therianthropes, part bird and part human in form. As I dug deeper, going back and carefully rereading the accounts of the Babylonian priest Berossos that I had first touched upon when I was researching *Fingerprints of the Gods*, I was reminded that Oannes and the Apkallu sages were also sometimes depicted in a different therianthropic form, in this case part fish, part human. Each of them was paired as a 'counsellor' to an antediluvian King and they were renowned for their wisdom in affairs of state and for their skills as architects, builders and engineers.[51]

Berossos compiled his *History* from the temple archives of Babylon (reputed to have contained 'public records' that had been preserved for 'over 150,000 years'[52]). He has passed on to us a description of Oannes as a 'monster', or a 'creature'. However, what Berossos has to say is surely more suggestive of a man wearing some sort of fish-costume – in short, some sort of disguise. The monster, Berossos tells us:

> had the whole body of a fish, but underneath and attached to the head of the fish there was another head, human, and joined to the tail of the fish, feet like those of a man, and it had a human voice . . . At the end of the day, this monster, Oannes, went back to the sea and spent the night. It was amphibious, able to live both on land and in the sea . . . Later, other monsters similar to Oannes appeared.[53]

Bearing in mind that the curious containers carried by Oannes and the Apkallu sages are also depicted on one of the megalithic pillars at Göbekli Tepe (and, as we saw in Chapter One, as far afield as ancient Mexico as well) what are we to make of all this?

The mystery deepens when we follow the Mesopotamian traditions further. In summary, Oannes and the brotherhood of Apkallu sages are depicted as tutoring mankind for many thousands of years. It is during this long passage of time that the five antediluvian cities arise, the centres of a great civilization, and that kingship is 'lowered from heaven'. Prior to the first appearance of Oannes, Berossos says, the people of Mesopotamia 'lived in a lawless manner, like the beasts of the field'.[54]

Berossos wrote his *History* some time between 290 and 278 BC, but only fragments of it have come down to us, preserved as quotations and summaries in the works of other writers such as Syncellus and

Figure 28: Oannes and the brotherhood of Apkallu sages.

Eusebius. However, scholars recognise that what has been transmitted to us in this way does accurately reflect much more ancient Mesopotamian traditions inscribed on cuneiform tablets going back to the very earliest times.[55] For example, the name Oannes, which has perhaps been distorted by the writers who passed it on to us, turns out to be derived from *Uannadapa* in cuneiform, often abbreviated simply to *Adapa* or to *U-Anna* – with the *Adapa* element originally being a title meaning (appropriately for a sage) 'Wise'.[56] It is said in the ancient Mesopotamian inscriptions that U-Anna 'accomplishes the plans of heaven and earth'.[57] Others of the group of antediluvian sages include *U-Anne-dugga* 'who is endowed with comprehensive understanding' and *An-Enlilda*, described as 'the conjurer of the city of Eridu'.[58]

This last point – that the seven antediluvian sages were 'conjurers', 'sorcerers', 'warlocks', 'magicians' – is driven home repeatedly in the cuneiform texts.[59] But at the same time, associated with their magical abilities are obviously practical, technological or even scientific skills.[60] Thus they were masters of 'the chemical recipes',[61] they were medical doctors,[62] they were carpenters, stone cutters, metal workers and goldsmiths,[63] and they laid the foundations of cities.[64] Indeed, in later times, all crafts used in royal building and renovation projects were attributed to knowledge that had originated with the antediluvian sages.[65] As Amar Annus of the University of Tartu, Estonia, summarises in a detailed study:

> The period before the deluge was the one of revelation in the Mesopotamian mythology, when the basis of all later knowledge was laid down. The antediluvian sages were culture-heroes, who brought the arts of civilization to the land. During the time that follows this period, nothing new is invented, the original revelation is only transmitted and unfolded. Oannes and other sages taught all foundations of civilization to ante-diluvian humankind.[66]

The cuneiform tablets of ancient Mesopotamia also shed at least some light on the containers that the Apkallu sages are so often depicted as holding. They are referred to as *banduddu* – 'buckets',[67] and are presumed to have held 'holy water'.[68] Very often, too, as the reader will recall from Chapter One, the sage holds in his other hand a cone-like object. These are referred to in the inscriptions as *mullilu* – meaning 'purifiers'.[69] In the same scenes the sages frequently appear in conjunction with a stylised tree or sometimes with the figure of a king, or sometimes both. No specific textual references to the tree have survived but the general assumption of scholars is that it must be a 'sacred tree' while many believe it represents 'the tree of life'[70] and that it symbolises 'both the divine world order and the king, who functioned as its earthly administrator'.[71] The conclusion therefore, is that we are looking at 'a magically protective rite, a benediction, an anointing':[72]

> By sprinkling the tree with holy water the sages imparted to it their own sanctity, upheld the cosmic harmony and thus ensured the correct functioning of the plans of heaven and earth.[73]

The Seven Apkallus were believed to have been created by Enki (Enki is his Sumerian name; the Akkadians called him Ea), revealed in the

Figure 29: Enki, the Sumerian god of wisdom and magic whose special responsibility was the subterranean freshwater ocean known as the Abzu. Because of this connection with the Abzu he was often depicted with streams of water bearing fishes flowing from his shoulders. The Akkadians called him Ea.

Schøyen tablet as Zisudra's patron, the great god of the subterranean freshwater ocean known as the Abzu.[74] Enki's particular attributes, in addition to his connection to this watery realm, were wisdom, magic, and the arts and crafts of civilization,[75] so it is appropriate that the sages would be amongst his creatures and that they would frequently be symbolised as fish. The form of the fish Apkallu, as one scholar notes:

> is linked with the secrets that dwell in the deep; and its never-closing, ever-watchful eyes lend it an omniscient sagacity.[76]

Thanks to the advice and teachings of these extraordinary sages, these magicians of the wisdom-god Enki, we learn from the cuneiform texts that human civilization achieved rapid technological and scientific advances and entered a phase of 'exceptional splendour and plenty, the golden age before the flood'.[77] All seemed to be for the best, in the best of all possible worlds. But as the millennia passed, mankind fell out of harmony with the universe and with the deities – and with one deity in particular, the great Enlil, described as 'the King, supreme lord, father and creator', and (perhaps giving more sense of his personality) as a 'raging storm'.[78] Although the sky god Anu was technically ranked first in the Sumerian pantheon, he was usually a rather remote, impotent figure. Enlil was his second in command but in fact responsible for most 'executive decisions'. Enki – nominated in some texts as Enlil's younger brother – was ranked third.[79]

The Sumerian flood story, as we have seen, has many gaps but other tablets, such as those containing the Epic of Gilgamesh, arguably the most famous of all surviving Mesopotamian texts, fill in the details and leave us in no doubt of Enlil's role:

In those days the world teemed, the people multiplied, the world bellowed like a wild bull, and the great god was aroused by the clamour. Enlil heard the clamour and he said to the gods in council, 'The uproar of mankind is intolerable and sleep is no

Figure 30: The powerful Sumerian deity Enlil (seated, right). Often described as a 'raging storm', it was he who ordered the extermination of mankind by the agency of the Flood.

longer possible by reason of the babel.' So the gods agreed to exterminate mankind.[80]

We know what happened next. The god Enki (in addition to the Schøyen tablet, other later texts also confirm it was he) intervened to warn Zisudra that the instrument of extermination, a great, life-destroying flood, was about to be unleashed.[81] Berossos, who calls Zisudra 'Xisouthros', gives us the next chapter of the story:

[Enki] appeared to Xisouthros in a dream and revealed that . . . mankind would be destroyed by a great flood. He then ordered him to bury together all the tablets, the first, the middle and the last, and hide them in Sippar, the city of the sun. Then he was to build a boat and board it with his family and his best friends. He was to provision it with food and drink and also take on board wild animals and birds and all four-footed animals. Then, when all was prepared, he was to make ready to sail . . . He did not stop working until the ship was built. Its length was five stades [3,000 feet or 914 metres] and its breadth two stades [1,200 feet or 366 metres]. He boarded the finished ship, equipped for everything as he had been commanded, with his wife, children and closest friends . . .[82]

The surviving fragments of Berossos do not tell us of the experience of the Flood, but the Epic of Gilgamesh does, putting the words into the mouth of Zisudra/Xisouthros himself:[83]

For six days and nights the wind blew, torrent and tempest and flood overwhelmed the world, tempest and flood raged together like warring hosts. When the seventh day dawned the storm from the south subsided, the sea grew calm, the flood was stilled. I looked at the face of the world and there was silence. The surface of the sea stretched as flat as a rooftop. All mankind had returned to clay . . . I opened a hatch and light fell on my face. Then I bowed low, I sat down and I wept, the tears streamed down my face, for on every side was a waste of water . . . Fourteen leagues distant there appeared a mountain, and there the boat grounded . . .[84]

Figure 31: The Sumerian Flood survivor and the Ark: 'The surface of the sea stretched as flat as a rooftop. All mankind had returned to clay... Fourteen leagues distant there appeared a mountain, and there the boat grounded.'

Berossos again:

> Then Xisouthros knew that the earth had once again appeared . . . He disembarked, accompanied by his wife and daughter together with the steersman. He prostrated himself in worship of the earth and set up an altar and sacrificed to the gods. After this he disappeared together with those who had left the ship with him. Those who had remained on the ship and had not gone out with Xisouthros . . . searched for him and called out for him by name all about. But Xisouthros from then on was seen no more, and then the sound of a voice that came out of the air gave instruction that it was their duty to honour the gods

and that Xisouthros, because of the great honour he had shown the gods, had gone to the dwelling place of the gods and that his wife and daughter and the steersman had enjoyed the same honour. The voice then instructed them to return to . . . the city of Sippar, to dig up the tablets that were buried there and to turn them over to mankind. The place where they had come to rest was in the land of Armenia.[85]

So, in summary, both the Biblical and Mesopotamian accounts agree that Armenia was the place of refuge for the survivors of the Flood. Berossos, however, adds some important details missing from the Old Testament story. These are, first, the reference to Sippar, which, as we've seen, was one of the five antediluvian cities remembered in Sumerian traditions; secondly, the intriguing information that writings or archives from antediluvian times ('all the tablets, the first, the middle and the last') were buried at Sippar before the Flood struck; and thirdly that the survivors were to return to Sippar when the waters had receded in order to dig up the buried tablets and 'turn them over to mankind'.

What is envisaged here, therefore, is nothing less than a renewal of civilization after a global cataclysm – a renewal in which antediluvian knowledge was to be recovered and repromulgated. The Seven Sages, however, would no longer have any part to play in the spread of that knowledge. The cuneiform texts tell us that they had been sent back to the depths of the Abzu at the time of the Flood and ordered never to return.[86] Other sages 'of human descent' – though in one case described as being 'two-thirds Apkallu'[87] – would take their place, some continuity would be maintained and civilization would rise again. In due course, later kings would speak of their link to the antediluvian world. In the late first millennium BC, Nebuchadnezzar I of Babylon described himself as a 'seed preserved from before the flood'[88] while Ashurbanipal, who ruled the central Mesopotamian empire of Assyria in the seventh century BC boasted: 'I learned the craft of Adapa, the sage, which is the secret knowledge . . . I am well acquainted with the signs of heaven and earth . . . I am enjoying the writings on stones from before the flood.'[89]

It is a curious mystery, as we shall see in the next chapter, that the exact same notions of the Seven Sages as the bringers of civilization in the remotest antiquity, and of the preservation and repromulgation of 'writings on stones from before the flood', turn up in the supposedly completely distinct and unrelated culture of Ancient Egypt.

Part IV

Resurrection

Chapter 9
Island of the Ka

━━◆━━

The banks of the Nile are lush, lined with palms and green fields, but they are narrow, won from the surrounding deserts thanks only to the gift of fertility bestowed upon them by the eternal river. It's the same story all the way from Cairo to Aswan, where the High Dam has permanently changed the divine landscape of the pharaohs by creating Lake Nasser, one of the largest man-made bodies of water in the world, which continues south to cross the border with the Sudan. As the level of the lake rose during the 1960s many Ancient Egyptian sites, such as the Fortress of Buhen, were submerged. Others such as world famous Abu Simbel, and the stunningly beautiful little Temple of Isis at Philae, were rescued by being moved block by block and re-erected on higher ground.

Others still were dismantled and shipped overseas – for example the Temple of Dendur, now in New York's Metropolitan Museum of Art, the Temple of Debod, now in the Parque del Oeste in Madrid, and the Temple of Taffeh, now in the Rijksmuseum Van Oudheden in Leiden, in the Netherlands. By such means, the sacred realm of the gods that continuously remade and remanifested itself in Egypt over untold thousands of years in antiquity can be said still to undergo resurrection and rebirth in far-off lands even today.

So it was, too, according to its own inscriptions, with the Temple of Horus at Edfu. Known as Behdet in ancient times (hence its patron, the falcon god Horus, is often referred to as Horus the Behdetite) Edfu stands on the west bank of the Nile 110 kilometres (68 miles) north of Aswan and was thus spared from flooding by Lake Nasser. The temple as we see it today, its golden sandstone blocks radiant and

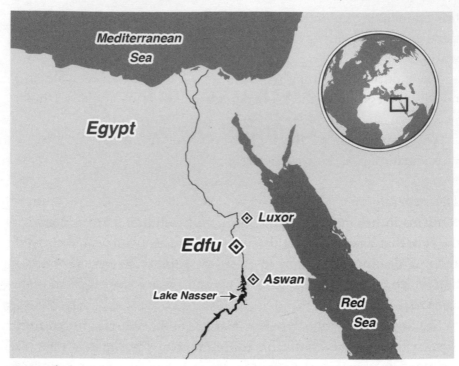

Figure 32

graceful beneath the fierce sun of Upper Egypt, is relatively young, the whole complex having been completed during the Ptolemaic period in a series of stages between 237 BC and 57 BC.[1] In every meaningful sense, however, what confronts us here is merely the latest incarnation of much older temples that previously occupied this site dating at least to the Old Kingdom (2575-2134 BC)[2] – and perhaps far beyond.

Of the greatest interest, at any rate, is the temple's *idea* of itself expressed in the acres of enigmatic inscriptions that cover its walls. These inscriptions, the so-called Edfu Building Texts, take us back to a very remote period called the 'Early Primeval Age of the Gods'[3] – and these gods, it transpires, were not originally Egyptian,[4] but lived on a sacred island, the 'Homeland of the Primeval Ones', in the midst of a great ocean.[5] Then, at some unspecified time in the past, a terrible disaster – a true cataclysm of flood and fire as we shall see – overtook this island, where 'the earliest mansions of the gods' had been founded,[6] destroying it utterly, inundating all its holy places and killing most of its divine inhabitants.[7] Some survived, however, and we are told that this remnant set sail in their ships (for the texts leave us in no doubt these gods of the early primeval age were navigators[8]) to 'wander' the world.[9]

Their purpose in doing so was nothing less than to recreate and revivify the essence of their lost homeland,[10] to bring about, in short:

> The resurrection of the former world of the gods . . .[11] The re-creation of a destroyed world.[12]

The general tone, as Egyptologist Eve Anne Elizabeth Reymond confirms in her masterful study of the Edfu Building Texts, conveys the view that 'an ancient world, having been constituted, was destroyed and as a dead world it came to be the basis of a new period of creation which at first was the re-creation and resurrection of what once had existed in the past.'[13]

Important in the evaluation of the texts is the realization that they were not *composed* in the historical temple. On the contrary, as Reymond informs us, the priests and scribes of Edfu merely *copied* what they regarded as the more important extracts from a vast archive of ancient documents that they had at their disposal.[14] By the fifth century AD the weight of Roman and Christian fanaticism had brought about the final collapse of Ancient Egyptian civilization.[15] Thereafter (with Islamic hatred of the past soon making things even worse) care ceased to be taken of the temples which were used as storerooms, stables and homes by local people who no longer venerated the ancient gods. In 1837 the English explorer Howard Vyse visited Edfu and described the mess that he found inside:

> The temple itself, one of the most imposing in Egypt, affords a striking contrast to the miserable hovels, many of which are built upon it, and others on vast mounds of rubbish with which it is surrounded. The interior, covered with painted hieroglyphics, has been divided by earthen walls to form a magazine for corn, and beneath it are enormous substructions which I entered by a hole from an Arab house. They were full of dirt and filth of every description, but had been built in the most solid manner . . .[16]

Fortunate for us, then, when Edfu still thrived, that priests and scribes who could read the mysterious texts in the temple's library committed themselves to the project of selecting extracts and carving them deeply into the 'solid' and 'imposing' walls of the temple itself. In so doing, whether by accident or design, they ensured that at least these fragments have survived to the present day, whereas the original source documents – looted, used as kindling, thrown into the Nile during the centuries of neglect and mistreatment – have long gone.

Inevitably, since they lack their original context, the fragments are often confusing and deeply tantalizing. Even so, they give us a glimpse into wonders and secrets of our past that the source documents – if only we had them! – might have revealed to us much more completely.

Atlantis in Egypt

The famed Greek philosopher Plato, who passed down to us the extraordinary story of Atlantis destroyed in a terrible cataclysm of flood and fire 9,000 years before the time of Solon – i.e. in 9600 BC in our calendar – is generally regarded by archaeologists as having made up the whole tale of the lost Ice Age civilization. The fallback position, amongst those grudgingly willing to admit some veracity to the information conveyed in the *Timaeus* and *Critias*, is that Plato had perhaps based his account on a much more recent cataclysm centred on the Mediterranean – for example the eruption of Thera (Santorini) in the mid-second millennium BC. The notion of a global disaster more than 11,000 years ago, and particularly the heretical idea that it could have wiped out a high civilization of that epoch, is strenuously resisted and indeed ridiculed by the archaeological establishment because, of course, archaeologists claim to 'know' that there was not, and never under any circumstances could have been, a high civilization at that time.

They 'know' this not because of any hard evidence which absolutely rules out the existence of an Atlantis-type civilization in the Upper Paleolithic, but rather on the general principle that the result of less than two hundred years of 'scientific' archaeology is an agreed timeline for civilization that sees our ancestors moving smoothly out of the Upper Palaeolithic, into the Neolithic (both, by definition, Stone

Age cultures) at around 9600 BC, and thence onwards through the development and perfection of agriculture in the millennia that followed – a process that also witnessed the founding of some very large permanent settlements such as Catalhoyuk in Turkey around 7500 BC.

By about 4000 BC the increasing sophistication of economic and social structures, and growing organizational abilities, made possible the creation of the earliest megalithic sites (such as Gigantija on the Maltese island of Gozo, for example) while the first city states emerged around 3500 BC in Mesopotamia and the Indus Valley and soon afterwards in Egypt and on the other side of the world in Peru.[17] The Pyramids of Giza are megalithic monuments; so too the Great Sphinx. In the British Isles, Callanish in the Outer Hebrides and Avebury in southwest England, both dated to around 3000 BC, are the oldest examples of true megalithic sites. The megalithic phase of Stonehenge is thought to have begun around 2400 BC and to have continued to around 1800 BC.

Within this well-worked-out and long-established chronology there is simply no room for any prehistoric civilization such as Atlantis, hence the wish of the mainstream to dismiss Plato's 'outlandish' story by any and every possible means. These means include ridicule of the supposed 'Egyptian' basis for the tale – specifically, of the claim, made in the *Timaeus*, that priests of Sais in the Delta said Atlantis, and its cruel fate, were described in 'sacred records'[18] in their Temple going back thousands of years before the established beginning of Egyptian civilization in the late fourth millennium BC.[19] To those wedded to the orthodox chronology, the very idea that the priests of Sais might have given Solon a true account of such 'impossible' records, which in due course reached Plato, seems preposterous – an obvious historical oxymoron which deserves only to be ignored. Furthermore the claim is frequently made that there are no references to Atlantis anywhere in surviving Ancient Egyptian papyri and inscriptions.

Only one Egyptologist, the late Professor John Gwyn Griffiths of the University of Wales at Swansea (who passed away in 2004) had the courage to challenge the consensus. The challenge he presented, however, had nothing to do with the fundamental point of whether Atlantis existed and was destroyed in the tenth millennium BC, but rather with the lesser point of whether Plato, through his ancestor

Solon, could indeed have been influenced by genuine Ancient Egyptian traditions.[20] Oddly enough for so learned a man, Griffiths seems to have known nothing of Edfu with its tempting account of a sacred island inhabited by 'gods' and destroyed by flood and fire in primeval times – an obvious prototype for Plato's Atlantis, as we shall see. The Professor's focus, instead, was on a papyrus, catalogued as P. Leningrad 1115 and now kept in Moscow, which contains an intriguing prose story known as the *Tale of the Shipwrecked Sailor*. In this 'fairytale', dating to Egypt's Middle Kingdom between 2000 BC and 1700 BC, Griffiths – quite correctly in my view – did find convincing resemblances to Plato's account of Atlantis.

The eponymous 'shipwrecked sailor' in the papyrus tells us of a time when he made a voyage in a great ocean-going vessel that was struck by a giant wave:

> Then the ship died. Of those in it not one remained. I was cast on an island by the sea. I spent three days alone . . . Lying in the shelter of trees, I hugged the shade . . . Then I stretched my legs to discover what I might put in my mouth. I found figs and grapes there, all sorts of fine vegetables, sycamore figs . . . and cucumbers that were as if tended. Fish there were and fowl; there is nothing that was not there. I stuffed myself and put some down, because I had too much in my arms.[21]

The shipwrecked sailor cuts a fire drill, makes fire and gives a burnt offering to the gods:

> Then I heard a thundering noise . . . Trees splintered, the ground trembled. Uncovering my face, I found it was a snake that was coming. He was of thirty cubits [15 metres or 50 feet] . . . His body was overlaid with gold; his eyebrows were of real lapis lazuli . . . Then he took me in his mouth and carried me to the place where he lived, and set me down unhurt . . .[22]

The serpent questions the sailor on how he came to be on the island and on hearing his reply, tells him not to be afraid:

It is a god who has let you live and brought you to this Island of the *Ka*. There is nothing that is not upon it; it is full of good things . . .

The name 'Island of the *Ka*' is 'curious' notes Miriam Lichtheim, the translator of the tale. She adds that the renowned Egyptologist Sir Alan Gardiner 'rendered it as "phantom island".'[23] It is beyond the scope of this book to present a detailed treatise on the concept of the *Ka* – the 'double', the astral or spiritual essence of a person or thing. It existed with the human being during his or her mortal life but was 'the superior power in the realms beyond the grave'. Indeed, the term for death in the Ancient Egyptian language meant 'Going to one's *ka*', or 'Going to one's *ka* in the sky'.[24] The gods were also believed to have their *kas* and so, too, were the great monuments of Egypt. Of particular relevance here is that the high god Osiris, lord of the celestial afterlife kingdom known as the *Duat*, was always referred to as 'the *Ka* of the Pyramids' of Giza:[25]

> The *Ka* entered eternity before its human host, having served its function by walking at the human's side to urge kindness, quietude, honour and compassion. Throughout the life of the human, the *Ka* was the conscience, the guardian, the guide. After death, however, the *Ka* became supreme . . .[26]

With this in mind, Gardiner's suggestion that a 'phantom island' is implicated in the *Tale of the Shipwrecked Sailor*, makes sense. The sailor has set out in a boat from the physical realm of Middle Kingdom Egypt, but he has been cast ashore on 'the Island of the *Ka*', a ghost realm – a place that no longer exists in this world except in the form of its spiritual essence.

The same theme continues as the huge snake that rules the island tells the sailor his sad story:

> I was here with my brothers and there were children with them.
> In all we were seventy-five serpents, children and brothers without
> mentioning a little daughter whom I had obtained through prayer.

Then a star fell, and they went up in flames through it. It so happened that I was not with them in the fire. I was not among them. I could have died for their sake when I found them as one heap of corpses.[27]

In due course a ship passes by and the sailor is rescued. The snake-king of the island sends him away with rich presents – myrrh, oils, laudanum, spices, 'perfume, eye-paint, giraffe's tails, great lumps of incense, elephant's tusks, greyhounds, monkeys, baboons, and all kinds of precious things'.[28] The sailor, filled with gratitude, wants to return with gifts from Egypt, but before he boards the ship the serpent takes him aside and tells him:

When you have left this place, you will not see this island again; it will have become water.[29]

The comparisons with Plato's story of Atlantis that John Gwyn Griffiths draws relate primarily to the rich variety of plant and animal life, including the elephants said to be found on both islands. Here's Plato on Atlantis:

There were a great number of elephants in the island; for as there was provision for all other sorts of animals, both for those which live in lakes and marshes and rivers, and also for those which live in mountains and on plains, so there was for the animal which is the largest and most voracious of all. Also whatever fragrant things there now are in the earth, whether roots, or herbage, or woods, or essences which distil from fruit and flower, grew and thrived in that land; also the fruit which admits of cultivation, both the dry sort, which is given us for nourishment and any other which we use for food – we call them all by the common name 'pulse' – and the fruits having a hard rind, affording drinks and meats and ointments . . . all these that sacred island which then beheld the light of the sun, brought forth fair and wondrous and in infinite abundance. With such blessings the earth freely furnished them . . .[30]

In addition there is the fact that Atlantis is a sacred island and so, too, of course, is the Island of the *Ka*, to which the shipwrecked sailor has been brought by a god. The closest resemblance by far, however, is in the fate of Atlantis which was 'swallowed up by the sea and vanished',[31] just as the Island of the *Ka* would never be seen again because it had 'become water'.

Taking such elements into account Griffiths concludes that although Plato's story may 'not derive from Egypt *in toto*', it nonetheless, most certainly owes a 'conceptual debt to Egypt'.[32] His argument is well made, but if he had been familiar with the Edfu Building Texts he might, I think, have stated his case more strongly.

Bringing some threads together

We no longer have access to the sacred records once kept at the Temple of Sais in the Delta that Plato tells us contained the story of Atlantis. That temple, which Solon visited around 600 BC, was dedicated to the goddess Neith and was extremely ancient, dating back at least as far as the First Dynasty, *circa* 3200 BC.[33] Unfortunately it had been completely destroyed by AD 1400, leaving only rubbish heaps and a few scattered blocks on the site that is today occupied by the village of Sa el Hagar.[34] At Edfu, on the other hand, although the original sacred records are also gone, the extracts preserved in the Building Texts do seem to tell essentially the same story that Solon heard and passed on to Plato and that Griffiths argues also reaches us, albeit in a more fragmentary and literary form, in the *Tale of the Shipwrecked Sailor*.

We've already seen that the Homeland of the Primeval Ones in the Edfu texts is described as a sacred island in the midst of a great ocean, so a comparison to the Island of the *Ka* in the *Tale of the Shipwrecked Sailor* is obvious at the level of the basic geographical setting. The resemblance goes deeper than this, however, since there are many passages in the Building Texts which make it clear that the first and original god who presided over the Homeland of the Primeval Ones was 'a dead deity, the *Ka*'.[35] Indeed, we read that the island was also known as the 'Home of the *Ka*'[36] and that 'the *Ka* ruled therein'[37] – 'this

Ka who dwelt among the reeds of the island'.[38] In other words, the Homeland of the Primeval Ones in the Edfu texts is nothing more nor less than the Island of the *Ka* and, to the extent that Griffiths is correct to see a prototype for Plato's Atlantis in the Island of the *Ka*, then the Homeland of the Primeval Ones is also a prototype.

What helps to firm up the comparison are certain details given in the Building Texts that do *not* appear in the *Tale of the Shipwrecked Sailor*. Of particular interest is a passage at Edfu in which we read of a circular, water-filled 'channel' surrounding the original sacred domain that lay at the heart of the island of the Primeval Ones – a ring of water that was intended to fortify and protect that domain.[39] In this there is, of course, a direct parallel to Atlantis, where the sacred domain on which stood the temple and palace of the god, whom Plato names as 'Poseidon', was likewise surrounded by a ring of water, itself placed in the midst of further such concentric rings separated by rings of land, again with the purpose of fortification and protection.[40]

Other details are found in all three stories. For example, the striking parallel between the inundation of the island of Atlantis as Plato recounts it, and the inundation of the Island of the *Ka* in the *Tale of the Shipwrecked Sailor*, is eerily duplicated in the inundation of the Homeland of the Primeval Ones as described in the Edfu texts where we read of an upheaval:

> so violent that it destroyed the sacred land . . .[41] The primeval water . . . submerged the island . . . and the island became the tomb of the original divine inhabitants . . .[42] the Homeland ended in darkness beneath the primeval waters.[43]

Compare this with Plato who tells us of 'earthquakes and floods of extraordinary violence'[44] as a result of which:

> in a single terrible day and night . . . the island of Atlantis was . . . swallowed up by the sea and vanished.[45]

Intriguingly, Plato also hints at the immediate cause of the earthquakes and floods that destroyed Atlantis. In the *Timaeus*, as a prelude to his account of the lost civilization and its demise, he reports that the Egyptian priests from whom Solon received the story began by speaking of a *celestial cataclysm*:

> There have been and will be many different calamities to destroy mankind, the greatest of them being by fire and water, lesser ones by countless other means. Your own [i.e. the Greeks'] story of how Phaethon, child of the sun, harnessed his father's chariot, but was unable to guide it along his father's course and so burnt up things on earth and was himself destroyed by a thunderbolt, is a mythical version of the truth that there is at long intervals a variation in the course of the heavenly bodies and a consequent widespread destruction by fire of things on earth.[46]

In the *Tale of the Shipwrecked Sailor*, too, we find that a celestial cataclysm plays a part. As the reader will recall, the serpent king speaks of the destruction of his race when 'a star fell, and they went up in flames through it'. The same ominous agency turns up in the Edfu Building Texts where a serpent is again invoked, but with the significant twist that here it is not the sad and wise ruler of the island but rather the fatal 'enemy' of the island and its divine inhabitants.[47] To place what the Edfu texts have to say about this in a wider context, let us first revisit the Zoroastrian tradition of an 'evil spirit' that:

> sprang like a snake out of the sky down to the earth . . . He rushed in at noon, and thereby the sky was as shattered and frightened by him as a sheep by a wolf. He came onto the water which was arranged below the earth, and then the middle of this earth was pierced and entered by him . . . He rushed out upon the whole creation and he made the world quite as injured and dark at midday as though it were dark night.[48]

To my mind, as I argued in Chapter Seven, what we have here is 'a mythical version of the truth' – with the underlying truth being a cataclysmic encounter with a comet. Now let's look at the relevant passages from the Edfu Building Texts where a snake called the *nhp-wer*, the 'Great Leaping One', is described as 'the chief enemy of the god'.[49] It is his 'assault' that causes the Homeland of the Primeval Ones to be swallowed up by the sea, but first the feet of the deity of the island – the *Ka*, here explicitly described as the 'Earth God'[50] – are 'pierced, and the domain was split'.[51]

This, as Reymond comments:

> is a clear picture of a disaster . . . It destroyed the sacred land with the result that its divine inhabitants died. This interpretation accords with other parts of the first Edfu record which allude to the death of the 'Company' [a group of divine beings] and to the darkness that covered the primeval island.[52]

Multiple threads seem to come together here: Plato's variation in the course of heavenly bodies leading to widespread destruction on earth, the murderous falling star in the *Tale of the Shipwrecked Sailor*, the snake of Zoroastrian tradition that springs out of the sky, pierces the earth and makes the world dark, and the Great Leaping Serpent of the Edfu texts whose assault pierces the feet of the Earth God, leads to death for the divine Company and cloaks the primeval island in darkness. I'm reminded, too, of the Ojibwa 'myth' reported in Chapter Three of the 'star with the long wide tail that came down here once, thousands of years ago' – a 'star' specifically recognised as a comet,[53] that caused 'the first flooding of the earth'. [54]

Comet and asteroid impacts not only cause floods but can also impose huge stresses on the crust of the earth resulting in increased earthquake and volcanic activity. How likely, therefore, is it to be an accident that Plato, who was at pains to preface his story with the 'thunderbolts' of Phaethon, implicated both earthquakes and floods in the demise of Atlantis and carefully dated the whole episode to 9,000 years before the time of Solon, i.e. 9600 BC? I suggest there's a real possibility that all these traditions are pointing to the same horrific epoch of prehistory.

This epoch, as I've argued in earlier chapters, is the Younger Dryas which began cataclysmically 12,800 years ago and ended equally cataclysmically 11,600 years ago with large-scale floods – associated with the cascading collapse of the North American and northern European ice caps – occurring at both dates. The case for multiple impacts from a large, fragmented comet initiating the Younger Dryas is, I believe, a very strong one. In the light of the mythological evidence, the possibility must also be considered that it was further encounters with the orbiting debris stream of the same giant comet that brought the Younger Dryas to an end.

In the process, I suggest, as so many myths and traditions from all around the world maintain, an advanced civilization was lost to history.

Mystery of the Sound Eye

Archaeology is not wrong when it tells us that most of the world in the epoch of 12,800 to 11,600 years ago, was populated by hunter-gatherers, locked in the Stone Age and lacking even the beginnings of agriculture. But Plato, to the eternal frustration of archaeologists, leaves us in no doubt that Atlantis was very different. In brief, it was a great and wonderful empire commanding a large navy of ocean-going ships that gave it the ability to project its power into Africa as far as Egypt, into Europe as far as Italy,[55] and onto the mainland of what Plato calls 'the whole opposite continent' – by which many believe he meant the Americas[56] – 'which surrounds what can truly be called the ocean'.[57] Atlantis was a fully-developed city-state, drawing its wealth from a mature and prosperous agricultural economy and boasting advanced metallurgy and sophisticated architectural and engineering works, all enhanced by an immense wealth of natural resources:

> With such blessings the earth freely furnished them; meanwhile they went on constructing their temples and palaces and harbours and docks. And they arranged the whole country in the following manner: First of all they bridged over the zones of sea which surrounded the ancient metropolis, making a road to and from the royal palace . . . which they continued to ornament in successive generations . . . until they made the building a marvel to behold for size and for beauty.
>
> And beginning from the sea they bored a canal of three

hundred feet in width and one hundred feet in depth and fifty stadia in length, which they carried through to the outermost zone, making a passage from the sea up to this, which became a harbour, and leaving an opening sufficient to enable the largest vessels to find ingress. Moreover, they divided at the bridges the zones of land which parted the zones of sea, leaving room for a single trireme to pass out of one zone into another, and they covered over the channels so as to leave a way underneath for the ships; for the banks were raised considerably above the water.

Now the largest of the zones into which a passage was cut from the sea was three stadia in breadth, and the zone of land which came next of equal breadth; but the next two zones, the one of water, the other of land, were two stadia, and the one which surrounded the central island was a stadium only in width. The island in which the palace was situated had a diameter of five stadia. All this including the zones and the bridge, which was the sixth part of a stadium in width, they surrounded by a stone wall on every side, placing towers and gates on the bridges where the sea passed in.

The stone which was used in the work they quarried from underneath the centre island, and from underneath the zones, on the outer as well as the inner side. One kind was white, another black, and a third red, and as they quarried, they at the same time hollowed out double docks, having roofs formed out of the native rock. Some of their buildings were simple, but in others they put together different stones, varying the colour to please the eye, and to be a natural source of delight. The entire circuit of the wall, which went round the outermost zone, they covered with a coating of brass, and the circuit of the next wall they coated with tin, and the third, which encompassed the citadel, flashed with the red light of orichalcum.[58]

Nobody now knows exactly what metal the fabled orichalcum of Atlantis was, since Plato tells us that it survived in his day 'only in name',[59] but it adds to the aura of technological mastery that still surrounds the fabled lost civilization.

8. Mount Ararat viewed over the ruins of Zvarnots Cathedral, Armenia.

9. Entrance passageway and stone door -- Derinkuyu underground 'city', Turkey.

20. The Temple of Horus at Edfu, Upper Egypt.

21. Vignette from the mysterious Edfu Building Texts. The texts leave us in no doubt that the 'gods' of the 'early primeval age' were sailors and navigators. After the destruction of their island homeland they are said to have wandered the world in ships.

22–27. Enigmatic Building Texts and scenes from the Temple of Horus at Edfu.

28. Above: Scene from the Temple of Horus at Edfu. Horus does battle with his rival Set who takes the form of a hippopotamus.

29. Edfu hieroglyphs.

30. Right: Thoth, the scribe of the gods who wrote down the words of the Seven Sages.

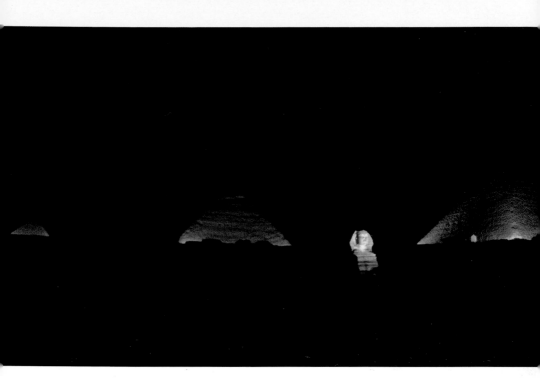

31, 32. The astronomically-aligned monuments of Egypt's Giza Plateau: A 'book descended from the sky'?

33. Aerial view of the Sphinx and its Temples.

34. The ancient megalithic limestone core of the 'Valley Temple'. Its blocks weigh up to 100 tons.

Facing page: 35. The Sphinx with the 'Dream Stela' between its paws.

36. The granite elements of the 'Valley Temple' (above) were added in Dynastic times to the ancient, pre-existing limestone structure.

37. The huge limestone blocks of the 'Valley Temple' were quarried from around the core body of the Sphinx when the Sphinx was made, and are therefore the work of the same culture.

Seagoing navigation, advanced agriculture and large-scale architectural and engineering works are also amongst the notable characteristics of the Homeland of the Primeval Ones described in the Edfu texts. We have already seen how the ring system of canals is prefigured there but so too are the grand temples of Atlantis. We read, for example, of a chapel 'measuring 90 by 20 cubits' (approximately 45 by 10 metres or 150 by 35 feet):

> At its front was erected a large forecourt of 90 by 90 cubits . . .
> Then a hypostyle hall of 50 by 30 cubits was constructed . . .
> then another hall of 20 by 30 cubits and two consecutive halls,
> each 45 by 20 cubits were added at the front of the first hypostyle
> hall.[60]

An enclosure is described measuring 300 cubits (150 metres or 500 feet) from west to east and 400 cubits from north to south. Within it is a temple, the 'Mansion of the God' and within that a Holy of Holies measuring 90 cubits from east to west.[61]

We also read of a third enclosure on the same grand scale of 300 by 400 cubits. It too contains an inner sanctuary measuring 90 cubits from west to east and 20 cubits from north to south, subdivided into three rooms each of which was 30 cubits by 20 cubits.[62]

But the strongest hint of high technology in the Homeland of the Primeval Ones is given in one of the Edfu extracts that describes the cataclysmic demise of the island following the assault of the celestial 'snake' called 'the Great Leaping One' that 'pierces' the Earth God and 'splits' the domain. Then we read – and it is most mysterious – that 'the Sound Eye fell'.[63]

'The mention of the Sound Eye . . . appears a little strange,' admits Reymond. But she explains, though the texts are obscure on the point, that it seems to be:

> the name of the centre of the light which illumined the island.[64]

We are, in short, to envisage some artificial system of illumination which lights up the primeval island of the gods. Beyond that:

All that can be said, with due reserve, is that it looks as though there is an allusion to a disaster which caused the fall of the Sound Eye, with the result that complete darkness fell upon the domain of the Creator.[65]

The gods sailed . . .

What happened after the disaster that struck Atlantis? Were there survivors? If there were, what did they do with the advanced knowledge that they possessed?

Plato's *Timaeus* and *Critias* provide no answers to these questions, but the Edfu Building Texts do, making it clear that there were survivors of the disaster that struck the Homeland of the Primeval Ones – 'companies of gods' who were already at sea when the sacred island was flooded. They sailed back to the former location of the island after the cataclysm but:

saw only reeds on the surface of the water.[66]

There was a great deal of mud there also,[67] a scene reminiscent of Plato's description of the vicinity of Atlantis after the flood:

the sea in that area is impassable to navigation, which is hindered by mud just below the surface, the remains of the sunken island.[68]

In the case of the Homeland of the Primeval Ones it seems that enough of the sunken island remained close to the surface for the survivors to attempt to win some of it back from the sea – an endeavour referred to in the Edfu texts as the 'creation of the *pāy*-lands', where the term '*pāy*-land' clearly means lands reclaimed from the sea.[69] Thus we read how 'the *Shebtiw* recited sacred spells, the water gradually receded from the edge of the island, and the actual land of the *pāy*-land was brought out.'[70] The texts then describe:

a process of . . . continuous creation by the emergence of a progressive series of plots of land . . . [71] The creation of these

. . . sacred domains was, in fact, a resurrection and restoration of what had been in the past but had vanished . . .[72] At the end there appeared further *pāy*-lands which brought to a new life the former homeland.[73]

Nonetheless, despite these efforts, the fact remained that the cataclysm had so utterly devastated the primeval island that no amount of reclamation could restore it to its former glory. The only solution for the survivors, therefore, was to attempt to recreate it elsewhere in regions that had not been as badly affected by the catastrophe. The result saw the beginning of a great project of which the world we live in today is the result. What the Edfu texts say, explains Reymond, is:

> that the gods left the original *pāy*-lands . . .[74] They . . . sailed to another part of the primeval world . . .[75] [and] journeyed through the . . . lands of the primeval age . . .[76] In any place in which they settled they founded new sacred domains.[77]

Their mission, in short, was to repromulgate the lost civilization and the lost religion of the days before the flood. As Reymond puts it, this 'second era of the primeval age' saw 'the development of the domains that survived in historical times.'[78]

Begin again like children

The Edfu texts make allusion to the *smd*, 'wandering', of the 'company of gods'[79] who initiated the civilizing project. Their leader was the Falcon Horus, after whom the temple at Edfu was much later dedicated, but present, also, was Thoth, the god of wisdom.[80] Accompanying Horus and Thoth were the *Shebtiw*, a group of deities charged with a specific responsibility for 'creation',[81] the 'Builder Gods' who accomplished 'the actual work of building',[82] and the 'Seven Sages'.[83] This is a matter of interest in the light of the Mesopotamian traditions of the Apkallus explored in Chapter Eight and it seems that something more than coincidence is involved.

The reader will recall that the Apkallus were often depicted as hybrid creatures, part bird of prey, part human in appearance. Similarly, the Seven Sages of the Edfu texts are described as primeval deities who were capable of assuming 'the form of falcons' and of 'resembling falcons'.[84]

Also exactly like the antediluvian Apkallus, the Seven Sages of the Edfu texts (who are not mentioned elsewhere in Ancient Egyptian inscriptions) were the magicians amongst the gods. They were seers who could foretell the future,[85] and they could *swr iht ti* – 'endue with power the substances of the earth'[86] – a process of creation 'by the word of the creators'[87] that, Reymond notes, 'has no equivalent'.[88] They were, in addition, believed to have the ability 'to magnify things', and thus to provide magical protection.[89] On this point, the best sense Reymond is able to make of what she describes as an 'unusually obscure' text, is that 'the protection was constituted by means of symbols. The magical power of protecting was conferred by a giving of names.'[90]

The Apkallus mingled their magic with practical skills – such as laying the foundations of cities and temples. Similarly, the Seven Sages of the Edfu texts also had their practical, architectural side and many passages testify to their involvement in the setting out and construction of buildings and in the laying of foundations.[91] Moreover, the Egyptians believed that 'the ground plans of the historical temples were established according to what the Sages of the primeval age revealed to Thoth.'[92]

This hint of a special connection between the Sages and Thoth is, of course, a further parallel for, as we've seen, the Apkallus were linked to Enki, the Mesopotamian god of wisdom. In the Mesopotamian inscriptions, however, Enki is clearly superior to the Sages – indeed, he is their maker. But in the Edfu texts, strangely, it appears that the knowledge of the Sages is regarded as superior to that of the wisdom-god Thoth. Indeed, it was the tradition at Edfu that the original records and archives from which the texts were extracted were nothing less than 'the words of the Sages' given as dictation to Thoth, who had then consigned them to writing.[93] The texts further disclose that the Sages of the mythical age were believed to be 'the only divine beings who knew how the temples and sacred places were created'[94] and were themselves the very *creators* of knowledge,[95] which thereafter could only be passed on but not invented anew. This finds parallels in the Mesopotamian notion that since the time of the antediluvian Apkallus nothing new had been invented – with the original revelation simply being retransmitted and unfolded in later epochs.

Without labouring the point further, therefore, it seems to me that the idea conveyed so strongly in the cuneiform inscriptions of ancient Mesopotamia of a project to recover and repromulgate antediluvian knowledge after a global cataclysm is, rather exactly, the same project that is set out in the Edfu Building Texts, which in turn bear uncanny and troubling resemblances to Plato's report of the destroyed Ice Age civilization of Atlantis.

More than that, the Edfu texts invite us to consider the possibility that the survivors of the lost civilization, thought of as 'gods' but manifestly human – albeit with mysterious 'powers' – set about 'wandering' the world after the flood. By happenstance it was only hunter-gatherer populations, the peoples of the mountains and the deserts – 'the unlettered and the uncultured', as Plato so eloquently put it in his *Timaeus* – who had been 'spared the scourge of the deluge'.[96] But the civilisers entertained the desperate hope, if their mission would succeed, that mankind might not have to 'begin again like children, in complete ignorance of what happened in early times'.[97]

The evidence of the Mesopotamian inscriptions, and of Göbekli Tepe to which we will return, is that the mountain lands of ancient Armenia and eastern Turkey were amongst the primal wildernesses to which the civilisers made their way after the flood. But the testimony of Edfu is that they also came to the Nile flowing in its fertile valley through the deserts of Egypt.

Moreover the Building Texts say very clearly which part of Egypt they came to first – and it was not Edfu, as we'll see in the next chapter.

Chapter 10
Monastery of the Seven Sages

———◆———

In his *Timaeus*, we've seen how Plato speaks of events, described in Ancient Egyptian temple records, that took place 9,000 years before the time of Solon, i.e. in 9600 BC. Nor is the *Timaeus* the only place where Plato alludes to such vast antiquity. In his *Laws*, for example, he says of the Ancient Egyptians:

> If you examine their art on the spot, you will find that ten thousand years ago (and I'm not speaking loosely; I mean literally ten thousand), paintings and reliefs were produced that are no better and no worse than those of today.[1]

It's interesting how the Greek philosopher makes a point of this 'ten thousand years ago', emphasizing that he's not speaking loosely – that he really means it. But we live, supposedly, in a more scientific age with the benefit of objective dating techniques, so what are we to make of such a chronology?

Plato was born around 428 BC, so his reference to 'ten thousand years' ago translates to around 10,400 BC in our calendar, within a whisker of the date of 10,450 BC that I proposed in *Fingerprints of the Gods* for the remote epoch, *Zep Tepi* – 'the First Time' – when the Ancient Egyptians believed that the gods walked the earth and the civilization of the Nile Valley had its true beginnings.[2]

This date, based on findings that arose from research underlying *The Orion Mystery*, my friend Robert Bauval's ground-breaking 1994 study of the astronomical aspects of the world-famous pyramids of Giza in Egypt,[3] was developed further by the two of us in 1996 in our co-authored book *Keeper of Genesis* (titled *The Message of the Sphinx* in the US).[4] In brief, the date arises from the extraordinarily precise layout of the principal monuments of the Giza plateau and the relationship of these monuments to certain stars in the sky. For full details I refer the reader to *Fingerprints of the Gods* and to *Keeper of Genesis*, where this issue is explored in depth, but the heart of the matter lies in the fact that the positions of the stars in the sky are not fixed and finite but change very gradually over a great cycle – known to astronomers as the precessional cycle – that unfolds in a period of 25,920 years.

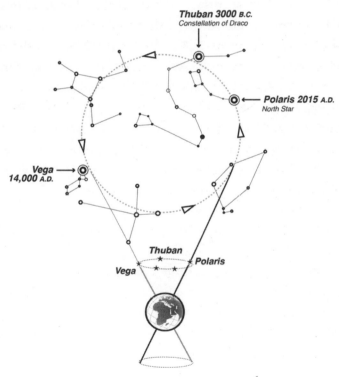

Figure 33: The effect of precession is to change the Pole Star over very long periods of time.

The cycle is the result of a motion of the earth itself, a slow circular wobble of the planet's axis of rotation unfolding at the rate of one degree every 72 years; since the earth is the viewing platform from which we observe the stars, these changes in orientation inevitably affect the positions and rising times of all stars as viewed from earth.

Our Pole Star, for example, around which the remainder of the heavens appear to revolve, is simply the star at which the earth's extended axis, passing through the geographical north pole, points most directly. Presently it is Polaris (Alpha Ursae Minoris, in the constellation of the Little Bear), but the effect of precession is to change the Pole Star over very long periods of time. Thus around 3000 BC, just before the start of the Pyramid Age in Egypt, the Pole Star was Thuban (Alpha Draconis) in the constellation of Draco. At the time of the Greeks it was Beta Ursae Minoris. In AD 14,000 it will be Vega.[5] Sometimes in this long cyclical journey the extended north pole of the earth will point at empty space and then there will be no useful 'Pole Star'.

The most dramatic, and indeed beautiful and aesthetically pleasing effects of precession, however, are those observed at the horizon on the March equinox, when night and day are of equal length and when the sun rises perfectly due east against the background of the twelve constellations of the zodiac. The rate of change is the same as at the pole, i.e. just one degree every 72 years, so it cannot easily be observed – let alone measured – in a single human lifetime. But if yours is a culture that keeps careful records over very long periods, it will be noted that the zodiacal constellation that 'houses' the sun on that special day (marking the beginning of spring in the northern hemisphere) does, indeed, very slowly shift along the horizon until eventually, the next constellation takes its place.

Broadly speaking the sun spends 2,160 years 'in' each house of the zodiac (30 degrees x 72 years) and, since there are twelve zodiacal houses, the result is that 'the Great Year' – the full precessional cycle – unfolds in 12 x 2,160 years, i.e. 25,920 years, at which point the cycle is back at its starting point and a new Great Year begins. In the sun's annual path through the zodiac, spending approximately one month in each sign as all of us who check our horoscopes are aware, Aquarius is followed by Pisces, which in turn is followed by Aries, which is followed by Taurus, then Gemini, then Cancer, then Leo, etc, etc, etc. But the slow, majestic precessional course of the sun through the Great Year is a *backwards* motion that unfolds in exactly the opposite direction – thus Leo → Cancer → Gemini → Taurus → Aries → Pisces → Aquarius – with each 'month' being 2,160 years in length.

So, to give some specific examples, it is not an accident that the early Christians used the fish as their symbol, since the constellation of Pisces housed the sun on the spring equinox from the very beginning of the Christian era until today. Nor is the famous song wrong to state that 'we live in the dawning of the Age of Aquarius', for the early twenty-first century does indeed stand in the astrological no-man's land near the end of the 'Age of Pisces' and on the threshold of the 'New Age' of Aquarius. Going back before the Age of Pisces we come to the age of Aries (2330 BC–170 BC) when, in Ancient Egypt, rams were the dominant symbolic motif (for example, the ram-headed sphinxes at the temple of Karnak in Luxor), and before that to the Age of Taurus (4490 BC–2330 BC) when the cult of the Apis Bull was initiated as early as the First Dynasty, or perhaps before.

Different astrologers and astronomers might choose to move the

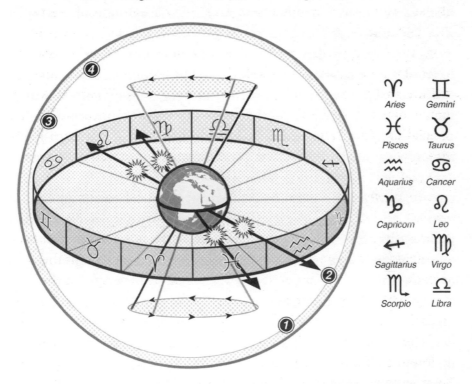

Figure 34: The sun has been in Pisces (1) at the spring equinox for the past 2,000 years, defining the astrological 'Age of Pisces', but will in due course shift into Aquarius (2) as a result of precession and the 'Age of Aquarius' will begin. At the same time the constellations marking the autumnal equinox will shift from Virgo (4) into Leo (3).

constellation boundaries a few degrees (and thus a century or two) in one direction or another, but the general schema is well understood and the dates given above stand as a good approximation to the facts. Moving back in time further, as it is easy to do with modern computer programs that simulate ancient skies, we come eventually to the Age of Leo when the constellation of Leo, the lion, housed the sun on the spring equinox. This astrological age spans the period between 10,970 BC and 8810 BC – although, again, depending on where one sets the constellation boundaries, the dates might be pushed back or forward by a couple of centuries. What is clear, however, even with a little boundary juggling, is that the Age of Leo pretty much perfectly encloses the Younger Dryas (10,800 BC to 9600 BC), something that I was unaware of when I wrote *Fingerprints of the Gods*. And, of course, it was also the Age of Leo that I signalled in *Fingerprints* as the most likely candidate for the remote epoch that the Ancient Egyptians called *Zep Tepi*, the 'First Time'.

Again, I refer readers to *Fingerprints* and to *Keeper of Genesis*, and to my later book *Heaven's Mirror*,[6] for more detailed discussions of the astronomical facts, and of the ideas behind them. The essence of the argument, however, is that there was an ancient globally-distributed doctrine – 'as above so below' – that set out quite deliberately to create monuments on the ground that copied the patterns of certain significant constellations in the sky. Moreover, since the positions of all stars change slowly but continuously as a result of the precession, it is possible to use particular configurations of astronomically aligned monuments to deduce the dates that they represent – i.e. the dates when the stars were last in the positions depicted by the monuments on the ground.

The Giza plateau contains the world's most striking array of astronomically-aligned monuments and, for purposes of clarity, let me emphasise that these alignments have nothing to do with compass directions. The 'north' indicated by a compass is magnetic north which can vary by 10 degrees or more from true north and wanders constantly because of magnetic changes in the earth's core. True north is the geographical north pole of the earth, in other words the pivot of our planet's axis of rotation; from it true south, east and west are derived.

It is therefore significant that the gaze of the Great Sphinx is perfectly targeted on true east, while the three great pyramids are aligned with uncanny precision to true north and south – indeed, the error in the case of the Great Pyramid is just 3/60ths of a single degree.

What this tells us is that all these monuments were set out using astronomy, for it is not possible to achieve such precision by any other means. In other words, even if there were no additional astronomical characteristics present, we would have to say, on grounds of accuracy of alignment alone, that astronomers had been at work here. But in fact there are many other astronomical characteristics – not only in the monuments themselves but also in Ancient Egyptian scriptures such as the Pyramid Texts – and for these, since I wish to avoid unnecessary repetition, I again refer the reader to my earlier books.

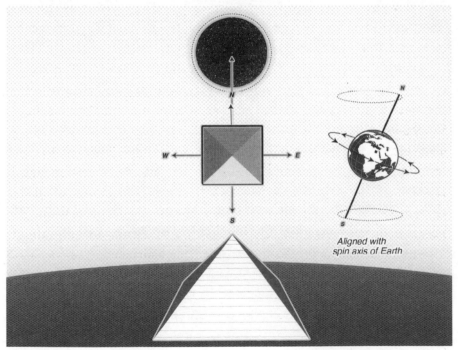

Figure 35: The alignment of the Great Pyramid is only 3/60th of a single degree off true north.

The heart of the matter, however, involves two constellations – the constellation of Leo, rising due east above the sun at dawn on the spring equinox in the epoch of 10,500 BC, and the constellation of Orion, which the Ancient Egyptians visualised as the celestial figure

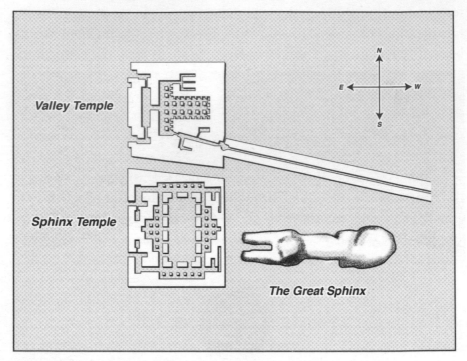

Figure 36: The gaze of the Great Sphinx is perfectly targeted on true east.

of the god Osiris, the deceased god-king who ruled over the afterlife kingdom known as the *Duat*. As we saw in Chapter Nine, Osiris was also believed in some way to be the *Ka* – the 'double', or spiritual essence – of the Pyramids of Giza.

I will not vex the reader with lengthy substantiations of the assertions that follow since they are fully backed up, referenced and documented in my earlier books, but an uncanny sky-ground 'lock' occurs at Giza in the epoch of 10,500 BC. I had opted for a date fifty years later – 10,450 BC – in *Fingerprints*, but such minor details are not really significant since the stellar changes are so slow, even within a single astrological age, that the same general configuration holds good for many centuries. Indeed, it is true to say that the Giza sky-ground lock stays in place throughout most, if not all, of the Younger Dryas from 10,800 BC down to 9600 BC.

Effectively, therefore, the epoch of the 'First Time', which I will continue, for ease of reference, to refer to as the epoch of 10,500 BC, *is* the epoch of the Younger Dryas. And while it was a time of freezing temperatures further north – particularly in North America and northern Europe – indications are that the climate in Egypt would have been much more comfortable and conducive and much wetter and

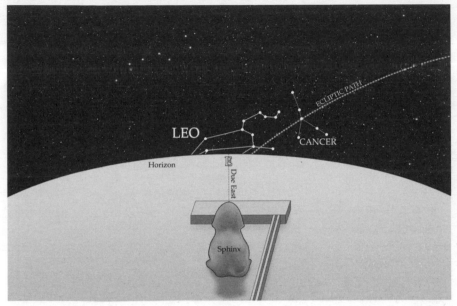

Figure 37: Looking east in the dawn, about an hour before sunrise on the morning of the spring equinox in the epoch of 10,500 BC, we see the constellation of Leo lying with its belly on the horizon, directly in line with the gaze of the Sphinx.

more fertile than it is today. This is not to say that Egypt was entirely spared the cataclysms of the Younger Dryas – there were powerful and destructive Nile floods as we shall see – but by comparison with many other parts of the world it would have stood out as an inviting refuge.

As above, so below . . . To return to the matter of the sky-ground lock at Giza in the epoch of 10,500 BC, let us consider first the lion-bodied (and very likely once lion-headed) monument, oriented perfectly due east, that we call the Great Sphinx. It looks not only at the rising sun on the spring equinox but also at the constellation that houses the sun on the equinox. Today, therefore, this monument gazes at the cusp between Pisces and Aquarius. At the time of the building of the Temple of Karnak it gazed at the constellation of Aries, and in the Old Kingdom, when the Sphinx was supposedly built, it gazed at the constellation of Taurus, the Bull – clearly not a perfect sky-ground match.

Indeed, only in one epoch in the last 25,920 years has the lion-

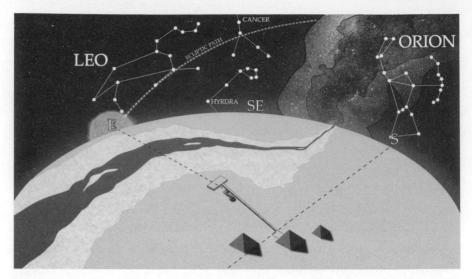

Figure 38: On the spring equinox in the epoch of 10,500 BC, at the exact moment that the sun bisected the horizon due east, the three belt stars of the constellation of Orion lay due south on the meridian – in a pattern that very precisely matches the pattern of the three Great Pyramids on the ground.

bodied Sphinx looked out at its own celestial counterpart, the constellation of Leo, in the pre-dawn on the spring equinox, and that was in the epoch of 10,500 BC.

But there is more. In that same epoch, at the exact moment that the sun bisected the horizon due east, the three belt stars of the constellation of Orion lay due south on the meridian – and they did so in a pattern that very precisely matches the pattern of the three Great Pyramids on the ground, thus making sublime sense of the image of Osiris/Orion as the *Ka*, or 'double', of the Pyramids.

After Robert Bauval presented the Orion correlation to a global readership in his 1994 book *The Orion Mystery*, and after the further work I did on the subject in *Fingerprints of the Gods*, and that Robert and I did together in *Keeper of Genesis*, the hypothesis came in for a great deal of criticism from the mainstream archaeoastronomer Ed Krupp of the Griffiths Observatory of Los Angeles.

Krupp claimed that the correlation was 'upside down', an argument of some sophistry based on the apparent curvature of the sky which means that the highest of the three stars of Orion's belt (matched, in the Orion correlation, by the southernmost of the three pyramids), is effectively the northernmost star. Refuting this, we were able to demonstrate that laying the pyramids out on the ground in the way that would satisfy Krupp might be technically 'correct' in terms of modern astronomical conventions, but would not produce an immediately recognizable and visually pleasing similitude between what is seen in the sky and what is seen on the ground. If, on the other hand, one steers clear of twenty first century astronomical conventions (in which north is 'up'), and simply models on the ground – rather as an artist or a sculptor would – what would have been seen in the sky at dawn on the spring equinox in the epoch of 10,500 BC, then the result is indeed a very good match, as Robert Bauval always claimed, between the three great pyramids and the three stars of Orion's Belt (see Appendix, *The Orion correlation is not upside down*, for further details).

Moreover, as noted above, the particularly striking feature of this match is its lock with the Sphinx/Leo. The point is worth re-emphasizing. Looking east in the predawn, about an hour before sunrise on the morning of the spring equinox in the epoch of 10,500 BC, we see the constellation of Leo lying with its belly on the horizon, directly in line with the gaze of the Sphinx. There is an unmissable sky/ground correlation here – for the constellation of Leo, in profile as seen at this moment, does very closely resemble the profile of the leonine Sphinx.

The earth turns, the stars and the sun rise, light floods the sky, and in due course – after about an hour – the solar disc bisects the horizon precisely due east, again exactly in line with the gaze of the Sphinx. At the precise moment it does so, the three stars of Orion's belt fall into place centred due south over the meridian. This is confirmed absolutely by modern astronomical software and it would have been known absolutely by anyone with sophisticated knowledge of the motions of the heavens, should such a person have been present at Giza in the epoch of 10,500 BC. Indeed, one can almost feel the ponderous gears of the sky at work, like a huge clock: the hour hand is the Sphinx/Leo correlation and the minute hand is the pyramids/ Orion's belt correlation, and both work together to point unmistakably to the epoch of 10,500 BC. This is the epoch that I long ago suggested was the mysterious Ancient Egyptian 'First Time', but that I now understand was significant for the world-changing cataclysm of the Younger Dryas as well.

Dating with stars

The use of combinations of stars in the sky and large-scale constructions on the ground to point symbolically to significant moments in history was a practice widely pursued in antiquity, as extensively documented in my 1998 book *Heaven's Mirror*.[7] Indeed, examples of such sky-ground mirroring, once they are properly understood, frequently shed new light on archaeological inquiries. For example, in 2014 an ancient mound in the Republic of Macedonia was identified as man-made by archaeoacoustic analysis. The mound's dimensions are 85 metres x 45 metres, it is very precisely oriented north–south and at its summit, placed within an oval ditch, a giant earthwork has been identified by researchers from the University of Trieste as a representation of the constellation of Cassiopeia, as it would have appeared from the site at dawn on 21 July 356 BC, the birthday of the famed Macedonian ruler Alexander the Great. 'Cassiopeia, lies directly to the north,' the researchers conclude:

> and stands vertically above the geoglyph in the sky's zenith, forming a perfect picture of the sky on the earth.[8]

Nor are such sky-ground endeavours confined to the ancient world. A relatively recent example is the Hoover Dam in the United States. There at the base of the towering Monument of Dedication with its black diorite pedestals supporting two colossal and imposing winged figures – themselves reminiscent of Mesopotamian and Ancient Egyptian deities – the sculptor Oscar Hansen created a spectacular terrazzo floor with an inbuilt star chart. Here's how the US Department of the Interior's Bureau of Reclamation describes the artwork, and its purpose:

> The chart preserves for future generations the date on which President Franklin D. Roosevelt dedicated Hoover Dam, September 30, 1935 . . .

In this celestial map, the bodies of the solar system are placed so exactly that those versed in astronomy could calculate the precession (progressively earlier occurrence) of the Pole Star for approximately the next 14,000 years. Conversely, future generations could look upon this monument and determine, if no other means were available, the exact date on which Hoover Dam was dedicated.[9]

Hansen, who explicitly compared the dam to the Great Pyramid as 'a monument to collective genius exerting itself in community efforts around a common need or ideal',[10] also incorporated the signs of the zodiac into his design.[11] Such elements, he said, were all put there as clues and pointers, so that 'in remote ages to come, intelligent people' would be able to discern 'the astronomical time of the dam's dedication.'[12]

It so happens that the Hoover Dam and its monumental sculptures were completed in the same year, 1935, but it is, of course, possible to use symbolic architecture and astronomical alignments to make a permanent statement about significant moments in the past *at any time*. A parallel might be the great Gothic cathedrals of Europe built in the twelfth and thirteenth centuries of our era but referring in every symbolic detail and in the sacred astronomy built into their stones and stained glass,[13] to much earlier periods – notably to the time of Christ and the time of the Old Testament patriarchs.

From a purely astronomical point of view, what can be said about the huge effort and endeavour of the Giza monuments is that the ground-plan of the pyramids and the Sphinx does speak clearly of the epoch of 10,500 BC. But as readers of my previous books will be aware, the monuments also include features, such as the four narrow shafts angled up through the body of the Great Pyramid, that target significant stars in the epoch of 2500 BC when Egyptologists believe the pyramids were built.[14]

In other words *both* epochs are symbolised – 2500 BC by the shafts and 10,500 BC by the ground plan.

Long lived cult of the Sages

The hypothesis I derive from this is that Giza was one of several sites around the world – Göbekli Tepe was another – where survivors of a great prehistoric civilization that had been all-but destroyed in the global cataclysm at the onset of the Younger Dryas chose to settle, and where their sages set in motion a long-term plan to bring about 'the resurrection of the former world of the gods . . . The re-creation of the destroyed world'.[15] Perhaps they felt that their own civilization had made some terrible error, some ghastly mistake, that had brought down the punishment of the universe upon them in the form of the Younger Dryas comet, and that it would therefore be impious or unwise to seek to refashion the destroyed world all at once and straight away. Indeed, perhaps it proved *impossible* for them to do so. Though its climate would have been attractive, at a time when much of the world was in the midst of a sudden deep freeze, the Nile Valley, like so many other places, did suffer cataclysmic events both at the beginning and at the end of the Younger Dryas. These events included episodes of extreme river floods, the so-called 'Wild Nile', that recurred several times in the epoch of 10,500 BC, with calmer and more predictable conditions not being restored until about 9000 BC.[16]

Located on higher ground, well above the valley floor, there is no evidence to suggest that Giza itself was ever scoured by those floods and it would, therefore, have been an obvious choice in Egypt for the survivors to have established a base and begun work on an architectural project, perhaps focused around certain natural features of the plateau itself. Amongst these I would draw particular attention to the rocky hill more than thirty feet high – an excellent contender for the 'Great Primeval Mound' described in the Edfu texts, as we shall see – that would much later be incorporated into the core of the Great Pyramid.

I suggest that a shaft was cut down into this hill and deep into the bedrock beneath it to create the rectangular cavity that is now nominated as the Subterranean Chamber – which can still only be accessed today through that same 300-foot-long shaft (now known as 'the Descending Corridor') that dives deeply into the bowels of the earth at an angle of 26 degrees. In my view, it is probably only one of several underground features that were created at that time, with others – far more extensive – still awaiting discovery.

Likewise these visitors to primeval Giza of the epoch of 10,500 BC would also have found a crest or ridge of rock (the technical term for such a feature is a 'yardang'), protruding downslope that had perhaps already been sculpted by the prevailing winds into something resembling the head of a lion. It faced east and overlooked the Nile Valley and it would, in due course, be extensively excavated and carved to form the Great Sphinx. It is likely that some substantial work was done in the epoch of 10,500 BC to free at least the front quarters of the core body of the Sphinx from its surrounding bedrock. But my view, unchanged since I wrote *Fingerprints of the Gods*, is that the majority of the work on this project, as on the pyramids themselves, was done later and finally completed in epoch of 2500 BC when the original leonine head of the Sphinx, perhaps heavily eroded, was recarved into the disproportionately-small human head that it still has today. My hypothesis, then and now, is that the same sacred 'cult', housed in something perhaps like a monastery, with a very small, even negligible, archaeological footprint – let us call it the Monastery of the Seven Sages – was involved in both major phases of the work and in everything that happened at Giza in between. As I wrote in 1995, this hypothesis resolves the anomaly of the 'missing' 8,000 years between the two epochs:

> by supposing the star shafts [of the Great Pyramid] to be merely the later work of the same long-lived cult that originally laid out the Giza ground plan in 10,450 BC. Naturally the hypothesis also suggests that it was this same cult, towards the end of those 8,000 missing years, that provided the initiating spark for the sudden and 'fully formed' emergence of the literate and accomplished historical civilization of dynastic Egypt.[17]

Dating with light

Since the publication of *Fingerprints of the Gods* I have had many years to reflect on the mysteries of Giza. It remains my view that the role of the historical pharaohs of the Fourth Dynasty was to complete, and finally fulfil, a much more ancient plan first brought to Egypt in the epoch of 10,500 BC. As noted above, however, the subterranean elements of the Giza plateau, and the earliest work on the Sphinx, may actually date back to the epoch of 10,500 BC. By virtue of the distinctive weathering patterns on that monument's flanks and on sections of the trench that surrounds it – highlighted in the analysis of geology professor Robert Schoch of Boston University – a proto-Sphinx does appear to have existed when heavy rains fell across Egypt at the end of the Ice Age,[18] perhaps even as early as the Wild Nile period.

I have long been convinced by the geological evidence that the Sphinx does in fact date back in some form to the epoch of 10,500 BC. But there is a grey area to do with events between 10,500 BC and 2500 BC and this concerns the megalithic temples of the plateau, particularly the Sphinx Temple (directly in front, i.e. to the east, of the Sphinx itself) and the Valley Temple which lies immediately southeast of the Sphinx, both of which are built for the most part of limestone blocks excavated from around the core body of the Sphinx, although in many cases the limestone blocks are surfaced with a veneer of granite. The orthodox archaeological dating of these structures (both of their limestone and of their granite elements) is to the Old Kingdom – specifically to the Fourth Dynasty, approximately 2613 BC to 2494 BC[19] – i.e. to the epoch of 2500 BC.

When I wrote *Fingerprints of the Gods*, however, I was open to the possibility that they might date back to the epoch of 10,500 BC. I remain so, but in the light of recent evidence some careful consideration is required. This is the case because an advanced scientific technique known as surface luminescence dating (which measures light energy stored in stone) has been applied to these temples. This technique seems, on the face of things, to rule out rather conclusively any possibility that the temples were created in the form we see them now in the epoch of 10,500 BC.[20]

I say 'on the face of things' because there are certain problems with the new technique which mean that any conclusions drawn from it must be carefully thought through. Most significantly, as the researchers themselves admit, surface luminescence dating relies upon the assumption that the sample being tested has not been exposed to sunlight since it was set into place in the building of which it is a part. Should there have been exposure to sunlight, even if 'just minutes' in duration – as would happen, for example, if any later reworking of the sampled area had been undertaken without cover of a roof – then 'the latent luminescence is released . . . setting the signal to zero or near zero', and thus yielding a date that reflects the most recent reworking rather than the original date at which the building was constructed.[21]

The Giza Surface Luminescence Dating study was conducted by nuclear physicist Professor Ioannis Liritzis and his colleague Asimina Vafiadou, both of the Laboratory of Archaeometry at the University of the Aegean. They reported their results in detail in 2015 in the *Journal of Cultural Heritage*.[22] Conclusive indications that at least some of the structures they sampled had indeed been reworked, with their latent luminescence zeroed and the clock set ticking again at the time of the reworking, are provided by Sample No. 4 (Valley Temple limestone) and Sample No. 6 (Sphinx Temple granite). The former yielded a very young surface luminescence date of 1050 BC, plus or minus 540 years, while the latter yielded a surface luminescence date of 1190 BC, plus or minus 340 years.[23] These are, effectively, dates from Ancient Egypt's New Kingdom (Eighteenth Dynasty and later) and we have firm archaeological and epigraphic evidence that both the Sphinx Temple and the Valley Temple were already very ancient by New Kingdom times.

Since this is so, the other dates yielded by the study must also be regarded with caution and certainly cannot be taken as firm evidence of the date of construction of the temples – particularly in the case of Sample No. 3 (Valley Temple granite), and Samples No. 7 and 8 (both Sphinx Temple granite). These yielded surface luminescence dates, respectively, of 3060 BC, plus or minus 470 years; 2740 BC, plus or minus 640 years; and 3100 BC, plus or minus 540 years.[24] These dates are *broadly* compatible with the Old Kingdom – although with some reservations which we will explore below – but they do not under any circumstance rule out a much more ancient date of construction for the limestone core masonry of the temples, since it has always been Robert Schoch's contention that:

this granite sheathing was added in the Old Kingdom to repair and restore the earlier (much earlier – 'Sphinx Age') limestone temples.[25]

We are left, then, with only a single sample (Sample No. 5) which was taken from the original limestone core masonry of the Sphinx Temple. It yielded a surface luminescence date of 2220, plus or minus 220 years,[26] but really nothing very conclusive can be said about it or deduced from it since its location does not rule out the possibility, as Schoch observed when I asked him to comment on these findings, that it 'may also have been exposed or reworked during repairs to the structure during the Old Kingdom.'[27]

In summary, the new study does not provide any evidence to confirm beyond doubt that the original limestone megalithic elements of the Sphinx and Valley Temples were built by the Fourth Dynasty Pharaoh Khafre, as archaeologists maintain. On the contrary, the only thing the study seems to demonstrate for sure is that these temples were reworked during the New Kingdom. More alarming for the mainstream chronology, the surface luminescence dating raises the possibility that the granite sheathing on the temples (with the exception of Sample No. 6 with its New Kingdom date) was not added in the Fourth Dynasty at all but many centuries earlier – indeed as early as 3380 BC at the extreme end of the dating range for Sample No. 7, as early as 3530 BC for Sample No. 3, and as early as 3640 BC for Sample No. 8.[28]

This potentially pushes what Robert Schoch has always regarded as restoration work on the Sphinx Temple (the adding of a granite veneer on top of much older and extensively eroded megalithic limestone blocks) far back into the pre-dynastic period, i.e. long before any large-scale construction is supposed to have been undertaken in Egypt. And needless to say if these temples were in need of such radical restoration in the pre-dynastic period then their core masonry is likely to be very ancient indeed, perhaps even going back as far as the epoch of 10,500 BC.

So much then for the Sphinx Temple and the Valley Temple, but what of the enigmatic pyramids that loom over them?

The researchers were not able to study the second pyramid at Giza, conventionally attributed (like the Sphinx and its temples) to Khafre. Nor did they investigate the Great Pyramid, attributed to Khufu. But they did test a single sample from the smallest of the three pyramids, which Egyptology attributes to Menkaure, the Pharaoh who succeeded Khafre to the throne. Taken from the granite facing stones of the pyramid, and not from its core masonry, this sample produced yet another strikingly anomalous date – 3450 BC, plus or minus 950 years – when assayed for surface luminescence.[29] Only at the youngest end of the range (3450 minus 950 = 2500 BC) does this date approximate to the reign of Menkaure – although many authorities do not see that pharaoh taking the throne until 2490 BC,[30] and thus *after* 'his' pyramid was completed even at the most recent date offered by the surface luminescence spectrum. But what is more disturbing are the other possibilities raised by the dating, i.e. that the facing stones of the so-called 'Pyramid of Menkaure' could have been put in place as early as 3450 BC or even, perhaps, 950 years before that, i.e. in 4400 BC and thus deep in the pre-dynastic period almost two thousand years prior to the Old Kingdom.

More work needs to be done to settle all this. As I've said, I remain willing, for the moment, to accept the still prevailing mainstream view that dates the pyramids to the Old Kingdom. But what is in the process of emerging, I think, is recognition of the need for a more nuanced view of the whole site with strong indications from geology, from astronomy, and now from surface luminescence dating as well, that it can no longer be attributed exclusively to the epoch of 2500 BC, but rather appears to be the result of a series of developments over an immensely long time-frame going back more than 12,000 years. As Professor Ioannis Liritzis of the University of the Aegean, lead author of the surface luminescence study, concludes, parts of the site appear to have been reused and:

> it is a reasonable assumption that some of the structures were already present at Giza when the large-scale works of the Fourth Dynasty began.[31]

Nor is the question of the *age* of the site the only open one. Its *function*, too, is up for grabs. Egyptologists like to define the pyramids as 'tombs and tombs only', but as Professor Liritzis notes:

The lack of contemporary human funerary remains from any Egyptian pyramid, and the obvious astronomical and geometric nature of the site, that prove their orientation was not by chance but inhere knowledge and star configuration patterns at the period of construction, imply that the 'pyramids as tombs' theory is no longer sufficient and a broader determination of age, function and re-use of both pyramids and Giza is required . . .[32]

'This book which descended from the sky . . .'

We've seen that there are many passages in the Edfu Building Texts which tell us that those amongst the 'gods' of the Early Primeval Age who survived the flood that destroyed their former Homeland set about 'wandering' the world with the purpose of establishing new sacred domains in suitable locations. One passage names a specific location that some of these 'gods' found their way to, the first place they settled in Egypt. This turns out not to have been Edfu in Upper (southern) Egypt but rather the city that the Greeks later came to know as Heracleopolis,[33] which is located in Lower (northern) Egypt and which the Egyptians themselves named *Henen-nesut*, meaning 'the house of the royal child'. Archaeologists do not know when *Henen-nesut* was established, but a reference to it on the Palermo Stone (so-called because it is now kept in the Archaeological Museum of the city of Palermo in Italy) sheds some light on the matter. An ancient fragment of inscribed diorite, the Palermo Stone provides information (dismissed as 'mythological' by Egyptologists) of some 120 pre-dynastic kings said to have ruled in Egypt prior to 3000 BC. But it also gives details of the early Dynastic period which Egyptologists accept as 'historical'. An entry on the Stone dating to the reign of Den, the second King of the First Dynasty, suggests strongly that the origins of Heracleopolis/*Henen-nesut* go very far back into the pre-dynastic period.[34]

But *Henen-nesut* is just where the trail begins, because it turns out it was closely associated with the ancient religious centre of Memphis, *Inbu-Hedj* (later *Mn-nfr*), which stands about 60 miles (100 kilometres) further north and was, according to legend, established by Menes, the first king of the First Dynasty – although again its origins are likely to be far earlier. It is therefore of interest, as Eve Reymond, the translator of the Edfu Building Texts, observes, that:

> It is impossible to read the principal Edfu records and not be struck by the very pronounced Memphite background and tone that is still preserved in them.[35]

In her view the Edfu texts 'preserve the memory of a pre-dynastic religious centre which once existed near Memphis' – a centre which 'the Egyptians looked on as the homeland of the Egyptian temple.'[36] Note, she is not saying 'which once existed *in* Henen-nesut', nor even '*in* Memphis' itself, but rather '*near* Memphis'. In short, the location is a bit of a mystery; Reymond supposes that archaeology has not yet identified it.[37] But wherever it was, it was believed to be a place carefully selected by the gods for the foundation of the first of the new generation of temples dedicated to the god Horus – the essential opening gambit in the long-term project to recreate the destroyed former world.[38] A text on the inner face of the enclosure wall at Edfu was recognised as an important clue by Reymond in her own search for the mystery location, since it tells us that the primordial Temple of Horus was:

> built at the dictates of the ancestors according to what was written in this book which descended from the sky to the north of Memphis.[39]

An extensive burial ground for the ancient kings of Memphis, known to Egyptologists as the 'Memphite Necropolis', rose to particular prominence during the Fourth Dynasty, 2613 BC to 2492 BC, when, according to orthodox chronology, both the Great Pyramid and the Great Sphinx are supposed to have been built. The pyramid fields of Dhashur, Saqqara and Giza were all integral parts of the Necropolis – so in theory all might be candidates.[40] But at Giza, as we've seen, the Sphinx models the constellation of Leo in 10,500 BC, the three pyramids model the Belt of Orion in the same epoch, and the four shafts of the Great

Pyramid lock on to specific stars in the later epoch of 2500 BC. Far more obviously than Dhashur and Saqqara, therefore, it seems to me that Giza absolutely merits description as 'book which descended from the sky' – a book written with the 'pen' of megalithic architecture in the 'script' of precession.

There is something else. The god Horus, for whom the primordial temple was built, is a complex figure who manifests in many different symbolic forms, notably the falcon; indeed, an imposing granite statue of Horus the Falcon stands in the forecourt at the Temple of Edfu to this day. Horus was likewise frequently depicted as a man with the head of a falcon – a classic therianthrope in other words, like the Apkallu sages of Mesopotamia. But Horus had another prominent avatar and that was as a lion.[41] Moreover this Horus lion was sometimes depicted as a therianthrope with a human head and there is a specific inscription in the Edfu Temple which tells us that:

> Horus of Edfu transformed himself into a lion which had the face of a man . . .[42]

Mystery of the Sphinx

Given the connection that the Edfu texts draw with the Giza area, and with that mysterious 'book descended from the sky', it is therefore impossible to ignore the fact that the Ancient Egyptians closely identified Horus with the Great Sphinx of Giza. In this capacity the lion-bodied (and probably once lion-headed) Sphinx was known both as *Hor-em-Akhet* – 'Horus in the Horizon' – and also as *Horakhti* which, with a subtle difference of emphasis, means 'Horus *of* the Horizon'.[43]

However, there is a very odd thing about the Sphinx. With the exception of Dr Rainer Stadelmann, who believes that it was the work of the Fourth Dynasty Pharaoh Khufu, all other modern Egyptologists are united in the opinion that the Sphinx was made by Khufu's son Khafre.[44] I use the word 'opinion' deliberately, because it is important to be clear at the outset that we are not dealing here with an established empirical 'fact' about the Sphinx, but rather with a received body of Egyptological conjecture which has gradually, through lack of opposition, begun to be treated as though it were a proven fact. 'As very often in our discipline, old and seemingly certain statements rest forever without further verification,' comments Dr Stadelmann,[45] who should know what he's talking about since he was Director of the German Archaeological Institute in Cairo from 1989 to 1998.

When we confine ourselves to the facts about the Sphinx rather than the opinions of Egyptologists, the first thing we discover is that no inscriptions have survived from the Old Kingdom which refer to this stupendous and imposing monument. Even the great Egyptologist Selim Hassan, who conducted extensive excavations at Giza in the 1930s, was therefore obliged to admit:

> As to the exact age of the Sphinx, and to whom we should attribute its erection, no definite facts are known, and we have not one single contemporary inscription to enlighten us on this point.[46]

Neither, for that matter, are there any inscriptions from the First Intermediate Period, or from the Middle Kingdom, or from the Second Intermediate Period. Indeed, it is not until we come to the New Kingdom, roughly 1550 BC onwards, supposedly about a thousand years *after* it was carved out of the bedrock of the Giza plateau, that the pharaohs of Ancient Egypt suddenly start talking about the Sphinx.

What Selim Hassan rightly describes as 'the earliest authentic opinion' is given by Amenhotep II (1427-1401 BC) who built a small temple that can still be seen today on the north side of the Sphinx enclosure.[47] There on a limestone stela, this New Kingdom pharaoh refers to the Sphinx under the names *Hor-em-Akhet* and *Horakhti*,[48] and also makes a direct reference to the Giza pyramids which – to the annoyance of Egyptologists – he does not ascribe to his Fourth Dynasty predecessors Khufu, Khafre and Menkaure, but rather nominates as 'the Pyramids of *Hor-em-akhet*'.[49] The clear implication is that in Amenhotep's time – far closer to the Fourth Dynasty than our own – there existed no historical archives, nor even any tradition, that linked the pyramids with the three pharaohs whom modern Egyptologists now insist were their builders. On the contrary, as Selim Hassan explains, the use of the epithet 'Pyramids of *Hor-em-Akhet*' suggests (since *Hor-em-Akhet* was one of the names by which the Sphinx was known) that Amenhotep:

considered the Sphinx to be older than the Pyramids.[50]

Chronologically, the next inscription referring to the Sphinx occurs on the famous 'Dream Stela' of Thutmosis IV. The story goes that before he ascended to the throne the future pharaoh was out hunting one day around Giza where the Sphinx lay forgotten, buried up to its neck in sand. Thutmosis took a siesta in the shade of the giant head at which point:

A vision of sleep seized him at the hour when the sun was in the zenith, and he found the majesty of this revered god speaking with his own mouth, as a father speaks with his son, saying: 'Behold thou me! See thou me my son Thutmosis! I am . . . Hor-em-Akhet . . . who will give thee my kingdom on earth' . . .[51]

However, there was a condition for, the Sphinx said, 'the sand of this desert upon which I am has reached me . . . My manner is as if I were ailing in my limbs . . . Thou shalt be to me a protector . . .'[52]

To cut a long story short, Thutmosis understood that if he were to clear the Sphinx of sand and restore it to its former glory he would become pharaoh. Accordingly he did as he was instructed and, when the restoration was complete, and the throne was his as prophesied, he erected the Dream Stela in commemoration.

If you visit the site today you can still see the huge stela – it's nearly 12 feet high and more than 7 feet wide – standing between the paws of the Sphinx directly in front of the monument's chest, but much of the original inscription, from the thirteenth line onwards, has flaked away. In the 1830s, however, a cast was taken of it, at which time some – though unfortunately not all – of the thirteenth line was still intact. There the single syllable Khaf (no longer present today) was noted and from this, as the American Egyptologist James Henry Breasted comments in his authoritative translation of the stela, many have been inclined to conclude that the Sphinx was the work of Khafre. Such a conclusion, Breasted adds dryly, 'does not follow'. He points out that there is in fact 'no trace of a cartouche' (the oval sign that normally enclosed royal names) on the copies and casts of the stela that were made in the nineteenth century – which suggests strongly that the syllable Khaf did not refer at all to the Fourth Dynasty Pharaoh Khafre.[53]

Moreover, as Selim Hassan later added, even if the cartouche had been there, we are not at liberty to conclude from the damaged line that Khafre made the Sphinx. At the most it would tell us that 'Thutmosis in some way connected the Sphinx with Khafre'.[54] Even Gaston Maspero, who was the Director of the Department of Antiquities at the Cairo Museum in the late nineteenth century, and who did believe the cartouche had once been present, saw no reason to deduce from such flimsy evidence that the Sphinx was Khafre's work. On the contrary, his preferred interpretation was that the purpose of Thutmosis in this part of the inscription was to recognise a former renovation and clearance of the Sphinx undertaken by Khafre. 'Consequently,' Maspero wrote, 'we have here almost certain proof that the Sphinx was already buried in sand in the time of Khufu [Khafre's father] and his predecessors.' [55]

Maspero would later change his view, grudgingly stating that the Sphinx 'probably represents Khafre himself'[56]and thus falling in line with the growing consensus amongst Egyptologists of the twentieth century. His initial opinion that the monument was older than Khafre, and indeed had been buried in sand in the time of Khufu, had in part been based on information contained in yet another stela, the so-called Inventory Stela, discovered at Giza in the 1850s by the French archae-ologist, Auguste Mariette. The gist of the Inventory Stela, once also referred to as the Stela of Khufu's Daughter,[57] was that the Great Sphinx and the Valley Temple, as well as a number of other structures on the plateau, were already in existence long before Khufu came to the throne.[58]

What apparently 'debunked' it, however, and no doubt contributed to Maspero's change of mind, was firm evidence that the hieroglyphic writing system used in the inscription was not consistent with the style of the Fourth Dynasty, but belonged to a much more recent period – Selim Hassan suggests the Twenty-sixth Dynasty.[59] This interesting little stela has therefore subsequently come to be regarded as a work of fiction, most likely fabricated by a group of priests who wished to magnify the name of the goddess Isis (who was popular in the Twenty-sixth Dynasty, 664-525 BC) and thus of no value in our attempts to determine what happened at Giza nearly 2000 years earlier in the Fourth Dynasty – or perhaps long before.

That is certainly how things look when viewed through the prism of 'Egyptologic' – i.e. that special form of reasoning, with a built-in double standard, deployed only by Egyptologists. According to Egyptologic, if evidence supports established theories then that evidence will be accepted. But if evidence undermines established theories, then that evidence must be rejected. Thus Egyptology uses *entirely* circum-stantial and non-contemporary data to support its present claim that the Sphinx and its megalithic temples were the work of the Pharaoh Khafre of the Fourth Dynasty (as we've seen, Selim Hassan admits that 'we have not one single contemporary inscription' to enlighten us as to the exact age of the Sphinx). So the dating of the monument to the Fourth Dynasty – something that Egyptologists tout as a 'fact', that is taught as such in universities and that is widely disseminated by the media – rests entirely on its 'context' (the nearby pyramids and megalithic temples) and on that single syllable Khaf, which was once present on the Eighteenth Dynasty Dream Stela.

The flimsy case of Egyptology

As to context, even if the pyramids were exclusively the work of the Fourth Dynasty – which is called into question, as we've seen, by the surface luminescence dating of the pyramid attributed to Menkaure – we could still not safely deduce that the Sphinx is also Fourth Dynasty work. Indeed, it could be the case that the pyramids were built where they are precisely *because* the Sphinx was already there, bestowing an air of ancient sanctity on the site.

Neither do the megalithic temples really prove anything about the Sphinx since there is no evidence that unequivocally dates their own construction to the Fourth Dynasty. The most that can be said is that a black diorite statue of Khafre (now in the Cairo Museum) was found dumped upside down in a deep pit in the Valley Temple. However, this tells us only that Khafre at some point required his statue to be placed in the temple and that he therefore identified with the temple in some way, not that he built it.

Superficially more persuasive is the claim made by some Egyptologists that Khafre's name was found inscribed at the Valley Temple. On his 'Guardians' website, National Geographic Explorer in Residence Dr Zahi Hawass, the former Director of the Giza Plateau and Secretary General of Egypt's Supreme Council of Antiquities, has this to say about the Valley Temple:

> inscriptions in the building are around the entrance doorways; they list the King's names and titles, those of the goddess Bastet (north doorway) and those of Hathor (south doorway).[60]

Wikipedia, which is influential in shaping public perceptions of Giza, and which routinely labels non-mainstream approaches as 'pseudoscience', goes even further than Hawass when it says of the Valley Temple that:

> Blocks have been found showing the partial remains of an inscription with the Horus name of Khafre (*Weser-ib*).[61]

On closer examination, however, Wikipedia turns out to be misinformed. Stephen Quirke, Professor of Egyptian Archaeology at University College London, was kind enough to look into this for me when I raised it with him and in due course reported the results of his investigation. The partial inscription with the Horus name of Khafre does not in fact appear on blocks from the Valley Temple, but rather on blocks from an entirely different building at Giza.[62]

What, then, of Dr Hawass's statement about 'the King's names and titles'. It is clear, at any rate, what his source is because in the first (1947) edition of his classic study *The Pyramids of Egypt*, I.E.S. Edwards, formerly Keeper of Egyptian Antiquities at the British Museum, wrote several pages about the Valley Temple which, along with the rest of the Egyptological profession by this time, he identified as being the work of Khafre.[63] 'Around each doorway,' he stated:

is a band of hieroglyphic inscription giving the name and titles of the King; no other inscriptions or reliefs occur anywhere else in the building.[64]

That would seem to settle the matter were it not for the fact that many years later, when Edwards produced the definitive final edition of his book, he revised the above passage with important information that he did not present in 1947. 'Around each doorway,' we now read:

> was carved a band of hieroglyphic inscriptions giving the name and titles of the King, *but only the last words 'Beloved [of the goddess] Bastet' and 'Beloved [of the goddess] Hathor' are preserved.* No other inscriptions occur anywhere else in the building.[65]

Needless to say the words 'Beloved of Bastet' and 'Beloved of Hathor' do not, in isolation like this, prove that Khafre was the King referred to as being the 'beloved' of these deities. They could apply to anybody and therefore cannot legitimately be used to support the claim that the Valley Temple was the work of Khafre.

Is there anything else to support that claim? The obscure and eye-wateringly expensive *Encyclopaedia of the Archaeology of Ancient Egypt* contains an entry on the 'Khafre pyramid complex'. Written again by Zahi Hawass, the entry informs us that the Valley Temple:

> is identified with Khafre from inscriptions on granite casing blocks from the western end of the Valley Temple. Reliefs from this complex were discovered at el-Lisht, where they were used as fill for the pyramid of Amenemhat I (Twelfth Dynasty).[66]

Now this is really clutching at straws! Since they are miles away at el-Lisht, cannibalised as filler material for a later monarch's pyramid, the reality is that these blocks tell us nothing reliable at all about the Valley Temple. Perhaps they were taken from there, but then again, perhaps they came from somewhere else entirely.

Besides, nobody is claiming that any of the inscriptions were made on the limestone core masonry of the Valley Temple. All of them appear on 'granite casing blocks' and as we've seen, the granite casing blocks of the Valley Temple give every appearance of being a veneer that was applied long after the core limestone blocks were set in place – in some cases perhaps as early as 3640 BC and in others perhaps as late as 1190 BC. That Khafre may well have been one of several pharaohs who carried out restoration work on the Valley Temple during this long period, and that he commemorated his good deeds with an official inscription and some statues of himself – perhaps at the same time as he also appears to have carried out a restoration project on the Sphinx – does not mean that he was the original builder either of the Sphinx or the Temple.

So we are left, then, with that single syllable Khaf on the Eighteenth Dynasty Dream Stela, which modern Egyptologists (unlike their nineteenth century predecessors) have eagerly grasped as 'proof' that Khafre built the Sphinx. Needless to say the Eighteenth Dynasty and the Fourth Dynasty are not contemporary with one another. Moreover, there is a strong case to be made that even the Eighteenth Dynasty attribution of the stela is questionable. Breasted, for example, points to 'errors and striking irregularities in orthography' and to a number of other 'suspicious peculiarities' leading him to conclude that the inscription was not in fact the work of Thutmosis IV but was a 'late restoration' dating to between the Twenty-first Dynasty and the Twenty-sixth (Saitic) Dynasty.[67]

In other words, it is quite possible that the Dream Stela is as young as the Inventory Stela. Yet 'Egyptologic' requires the shaky evidence of the Khaf syllable on the former to be accepted as proof that Khafre made the Sphinx, whereas the several clear statements on the latter that absolutely contradict the attribution to Khafre are rejected as 'preposterous fictions'.

Dynamite revelations

Here are some extracts from the text of the Inventory Stela. Note before reading that all the pharaohs of Egypt were regarded as incarnations of the god Horus[68] and the name Horus was therefore routinely included in their titles. Each King also had a 'Horus name', which in Khufu's case was Mezer:[69]

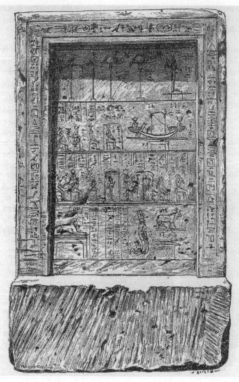

Figure 39: The Inventory Stela. The gist of the inscriptions, which Egyptologists reject, is that the Great Sphinx and the Valley Temple, as well as a number of other structures on the Giza plateau, were already in existence long before Khufu came to the throne.

Live Horus, the Mezer, the King of Upper and Lower Egypt, Khufu, given life. He found the House of Isis, Mistress of the Pyramid, by the side of cavity of the Sphinx, on the north-west of the House of Osiris, Lord of Rostau . . . The plans of the Image of Hor-em-akhet were brought in order to bring to revision the sayings of the disposition of the Image . . . He restored the statue all covered in painting . . . He made to quarry the hind part of the nemes headdress, which was lacking, from gilded stone, and which had a length of about 7 ells (3.7 metres). He came to make a tour, in order to see the thunderbolt, which stands in the Place of the Sycamore, so named because of a great sycamore, whose branches were struck when the Lord of Heaven descended upon the place of Hor-em-akhet . . . The figure of this God, being cut in stone, is solid, and will exist to eternity, having always its face regarding the East.[70]

The language of the Inventory Stela is obscure, but Selim Hassan's analysis brings some clarity. 'If we could believe its inscriptions,' he writes:

> we should have to credit Khufu with having repaired the Sphinx, apparently after it had been damaged by a thunderbolt. As a matter of fact, there may be a grain of truth in this story, for the tail of the *nemes* headdress of the Sphinx is certainly missing, and it is not a part, which, by reason of its shape and position, could be easily broken off, except by a direct blow from some heavy object, delivered with terrific force. There is actually to be seen on the back of the Sphinx the scar of this breakage, and traces of the old mortar with which it was repaired. This scar measures about 4 metres which accords with the measurements recorded on the stela . . . Therefore, it is perhaps likely that the Sphinx was struck by lightning, but there is not a particle of evidence to show that this accident happened in the reign of Khufu.[71]

Neither, however, is there any evidence to prove that the 'accident' to the Sphinx did *not* happen in the reign of Khufu. All we have is the Egyptological bias that it could not have happened then, because the Sphinx is supposed to be the work of Khafre, undertaken after Khufu's death, and therefore – obviously – should not have existed in Khufu's time.

The same goes for the second dynamite revelation of the Inventory Stela, namely the mention of 'the House of Osiris, Lord of Rostau'.[72] We can gather the location of this structure because 'the cavity of the Sphinx' is said to lie on its 'north-west'[73] – which means, to put things the other way round, that 'the House of Osiris, Lord of Rostau' is located immediately south-east of the Sphinx. The only structure which fits these co-ordinates is the Valley Temple which does indeed lie immediately south-east of the Sphinx. As with the references to the Sphinx itself, therefore, the testimony of the Inventory Stela is that the Valley Temple was not made by Khafre since it was already in existence in the time of his predecessor Khufu.

These, then, are the real reasons why the Inventory Stela has been rejected by Egyptologists as a preposterous fiction – rather, say, than as an inscription that preserves and transmits to a later age, using language and terminology suitable to that age, a much older but genuine tradition. Certainly the rejection cannot be because the Inventory Stela is not contemporary with the reign of Khufu, or because of its Twenty-sixth Dynasty 'orthography' – since such factors do not prevent Egyptologists from accepting the Dream Stela, which suffers from the same non-contemporaneity and the same 'striking irregularities in orthography'. In short, is it not obvious that the Inventory Stela has been rejected and ignored, while the Dream Stela has been accepted and embraced, because the former blows the established theory of Egyptian history completely out of the water, while the latter can be conveniently 'spun' to support the established theory?

A bolt from heaven and an ancient archive

Quite apart from its implications of a much older Sphinx, there are two other aspects of the Inventory Stela that merit further investigation.

The first is the information that the Sphinx had been damaged by a 'thunderbolt'. Selim Hassan is willing to accept there might be some truth to that, but we cannot be sure that a thunderbolt means a lightning strike as he assumes. The thunderbolt in question is said in the inscription still to have been present for Khufu to 'see' when he made his 'tour'. This would not be the case with lightning, which would leave damage but not a physical object that could be viewed. On the other hand a meteorite, after striking and damaging the Sphinx, would have been there, on the spot, for inspection by the King – and descending in fire from the sky amidst awesome noise, burning a great old tree in its passage, a meteorite might easily be described as a thunderbolt (indeed in a number of cultures that was exactly how meteorites were described).[74]

Equally intriguing is the Inventory Stela's statement that 'the plans of the Image of Hor-em-akhet' – i.e. of the Sphinx – were brought to the site by Khufu, presumably for reference purposes while the repair of the monument was undertaken. This very obviously implies the existence of an ancient 'archive' pertaining to Giza, perhaps a 'Hall of Records' reminiscent of the lost records in the temple library at Edfu from which we know the Building Texts were extracted.

These, as we've seen, were said to be the words of the Seven Sages, taken down in writing by no lesser personage than the wisdom god Thoth himself. Reymond even suggests that there may once have existed a *Sacred Book of the Early Primeval Age of the Gods*, in which the whole 'divine' plan in Egypt was set out.[75] And the indications are, she says, that this was linked to a second ancient book, *The Specifications of the Mounds of the Early Primeval Age*, which was believed to contain records not only of all the lesser 'mounds' and the temples that would ultimately be built upon them as part of the project to bring about the rebirth of the destroyed world of the 'gods', but also of the Great Primeval Mound itself.[76]

Unfortunately nothing more is known about either of these lost 'books' than the few very brief and tantalizing references to them at Edfu. Nonetheless, as I suggested earlier, there is every possibility that this Great Primeval Mound, where the time of the present age of the earth supposedly began, was the rocky hill at Giza around which the Great Pyramid would in due course be built. There is, too, an extraordinary text, preserved on papyrus from Egypt's Middle Kingdom, which speaks of a search for 'the secret chambers of the sanctuary of Thoth' – secret chambers that Khufu wished to 'copy' for his temple.

A deep and ancient mystery that we'll explore in the next chapter lies concealed in these strange references.

Chapter 11
The Books of Thoth

A quick summary.

The Edfu Building Texts speak of the 'Homeland of the Primeval Ones' – an island, the location of which is never specified – that was destroyed by an 'enemy', described as a 'serpent', 'the Great Leaping One'. The 'serpent's' assault caused a flood that inundated this 'primeval world of the gods', killing the majority of its 'divine' inhabitants. A few of them, however, escaped the disaster and fled the scene in boats to wander the earth. Their purpose in so doing was to identify suitable sites where they might set in motion a sacred design to bring about

> the resurrection of the former world of the gods . . . The re-creation of a destroyed world.

And all of these events took place in the 'early primeval age' – a very, very long time ago, so long ago that they would have passed beyond human remembering if great efforts had not been made to preserve them. 'In our temples,' the Egyptian priests of Sais reportedly told Solon:

> we have preserved from earliest times a written record of any great or splendid achievement or notable event which has come to our ears.[1]

This was the case, too, at Edfu where Reymond's detailed study reveals that a vast and extensive archive once existed, from which the extracts were taken that the priests carved into the temple walls and that thus still survive. It is by following the trail of clues in these extracts, as we did in the last chapter, that we have arrived at the Great Sphinx, perhaps the very 'lion which had the face of a man' that Horus was said in the Edfu texts to have transformed himself into.

In this context, the reference in the Inventory Stela to Khufu having access to plans of the Sphinx, which he refers to when he 'restores the statue', is suggestive of the existence of an ancient archive of Giza – perhaps an archive dating back to the remote age when the site was founded by the 'gods' with distinctive astronomical characteristics that would later allow the whole complex to be described as a 'book which descended from the sky'. Does this 'book' refer to the constellation of Leo as it appeared at dawn on the spring equinox in the epoch of 10,500 BC – a constellation that 'descended from the sky' at Giza in the form of the Great Sphinx? And did the three belt stars of the constellation of Orion as they looked in that distant epoch 'descend from the sky' at Giza in the form of the ground plans of the three great pyramids?

We've seen that the Sphinx, or at any rate large parts of it, could very well have been carved in the epoch of 10,500 BC. The pyramids were certainly *completed* much later, but it's my belief that they were built over pre-existing structures dating back to the time of the gods – gods whom the Edfu texts tell us quite explicitly were 'capable of uniting with the sky'.[2] These pre-existing structures would, of course, have been hidden when they were replaced by the pyramids,[3] amongst them the original natural hill that anchors the whole plan and which was later incorporated into the structure of the Great Pyramid.

Since the Edfu texts envisage the work of the gods as the re-creation in other lands of their lost world, and since the key feature of that lost homeland was 'a primeval temple that was erected on a low mound',[4] it becomes all the more likely they would have sought to reproduce these features at Giza. At any rate, no lesser authority than Professor I.E.S. Edwards, formerly Keeper of Egyptian Antiquities at the British Museum, was of the view that the natural hill, now incorporated within the Great Pyramid, was indeed the Great Primeval Mound that is referred to so often in Ancient Egyptian texts[5] – a mound, we now understand, that drew its sanctity from its predecessor that had once stood in the lost world of the gods. That mound, Reymond tells us, formed 'the original nucleus of the world of the gods in the primeval age',[6] so it follows that the rocky mound at the heart of the Great Pyramid, and later the Great Pyramid itself, served the same function in the project to resurrect that lost world in Egypt.

The Inventory Stela is by no means the only testimony to the existence of ancient plans connected with that project. We've seen in the Edfu texts how these plans were part of an archive believed to have been set down in writing by the wisdom god Thoth 'according to the words of the Sages',[7] so it is not surprising that the Ancient Egyptians of later times became obsessed with 'the books of Thoth', which they appear to have lost access to and which came to be regarded as the fount of all knowledge. A number of papyri have survived documenting searches for the books of Thoth, and these searches, not surprisingly, are always said to have taken place in the vicinity of Giza and the Memphite necropolis.

There is, for example, the story of Setnau-Khaem-Uast, a son of Rameses II, one of the great pharaohs of the thirteenth century BC. Informed that a 'book written by Thoth himself' lay concealed in an ancient tomb near Giza:

> Setnau went there with his brother and passed three days and nights seeking for the tomb . . . and on the third day they found it [and] . . . went down to the place where the book was. When the two brothers came into the tomb they found it to be brilliantly lit by the light which came forth from the book.[8]

There seems to be a hint of an ancient technology here, reminiscent of Yima's underground Vara, which 'glowed with its own light', or of the mysterious illumination of Noah's Ark, described in Chapter Seven. What sound like the artifices of a lost technology are also mentioned in Arab traditions concerning Giza. The Egyptian historian Ibn Abd El Hakem believed that the pyramids were built as places of safekeeping for antediluvian knowledge, prominently including archives of books containing:

The profound sciences, and the names of drugs and their uses and hurts, and the science of astrology, and arithmetic and geometry and medicine . . . [and] everything that is and shall be from the beginning to the end of time . . .[9]

Hakem, who lived in the ninth century AD, could have known nothing of advanced metallurgy or plastics, yet he stated that amongst the treasures from the time before the flood that were hidden away in the bowels of the pyramids were:

arms which did not rust, and glass which might be bent but not broken.[10]

He likewise described machines that guarded these antediluvian remnants including:

an idol of black agate sitting upon a throne with a lance. His eyes were open and shining. When anyone looked upon him, he heard on one side of him a voice which took away his sense, so that he fell prostrate upon his face, and did not cease until he died.[11]

A second machine also took the form of a statue:

He who looked towards it was drawn by the statue until he stuck to it, and could not be separated from it until such time as he died.[12]

Returning to the traditions of the Ancient Egyptians themselves, we have a text from the Westcar Papyrus, which dates to the Middle Kingdom, around 1650 BC, but was copied from an older document now lost.[13] The text makes reference to a 'building called "Inventory",' located in the sacred city that the Ancient Egyptians knew as *Innu*, that the Bible calls *On*, and that the Greeks later made famous under the name of Heliopolis – the 'City of the Sun' – eleven miles north-east of Giza. According to the papyrus 'a chest of flint' was stored in Heliopolis containing a mysterious document that Pharaoh Khufu himself is reported to have 'spent much time searching for' – a document that recorded 'the number of the secret chambers of the sanctuary of Thoth' which Khufu wished 'to copy for his temple'.[14]

What are we dealing with here?

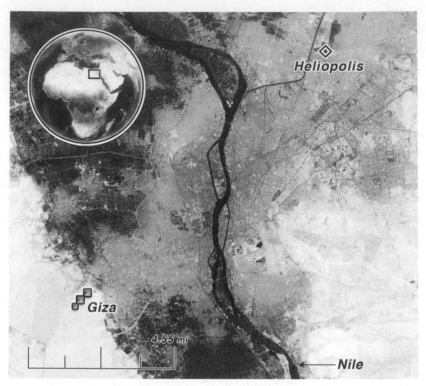

Figure 40: Heliopolis stands about eleven miles north-east of the pyramids of Giza. Other than an obelisk in what is now the Cairo suburb of El Matariya almost nothing remains today of the ancient 'City of the Sun'

I.E.S. Edwards points out that Heliopolis, the site of the 'Inventory Building', had been a centre of astronomical science closely connected to Giza since time immemorial, and that the title of the high priest of that city was 'Chief of the Astronomers'.[15] To this the Egyptologist F.W. Green adds that the 'Inventory Building' appears to have been a 'chart room' at Heliopolis 'or perhaps a "drawing room" where plans were made and stored.'[16] Similarly, Sir Alan H. Gardiner argues that 'the room in question must have been an archive' and that Khufu 'was seeking for details concerning the secret chambers of the primeval sanctuary of Thoth.'[17]

So once again we are confronted by a report that Khufu sought out and consulted ancient documents to guide his works at Giza – whether to restore the Sphinx to its original appearance, as we are told in the Inventory Stela, or to build his 'temple' in the correct way, incorporating an ancient design as the Westcar Papyrus suggests. Such traditions, in my view, further strengthen the notion that whatever Khufu and the other pharaohs of the Fourth Dynasty were doing at Giza was more of the order of the fulfilment and completion of plans they had inherited from the time of the gods – antediluvian plans, in other words – than the implementation of some novel scheme of their own. They were, in short, playing their part in the resurrection of the former world of the gods. Moreover, the surface luminescence dating results reported in Chapter Ten, when taken together with the geological arguments about the age of the Sphinx and its temples, invite us to consider that this process had originated in the flood epoch of 10,500 BC, had then lain practically dormant for many millennia during which the ancient knowledge and archives were maintained by initiates in something like a monastery, and then got underway again perhaps as early as the fourth millennium BC with a gradual build-up to its completion and fulfilment in the epoch of 2500 BC.

The existence of such a college of initiates is signalled clearly in the Edfu texts which speak of the long-term mission of:

the Builder Gods, who fashioned in the primeval time, the Lords of the Light . . . the Ghosts, the Ancestors . . . who raised the seed for gods and men . . . the Senior Ones who came into being at the beginning, who illumined this land when they came forth unitedly.[18]

The Edfu texts do not claim that these beings were immortal. After their deaths, we are told, the next generation 'came to their graves to perform the funerary rights on their behalf'[19] and then took their places. In this way, through an unbroken chain of initiation and transmission of knowledge, the 'Builder Gods', the 'Sages', the 'Ghosts', the 'Lords of the Light', the 'Shining Ones' described in the Edfu texts were able to renew themselves constantly, like the mythical phoenix

– thus passing down to the future traditions and wisdoms stemming from a previous epoch of the earth.

Another name for these initiates, and an appropriate one given the importance of Horus at Edfu, was the *Shemsu Hor*, the 'Followers of Horus'.[20] Under this name they were particularly closely associated with Heliopolis/*Innu*, the sacred city where the records of the secret chambers of the sanctuary of Thoth were kept. The reader will recall that at Edfu it was the Seven Sages who specified the plans and designs that were to be used for all future temples throughout the length and breadth of Egypt, so it is interesting that at Dendera, a little to the north of Edfu, inscriptions tell us that the 'great plan' used by its architects was 'recorded in ancient writings handed down from the Followers of Horus'.[21] Identical in all respects to the 'Sages' and the 'Builder Gods' these Followers of Horus were said to have carried with them a 'knowledge of the divine origins' of Egypt[22] and of the divine purpose of this land, 'which once was holy and wherein, alone, in reward for her devotion, the gods deigned to sojourn upon earth'.[23]

Stones fallen from heaven

The nexus interlinking the Sages of the Edfu texts with Giza, Heliopolis, and the Followers of Horus offers a number of clues that will enable us to take this inquiry forward. Amongst these, of the first importance, is the fact that Heliopolis, an uninteresting suburb of Cairo today, was once the site of the Temple of the Phoenix – known in Ancient Egypt as the *Bennu* bird – that famous symbol of resurrection and rebirth.[24] In this temple, often referred to as the 'Mansion of the Phoenix', was kept a mysterious object, long since lost to history, a 'stone' called the *Benben* (a word closely linked etymologically to *Bennu*[25]) said to have fallen from heaven and depicted as the seed, the sperm, of Ra-Atum, the Father of the Gods. In the Ancient Egyptian language the determinative of the word Benben, as one expert explains:

> shows a tapering, somewhat conical shape for the Benben stone which became stylised for use in architecture as a small pyramid, the pyramidion; covered in gold foil it was held aloft by the long

shaft of the obelisk and shone in the rays of the sun, whom the obelisks glorified.[26]

Likewise the capstone of every pyramid was also referred to as its Benben[27] – an example in excellent condition has survived from the pyramid of the Twelfth Dynasty Pharaoh Amenemhat III and can be seen in the Cairo Museum.

Numerous theories have been put forward as to where the concept of the Benben came from, but the most compelling, in my view, is the work of my friend and colleague Robert Bauval that first appeared in the scholarly journal *Discussions in Egyptology* in 1989 under the title 'Investigation on the Origins of the Benben Stone: Was it an Iron Meteorite?' Similar to many other cases of the worship of meteorites by ancient peoples, Robert argued:

> it is likely that the Benben stone once worshipped in the Mansion of the Phoenix was a meteorite. Its conical shape . . . is very suggestive of an oriented iron meteorite, possibly a mass within the 1-15 ton range. Such objects fallen from heaven were generally representative of 'fallen stars' and likely provided the Egyptian clergy with a tangible star object, a 'seed' of Ra-Atum.[28]

A linked possibility was considered by the Egyptologist R.T. Rundle Clark in 1949 in a paper entitled 'The Origin of the Phoenix' for the *University of Birmingham Historical Journal*. He drew attention to the earliest surviving mention of the Bennu bird, which is found in the *Pyramid Texts* (Old Kingdom, Fifth and Sixth Dynasties) and reads as follows:

> Thou [the god Ra-Atum is addressed] did shine upon the *Benben* Stone in the House of the *Bennu* bird in Heliopolis.[29]

But curiously, the Benben stone, always shown in later texts as a geometrical pyramidion,[30] is depicted in the Pyramid Texts as a rough stone with slightly curved sides. 'This is an important fact,' observed Rundle Clark, 'since it shows that the pyramids were not exact copies of the original benben stone in Heliopolis . . . One can assume that the Benben stone became a pyramidion during the Old Empire, but whether influenced by the actual developed contour of the Fourth Dynasty pyramids cannot be determined.[31]

He went on to note something else that caught my attention:

> The form of the Benben stone in [the Pyramid Texts] is that of an omphalos or *betyl*, the umbilical stone which is so widespread in the early religion of Asia . . . It is a lesson of this text . . . that the Benben stone is a *betyl*-like object and that it is modified into a pyramidion by the Fourth Dynasty.[32]

What Rundle Clark did not appear to realise in his 1949 paper, and that strongly reinforces Robert Bauval's later argument, is that *betyls*, wherever they were worshipped, were nothing more nor less than *meteorites* – although often they were stony rather than iron meteorites. I had occasion to investigate this issue in some depth in the 1980s when I was researching my book *The Sign and The Seal* with specific reference to the two tablets of the Ten Commandments said to be contained within the Ark of the Covenant.[33]

Biblical scholar Menahem Haran, author of the authoritative *Temples and Temple Service in Ancient Israel*, argues persuasively that 'the Ark held not two tables of the law but . . . a meteorite from Mount Sinai.'[34] As such the ancient worship of the Ark and its contents fits in with a wider tradition, distributed across the whole of the Near and Middle East, of veneration of 'stones that fell from heaven'.[35]

An example that has survived into the modern world is the special reverence accorded by Muslims to the sacred Black Stone built into a corner of the wall of the *Ka'aba* in Mecca. Touched by every pilgrim making the *Haj* to the holy site, this stone was declared by the Prophet Muhammad to have fallen from heaven to earth where it was first given to Adam to absorb his sins after his expulsion from the Garden of Eden; later it was presented by the angel Gabriel to Abraham, the Hebrew Patriarch; finally it became the cornerstone of the *Ka'aba* – the 'beating heart' of the Islamic world.[36]

Geologists attribute a meteoric origin to the Black Stone.[37] Likewise the *betyls* – sacred stones – that some pre-Islamic Arab tribes carried on their desert wanderings were meteorites, and a direct line of cultural transmission is recognised linking these *betyls* (which were often placed in portable shrines) with the Black Stone of the *Ka'aba* and with the stone 'tablets of the law' contained within the Ark. In Europe *betyls* were also known and were called *lapis betilis*, a name:

> stemming from Semitic origins and taken over at a late date by the Greeks and Romans for sacred stones that were assumed to possess a divine life, stones with a soul [that were used] for divers superstitions, for magic and for fortune-telling. They were meteoric stones fallen from the sky.[38]

With all this in mind, the special interest of Khufu in the 'thunderbolt' mentioned in the Inventory Stela takes on a new significance. As the reader will recall, the inscription speaks of the 'Lord of Heaven' – an epithet for Ra-Atum – 'descending' on the Sphinx and inflicting the damage that Khufu would later repair according to the ancient 'plans' to which he had access. For such a thunderbolt to be merely a lightning strike, as Selim Hassan suggests, makes no sense since the Inventory Stela tells us very clearly that Khufu visited the site 'in order to *see* the thunderbolt'.

In short, an object that had fallen from the sky, and that could reasonably be described as the result of the Lord of Heaven 'descending' on the Sphinx, must still have been physically present there. A meteorite satisfies this context but it could not, of course have been *the* Benben kept at Heliopolis – for the Mansion of the Phoenix and the Benben already existed in Khufu's time.[39] The Pharaoh's eagerness to 'see the thunderbolt' does, however, testify to the special reverence that was accorded to this class of objects, and it is natural to wonder what specific event that reverence goes back to – and how far it goes back.

Could it, for example, go back all the way to the time memorialised in the Edfu texts – the time when the island of the gods was destroyed in the cataclysmic flood caused by the assault of the 'enemy serpent', so evocatively described as the 'Great Leaping One'?

Before attempting to answer that question, let's consider the Benben stone, and the Bennu bird with which it is associated, a little more closely.

The flight of the Phoenix

R.T. Rundle Clark, who made an in-depth study of the Bennu–Phoenix, reports that the Ancient Egyptians believed in a 'vital essence' – *Hike* – that had been brought to their land:

> from a distant, magical source. The latter was 'the Isle of Fire' – the place of everlasting light beyond the limits of the world, where the gods were born or revived and whence they were sent into the world. The Phoenix is the chief messenger from this inaccessible land of divinity. A Coffin Text makes the victorious soul say: 'I came from the Isle of Fire, having filled my body with *Hike*, like that bird who [came and] filled the world with that which it had not known'.[40]

So the Phoenix came from far away, Rundle Clark concludes, 'bringing the message of light and life to a world wrapped in the helplessness of primeval night. Its flight is the width of the world, "over oceans, seas and rivers", to land at last in Heliopolis, the symbolic centre of the earth where it will announce a new age.'[41]

There is much in this summary that is evocative of the Edfu texts – the far-off island from which the gods are sent out, the return of the light after an episode of primeval darkness, and an arrival at Heliopolis where a new age is set in motion. Indeed the Phoenix might almost be said to symbolise the mission of those 'gods' who fled their drowned homeland with a long-term plan to bring about the rebirth and renewal of the former world.

But the symbolic crossovers go deeper than this and become more complex. The Phoenix, remember, is closely associated not just with light but also with fire. Thus Lactantius writing in the fourth century AD tells us that the Phoenix:

> bathes in holy waters and feeds on living spray. After a thousand years . . . it builds a nest as a sepulchre, supplied with various rich juices and odours. As it sits on the nest its body grows hot enough to produce flames which in turn burn the body to ashes

destined to produce a milky white worm; the latter falls asleep and then forms into an egg, eventually to sprout forth as a bird from the broken shell. After taking nourishment it rolls the ashes into a ball enclosed in myrrh and frankincense, which the new-born bird transports to an altar in the city of Heliopolis.[42]

This theme of fire and of regeneration and new life emerging from a fiery death, also crops up in ancient Iran where Yima built his Vara, and where the Phoenix was called the *Simorgh*. As folklorist E.V.A. Kenealy explains, the accounts of the *Simorgh* decisively establish:

> that the death and revival of the Phoenix exhibit the successive destruction and reproduction of the world, which many believed to be effected by the agency of a fiery deluge.[43]

Different lengthy periods – 1000 years, 500 years, 540 years, 7006 years – are given for the life of the Phoenix before it dies in fire and then renews itself.[44] There is, however, a strong and very specific tradition, relayed, for example, by Solinus in the early third century AD, which sets the period of the Phoenix at what seems to be a completely arbitrary and bizarre number – 12,954 years.[45] But further investigation reveals that 'the period of the Phoenix's return was thought to correspond to the Great Year'[46] and the 'Great Year', we already know, is an ancient concept linked to the Precession of the Equinoxes with its twelve 'Great Months' (one for the sun's passage through each house of the zodiac) of 2,160 years each – thus 12 x 2,160 = 25,920 years. That figure of 25,920 years is in turn, of course, very close to twice 12,954 years (2 x 12,954 = 25,908 years) – too close to be a coincidence, in my opinion, especially when we remember that Cicero in his *Hortensius* specifically linked the Great Year to the number 12,954.[47]

The figure of 540 years given in other sources for the period of the Phoenix also turns out to be derived from the Great Year as Giorgo de Santillana and Hertha von Dechend demonstrated in *Hamlet's Mill*, their masterly study of precessional knowledge transmitted through myth. As we saw in Chapter Ten, the heartbeat of the precessional cycle is the number 72 – the number of years required for one degree of precession. We then add 36 (half of 72) to the number 72 to get 108; next we half 108 to get 54 and, finally, multiply 54 by 10 to get 540. I went into all this in great detail in *Fingerprints of the Gods* twenty years ago and refer the reader to that book for a full exposition of these precessional numbers,[48] which are found in ancient myths and traditions from all around the world and which Santillana and von Dechend long ago demonstrated are proof of advanced astronomical knowledge in the deepest antiquity – knowledge that they attributed to some as yet unidentified and 'almost unbelievable' ancestor civilization.[49]

What is particularly intriguing is how often ancient authorities connect the passage of the Great Year, which we now see to be linked to the period of the Phoenix, to a 'world conflagration' and a 'world flood' – not necessarily as the cause of those cataclysms, but as a timer that records and predicts them.[50] Confronted by such material, despite all the oddities and contradictions it has been weighed down with during the passage of several millennia, I am forcibly reminded of the Younger Dryas comet and the conflagration and global flood that it brought in its wake – the latter caused by the catastrophic collapse of large segments of the North American and northern European ice caps as they were hit by multiple large fragments, the former caused by superheated ejecta setting off forest fires across the minimum 50 million square kilometres of the earth's surface that were directly affected.

What goes around comes around

Suppose you wished to pass a message to the future, and not just the near future but the very distant future? You would be unwise to entrust it to writing, because you could not be certain that any civilization 12,000 years from now would be able to decipher your script. Besides, even if the script could be deciphered, the written document on which you had placed your message might not survive the ravages of time. If you were really determined to be understood by some distant future generation, you might therefore do better to devise your message using gigantic architectural monuments that 'time itself would fear' – monuments like the pyramids and the Great Sphinx of Giza – and to associate those monuments with a universal language such as the slow precessional changes in the sky that any astronomically literate culture would be able to read.

Ideally, also, your message should be a simple one.

We saw in Chapter Ten how the Giza-Heliopolis-Memphis area perfectly fits the bill as one of the new sacred domains that the Edfu texts tell us were established at various locations by the wandering 'companies' of gods seeking to bring about the resurrection of the former world destroyed in the flood. It is, moreover, a domain that fully justifies the description of 'a book descended from the sky'. And when we 'read' that book, written in the 'script' of precession with the 'pen' of megalithic architecture, it compels us to look at the *epoch* of 10,500 BC – not an exact date, because the precessional 'clock' gives indications that are too general to allow us to specify 'seconds' or even 'minutes', but quite definitely to the epoch of 10,500 BC, i.e. about 12,500 years ago. The same general astronomical configurations that are symbolised on the ground by the great monuments of Giza would have held true for the best part of 500 years before 10,500 BC and for about 1000 years afterwards.

In other words, as we have seen, the 'message' of the monuments exactly encapsulates the cataclysmic episode of the Younger Dryas which began suddenly and shockingly with the impacts of multiple fragments of a giant comet around 10,800 BC, i.e. around 12,800 years ago, and which ended equally suddenly – we do not yet know why – around 9600 BC, i.e. around 11,600 years ago. The most likely explanation is that the earth interacted again in 9600 BC with the debris stream of the same fragmenting comet that had caused the Younger Dryas to start in 10,800 BC. On the second occasion, however, the effects of the impacts were global warming rather than global cooling.

With comets, as with the mythical Phoenix, what goes around comes around.

Since they are in orbit, they return to our skies at cyclic intervals – some as short at 3.3 years (like Comet Encke for example), some longer than 4,000 years (such as Comet Hale-Bopp), some even running into tens of thousands of years.

Like the mythical Phoenix, also, comets do literally undergo a process of 'renewal' – indeed 'rebirth' – on each appearance in our skies. This is because comet nuclei are usually inert and utterly dark while travelling through deep space, producing no characteristic glowing 'coma' and sparkling 'tail'. However, as a comet approaches the sun (and thus also the earth) the solar rays cause volatile materials buried in its interior to burst into boiling, seething activity, producing jets of gas – scientists call the process 'outgassing' – and shedding millions of tons of exceptionally fine dust and debris to form the coma and tail.

Last but not least, outgassing comets, like the Phoenix, do have the appearance of being consumed in flames. Moreover, the collision of large cometary fragments with the earth itself, as the scientists studying the Younger Dryas impact event of 12,800 years ago have so graphically indicated, can be expected to result in conflagrations on a continent-wide scale followed, if impacts occur on ice sheets, by global flooding.

It is possible, indeed highly probable, that we are not yet done with the comet that changed the face of the earth between 10,800 BC and 9600 BC. To be quite clear, as we will see in Chapter Nineteen, some suspect that 'the return of the Phoenix' will take place in our own time – indeed by or before the year 2040 – and there is a danger that one of the objects in its debris stream may be as much as 30 kilometres in diameter. A collision with such a large cometary fragment would, at the very least, mean the end of civilization as we know it, and perhaps even the end of all human life on this planet. Its consequences would be orders of magnitude more devastating than the Younger Dryas impacts 12,800 years ago that left us as a species with amnesia, obliged to begin again like children with no memory of what went before.

Or rather with *almost* no memory.

Because in our beginning again it seems we had the guidance, the leadership, the teachings, and the high wisdom of 'the Sages', 'the Shining Ones' – those 'Magicians of the Gods' – who had survived from antediluvian times and whose mission was to ensure that all was not after all lost. It doesn't make sense that they would have gone to such great lengths to spell out the epoch of 10,500 BC at Giza just to say they were there. I suggest the science of their civilization was high enough for them to have understood exactly what had happened to the world and to predict when it would happen again.

I think, in short, that their purpose may have been to send us a message

We will look more deeply into that message, and its implications, in later chapters, but first there is another trail of clues to follow, a trail that may lead us closer to the 'Magicians' and their 'magic'.

Part V

Stones

Chapter 12
Baalbek

———◆———

We land at Beirut's International Airport in the late evening of 9 July 2014. The airport is named after former Prime Minister Rafic Hariri, who was assassinated on 14 February 2005 when his motorcade drove past a Mitsubishi van parked outside the Saint George Hotel on the city's fashionable Mediterranean seafront – known as the Corniche. The van contained a young male suicide bomber (or so the very fragmentary DNA evidence suggests) and an estimated 1,800 kilos (about 4,000 pounds) of TNT. Twenty-three people, amongst them Hariri, several of his bodyguards, and his close friend and former Minister of the Economy Bassel Fleihan, were killed. Those suspected of organizing the massacre include senior members of Hezbollah, the Shia militant and political group that controls the town of Baalbek in the Bekaa Valley, where there are certain intriguing ancient ruins that I'm determined to see on this research visit to Lebanon. Hezbollah itself blames Israel. In addition, some suspect that President Bashar al-Assad of Syria was directly involved.[1]

The Syrian border runs along the eastern edge of the Bekaa Valley and very close to Baalbek itself, which was hit by missiles in June 2013 and where there are repeated violent incidents.[2] With the horrendous Syrian civil war still in full swing, and huge numbers of refugees adding to the general state of chaos and instability, we've been advised to stay away. But I've wanted to see Baalbek for years and I feel all the more strongly drawn to the ruins there after what I've learnt researching Ancient Egypt.

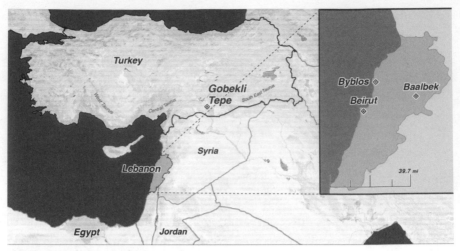

Figure 41: Lebanon in its regional context.

There are, you see, a number of puzzling connections and I have these very much in mind, having been re-reading my notes on the flight, as Santha and I step down out of the plane onto the tarmac and make our way into the terminal building. The night air is warm but a refreshing breeze blows in off the Mediterranean, and I find myself looking forward to whatever adventures lie ahead.

Our first encounter is with bureaucracy in the form of an immigration officer wearing a grey uniform over an open-necked shirt. He is young but he has a sallow, unhealthy complexion and an unshaved, suspicious look about him. Indeed, he is *extremely* suspicious, as he makes clear each time he glances up from my passport to glare at me before returning to his forensic examination of the pages. My passport contains 41 pages with space for visas and I travel frequently, so there are stamps from all over the world – Malaysia, Indonesia, Australia, South Africa, India, the United States, Brazil, Bolivia, Peru, Egypt, the United Arab Emirates, Canada, Turkey . . . The young officer studies each stamp minutely, slowly leafing through the pages from front to back, glaring at me, returning to the investigation, glaring at me again. Then when he has reached the very last page, he repeats the procedure, this time leafing through from back to front.

I know what he's looking for – a visa stamp for Israel, the presence of which will allow him to deny me entry. He won't find one.

240

Although my research has taken me to Israel several times, I'm always careful to get the entrance and exit stamps on a loose sheet of paper placed inside my passport, rather than on the passport itself. Besides, my last visit was in 1999 and I've changed my passport twice since then, so there's nothing to be in the least bit concerned about. Even so, I have to admit I feel uncomfortable at this intense, sustained scrutiny.

After going through the passport a third time, the officer gives me another hostile glare and asks: 'Why you come to our country?'

'Tourist,' I reply. I know from long experience that saying anything about researching a book can lead to all manner of additional problems and suspicions that are best avoided.

He raises a sceptical eyebrow. 'Tourist?'

'Yes. Tourist.'

'And you see what, in our country?'

I'm ready for the question. 'Beirut. The beautiful Corniche. I've heard there are some great restaurants. Then we're going to Byblos and of course to Baalbek.'

The eyebrow shoots up again. 'Baalbek?'

'Yes, of course! Wouldn't miss it for anything.' This at least is true. 'The temples. The big stones. I've heard it's one of the wonders of the world.'

Suddenly a smile. 'Wonderful, yes! I am from Baalbek. My home town.' He stamps my passport with a flourish and scrawls something in handwriting over the visa. 'Welcome to Lebanon,' he says.

Now it's Santha's turn, but with the ice broken, the officer only flips through the pages of her passport once before stamping it and directing us onwards into the baggage hall.

Well of Souls

On the drive in from the airport to our hotel we pass the place where Rafic Hariri was assassinated. The damage was long ago cleared away, of course, everything seems very chic and despite the late hour there are still a great many people, mostly young, mostly fashionably dressed, promenading along the Corniche overlooking the glittering waters of the Mediterranean, in which the street lights and the stars are pleasingly reflected. Amidst such a scene, it's hard to imagine the violence this city has witnessed during the past forty years and my thoughts turn again to the reasons we've come here.

While I've been researching Egypt, and the hints of an ancient civilizing mission after a global cataclysm described in the Edfu texts, I've found something odd that seems to suggest a possible link between the megalithic monuments of the Giza plateau and Lebanon.

A few thousand years ago Lebanon formed the northern sector of the land the Bible refers to as Canaan, which also included the region covered, roughly, by modern Israel, the Palestinian Territories, western Jordan and southwestern Syria. What interests me is that both in Israel and in Lebanon there are mysterious megalithic structures on a scale that not only rival those of Giza, but seem to express the same underlying purpose to create something that would last – sacred mounds, holy places, that would withstand the test of time and that would continue to be venerated down the ages, even if the religions and cultures associated with them changed.

The Temple Mount in Jerusalem is one such place. Both orthodox archaeology and Biblical testimony put the construction of the first great edifices there back to the almost mythical time of King Solomon – that renowned magician amongst monarchs, who supposedly ruled in the tenth century BC. The structure known as Solomon's Temple, the 'First Temple' of the Jews, was destroyed by the Babylonians in 587 BC and rebuilt by Zerubbabel in the 520s BC.[3] A further ambitious restoration was undertaken by the Romanised Jewish monarch Herod the Great in the first century BC and completed around 20 BC.[4] Some ninety years after his death, Herod's Temple in its turn was destroyed by the Romans, along with much of the city of Jerusalem, in 70 AD.[5]

What survived was the immense trapezoidal platform, known today as the *Haram esh-Sharif*, where stand the Al Aqsa Mosque and the Dome of the Rock, the third and fourth most sacred places in Islam.[6] We need not concern ourselves here with the recent history of this place, or how it came to be in Muslim hands, but the Dome of the Rock is so called because within it lies an enormous megalith, known to the Jews as the *Shetiyah* (literally the 'Foundation'). When the Temple of Solomon was erected over this exact spot in the tenth century BC, the *Shetiyah* formed the floor of the Holy of Holies and the Ark of the Covenant, that enigmatic object which I have investigated extensively in another book, stood upon it.[7]

The *Shetiyah* is not the only megalith in Jerusalem that dates back, potentially, to what the Edfu texts would call 'the time of the gods'. Of course this huge natural rock has been in this place, at the summit of a primeval mound, rather similar to the natural hill now enclosed within the Great Pyramid of Giza, for an incalculable period. But at some point, perhaps at the date in the tenth century BC that archaeologists accept for Solomon's Temple, perhaps later, perhaps much earlier, it was modified by human beings and there is now a hole cut through it which sheds a beam of light into the natural cave, also modified by human hands and evocatively known as the 'Well of Souls', that lies directly beneath it.

I've been in the Well of Souls several times. If it doesn't have the raw atmospheric power of the Subterranean Chamber beneath the Great Pyramid, it is only because local bad taste has allowed the Well to be tiled, carpeted, furnished and lit as a prayer room. But the way the great rock that covers it has been cut and shaped is highly reminiscent of patterns that are found on rock-hewn surfaces at Giza. My guess, in short, as at Giza with its underground chamber beneath a natural hill, is that the rock and the Well formed the original sacred shrine around which everything else on Jerusalem's Temple Mount was built.

What came next was a platform, solidly founded, of gigantic stones, to create the level, elevated surface upon which all later temples (and mosques) would be built. It is not my intention to explore the mysteries of Jerusalem here, but before moving on to Baalbek, the main focus of the present chapter, I will simply register surprise that the huge megalithic blocks which have been discovered in the so-called Hasmonean Tunnel lying to the north of, and directly extending, the famous Wailing Wall – blocks weighing in some cases more than 500 tons[8] – have been so readily assumed to be Herod's work.

In the same way, the very similar gigantic megalithic blocks of Baalbek are assumed to be of relatively recent date – spanning the late first century BC to the second half of the first century AD – and to be the work of the Romans, with perhaps some early contribution by Herod himself.[9] But just as the history of the Giza plateau has been forced between narrow and restricting bounds so, too, with Baalbek. Parts of it may be much older than presently believed.

What led me to consider this possibility at all – indeed the entire reason I'm in Beirut in July 2014 and about to take a run over to the Bekaa Valley, Hezbollah and the Syrian border – is the weird connection that I've found linking Giza with ancient Canaan, and with the ancient Semitic people known in the Bible as the Canaanites.

The magician among the gods

Selim Hassan (1887-1961) was what a real Egyptologist should be – passionate, erudite, deeply versed in his subject and open-minded. He was also a hands-on excavator and, in the 1930s, carried out the most thorough and detailed investigation of just about every major structure on the Giza Plateau. In the process, while excavating the Sphinx enclosure, he came across evidence of a Canaanite presence at Giza – indeed a long-term Canaanite settlement – which, for some reason, had been particularly focused on the Sphinx and its megalithic temples. 'How these people came to settle in Egypt, and why and when they left, we have not, as yet, any written inscription to tell us,' Hassan admits.[10] That they were there from at least the Eighteenth Dynasty (1543 BC– 1292 BC) is well attested, but the possibility cannot be ruled out that their stay in Egypt dates back long before that time.

At any rate, numerous votive stele and other marks of respect to the Great Sphinx of Giza, inscribed and offered by members of this Canaanite community, have been found. We have seen already that the Sphinx was identified with the Egyptian god Horus, who could appear in many forms but most often as a falcon. Of interest, then, is the fact that the Sphinx in the Canaanite inscriptions is called *Hurna*, and sometimes *Hauron*. These are not Egyptian words at all, but instead are the names of a Canaanite falcon deity.[11] The reader will also recall from Chapter Ten that the Ancient Egyptians often called the Sphinx *Hor-em-Akhet* ('Horus in the Horizon'). It turns out that this name is directly linked with *Hurna* in a number of inscriptions, not only left by members of the Canaanite community that had settled near Giza, but also by the Ancient Egyptians themselves – for example, a plaque of Amenhotep II where the Pharaoh is referred to as 'beloved of *Hurna-Hor-em-Akhet*.'[12]

Selim Hassan comments on 'the assimilation of the names *Hurna* and *Hor-em-Akhet*' on Amenhotep's plaque, which succinctly confirms the use of 'the name of the god *Hurna* in Egypt and its association with *Hor-em-Akhet* and application to the Sphinx.'[13] Likewise a stela found at Giza reads: 'Adoration to *Hor-em-Akhet* in his name of *Hurna* . . . Thou art the only one who will exist till eternity, while all people die'.[14] And a second Giza stela represents *Hurna* in the form of a falcon beside an inscription which reads: 'O *Hurna-Hor-em-Akhet*, may he give favour and love . . .'[15] Christiane Zivie-Coche, Director of Religious Studies at the *Ecole pratique des hautes études* in Paris, adds that the variant *Hauron* was also frequently used in the same way:

> *Hauron* was so closely associated with *Hor-em-Akhet*, name of the Great Sphinx of Giza . . . that one addressed him indifferently as *Hor-em-Akhet*, *Hauron*, or *Hauron-Hor-em-Akhet*.[16]

What really caught my attention, however, and put me on the plane to Beirut, was a further observation from Zivie-Coche. 'An epithet on a Sphinx statuette,' she reported:

> indicates that *Hauron* is originally from Lebanon.[17]

Intriguing, too, in light of the civilizing work of 'Sages' and 'Magicians', of which there are so many traces in the Edfu texts and in the Mesopotamian inscriptions, is a baked clay tablet from the ancient city of Ugarit on the Mediterranean coast of what is now Syria, a little to the north of Byblos in Lebanon. *Hauron* is the subject of the tablet and, exactly like the Apkallu Sages of Mesopotamia, he is portrayed as a 'conjurer'[18] – indeed, notes Egyptologist Jacobus van Dijk, as:

> the magician among the gods . . .[19]

With further echoes of the Apkallu, *Hauron's* 'magic' consists of what sounds to the modern ear like advanced scientific knowledge, in this case providing anti-venom, extracted 'from among the shrubs of the tree of death'[20] that cured the victim of a deadly snakebite. The poison was neutralised, we read, so that it 'became weak' and 'flowed away like a stream'.[21]

And there is something else – something that points directly towards Baalbek with its mysterious megaliths – for not only was *Hauron/Hurna* worshipped at Giza and assimilated to the Sphinx and to the falcon Horus, but Baal, the Canaanite deity after whom Baalbek is named,[22] also had a cult in Egypt where he was associated with Set, the god of deserts and storms.[23]

Last but not least, there is the fact that Baalbek was renamed 'Heliopolis' – Greek for 'City of the Sun' – after Alexander the Great conquered the Levant and Syria in 332 BC.[24] The reader will recall from Chapter Eleven that *Innu*, the sacred city of the Ancient Egyptians, where stood the Temple of the Phoenix attended by the priesthood of Giza, was also called 'Heliopolis' by the Greeks. They referred to it as such from at least the time of Herodotus in the fifth century BC,[25] and the Romans followed suit. Likewise Baalbek continued to be called 'Heliopolis' throughout Roman times.

Marching in Alexander's footsteps, Pompey annexed the Levant and Syria in 64 BC and Roman power here reached its height in the first and second centuries AD, when a statue of 'Jupiter the Most High and the Most Great of Heliopolis' stood in the courtyard of the great temple that the Romans built at Baalbek in honour of this god.[26] As well as its usual Roman attributes, the statue, which may be seen today in the Louvre Museum in Paris, displays a winged sun-disc on its chest – a possible reference, argues Friedrich Ragette, formerly Professor of Architecture at the American University of Beirut, 'to the god of Egyptian Heliopolis'.[27]

It was not until the Arab conquests in the seventh century AD that the original Canaanite name 'Baalbek' began to reappear in Levantine annals, and it was only then that the city's Graeco-Roman designation as 'Heliopolis' fell entirely out of use. [28]

Between Lebanon and Anti-Lebanon ranges

The morning after our late-night arrival in Beirut, Lebanese friends kindly join us at our hotel to drive us to Baalbek. Over coffee before we go, they tell us of our good fortune: there is a lull in the fighting in Syria, all is calm along the border, and they expect no trouble.

Seen in daylight the Lebanese capital is almost as charming and beautiful as it was at midnight. One hundred and twenty thousand people were killed in this country during the terrible and protracted civil war between 1975 and 1990, but the city which was the focus of so much of the fighting seems to have put that ghastly episode behind it. Most of the bullet holes, shrapnel and blast wounds in the buildings have been repaired, there's a lot of new construction going on and the atmosphere is one of optimism and vigorous enterprise. Yes, there is sadness in the air – it's unavoidable after so much murder and mayhem – but the sense I get is of a nation recovering from its trauma, not wallowing in it, filled with bright, intelligent young people who are determined to move ahead.

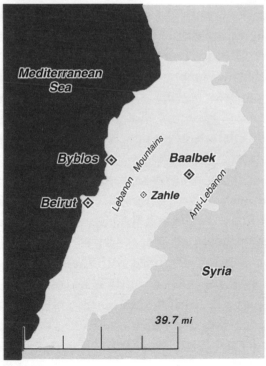

Figure 42

247

The traffic is heavy as we wind our way up the steep foothills of the Lebanon Mountains to the east of the capital. It's only 86 kilometres (about 53 miles) to Baalbek but there are frequent military checkpoints, where we're filtered through chicanes and inspected by attentive, heavily-armed soldiers. Inevitably this slows us down. The views, however, get more and more spectacular with the Mediterranean gleaming behind us and the great, green, tree-strewn ridges of the Lebanon range rising ahead of us. The road wraps itself around multiple tight hairpin bends above vertiginous drops, the air becomes notably cooler and the landscape more barren. Then we're over the top through the Dahar el Baydar pass at an altitude of 1,556 metres (5,100 feet) and motoring down the other side with the broad, intensively cultivated sweep of the Bekaa Valley opening out below us. We pass the edge of the urban sprawl of Zahle, famous for its Ksara Winery, and pretty soon we're running through the Bekaa proper – although it is really a plateau rather than a valley since its average elevation is more than 1,000 metres (3,280 feet) above sea level.

Bounded on the west by the Lebanon Mountains over which we've just driven, and on the east by the Anti-Lebanon range, the Bekaa is watered by two historic rivers – the Litani and the Orontes. When the Romans colonised the region two thousand years ago, this fertile plateau was one of their breadbaskets, exporting grain to feed the empire. Today a more lucrative crop, though largely hidden from view, is cannabis. In the interests of keeping local farmers happy, the authorities generally turn a blind eye.

After another thirty or forty minutes of mainly level driving on a long, straight stretch of road with cultivated fields on either side, we enter the outskirts of Baalbek at the edge of the Anti-Lebanon foothills. It's a shabby town of shops, offices and dilapidated low-rise apartment blocks, many festooned with the Hezbollah flag featuring an upraised arm at the end of which is a hand clenched into a fist around an AK-47 assault rifle. Hand, arm and Kalashnikov emerge from a line of calligraphy spelling out Hezbollah's name – 'Party of God'. Other lettering states 'Then surely the party of Allah are they that shall be triumphant' and, separately, 'the Islamic resistance in

Lebanon'. The background colour of the flags is a strident yellow, while the logo and calligraphy are picked out in green.

Fashions and preferences in gods come and go, but the sacred landscape endures. On an eminence above the town we can clearly see the spectacular remains, the soaring columns, and the lofty pediments of the group of three Roman temples that bestowed such renown upon Baalbek in the ancient world. Dedicated, supposedly, to Jupiter, Bacchus and Venus, they were built on a scale larger and more imposing than almost any other Roman structures, including those in Rome itself. What really interests me, however, is the megalithic wall that surrounds the Temple of Jupiter on three sides, and in particular the three gigantic blocks, known as the Trilithon, that are embedded in it. Much that I've learned about the Trilithon in my prior research has led me to suspect that it may be older – far older – and dedicated to a far more enigmatic purpose than anything the Romans built here.

Now's my chance to find out.

Centuries of darkness

The mid-morning sun is beating down out of an absolutely cloudless clear blue sky and I'm sitting on a big limestone block roughly in the middle of what was once the Temple of Jupiter. I say 'once' because there's very little of this towering edifice left standing now, other than the six immense columns that rear skywards about the width of a football field behind me – the last six out of the total of fifty-four that originally demarcated the exterior of the vast rectangular structure. This site is so enormous, the complex of temples so colossal and at the same time so ruined that I'm finding it difficult to get my bearings. Also, I have to confess, the long echoing booms of distant artillery, punctuated by the rapid, stuttering coughs of heavy machine guns, and an occasional very loud explosion, are a little disconcerting.

OK, I think, deliberately shutting my ears to the sounds that are, almost certainly, only the Lebanese military doing some practice firing, let's figure out what we've got here. I glance over my shoulder and when I do I'm looking roughly south-east, through the six big columns which stand on the edge of the massive platform I'm in the midst of, across a sunken plaza, to the row of a dozen columns that line the northern perimeter of the smaller, but more intact and still very beautiful Temple of Bacchus, the Roman god of wine.

I'm not here to research or write about Roman architecture but still I'm impressed. Not only did the Romans have the sense of fun to dedicate a temple to wine and all its pleasures – reportedly joyous acts of sexual licence regularly took place within – but also, let's not beat around the bush here, these people really knew how to *build*! The columns themselves are extraordinary feats of megalithic architecture, and the Romans seem to have had no difficulty in hauling the ponderous blocks of the pediment, each weighing tens of tons – and in some cases hundreds of tons – up to the top of them.

So let's be clear about this, right from the start, because there is so much ignorant baloney talked on the subject: the Romans were *incredibly* accomplished builders and they were absolutely capable of moving and placing monstrously huge and heavy blocks of stone. If there's an argument to be made for a lost civilization at Baalbek then it can't be based on the block weights, or on naïve, ill-informed notions about what the Romans could or couldn't do, because in the realm of building, the evidence all around me confirms they could do pretty much anything they chose to.

One of the things they frequently did was build their temples on pre-existing sacred sites. Their objective was not to obliterate the indigenous gods and religions (as the Spanish sought to do in Mexico, for example, when they installed churches on the site of Aztec temples), but rather to associate the gods and religion of Rome in a positive way with what had gone before. The pre-Roman cults usually continued to flourish and the pre-Roman deities were honoured and absorbed in a rich, creative and endlessly proliferating syncretism. But for those doing archaeological forensic work to try to establish exactly who was responsible for what, and when, this practice of overbuilding inevitably presents some challenges – particularly so, as is the case at Baalbek, when other later cultures, and the ravages of time, have also continuously modified the site.

Towards the end of the Roman era bad things began to happen here. The turning point was Rome's conversion, under the Emperor

Constantine (AD 306-37), to the new fanatical, exclusivist religion of Christianity. The militants of that faith focused their beady eyes first on the Temple of Venus, described by the Christian chronicler Eusebius as 'a school to learn sensual practices', where initiates indulged 'in all kinds of debauchery'.[29] Constantine gave orders that the temple should be destroyed completely (in the event it wasn't).[30] Julian the Apostate (AD 361-3) detested Christianity and reinstated the old gods. Then Theodosius (AD 379-95) took the throne and the Christians were back in power with a vengeance. 'Constantine the Great contented himself with closing the temples,' reports the *Chronicon Paschale*:

> but Theodosius destroyed them. He transformed into a Christian Church the temple of Heliopolis, that of Baal-Helios, the Great Sun-Baal, the celebrated Trilithon.[31]

Some hundreds of years later the Islamic era began. Around AD 664 Baalbek was besieged and captured by a Muslim army that converted the Temple of Jupiter and the Temple of Bacchus, immediately south of it, into a single large fortress. Various factions then held Baalbek and continued to fortify it (indeed, to this day, it is often still referred to in Arabic as the *Kala'a*, meaning the 'fortress'[32]). In the process, of course, the ancient temples suffered further destruction. In AD 902 the Karmates, a dissident Shia sect, besieged and captured Baalbek, slaughtering the defenders. The Fatimites seized it in AD 969. Four years later, a Moslem General named Zamithes arrived with a huge army and another devastating siege and massacre followed.[33]

A Greek Christian army set Baalbek on fire in 996; by 1100 it was in the hands of the Seljuk, Tadj Eddolat Toutoush. In 1134 it was besieged by Zinki, who 'for three months hurled on its ramparts a storm of projectiles' using 'fourteen catapaults working day and night'.[34]

In 1158 Baalbek was struck by an earthquake of 'unparalleled violence' that 'destroyed the fortress and the temples'. Noureddin, the son of Zinki 'hastened to Baalbek to repair the damage which the earthquake had done to the ramparts.'[35]

In 1171 a force of captured European Crusaders who were being held prisoner in the fortress staged an uprising, in which they slaughtered the garrison and took possession of the citadel, but were soon slaughtered in their turn by a Muslim army that broke in through an underground passage. In 1176 the Crusaders were back. They attacked and pillaged Baalbek. Soon afterwards, in 1203 there was another massive earthquake that caused further extensive damage.[36]

In 1260 the Tartar Sultan, Holako, besieged Baalbek, captured it and destroyed it. 'Not even the fortifications were spared' – a folly that the Tartars came to regret when King Daher Bibars attacked them and expelled them. He gave orders that the fortress of Baalbek – which, let us not forget, was the site of the ancient temples – should immediately be rebuilt and its walls reconstructed. In 1318, however, nature took a hand again and a fearsome flood undermined the ramparts making several wide breaches. 'The water rushed in with such force that it lifted a tower 12 metres square to a distance of 400 metres.'[37]

Next came the Turko–Mongol conqueror, Timur. In 1491, after capturing the citadel and subduing all resistance there, he gave it up 'to the rapacity of his soldiers who pillaged it ruthlessly'. By 1516, when Baalbek became part of the Ottoman empire, the fortress and its temples were 'completely ruined'.[38]

In this state they were seen by the English architect Robert Wood in 1751, whose detailed drawings of the site show nine of the original fifty-four columns of the Temple of Jupiter still intact. Then in 1759 another fearsome earthquake struck, leaving only the six standing columns that I now sit in front of as I mull over the tumultuous history of this ancient sacred place.[39]

The question I'm asking myself is this – after so many cycles of construction, destruction and rebuilding, how much can archaeology really claim to *know* about the site? As Michael Alouf, the former Curator of Baalbek, confirms:

Unfortunately this temple has suffered greatly through the ravages of time and the vandalism of the ignorant; its walls have been demolished, its columns overthrown and its foundations undermined. There only remain the six columns of the southern peristyle, four broken columns on their bases in the northern peristyle within the Arab fortifications, and the socles [plinths] of the peristyle of the façade. The Byzantine Emperors were the first who began to destroy the temple, using the building material thus obtained for the construction of [a] basilica. The Arabs followed their example, extracting from the walls and the foundations of the temple any blocks of stone likely to be useful in fortifying the weak spots of the ramparts.[40]

Undoubtedly the German Archaeological Institute, who have the concession for this site (as they have also for Göbekli Tepe in Turkey) are doing their best. In the process, however, they have revealed even more deeply confusing layers of complexity and have been obliged to overturn what was for a long while the mainstream consensus that the first builders at Baalbek were the Romans.[41] Far from it! Indeed, under the place where I'm sitting now, which was in the midst of the area that once formed the *cella* – the inner chamber – of the Temple of Jupiter, are the remains of a far more ancient sacred mound. Such mounds are known as 'Tells' in this region, and archaeologists now admit that 'Tell Baalbek' goes back *at least* 10,000 years[42] – i.e. 8,000 or more years *before* the Romans arrived here! 'A long sequence of Neolithic settlement layers . . . most probably the Pre-Pottery Neolithic',[43] has been excavated, pushing the origins of Baalbek very close to the time when Göbekli Tepe flourished in nearby Turkey.

Megalithic wall north

The artillery fire is still going on in the background, but it's one of those noises you tune out after a while. I get up off the warm comfortable block I've been sitting on and make my way a few dozen paces north, across what would have been the floor of the Temple of Jupiter, until I come to its northern edge (marked by a few broken columns, still upright on their plinths like the stubs of rotten teeth) set into a later – very makeshift and higgledy-piggledy – Arab fortification wall. Into the wall, at intervals, are built embrasures with loop holes through which defenders fired arrows down on their attackers. Peering north through one of these loopholes, I can just see the top of a truly massive row of megaliths perhaps (I'm guessing) 20 or 25 feet below me. I count nine of them and note that they're separated from the base of the wall in which the embrasure is set by a horizontal distance of – another rough guess – 35 feet. In the gap, which is overgrown with grass and bushes, are many fallen, broken, blocks of stone.

In order to get a better view of this strange megalithic wall I continue

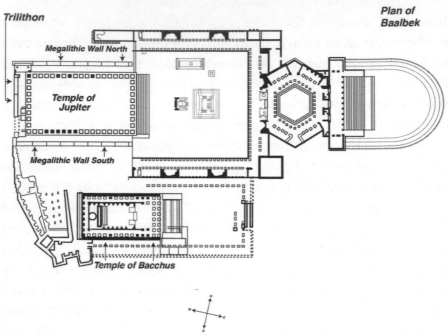

Figure 43

to walk westwards along the northern margin of the Temple of Jupiter, until I get to another part of the Arab fortifications that were later added onto it, the so-called 'Northwest Tower'. I can step out onto this – there's a convenient terrace with a commanding view – and look back from it in an eastwards direction along the huge megaliths, set out in a row below me, and down into the overgrown grassy gap that separates them from the wall of the temple platform.

I'll not try to explain yet what those megaliths are. There are enough confusing factors already! But we'll return to them shortly when, hopefully, all will become clear. Meanwhile I exit the Arab tower, walk back into the huge rectangular space it leads off, where the Temple of Jupiter once stood, and cross it heading east until I come to the steps that once led up to the temple's entrance. I descend the steps, then turn westwards again into the sunken plaza, bounded by the platform of the Temple of Jupiter to the north and by the Temple of Bacchus to the south.

The transmission of knowledge

Naturally I check out the wine god's sanctuary. It's beautiful, with a strong energy of its own, and I'm sure a lot of joy was celebrated here in antiquity. But there's a more serious side, too, hinting that the Romans were the recipients of a stream of ancient knowledge and symbolism with its origins in the remotest antiquity – a stream, though divided into many channels, that continues to flow to this day.

Freemasons who have studied the Temple of Bacchus point to a number of reliefs and designs here that are meaningful to them. For example, on the underside of a huge stone ceiling block, still balanced on the columns of the temple, appears the device known as the 'Seal of Solomon' – a six-pointed star inscribed within a circle. According to leading US Freemason Timothy Hogan, Grand Master of the Knights Templar Order, the figure in the centre of the star is depicted 'giving a sign that would be familiar to Entered Apprentices'. Another relief shows two figures 'sitting side by side and making gestures that would have meaning to a Fellowcraft in Freemasonry'.[44]

It's also noteworthy at the Temple of Bacchus, and indeed throughout Baalbek, how much evidence there is for the veneration of the god of wisdom whom the Romans called Mercury – the Greek Hermes – whom the Ancient Egyptians knew as Thoth and connected, as we saw in Chapter Nine, to the traditions of the Seven Sages.[45] Another curious link is that the cult of Mercury in its earliest forms involved the use of *betyls*,[46] discussed in Chapter Eleven, which were originally 'stones fallen from heaven' – in other words, meteorites and thus often part of the debris stream of fragmenting comets. When we recall that the Black Stone of the *Ka'aba* in Mecca is said to be a meteorite, it's interesting that Baalbek in antiquity was the site of a famous oracle (the Roman Emperor Trajan reportedly held it in great esteem), and that it was 'a black stone which answered questions'.[47]

Some scholars believe the Temple of Bacchus was jointly dedicated to Mercury,[48] but since I'm not in Baalbek to explore Roman architecture I won't describe it further. It's the Temple of Jupiter, and its tangled prehistoric past that really interests me – particularly its relationship through the platform on which it stands with the earlier constructions going back to the time of Göbekli Tepe.

Again, sorting out the different phases is difficult and I'm determined not to be lured by the trap that so many 'alternative' historians have fallen into – namely to conclude, when we see huge megaliths, that super-advanced, even 'alien' technologies must have been involved in moving them and lifting them. As I've already said, I don't dispute that the Romans could and did move enormous blocks of stone when they wanted to. Indeed, the evidence for that is all around me in the space between the Temple of Bacchus and the Temple of Jupiter, where heaps of carved and engraved blocks from the fallen pediments of both structures lie scattered. They are, without question, Roman, some of them weigh in the range of 100 tons or more, one weighs 360 tons,[49] and all of them were raised almost 70 feet (21 metres) above the ground – the height of the columns on which they were perched.[50]

I walk north through these ruins, back towards the Temple of Jupiter, looking up now at its six remaining giant columns, each one of them composed of three enormous blocks and each standing on a monolithic stone plinth almost 9 feet (2.7 metres) high.[51] You'd have to be a fool to argue that the Romans didn't make and raise up those columns, or the pediments above them, because it's completely obvious on stylistic grounds, and on the basis of comprehensive archaeological research, that they did.

However, as noted earlier, the Romans were themselves both the inheritors and the transmitters of sometimes extremely archaic traditions and it may not be an accident that the Temple of Jupiter originally boasted fifty-four columns. The reader will recall the phenomenon of precession discussed in Chapters Ten and Eleven, and the mystery of 'precessional numbers', encoded in ancient myths and traditions from all around the world, which Professors Giorgio de Santillana and Hertha von Dechend take as proof of advanced astronomical knowledge handed down from some as yet unidentified and 'almost unbelievable' ancestor civilization. It so happens that 54 is one of the sequence of precessional numbers. It derives from 72, the number of years required for one degree of precessional motion. We then add 36 (half of 72) to 72 itself to get 108 and divide 108 by two to get 54. In their groundbreaking study *Hamlet's Mill*, Santillana and von Dechend point to the avenues of statues at Angkor in Cambodia, '108 per avenue, 54 on each side', as examples of deliberate precessional symbolism[52] – so why not the fifty-four columns of the Temple of Jupiter at Baalbek as well?

Megalithic wall south

My eye tracks down from the top of the six remaining columns past their huge plinths, to the wall of moderate quarter-ton blocks that they surmount (forming the southern edge of the Temple of Jupiter) and down again to the base of that wall which in turn is flanked by a row of nine colossal megaliths that are each about 32 feet long, 13 feet high and 10 feet wide (9.5 metres by 4 metres by 3 metres).[53] These monster blocks weigh somewhere in the range of 400 tons each. A number of them, those furthest towards the west, have a nicely finished appearance, with the stone smoothed and polished and the upper half trimmed in to be narrower than the base. But others are rough, still showing the 'boss', the protective layer that masons leave on the surface to protect the ashlar from damage while it is being transported to the site.[54]

The quarry these blocks were brought from has been identified. It's about 800 metres (half a mile) to the south. I don't doubt that cutting and moving them would have been within the technical capacity of the Romans, the greatest and most ingenious builders of the historical antiquity. Still the question must be asked – are these blocks their work? Or someone else's? The question must be asked, because the nine blocks I'm looking at now are part of the same stupendous, megalithic wall to which belong the nine equally gigantic blocks I saw earlier on the north side of the complex. That northern row of megaliths and this southern row of megaliths form the northern and southern 'arms' of a single gigantic 'U'-shaped wall that surrounds the Temple of Jupiter to the north, south and west with the base of the 'U' – in which is set the fabled Trilithon that I've come here to see – oriented west.

As usual with Baalbek, as though this were not complicated enough, there are further complications! These have been explored by Daniel Lohmann, an extremely thorough and really quite brilliant German architect and archaeologist, who has spent years excavating and closely examining this site and who, in February 2015, was gracious enough to engage in correspondence with me and to give me the benefit of his extensive knowledge. It's his opinion, which I'll go into in more depth in the next chapter, that the awe-inspiring U-shaped megalithic wall surrounding the Temple of Jupiter is one hundred per cent Roman.

His case is that it was part of what was intended to become an immense podium – let us follow the logic of his argument and call it 'Podium 2' – with which whoever commissioned the temple (and since there are *zero* contemporary records we don't know who that was[55]) wished to surround his 'megalomaniac' masterpiece.[56] The upshot of Lohmann's investigation is that within the U-shaped wall of Podium 2 are the remains of what he sees as an earlier building phase, which he refers to as 'Podium 1'.[57] His investigations show the dimensions of Podium 1 to be 12 metres in height by 48 metres north to south, by 95 metres east to west, but, he admits, 'the only certain clue' to its age 'is that it pre-dates the Julio Claudian temple'[58] (i.e. the Temple of Jupiter which was built in the main by the Julio-Claudian dynasty, spanning the reigns of the Emperors Augustus, Tiberius, Caligula, Claudius and Nero, 27 BC–AD 68). To cut a long story short, Lohmann argues that Podium 1 was the work of Herod the Great, the Roman client king who ruled Judea in the last decades of the first century BC. But there are no inscriptions or other documentary evidence that could settle the matter, so 'the only source of information is the well-preserved structure itself',[59] notably its stylistic features:

> such as the use of alternating rows of headers and stretchers, drafted-margin masonry and the reconstruction of the plan of this early structure. These elements reveal surprisingly close parallels to Herodian sanctuaries, and in particular the Temple at Jerusalem, not only in general appearance but in their precise

proportions and measurements. These correspondences between the two building projects strongly suggest Herodian involvement . . . even though its precise nature remains to be determined.[60]

As we've seen, the Jerusalem Temple was destroyed by the Romans in AD 70, so Lohmann is obliged to base his argument on 'the only surviving part of the Temple, the gigantic trapezoidal platform of the *Haram-esh-Sharif.*'[61] Nonetheless, the detailed comparisons he offers do, indeed, make an excellent case for 'Herodian involvement' in Baalbek's Podium 1. What remains to be settled, however, is how *extensive* this involvement was. To be specific, although Lohmann concedes that 'Tell Baalbek . . . was continuously inhabited since the pre-pottery Neolithic period'[62] – i.e. since the time of Göbekli Tepe – and although his whole argument is that the Julio-Claudian Emperors worked around Podium 1 at Baalbek when they started to build the massive and imposing U-shaped wall for Podium 2, he doesn't consider the possibility that there might have been a 'Podium 0', which Herod in turn overbuilt.

I can hardly blame him for that, since no mainstream archaeologist that I'm aware of is willing to consider the same possibility for Herod's restoration of the Jerusualem Temple – particularly with reference to the huge megalithic blocks, discussed earlier, that now stand exposed by the Hasmonean Tunnel. Nevertheless it's a possibility that shouldn't be ignored at Baalbek, especially in the light of what Lohmann himself describes as the 'great antiquity' of the site.[63]

And there's another possibility as well, which I intend to consider. It concerns the megalithic U-shaped wall that forms the base and boundary of the feature Lohmann calls Podium 2. Suppose that U-shaped wall isn't Roman at all? Suppose it was already in place *before, not after*, Herod built Podium 1? Suppose, further, that the Tell that antedates Podium 1 by thousands of years was itself situated where it is because of the prior existence of the U-shaped megalithic wall? In other words, suppose the U-shaped wall with its immense megaliths was the very *first* work of architecture to be built on this site, perhaps enshrining some central feature, some primeval mound, in front of which the Tell later evolved over thousands of years, until the Herodian Temple was built on top of it, and then a little later overbuilt by the Temple of Jupiter?

Trilithon

Having climbed a stairway set against the side of a monstrously large block – the scale of everything here is truly epic! – I make my way along the top of the row of 13-feet high, 400-ton megaliths that form the southern elevation of the U-shaped megalithic wall that Lohmann sees as part of the – never completed – Podium 2. I'm heading west now and I pass under the six standing columns, which seem less to loom than to take flight over me, so light and graceful do they appear despite their massive size. The wall they're perched on rises to about twice my height; its upper edge – where the columns stand – marks the level of the floor of the Temple of Jupiter, where I'd sat earlier. The space between the wall and the edge of the 10-feet wide megaliths I'm walking on is an obstacle-course of broken fragments of columns and ornate multi-ton chunks of the pediment they once supported.

At the end of the long row of megaliths I'm confronted by a warren of towers, archways and tumbledown, medieval Arab fortifications. I thread my way through these – it's all a bit bewildering! – climb a flight of stairs and take a right turn into a narrow alley at the western edge of the whole complex. I'm heading north now and the alley, which isn't wide enough for two people to pass abreast, runs between the outer fortification wall on my left – part Roman, part Arab recon-struction – and a row of rough-hewn megalithic blocks on my right. I don't know what to make of these blocks but a few months later, in correspondence we eventually engage in, Lohmann will tell me that they're:

> part of a filling layer . . . that was intended to fill up space between the Herodian wall and the later megaliths which make up the exterior shell of the second, Julio-Claudian podium. They were intended to be invisible behind the shell, so they remained undressed, and with a rough surface.[64]

Whatever they are, these massive blocks are separated by little more than the width of my shoulders from the hybrid Roman wall extended by Arab fortifications to my left. The feeling is one of constriction, almost claustrophobia. After twenty paces, or so, however, the alley widens as the outer fortification wall, previously several courses thick suddenly reduces to a single course which, just ahead, has a large gap in it through which I peer down onto a grassy border, some 35 or 40 feet below, edged by the modern fence that surrounds the whole of the Baalbek complex.

That's when I realise for sure – I'd been half expecting it, but I wasn't certain until this moment – that I'm standing on what I've come to Baalbek to see. It's just over 64 feet long, more than 14 feet high, nearly 12 feet wide and weighs more than 800 tons.[65]

It's the southernmost of the three famed megaliths of the Trilithon.

Chapter 13
And Then Came the Deluge . . .

——◆——

I'd hoped, I'd expected, I was almost sure, that the course I'd charted through the ruins would lead me to the Trilithon, but still I feel a minor sense of triumph that my wanderings in the labyrinth have actually brought me to this very special place!

It's a good moment to take stock. That single course of outer fortification masonry to my west barely covers a quarter of the Trilithon's immense width. There's part of the drum of a fallen column lying just by the gap in the fortifications that overlooks the grassy border within the perimeter fence surrounding the ruins. Pressed against the fortification wall this column covers approximately half the width of the huge megalith it rests on, the southernmost of the three in the Trilithon. All in all this is a sheltered spot, a quiet space, a little courtyard almost. Conveniently there's a loose block about the height of a stool for me to perch on, and what's more, since it's afternoon now, there's a patch of shade.

With a sigh of relief I sit down, haul out my notebook and compose my thoughts. I'm aware, as I do so, that my feet are placed not only on the Trilithon block, but also on something inscribed into it that effectively proves it is older than the Temple of Jupiter, though not how *much* older. The shade is working against me, the fifty years since it was first brought to light have not been kind to it, and honestly I can't see it. However, Professor Haroutune Kalayan, the engineer placed in charge of the restorations of Baalbek by the Lebanese Department of Antiquities, explains that back in the mid-1960s, 'In view of the scientific interest, Emir Maurice Chehab, Director General of the Antiquity Department, decided to have the top of the Trilithon cleared . . .' When this was done:

The south block . . . exposed a full-scale orthographic drawing of the pediment of the Temple of Jupiter. The drawing partly extends under Roman construction and partly it is hidden under an early period Arabic construction . . . This . . . discovery suggests that the Trilithon was already in place to serve as a trestle board for the dimensioning and ordering of the pediment blocks; that is, in the beginning of the second half of the first century AD. Further, it can be concluded that after the construction of the pediment, after the drawing had served its purpose, the constructional scheme above the level of the Trilithon [was] executed; this is why part of the drawings extend under the Roman constructions.[1]

So right here, at my feet, unfortunately invisible now without special lighting, is a convincing piece of evidence that a real mystery, not just one made up by alternative historians, surrounds the Trilithon. Obviously, since it was used for an architectural drawing of part of the Temple of Jupiter, as Kalayan admits, and particularly so since it was afterwards partially covered by Roman construction, the only logical deduction is that it must be older than the temple.

We'll look further into the implications of this, but it should be noted right at the outset that Daniel Lohmann doesn't agree. Presenting a paper for the Proceedings of the Third International Congress on Constructional History, held in the German city of Cottbus, in May 2009, he argued:

Kalayan suggested that this drawing proves the Trilithon to be older and already in place when the temple was built. Today, new indications show that this assumption is outdated, and that the Trilithon and temple were built synchronous. The upper surface of this block [the southernmost Trilithon block with the drawing on it] was practically used for a simultaneous construction, later simply to be covered by the next stone course.[2]

And in a follow-up paper in 2010, Lohmann expanded on his reasoning:

The unfinished pre-Roman sanctuary construction [Podium 1] was incorporated into a master plan of monumentalisation. Apparently challenged by the already huge pre-Roman construction, the early imperial Jupiter sanctuary shows both an architectural megalomaniac design and construction technique in the first half of the first century AD. The most famous example may be the Trilithon forming the middle layer of the western temple podium . . . The podium can be considered as an attempt to hide the older, inconveniently shaped temple terrace behind a podium in fashionable Roman manner . . .[3]

I understand Lohmann's logic but I have a number of problems with it. First and foremost there is the very concept of a 'podium' that is being bandied around here. The dictionary defines 'podium' as:

the masonry supporting a classical temple.[4]

Or, alternatively:

a stereobate for a classical temple, especially one with perpendicular sides.[5]

A 'stereobate' in turn is defined as:

the foundation or base upon which a building or the like is erected.[6]

Or, alternatively:

the solid foundation forming the floor and substructure of a classical temple; crepidoma; podium.[7]

A 'crepidoma', likewise, is 'the platform on which the superstructure of the building is erected.'[8]

What all these definitions hold in common is the notion that a podium is a structure on top of which a temple is built. But this is

264

not the case with Lohmann's Podium 2. It is not the 'foundation or base' upon which the Temple of Jupiter is erected, it is not the 'solid foundation forming the floor' of the Temple of Jupiter, and it is not 'the masonry supporting' the Temple of Jupiter. What the Temple of Jupiter in fact stands on, and is 'supported' by, as Lohmann himself makes clear, is the Herodian Podium 1. Lohmann's Podium 2, it turns out, does not 'support' any part of the Temple of Jupiter. It *surrounds* Podium 1 on three sides but it does not support it. It is, in other words, as I described it several times in Chapter Twelve, a U-shaped megalithic wall; but it is not a podium. If the Romans built it, as Lohmann believes, then they did not build it to serve any structural, load-bearing, podium-like purposes but purely for cosmetic reasons – 'as an attempt', to repeat his own words, 'to hide the older, inconveniently shaped temple terrace behind a podium in fashionable Roman manner.'

In response I can only repeat that 'podium' continues to be a misleading term, which does not describe what we actually see on the ground. If Lohmann's analysis of the pre-existing Herodian works is right, then we don't see evidence of the Romans hiding 'the older, inconveniently shaped temple terrace' behind a fashionable Roman 'podium'. Whatever plans they may have had for extension and development, which we cannot know and which there are no records of whatsoever, the evidence on the ground is limited to that massive U-shaped enclosure wall surrounding Podium 1 on three sides but not supporting it – a profoundly megalithic wall, larger in every dimension than any other that the Romans are known to have built anywhere in the world.

A wall that doesn't even *look* Roman, incorporating blocks weighing more than 800 tons – the Trilithon – that would have required truly spectacular efforts to move and put into place.

I'm not saying that the Romans weren't equal to such efforts, or that 800 ton blocks were beyond the limits of their building technology. I don't know, and don't claim to know, the limits of their technology. What I'm saying is that it is quite unlike the practical, phlegmatic cast of mind of the Romans, which Lohmann recognises,[9] to go to such extreme lengths for purely cosmetic purposes. Surely, therefore, there is room to consider an alternative possibility, namely that the megalithic

U-shaped wall was already in place long before – *perhaps even thousands of years before* – Podium 1 was built?

But in the very paper in which Kalayan asserts that the Trilithon predates the Temple of Jupiter he goes on to give another crucial piece of information that seems to pour cold water on speculation of this sort. Yes, the Trilithon is older than the superstructure of the Temple of Jupiter, but not much older, because:

> A part of a drum of a column similar in dimension to the columns of the Temple of Jupiter is used as a block in the foundation under the Trilithon. In the absence (to our knowledge) of a second monument with similar dimensions of columns in Baalbek, one can conclude that the drum was a discarded one and that the columns were already cut, or were in process of shaping when the foundations of the Trilithon had started.[10]

Is this the 'ugly little fact that destroys a beautiful theory'? Is my quest for a lost civilization at Baalbek fatally compromised by Kalayan's column drum? Might I just as well pack up and go home? You would think so from the sceptical literature on this subject, which endlessly regurgitates the paragraph quoted above as though it settles the matter once and for all, as though it proves beyond reasonable doubt that the Trilithon is the work of the Romans – as though any further thought and questioning on the matter is spurious, pseudo-scientific hogwash.

Sceptical author and self-styled 'debunker of fringe science and revisionist history' Jason Colavito, for example, claims that 'archaeology and engineering can explain all the individual aspects of the Trilithon' and that there is therefore no need for an alternative perspective.[11] Rather than do the work to back up this assertion himself, however, he refers us to the 'wonderful' writings of another self-styled 'sceptic', physicist Aaron Adair.[12] Adair in turn simply rehashes Kalayan's arguments, placing heavy reliance on the column drum in the foundations, and on the architectural drawing on top of the southernmost Trilithon block, to conclude:

we can be reasonably certain that the Trilithon stones were put into place contemporaneously with the construction of the Temple of Jupiter. So already, by having the Trilithon stones contemporaneous with the temple we have established the Roman provenance of the structure.[13]

It all sounds reasonable, wholesome and convincing. But actually, like so much else in the sceptical literature that is passed off as fact, it turns out, on close scrutiny, to be speculation, opinion, and bias masquerading as objectivity. That column drum, that Kalayan mentioned in passing, and that so many others have relied upon absolutely to reinforce established ideas about the chronology of the site, is much – *much!* – less than it seems.

Ironically, the central problem that I'm coming to here is illustrated by Adair himself in a black and white photograph of the western wall of the sanctuary (apparently taken from a *very* old postcard) that he reproduces with his article to support his argument – namely that there are blocks below the Trilithon, and that below these blocks, out of sight in the photo, is Kalayan's column drum. But what the photograph shows in the wall *above* the Trilithon is a section of a different Roman column drum that was redeployed by the Arabs during one of the many occasions when we know they repaired fortress Baalbek, after it had been attacked and pounded by enemy catapults.[14] Moreover, as though to underline the impermanence of every redeployable feature in the walls of Baalbek, even that bit of column drum (which can also be seen in a photograph 'taken before the First World War' and reproduced in 1980 by Friedrich Ragette[15]) was removed in more recent restorations – as Santha Faiia's images from 2014 in the plates section show.

Indeed the Arabs regularly and routinely cannibalised, reused and repurposed Roman column drums and parts of column drums.[16] Moreover, as we saw in Chapter Twelve, and as Michael Alouf, a man who knew the ruins intimately for more than fifty years, confirms, the foundations of Baalbek were repeatedly *undermined* during the numerous sieges that the sanctuary suffered while it served as a fortress.[17] After the sieges the foundations were naturally repaired (otherwise whole sections of wall would have collapsed) and it is my view that this, rather than original Roman construction, is the most plausible explanation for the column drum found in the foundations beneath the Trilithon. Why, after all, if the Romans made these foundations, as the orthodox theory requires us to accept, would they have suddenly used a column drum at this point, when they would surely have had plenty of regular blocks, specifically cut and dressed for the purpose, at their disposal?

It simply doesn't make sense. But Arab masons repairing an undermined foundation would have used whatever lay at hand and the centuries of warfare, earthquakes and other disasters that Baalbek suffered meant that there were enormous quantities of broken columns lying around, as there still are to this day. There is also another possibility, which is that the Romans did, in fact, put the column drum into the wall – but again as a repair, rather than as an act of original construction. If the megalithic wall was already very ancient when the Romans came on the scene, and if it was their intention to use it as a base for further construction, they would undoubtedly have surveyed the foundations and repaired any sectors that the years had not been kind to.

I scrawl 'FIND OUT MORE ABOUT THAT COLUMN DRUM' across a page of my notebook. The matter isn't closed yet – one way or the other – but the hypothesis that the Romans were *not* the original builders of the U-shaped megalithic wall of which the Trilithon is an integral part, continues to look viable to me, and worthy of further investigation.

It's time to see the Trilithon from the outside. I leave my welcome patch of shade, poke around a little longer on the top of the giant blocks and then retrace my steps eastwards through the Temple of Jupiter complex. Eventually – it's a long walk – I find my way back to the main entrance of the site, pass through the propylea and down the main stairs, turn right and follow the path that runs parallel to the southern exterior wall of the fortress the Arabs made of this place. The Temple of Venus comes into view a few hundred metres south-east of the main ruins. It's beautiful, but irrelevant to my purposes, so I ignore it and press on towards the south-west, passing two more Arab towers built into the fortification walls and eventually coming to a gateway in the fence through which I can see the Trilithon in the distance.

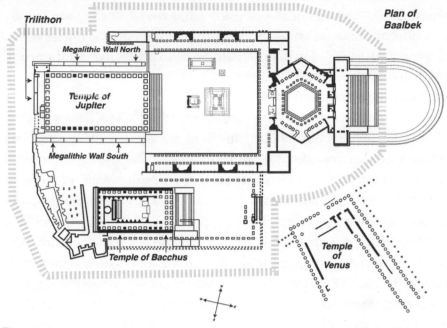

Figure 44

A guard is there. He makes a great show of keeping me out, but money changes hands, the gate is opened with a flourish, and I'm on my way through an orchard of shrivelled trees to get a better look at the three largest blocks ever used in any construction anywhere in the world . . .

'The highest pinnacle of power and science . . .'

In the nineteenth century David Urquhart, a learned Scotsman, travelled widely in Lebanon, eventually publishing his *History and Diary* in 1860. He never explained where he got the hint from, but it was his belief that Baalbek had played an important part in the secretive maritime empire of the Phoenicians, whose exploits started to be remarked upon by other cultures in the second millennium BC and who were descended from the original Canaanite people of this region. Indeed the Phoenicians usually referred to themselves as Canaanites.[18] Renowned for their seafaring abilities, and especially for their uncanny

– or perhaps one should say instead, precise and scientific – navigational skills, they established ports all around the coasts of the Mediterranean as far afield as Tunisia, Morocco, Spain, Italy, Turkey, Cyprus and Malta. Their heartland was in Lebanon, however, and their first city was Byblos, to the north of modern Beirut, with other important centres at Tyre and Sidon.

There is much that is mysterious about the Phoenicians, and they have often been reproached by frustrated researchers 'for having been so persistently silent about themselves and for having left no written history of their own. Everything we know about them comes from the annals of other races; they have only foreign advocates to plead their cause to posterity'.[19]

One of those foreign advocates was the Greek scholar Philo, who lived in Byblos in the first and second centuries AD – hence he is known as Philo of Byblos. His *Phoenician History* purported to be a translation of a book written by one Sanchuniathon, a Phoenician sage who had supposedly lived more than a thousand years earlier.[20] Sanchuniathon's writings have not come down to us in any other source. Moreover, like the works of the Babylonian priest Berossos, whom the reader will recall from earlier chapters, Philo's own *Phoenician History*, has also been lost. All that is left of it are fragments preserved as quotations and summaries by other authors – notably the fourth century Church Father Eusebius.[21]

In these fragments we read of the exploits of a 'god' identified with the Greek deity Ouranos, whose name means 'sky' or 'heaven' and who:

> invented *betyls* by devising stones endowed with life.[22]

There are a couple of points of interest here. First of all, obviously, we are back in the realm of *betyls*, those meteoritic 'stones fallen from heaven' that are so often part of the debris stream of fragmenting comets and that were treated as cult objects throughout the ancient Near East. If we look into the etymology of the word *betyl* we find that it means 'home of the god',[23] and the home of Ouranos is, of course, the sky, the right place for objects of meteoritic origin. Secondly, there is this curious reference to 'stones endowed with life' which, significantly, is given in some translations as 'stones that *moved* as having life'.[24] In this I couldn't help but be reminded of traditions from Ancient Egypt that spoke of huge stones being effortlessly moved around by 'magicians' using 'words of power'. For example, there is an account preserved on British Museum Papyrus No. 604 of the deeds of the magician Horus the Nubian, who:

> made a vault of stone 200 cubits long and 50 cubits wide rise above the head of Pharaoh and his nobles . . . When Pharaoh looked up at the sky he opened his mouth in a great cry, together with the people who were in the court.[25]

Since 200 cubits by 50 cubits equates to approximately 100 metres by 25 metres (328 feet by 82 feet) it is obvious that any magician who could raise such a massive block would have no difficulty raising the megaliths of the Trilithon, which are less than a quarter of that size. At any rate, this thought of the magicians of the gods brings us back, by a circuitous route, to David Urquhart who tells us in his *History and Diary* what it was that led him to Baalbek in the mid-nineteenth century:

> I was drawn thither by the *Betylia* [i.e. *betyls*], that mystery of the ancient writers . . . which I [believe] to have been Magnets used in the Phoenician vessels engaged in distant traffic, and which on the return of their fleets were conveyed in religious procession to the temple at Baalbek, to remain there until the fleets were again sent forth . . .[26]

Unfortunately Urquhart found no hints of the lost technology, 'the magical, magnetic stones'[27] he was looking for in Baalbek. 'Where is the temple that held the Betylia?' he asked. 'It has disappeared.' He deduced that 'it must have stood upon the platform and was probably pulled down', to make way for the Roman temples.[28] He therefore contented himself with an inquiry into the mysteries of the Trilithon and of an even larger cut-stone block that his local informants showed him lying abandoned in the quarry half a mile to the south of the ruins. These ruins, he noted, when you imagined them without the later temples 'now stuck on the top', were 'nothing but a quadrangular enclosure':[29]

> One can conceive the hewing out of enormous blocks for the statue of a king, the ornament of a palace, or the pomp of a temple, but here there is no such object; there is no conceivable object by which such an effort can be explained.[30]

This was one of a series of questions to which Urquhart could propose no answers of his own: first, why build with such huge blocks (beside which 'Stonehenge is a nursery toy'); second, why build *here*, since Baalbek was not a great capital or a great port, but stood far inland; third, why was the work suddenly stopped, as evidenced by the block in the quarry and by the unfinished state of the U-shaped wall in which the Trilithon is set; and fourth, why was Baalbek unique?[31]

> This structure is alone; there is nothing upon earth in the remotest degree resembling it.[32]

That night Urquhart dined with the Emir of Balabek and asked him whom the huge U-shaped enclosure had been built by. The Emir replied in rather matter-of-fact tones that there had been three phases of construction. The megalithic work had been done at the command of two different rulers in the primeval period before the Flood:

> And then came the Deluge. After that it was repaired by Solomon.[33]

When he was on his way back to Beirut, Urquhart reflected on what the Emir had told him, concluding that it touched on a fundamental truth and that 'the stones of Baalbek had to be considered as some of those sturdy fellows who the Deluge could not sweep away'.[34] More than that, it seemed to him that:

Before the Deluge the whole course of human society had been run . . . The builders of Baalbek must have been a people who had attained to the highest pinnacle of power and science; and this region must have been the centre of their domain.[35]

Noah, after all, had mastered the science to build the Ark:

A vessel 450 feet long, 75 broad, and 45 deep . . . He therefore shared in the knowledge of these men of renown, and navigation must have attained in these antediluvian times to an extra-ordinary degree of perfection. For the building of the Ark we have only the authority of the Bible . . . The sceptic, on the other hand, who visits Baalbek, will cease to doubt that the men who could build into its walls stones of the weight of a three-decker with its guns on board, could construct a vessel of [such immense] dimensions. I assume that the Antediluvian origin of the one can no more be contested by the critic than that of the other by the believer. [36]

Today, and rightly so, sceptics question everything that smacks of credulous superstition and easy belief. The traditions that so excited Urqhuart, however, are pervasive. Noah himself is said to be buried in the area, having returned there after the Flood to live out the remainder of his days.[37] And according to Estfan El Douaihy, Maronite Patriarch of Lebanon from 1670 to 1704:

Baalbek is the most ancient building in the world . . . It was . . . peopled with giants who were punished for their iniquities by the Flood.[38]

Other traditions implicate demons in the placing of the megaliths,[39] and an Arabic manuscript echoes the story Urquhart was told about an attempt to rebuild Baalbek after the Flood. In this account it was not Solomon but Nimrod, the great grandson of Noah, who sent giants to repair the damaged walls.[40]

Demons, giants, rollers, capstans, cranes . . . or aliens?

Looking up at the three massive blocks of the Trilithon, their bases more than 6 metres (20 feet) above ground level in Baalbek's western wall, I can understand why they were believed to be the work of demons or giants. There is, indeed, something supernatural – something seemingly *impossible* – about them. Their lengths are respectively 19.60 metres (64 feet 3 inches), 19.30 metres (63 feet 3 inches) and 19.10 metres (62 feet 8 inches) and they're all 4.34 metres (14 feet 3 inches) high and 3.65 metres (just a shade under 12 feet) wide.[41] They are fitted in place so precisely that it is impossible to insert even the edge of a razor blade into the joints.

'Go figure' is all I can say!

But if you want the orthodox take on the subject read Jean-Pierre Adam's 1977 paper, *A propos du trilithon de Baalbek: Le transport et la mise en oeuvre des megaliths.*[42] It's still the standard work of reference cited by all sceptics as though it proves their case, and it sets out a proposal deploying rollers of cedar wood, on which we are to envisage the blocks being placed.[43] To pull the blocks over the rollers Adam first considers, then (for logistical reasons) rejects, the use of a herd of 800 oxen.[44]

Finally, reasoning that weakness of human muscle power can be overcome by technical ingenuity, he settles on multiple arrays of pulleys rigged up to six capstans, each worked by a team of 24 men making a total of just 144 men to transport the blocks of the Trilithon, one by one, from the quarry half a mile (800 metres away) to the construction site.[45] At the end of the journey, he calculates that 16 larger capstans, each worked by a team of 32 men (i.e. 512 men in total) would have been required to manoeuvre the blocks into their final position.[46] The reason for the increased number of capstans and men at the end of the operation is that the wooden rollers would have to be removed, since obviously they could not be left in place in the wall. This would greatly increase the friction between the block and the surface over which it had to be dragged, but the deployment of some kind of lubricant would theoretically reduce the friction enough to avoid any need to lift the blocks – a problem that

Adam believes the Romans would have preferred not to confront with blocks of this size.[47]

Friedrich Ragette has a slightly different orthodox solution to the challenge of moving and placing the megaliths of the Trilithon.[48] In his case it does involve lifting the blocks at the end of the procedure, which he suggests would have been done using multiple 'Lewis' devices (metal pieces fitted into specially cut holes in the stones above their centre of mass, attached to chains or ropes and lifted by cranes or winches):

> The 800-ton block of the Trilithon must have been moved into position by rollers. Then it had to be lifted slightly to allow the removal of the rollers before the tremendous load was lowered inch by inch. If we figure five tons lifting capacity per Lewis hole we would need 160 attachments to the stone.[49]

It is not my intention to offer a detailed critique here. I simply note in passing that there are some difficulties with Adam's and Ragette's proposals. Both, for example, rely on wooden rollers but calculations indicate that the stress of supporting the huge blocks would very quickly have crushed such rollers, even if they were cut from the strongest Lebanon cedar.[50] Likewise, capstans are all very well and certainly multiply the 'muscle power' that each man is able to exert, but there is a danger, which Adam recognises, that unless massively anchored to the ground, it would be the capstans rather than the blocks that moved.[51] Finally, every mason understands the principle of Lewis devices and how they work, but there is no sign on the Trilithon blocks of even a single Lewis hole, let alone of 160 on each of them.[52]

Both Adam and Ragette, and others who want to reassure us how unremarkable and unmysterious the whole achievement of the Trilithon is, like to preface their accounts with reference to large megaliths that were moved using known technologies in historical times. For example a 25 metre (82 feet) tall Egyptian obelisk, weighing 320 tons, was brought to Rome in the first century AD by the Emperor Caligula. Transporting it from Egypt and across the Mediterranean in a specially built ship was, itself, an incredible feat of engineering, logistics and heavy lifting. Then, much later – in the sixteenth century – the same obelisk was moved from where it had stood since Caligula's time and re-erected in St Peter's Square on the orders of Pope Sixtus V.[53] Likewise in Russia in the late eighteenth century the 'Thunderstone', a 1,250 ton block of granite, the base for an equestrian statue of Peter the Great that still stands in the city of Saint Petersburg, was hauled seven kilometres overland on a special moveable track of bronze spheres.[54]

Mind you, it's one thing to drag a supersized megalith in a straight line over bronze ball-bearings, or to stand one up in the middle of a huge empty square, but it's quite another to build a series of such megaliths into a wall that looks like a titan's Lego project.

Still . . . let's accept that it can be done, that similar things have been done, and of course – for the evidence is before our eyes – that it *was* done at Baalbek. The only question that matters, therefore, is whether it was the Romans who did it, or whether they, and the cultures that preceded them here going back 10,000 years or more, found the U-shaped megalithic wall already in place and fitted their own structures into its embrace.

That's what it looks like to me.

The solid foundation rising above the plain at Baalbek that Daniel Lohmann identifies as pre-Roman and calls Podium 1, *and on top of which the Temple of Jupiter was built*, sits nicely inside the U-shaped wall which embraces it on its south, west and northern sides. At no point does the wall *support* the Temple of Jupiter. It is an entirely separate, exterior, structure.

I walk several times along the western wall, gazing up in stupefaction at the awesome megaliths of the Trilithon, trying to get to grips with what they mean. Regardless of whether it was the Romans or some unknown, antediluvian culture who put them here, what I'd like to know is *why* they put them 20 feet up? Why did they stack them on top of courses of smaller blocks, when surely the logic would have been to put the largest, heaviest blocks at ground level and add the smaller, lighter blocks above them. Why create the huge additional engineering and lifting challenge of doing it the other way round?

I walk along the wall. I'm counting blocks and courses. First of all, working upwards from ground level, there are three courses of really

276

quite small – let's say 1.5 metres high, quarter ton – ashlars. On top of these are six much bigger blocks, very nicely finished (although also very heavily eroded) with the upper half trimmed in to be narrower than the base. These six blocks, which are more or less identical to blocks in the south wall that I described earlier (see Chapter Twelve), weigh about 400 tons each. Finally on top of them, come the three monster, 800-ton, blocks of the Trilithon.

I walk north now, to the corner of the west and the north walls. The northernmost block of the Trilithon doesn't extend right to the end of the west wall. There's a gap, filled up by an Arab defensive tower extending out from Podium 1 and built over the corner. But if I remove that tower in my mind's eye, then I can see what's going on, because on the other side of it is another huge row of megaliths forming the northern arm of the 'U' shaped wall – the row that I'd looked down on earlier from above (see Chapter Twelve); indeed the Arab defensive tower was the very one I stepped out on to get a proper view of this part of the megalithic wall, which is separated by a grassy gap 35 feet wide from the north wall of Podium 1.

I know archaeologists see the U-shaped wall as the base of the Temple of Jupiter's grandiose but unfinished Podium 2. Lohmann makes a very good case for it being exactly that. But I'm still bothered by its non-load-bearing, purely cosmetic function, if that's the case, and I can't shake the feeling that it was a feature the Romans inherited from a much earlier time.

Where I do agree with the archaeologists, however, is that the even larger megaliths that I know are still in the quarry half a mile away, and that I'm going to take a look at as soon as I'm finished here, were definitely intended to sit on the top of the northern and southern arms of the U-shaped wall, thus raising them to the height that the western wall attained with the placement of the Trilithon. True, they are a bit longer and wider than the Trilithon blocks, but after trimming off the 'boss' left to protect them on their journey from the quarry they would match exactly, fitting like the pieces of a jigsaw puzzle. This remains the case, whether the Romans made the U-shaped wall as part of Podium 2 or whether it was the work of the architects and masons of a lost civilization of prehistoric antiquity.

And there's something else I agree with the archaeologists on.

Ideas put into circulation decades ago by 'ancient astronaut' enthusiasts, notably Zecharia Sitchin in his book *Stairway to Heaven*, first published in 1980 (and in other later volumes of his *Earth Chronicles* series), cannot possibly be right. Whatever Baalbek is, and for whatever reason megaliths of 800 tons and more were used here, and whoever it was who put those megaliths in place, they definitely did not do so in order to create 'a landing place for the aircraft of the gods'.[55] Sitchin's claim that the raised platform of Baalbek was 'intended to support some extremely heavy weight' and that the heavy weight in question was a 'rocket-like Flying Chamber',[56] could only have been made by a man who had no idea of the real appearance and layout of Baalbek itself, and could only be believed by others with no direct knowledge of the site.

The giant megalithic blocks of the Trilithon that seem to have convinced Sitchin the entire platform of Baalbek was megalithic all turn out to be parts of the U-shaped wall that embraces the (only modestly sized) Podium 1. And while an alien might conceivably land his spacecraft on even so modest a podium (if there were no other structure there) he certainly would not want to land it on top of a wall. It follows, therefore, that to use the megalithic character of the U-shaped wall to claim that a podium – which it is not even connected to, and does not support – was an alien 'landing platform', designed to bear extremely heavy weights, where 'all landings and take offs of the Shuttlecraft had to be conducted'[57] is either ignorant, or disingenuous or both.

Besides, even if the whole of the Baalbek complex was megalithic – which is not at all the case – we must ask ourselves why technologically advanced aliens capable of crossing the solar system in their spaceships would need such a platform to land on in the first place? If they could hop from planet to planet as Sitchin asks us to believe, wouldn't their science be up to constructing something a little more high-tech and fit for purpose than that? In short, isn't it obvious that Sitchin simply took 1970s NASA space technology as his template and projected it onto his imagined ancient astronauts?

I knew Zecharia Sitchin personally, had a few dinners with him in New York and once drove him from Stonehenge to London when he was on a visit to England. I liked him well enough, and I think he did some good research, but on Baalbek at least I have no doubt now – after exploring the site myself – that his whole 'landing platform' thesis is fundamentally flawed. This is not to say, however, that every idea set out in his books was equally compromised. The Mesopotamian cuneiform texts, which he could not read and translate as he claimed (his 'translations' were adapted and to some extent 'fictionalised' from the work of mainstream scholars) do in fact contain material of the greatest interest, and I think he was right to notice hints of high technology in them.

But were those technologies 'alien' or human? This is a question we'll return to in Chapter Sixteen, when we'll consider what is known about certain powerful beings referred to in Biblical and other ancient texts as 'the Nephilim' and 'the Watchers'.

The biggest cut stone block in the world

'I have found that archaeologists are seldom receptive to the notion of ancient astronauts,' wrote Elif Batuman in an article about Baalbek in the *New Yorker* on 18 December 2014, 'although one could argue that, when the archaeologists went looking for answers, all they managed to find was an even bigger and more mysterious block.'[58]

Indeed so! In June 2014, just a month before I arrived in Baalbek, the German Archaeological Institute made a stunning discovery in the quarries half a mile south of the Temple of Jupiter. There, it had long been known, lay two giant megaliths that are heavier, by a significant margin, than any of the stones in the Trilithon. What no one had suspected, however, despite a century of rather intensive investigations around Baalbek, was that a third immense block lay buried and hidden from view under the sediment that has accumulated in the quarry over the millennia. The archaeologists chose not to announce their discovery to the world until late November 2014, but since they had excavated it in June, it lay there in full view when I first visited the quarry on 10 July and a local shopkeeper – who claimed that the discovery was in fact his and that the Germans had merely appropriated it – made a point of drawing it to my attention.

The quarry is in two parts, divided by a road, and in the first area you come to as you approach from the direction of the temples lies the famous 'Stone of the Pregnant Woman', also known as the 'Stone of the South', which has been decorating postcards from Baalbek for a hundred years and was known to travellers like David Urquhart long before that. It measures 21.50 metres (almost 71 feet) in length, 4.20 metres (just under 14 feet) in height, and 4.30 metres (just over 14 feet) in width. It weighs 970 tons.[59] Across the road a second even bigger megalith, which had lain undiscovered since time immemorial, was unearthed in the 1990s. It measures 20.5 metres in length, 4.56 metres wide and 4.5 metres high; its weight has been calculated to be 1,242 tons.[60] But the megalith that was discovered in June 2014 has a mass greater than either of these, measuring 19.60 metres (64 feet 4 inches) long, 6 metres (19 feet 9 inches) wide, and 5.5 metres (18 feet) high, with an estimated weight of 1,650 tons.[61]

It was this newly excavated megalith, the single largest block of stone ever quarried in the ancient world, that the excited shopkeeper proudly pointed out to me during my visit. Its upper surface is less than two metres below the lower edge of the Stone of the Pregnant Woman, which it lies immediately beside and parallel to. And, like the Stone of the Pregnant Women, it is beautifully cut and shaped, ready, after removal of the 'boss', to go straight into the U-shaped wall for which all three giant blocks were undoubtedly intended.

I spend some hours clambering around these weird, otherworldly blocks. I feel as though I'm mountaineering. The scale is so immense, and in a way so 'alien', that a curious detachment from everyday reality sets in and I lose all track of time. I note that the Stone of the Pregnant Women appears to have been sliced through at the base, where it emerges from the bedrock, with a clean straight cut. How was that done? And no matter where I stand – above, below, beside – I am dwarfed by this monstrous product of ancient and unknowable minds. The very thought that someone, in some distant epoch, could conceive of this, could cut it out and shape it entire and then, at the end, just leave it here, abandon it, forget about it, is incomprehensible to me. The closer I examine it, the more details I observe of the precision of the workmanship, of the scale of the enterprise, and of the will and imagination that went into its creation, the more certain I become that it and its fellows here in the quarries, and the Trilithon, and the other giant megaliths of Baalbek, were not the work of the Romans.

I know how profoundly Daniel Lohmann disagrees! A few months later, in February 2015, he and I will correspond at some length over several days. He will graciously answer many questions and help me to understand some of the complexities of Baalbek that escaped me when I was there. He'll make an excellent case for the Roman provenance of the whole vast scheme. He will even send me a photograph of the column drum built into the foundations of the Trilithon wall and he'll write:

> In my recent work I located this column drum fragment, excavated it anew, and measured it millimetre precise to determine the drum diameter. I looked at the surface structure and masons dressing in comparison with the Jupiter temple columns and the lithology. All indications are exactly the same as the column drums of the Roman Jupiter temple. The fragment was neatly dressed at the edges to make a masonry ashlar out of it, and it received the beautifully sharply cut edges that all ashlars of the Roman Jupiter Temple phase have (including the megaliths).[62]

My reply:

> First of all, to be absolutely clear, *I don't* dispute that this fragment is from a column drum of the Roman Jupiter Temple. Clearly it is. And *I don't* dispute the generally agreed dating of the columns of the Roman Jupiter Temple. But this fragment is a very important part of the (formidable!) edifice of logic you and your colleagues use to establish the chronology of the Trilithon, and that many others have relied upon when reporting that chronology. What I'd like to interrogate a little further, therefore, is your level of certainty that this column drum fragment was put there at the same time as the original construction of the western wall. It's nicely cut and shaped, I agree, but still it sticks out like a sore thumb (especially now I see it cleared in

the photo you kindly sent me). It looks intrusive, odd and awkward – very different from the rest of the blocks in this course. In short I think the argument can be made that it is more likely to be a later repair of the wall than it is to be an integral part of the original wall. Lending some support to this argument is that we know the Arabs were constantly repairing the walls around the whole site, and sometimes using column drums to do so, so why shouldn't this be just one more of those repairs? *What is the absolutely compelling archaeological evidence that completely, effectively and once and for all rules this possibility out?* I'd be most grateful if you could address that specific point in your reply.[63]

Lohmann comes right back at me on this:

The fragment is just one of the indications that shows the synchronicity of the megalith podium and the temple, which was not our result, but known to science for over one hundred years – and at latest since the excavations by the German team of 1900-1904. Yes, it sticks out. But no – not unlike the others. The builders of the temple were rather pragmatic: once the structure was to be hidden underneath the soil or behind something else, they didn't bother to flatten the surfaces or make it look nice . . . What was important first when building is that the ashlar was perfectly flattened on the top and bottom, and then the two sides, in order to create a solid and stable wall – and that was done on the column drum exactly in the same Roman manner as it was done on the blocks around it. If you look at the length of the fragment, and imagine a hole in the wall instead, the two smaller ashlars in the course above would fall, causing further instability for the structures above. Here, frictional connection/ force closure (translations of *kraftschluss* from my dictionary – language barriers!) is needed, you can't just replace an ashlar in a row of 'stretchers'. Secondly, Arab repairs of Roman walls look a lot different: they used smaller blocks instead, and would never have been able to squeeze a block in so tightly . . . Medieval

282

repairs never have such tight joints. It's a comparison of precision that makes an engineer like me 100% certain.[64]

After examining our own photographs of the Trilithon wall – Santha took a great many while we were there – I find myself unpersuaded by Lohmann's argument. First of all (see Plate 40), this column drum is not 'hidden underneath soil or behind something else'. It's in plain view in the lowest visible course of the wall, and it does stick out like a sore thumb. It's made of a distinctively different, much darker, stone and it has a very different 'look' from any neighbouring block. It is quite unique in fact. Secondly, as to the precision, I don't agree with Lohmann that the column drum cannot be an Arab repair. In Plates 42 and 43 the reader will find an example of another column drum which is certainly part of an Arab repair to the walls of Baalbek and its precision is as good as that on the column drum in the foundations. Another possibility I've considered – that it could be a Roman repair to a pre-Roman wall – also remains very much in play. If the lower block which this improvised block replaced had been badly damaged, and a decision had been made to remove it, the two small rectangular blocks above it (the ones Lohmann said 'would fall, causing further instability for the structures above') would have had to be removed at the same time.

But the next course up is so set that none of the other blocks in it would have fallen, nor would any instability have been caused to the huge megalith in the course above that, which is supported on no less than five large horizontal blocks, three of which would be entirely unaffected by the removal of the two smaller blocks below, while the other two would have been held in place by 'frictional connection'. Once the column drum had been cut to shape and put in place at ground level, the two smaller blocks could have been slid back into the wall above it, completing a very neat and effective repair.

There's something else, a fundamental area of disagreement, concerning what I see as a U-shaped megalithic wall surrounding Podium 1, but that Lohmann sees as the first courses of Podium 2. He tells me that 'aside from the size of the ashlars' what I call a U-shaped megalithic wall is 'the bottom of a standard shape of a Roman temple podium after Augustus times.' He asks me to take a look at the podium of the *Maison Carée* in Nimes,[65] and suggests that the Temple of Bacchus in Baalbek itself also has a similar podium.[66] He sends me links to photographs. 'If you zoom in,' he writes, 'you can see the stones of the second layer above the bottom layer, corresponding to the Trilithon.'

My reply:

You write that the megalithic podium for the Temple of Jupiter, though obviously on a very different scale, is the 'standard shape of a Roman temple podium' but I'm not sure I see that from the pix you linked to. I attach here one of ours from the Temple of Bacchus . . . (same angle as the one you sent[67]). It shows a podium with a single straight side (apart from the lip at top and bottom), whereas the podium of the Temple of Jupiter gives more of a stepped effect with the row of huge megalithic blocks, that according to our correspondence form part of the lowest layer of the Julio-Claudian Temple podium, stepped out very far from the sheer wall above them, on top of which stood the peristasis. I suppose the resemblance would be better if the megalithic layer had been completed and extended all the way up to the top of the wall, but the peristasis would still have been set back a few metres from the top, instead of pretty much flush with the top as it is in the Temple of Bacchus. In short, when I zoom in to the Temple of Bacchus podium I don't really see blocks, regardless of scale, that correspond with the Trilithon blocks. Am I missing something obvious here?[68]

I also ask: 'Have you found organic materials with good provenance anywhere in "Podium 2" and have you done carbon dating on these?'[69]

On the carbon dating Lohmann replies that 'unfortunately' none had been done:

The history of constant change in the building, as well as deep excavation levels of the past 100 years have left no archaeological or organic material at all that would help us with this.[70]

In its own way this is quite a revelation to me, since it means – to deploy an appropriate metaphor – that the entire edifice of archaeological chronology for the so-called 'Julio-Claudian podium' – Podium 2 – of the Temple of Jupiter, rests on foundations in which there is no scientific dating evidence whatsoever. This not to say that radiocarbon dates for archaeological sites are unproblematic! As we've seen in earlier chapters, they are often very problematic indeed – unless it can be demonstrated, as is the case at Göbekli Tepe, that the dated organic remains have been 'sealed' at a particular moment and there is no possibility of subsequent intrusion of later materials that might give a falsely young date.

But there are simply no carbon dates, problematic or not, for Podium 2. It follows, therefore, that the orthodox chronology of this incredibly interesting and peculiar structure is based entirely on stylistic factors – that certain styles of building can be associated with specific cultures and specific periods and that the 'style' seen in Podium 2 is entirely appropriate to the 'Julio-Claudian' epoch of Roman construction.

It's my view that the stylistic argument at Baalbek is nowhere near as clear-cut as it should be, given how much of our understanding of the site depends on it. And in response to my question about the positioning of the peristasis (i.e. of the four-sided porch or hall of columns surrounding the *cella* – the inner building – of the temple), Lohmann admits there is a stylistic anomaly:

> yes, normally the peristasis would rest on the edge of the podium, as it does at the Bacchus temple. That would be following the Roman examples. (Mars-Ultor at the Roman Forum was a milestone building for that[71]). It is one of the oddities of Jupiter.[72]

On the other hand, Lohmann points out, temples do exist where the peristasis is set back in the way he envisages it would ultimately have been at Baalbek if Podium 2 had ever been completed – for example, the Bel temple in Palmyra, the temple of Zeus in Aizanoi, Turkey, and the colossal temple in Tarsos, Turkey. 'In my opinion,' he writes:

> this is due to the fact that both Bel temple, and Jupiter in Baalbek, were built onto older podia (Herodian in Baalbek, Hellenistic

in Palmyra), and had to find a solution how to squeeze a first-century, latest-fashion Roman podium underneath the (even only slightly) older temple building. Baalbek's terrace was immensely high, so the podium needed to be colossal, and in Palmyra the peristasis was already standing, so the podium was erected at a distance.[73]

Further, Lohmann stands his ground on the issue of the shape of Podium 2 which, despite its incompleteness, he sees as being quite normal:

> a standard podium consists of a bottom profile (lip, as you call it), the 'shaft' or the vertical part (that's the trilithon layer in Baalbek . . .) and a top lip layer . . .[74]

He attaches an architectural diagram of the podium of Hosn Niha, another Roman temple in Lebanon, to make his point.[75] To my eye, however, it looks astonishingly *unlike* Podium 2 at Baalbek and the layer in it that he wants me to compare to the Trilithon is just 1.58 metres (5 feet 3 inches) high, whereas the Trilithon, as we've seen, is 4.34 metres (14 feet 3 inches) high.

As I've already noted, I think Daniel Lohmann makes a strong case, but nothing in our correspondence proves to me that the U-shaped megalithic wall (that surrounds, but that does not support, Podium 1 on which the Temple of Jupiter in fact stands) is the work of the Romans. He could be right. But he could also be wrong and, in context of all the other indications from around the world of a lost civilization, I think it wise to keep an open mind on Baalbek.

Finally, however, it's what I see in the quarry that convinces me of this, because we have to ask ourselves why three huge blocks in the range of 1,000 to 1,650 tons were left there at all.

The conventional answer is that the Romans, having quarried these exceptionally large blocks, found that they could not move them and simply abandoned them. But that explanation makes very little sense. If the argument that the Romans were responsible for the U-shaped megalithic wall is correct, then we know that they went on to build an extensive temple complex dedicated to Jupiter using smaller blocks of stone. Surely their first source for the multiple smaller blocks they needed would have been the huge megaliths that, according to the argument of mainstream archaeology, they had discovered they could not move from the quarry? The Romans were practical people, who would not allow work that they had already so painstakingly done to go to waste. Rather than opening up fresh quarry faces, wouldn't they have used those massive, already almost completely quarried 1,000-ton-plus blocks and simply sliced them up into smaller, more moveable megaliths for the construction of the rest of the temple?

It's really puzzling that they didn't do so and therefore the fact that these gigantic, almost finished blocks remain in the quarry, and were never sliced up into smaller blocks and used in the general construction of the Temple of Jupiter, suggests to me very strongly that the Romans did not even know they were there – just as the German Archaeological Institute, despite a hundred years of excavations, didn't know until 2014 that a third massive block was there. In due course, I'm told, 'good new information about the dating and practicalities of the quarry megaliths' may be forthcoming, but that information was not available at the time of writing.[76] I await it with interest, but also with some doubt as to whether it will settle anything or simply raise further questions.

We are a species with amnesia. The devastating comet impacts that set the Younger Dryas in train 12,800 years ago and that caused two episodes of global flooding, one at the beginning and one at the end of the Younger Dryas, made us forget so much. The recovery of memory from the fragments that remain is logistically difficult and psychologically painful – as the complexities and decades of disputes around Baalbek show. But messages still reach us from the deep and distant past in the words of the Sages, in the deeds of the magicians, and in the mighty memorials that they left behind to awaken us at the time of the Great Return.

Part VI

Stars

Chapter 14
The Gates of the Sun

———◆———

Baalbek remains very much on my mind the next day as we drive the magnificent coastline around Jounieh Bay heading 38 kilometres north to Byblos, the ancient Phoenician port that claims, with some justification, to be the oldest continuously inhabited city in the world. Archaeologists have established that it was occupied as early as 8800 BC,[1] while Göbekli Tepe still functioned.[2] By 5000 BC, Byblos was a flourishing, stable settlement that has never since been without human population.[3] By 3000 BC, when it was known as Gubla or Gebel, it had grown to become the key port and city of the ancient Canaanite coast.[4] It was the Greeks who later called it Byblos, when it served as the centre of a lucrative papyrus trade with Egypt (*bublos* is the Greek word for papyrus).[5] Likewise the reader will recall from Chapter Thirteen that 'Phoenician' was the Greek name for the Canaanites and that the Phoenicians referred to themselves as Canaanites. For simplicity's sake, I will continue to use the terms 'Phoenician' and 'Canaanite' interchangeably here and continue to refer to ancient Gubla/Gebel as Byblos.

As we pull into Byblos with its street cafés and palms and the bright Mediterranean lapping at its beautiful, crescent-shaped harbour, what's on my mind about Baalbek is a question. Why didn't the Romans choose to build the greatest and most spectacular temple in their entire empire in Rome itself? Or failing that, if for some reason they felt compelled to build the Temple of Jupiter in Lebanon, then why didn't they build it in a prestigious and important entrepôt like Byblos? And if not in Byblos, then why not in another of the renowned Phoenician ports along the same coast such as Tyre or Sidon?

Why Baalbek for the Temple of Jupiter? That's the question. But there's no easy answer, because archaeologists and historians admit that not a single shred of evidence exists 'to tell us who commissioned, paid for, or designed any portion of the complex'.[6] We can therefore only speculate as to their motives. It is really rather surprising when you consider the scale of the enterprise that no Emperor, no general and no architect ever claimed credit for it, but the fact is that the temple remained peculiarly absent from the annals of the Romans and of all other peoples for many centuries after it was built.[7]

Not until Macrobius, who wrote in the fifth century AD (by which time Baalbek had long been Christianised) do we even get a reference to the god who was worshipped there.[8] It is almost as though a spell of silence was cast over the place by the magicians of a former age and that the Romans fell under its glamour, allowing themselves to be bound by it, even as they raised up the huge columns and pediments of their own temples. In consequence, as architectural historian Dell Upton observes, 'ancient Baalbek is a figment of our imaginations'.[9] Even the site itself, as we see it now, is in a sense a work of fantasy, since so much of it:

> was reconstructed by a German archaeological mission in the early twentieth century and by French and Lebanese archaeologists in the 1930s, 1950s and 1960s. The rest we know from reconstruction drawings of the complex in a mythical state of completion.[10]

It is a continuation of this archaeological 'myth-making', I believe, that leads Daniel Lohmann to his paradoxical speculation that the builders of Roman Baalbek were 'megalomaniacs' even though they were, in fact, so self-effacing that they never sought to associate themselves by name with any of the 'giant strides towards monumentality' that they took there.[11] The most gigantic of all these 'megalomaniac' strides, of course, if Lohmann is right, was the unfinished attempt to give the Temple of Jupiter a purely cosmetic, non-load-bearing podium, rising – had it ever been completed – to around 50 feet high (dwarfing any other Roman temple podium) and made up of blocks weighing hundreds of tons and, in the case of the Trilithon, close to a thousand tons. In Lohmann's reference frame, and the reference frame of every archaeologist for the past century, only megalomaniacs would contemplate such a task.

Since we're all speculating, however, I offer the alternative speculation that the Romans chose Baalbek for the Temple of Jupiter – that it was such a special place to them – precisely *because* the U-shaped wall that Lohmann thinks was the base of their 'megalomaniac' podium was already there, coming down from the time of the gods themselves and worthy of veneration in later ages purely in order to honour those ancient gods, rather than to exalt the names and stoke the egos of those who honoured them.

Star worshippers

Overlooking the ruins of Phoenician and Roman temples, a castle from the Crusader period (twelfth century AD) is the dominant landmark in Byblos today. And interestingly this Crusader castle, reconstructed and repaired many times, has at least a dozen Roman column drums re-used as masonry blocks in its walls – a reminder that, in this region, you can never take any piece of architecture entirely at face value.

But the castle is a wonderful spot to get a sense of the old, indeed the truly ancient, city of Byblos, from which Phoenician seafarers once sailed out to all points of the known world and beyond – for the suggestion that the Phoenicians reached the Americas thousands of years before Columbus continues to be supported by intriguing though fragmentary evidence.[12] There is also a mysterious connection with Ancient Egypt that goes far beyond the papyrus trade between these two ancient peoples.

This connection concerns the god Osiris, whose celestial image the Ancient Egyptians saw in the constellation of Orion. The father of Horus and the husband of Isis, the goddess of magic, Osiris was, according to tradition, a great king of primordial times, who offered the gifts of civilization to those who were willing to receive them.[13] After weaning the indigenous peoples of Egypt:

from their miserable and barbarous manners, he taught them how to till the earth, and how to sow and reap crops, he formulated a code of laws for them, and made them worship the gods and perform service to them. He then left Egypt and travelled over the rest of the world teaching the various nations to do what his own subjects were doing. He forced no man to carry out his instructions, but by means of gentle persuasion and an appeal to their reason, he succeeded in inducing them to practice what he preached.[14]

The deeds of this great civilizing teacher as they are recorded in the Ancient Egyptian annals are, of course, reminiscent of the mission of those companies of gods, magicians and sages whom the Edfu Building Texts tell us 'wandered the earth' in their great ships after the flood that destroyed their homeland, seeking to bring about the resurrection of the antediluvian world. And the antagonist, Set, who appears in the Edfu tradition and is eventually defeated and subdued by Horus, also plays a key role in the Osiris cycle of myths. He plots against the god-king while he is away on his civilizing mission and on his return he contrives to murder him with the help, significantly, of seventy-two co-conspirators.[15] There is code here for, as the reader will recall, the number 72 is the heartbeat of the precessional cycle – the number of years required for one degree of precessional motion.

The body of Osiris, we are told, is placed in a sarcophagus by Set and the other conspirators and thrown in the Nile, whence the current carries it north and out into the Mediterranean sea. The waves carried the box to the coast of Lebanon:

> and cast it up at Byblos, and as soon as it rested on the ground a large tree sprang up and, growing all around the box, enclosed it on every side. The King of Byblos marvelled at the size of this tree and had it cut down and caused a pillar for his palace to be made of that portion of the trunk which contained the box.[16]

Discovering the whereabouts of her husband's remains, Isis takes ship to Byblos, goes to the palace and contrives to have herself appointed

as nursemaid to the children of the King. When unobserved she trans-
forms into a swallow and flies round and round the pillar lamenting.
Eventually she reveals her true identity and persuades the monarch
to give her the pillar, from which she removes the sarcophagus
containing the dead body of Osiris and returns with it to Egypt.[17]

What happens next is a long story, that we needn't go into here,
but the upshot is the resurrection of Osiris in the heavens as the
constellation of Orion where, as a star god, he reigns over the afterlife
kingdom, his consort Isis by his side in the form of the bright star
Sirius (called Sopdu or Sept in the Ancient Egyptian language, often
rendered in Greek as Sothis).[18] In one text, which makes these stellar
identifications particularly clear, Isis speaks of Osiris as follows:

Thy sacred image, Orion in heaven, rises and sets every day; I
am Sothis following after him, and I will not forsake him.[19]

And in the Pyramid Texts we read, amongst many similar utterances,
that 'Osiris has come as Orion'.[20] Multiple other references also identify deceased pharaohs of Egypt with Osiris and with the stars of Orion
and Sirius, for example:

O flesh of the King, do not decay . . . You shall reach the sky as
Orion, your soul shall be as effective as Sothis . . .[21]

Likewise:

O King, the sky conceives you with Orion, the dawn light bears
you with Orion. He who lives, lives by the command of the gods,
and you live. You will regularly ascend with Orion from the
eastern region of the sky, you will regularly descend with Orion
into the western region of the sky.[22]

From such texts, notes Egyptologist Selim Hassan:

I think it cannot possibly be denied that, at one period in their
history, the Egyptians believed that the souls of their Kings either

mingled with the stars, or became a star . . . and this tradition never entirely died out. Moreover the association of the Giza Pyramids with the stellar cult was long maintained by tradition and those of Khufu and Khafre retained the reputation of being connected with star-worship as late as the Arab Period.[23]

In the same passage, Hassan then goes on to make an observation of the greatest relevance to my research. 'In the Geographical Dictionary, *Mo'gam-el-Buldan,* by Yakut el-Hamawi,' he writes, 'Vol. VIII, p. 457 (Cairo Edition)':

it is said, after giving the dimensions of the two largest of the Giza Pyramids: 'To both of them the Sabians made their pilgrimage.' Now, of course, these Sabians were star-worshippers, and if I guess rightly they had derived their name from the Egyptian word *sba,* 'star'. The Sabians were followers of an ancient religion . . . worshippers of the hosts of Heaven, the heavenly bodies . . . Whatever the origin of their name may have been, the fact remains that they fully recognised the Pyramids of Khufu and Khafre as being monuments connected with the stellar cult, and revered them as places of pilgrimage.[24]

The connection Hassan makes here is a remarkable one, because the home city of the Sabians, since time immemorial, was Harran in south-eastern Turkey,[25] within a few miles of Göbekli Tepe. Moreover, as well as being 'star-worshippers', these Sabians of Harran were followers of the 'Books of Thoth' – see Chapter Eleven – in which the Ancient Egyptian wisdom god had set down the 'words of the Sages'. Indeed in Islamic times (for hundreds of years after the revelation of the Koran to the Prophet Muhammad in the seventh century AD), the Sabians were able to win exemption from persecution at the hands of the Muslims by claiming not to be pagans but a 'people of the book', distinguished, like the Christians and Jews, by their possession of a divinely revealed Scripture.[26] When asked to show their 'book' they produced a copy of the Hermetic texts – the Greek and Latin writings purporting to be dialogues between Thoth (the Hermes of the Greeks, the Mercury of the Romans) and various of his pupils.[27] It is noteworthy that Thoth, as well as being the god of wisdom, was also 'Lord of the Moon',[28] and that the major temple of Harran was dedicated to the moon god of their own pantheon, whose name was Sin.[29] Last but not least, Philo of Byblos tells us that Sanchuniathon, the source of his *Phoenician History*:

> carefully searched out the works of Taautos. He did this since he realised that Taautos was the first person under the sun who thought of the invention of writing and who began to compose records, thereby laying the foundation, as it were, of learning. The Egyptians call him Thouth and the Alexandrians Thoth, and the Greeks translated his name as Hermes.[30]

We stay a few hours longer in Byblos. Excavations of the ancient city lie all around the Crusader castle. There's a Roman colonnade, a small theatre, Phoenician ramparts, the remains, little more than foundations, of the Temple of Baalat-Gebel, circa 2800 BC and dedicated to the Phoenician patron goddess of Byblos, and the so-called L-shaped temple, circa 2600 BC – a sacred lake once separated the two edifices. On top of a podium a number of small, crude obelisks still stand – the 'Temple of the Obelisks', circa 1900 to 1600 BC. There are the remains of the royal necropolis of the Kings of Byblos, circa eighteenth century BC down to tenth century BC, but mingled in with all this, very close to it, is the Neolithic quarter, dating back to 5000 BC and beyond, where the inhabitants of Byblos first started to make floors of crushed limestone around 4500 BC.[31]

All these ruins and remains are jumbled together promiscuously, one on top of the other, around one another, century upon century, millennium upon millennium, receding back into prehistory, very comprehensively picked clean by the archaeologists and left on show as tourist attractions. The site does not touch my heart and in the absence of Sanchuniathon's original text, in the absence even of Philo's *History*, other than in the fragments that have survived, I feel there's nothing more of use that I can do here.

It's time to move on.

Hill of pillars

It's a short flight from Beirut to Istanbul and from Istanbul it's only another short hop to the city of Şanlıurfa, which Santha and I will use as our base for visiting Harran, the city of the mysterious 'star-worshipping' Sabians, and for a return visit to Göbekli Tepe. Our first target, however, is neither of these places. Instead we seek out an as yet unexcavated site which shows every indication of being as old as Göbekli Tepe and which appears to have been dedicated to the same mysterious purpose. The name of this site, I've learned from my background research, is Karahan Tepe, but knowing its name is one thing; finding it is quite another.

It's baking hot in southeastern Turkey in July. Our driver speaks English so there's no problem communicating with him, and he in turn can communicate with others on our behalf, but nobody we pass as we drive through a landscape of irrigated fields and barren hills seems to have the faintest idea where Karahan Tepe is. Well, why should they, after all? It's just another hill and by all accounts it's in a fairly deserted spot. We do find it in the end, however, about 15 kilometres south of the main E90 highway and 65 kilometres east of Şanlıurfa. That's where we spot a little farmstead surrounded by low walls and poor fields at the end of a bumpy dirt track. The farmer points to a hill rising a few hundred metres to our north. It's on his land, he says, but we're welcome to take a look. He assigns his teenage son to show us how to drive our car as close as possible to the site, then we step out and go the rest of the way on foot.

The *tepe* is a ridge of limestone running roughly north to south with steep slopes, covered in loose crumbly soil, overgrown with yellow grass on its eastern and western flanks. The top of the ridge is about 705 metres above sea level, but the climb from where we've parked is only another 50 metres and almost immediately we start seeing the characteristic T-shapes of the pillars we're familiar with from Göbekli Tepe. They are everywhere around the sides of the ridge, dozens of them, some organised in circles, others in what appear to be parallel rows, but all of them are quite deeply buried with only the distinctive tops of the 'T' protruding above the ground.

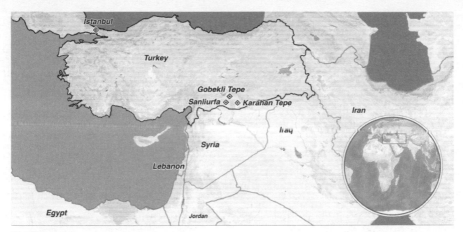

Figure 45

Extraordinarily, other than confirming that Karahan Tepe is the same age as Göbekli Tepe, i.e. between 11,000 and 12,000 years old, and that it was abandoned at around the same time, i.e. around 10,200 years ago, after which it was never resettled,[32] almost no archaeology has been done on the site at all. Local people, on the other hand, have been busy here looking for treasure and their efforts have exposed and broken a number of the pillars, two with serpents carved on them exactly in the manner that serpents are depicted on the pillars of Göbekli Tepe.

Along the top of the ridge we find numerous semi-spherical depressions, like little craters, cut into the rock. Some have very clean, sharply-defined edges that are typically about 30 centimetres (1 foot) in diameter and up to 15 centimetres (6 inches) deep – although there are also smaller and larger cupules present. In most cases they are grouped into arrays of a dozen or more, sometimes in rows, sometimes in circular or spiral patterns – but in such a random way that it is difficult to see the logic behind them.

As at Göbekli Tepe, it is clear that the quarrying of the pillars was done on site and we find a number of places where parallel grooves, marking out the shape of a pillar, have been cut into the bedrock of the ridge. There is one almost complete T-shaped pillar still in situ in the quarry that measures 4.5 metres (14 feet 10 inches) high, 1.5 metres (5 feet) wide and 80 centimetres (2 feet 7 inches) thick.[33] Looking from that to the forest of pillars with only their heads protruding above the flanks of the hill, I can't help but wonder what would be found here if a proper excavation was done. Göbekli Tepe has already rewritten the history of mankind and here is another Göbekli Tepe, pristine, practically untouched, and no one seems in the least bit interested. Indeed there is even a broken L-shaped fragment of a carefully cut block that once formed a complete square 'window' or 'porthole' – similar pieces have been found intact at Göbekli Tepe – that has been used here as part of the hearth for some shepherd's fire and now sits blackened with smoke in a sheltered corner near the top of the ridge.

It's incomprehensible to me that a place as important as Karahan Tepe, with so much to teach us, could be so ignored and so disregarded. I have often said, as I did at the end of the last chapter, that we are a species with amnesia. I attribute our great forgetfulness of our own past, the blank pages in our memory, to the terrible cataclysms the earth passed through at the end of the Ice Age, but here at Karahan Tepe I'm reminded that our collective stupor is also often wilfully self-inflicted – as though we no longer care to know where we come from or who we really are.

Control of the past

The next day Santha and I go back to Göbekli Tepe. Klaus Schmidt is still alive at this point in July 2014, but he's away in Germany for the summer and in just a few days' time he will die of a heart attack.

In his absence I want to take another look at the site. In particular, I'm hoping to arrange to be there at night, so that I can experience it under the open sky and get a sense of its relationship to the stars above as well as to the earth below. Instead, what I get is another forceful reminder of how we humans wilfully desecrate the precious gifts bequeathed to us by our ancestors.

Even in 2013 the archaeological vandalizing and defacing of the site was well advanced with a hideous raised walkway in place, but what has happened since our last visit is almost beyond words to describe. A massively ugly wooden roof now looms over the megalithic enclosures, entirely covering them, and hulking platforms loaded with tons of stones have been suspended beneath it to prevent the roof from blowing away in high winds. These platforms, together with the struts supporting the roof and the prominent 'no entry' signs scattered around, make it almost impossible to see the megalithic pillars or to appreciate their profound, original beauty and spiritual power.

What the archaeologists have done – of course, they claim they did it to 'protect' the site – is a travesty, an abomination, a masterpiece of ugliness, and we, the global public, whose heritage Göbekli Tepe is, are left cheated and bereft. I simply cannot understand the minds that could have boxed in, caged and imprisoned Göbekli Tepe in this way. I cannot begin to imagine what they were thinking. And even if the roof is 'temporary' as is presently claimed – until, no doubt, a larger one is put in place – that is no excuse. Better no roof at all (the site has managed very well without one for nearly nineteen years since the first excavations began) than even five minutes of this vile 'temporary' horror.

Besides, I have grave doubts about how 'temporary' it will be. It has taken almost a year for the German Archaeological Institute to put the roof up (they were already working on it during our previous visit in September 2013), a lot of money has been spent on it, and I fear we will not see it removed and replaced with something more aesthetically appropriate to the majesty and mystery of Göbekli Tepe for a very long while.

As to a night visit, and my plan to see the stars with the megaliths around me . . . What a joke! The roof has cut Göbekli Tepe off entirely from the cosmos. It feels almost like a deliberate, calculated act of disempowerment – as though someone amongst the powers that be suddenly woke up and realised how dangerous this ancient place has become to the established order of things and how subversive it potentially is to the system of mind control, very much including control of the past, that keeps modern society in order.

Ancient astronomers

That night back in our hotel I'm working on my laptop, going through a pile of research papers about Göbekli Tepe that I've downloaded and brought with me. Most of them are from academic journals, but one is from my own website. Written by registered engineer and environmental geologist Paul Burley, I published it in March 2013 and haven't read it since. I recall at the time feeling it was important, but I can't immediately remember why. Göbekli Tepe wasn't as central to my concerns then as it is today. Now as I read through Burley's paper in the light of everything I've learned since March 2013, its central message, and exactly why it matters, hits me like a shot of adrenaline.

Klaus Schmidt's opposition to any form of astronomical connection at Göbekli Tepe, which I reported briefly in Chapter One, was based more on his own profound ignorance of astronomy and distaste for the subject, than anything else. In the teeth of this hostility from the lead archaeologist, however, a number of scientists have studied Göbekli Tepe to see if any of the enclosures, or the groups of pillars within them, reveal any obvious astronomical alignments. It is the unanimous testimony of all these studies that Göbekli Tepe is *a profoundly astronomical site*, that its builders observed the stars closely, and that they were able to manifest these observations very successfully in the alignments of the structures on the ground.

I'll give a few examples here.

Dr Giulio Magli, Professor of Mathematical Physics at the Politecnico di Milano, is a leading Italian astrophysicist who has conducted archaeo-astronomical studies of a number of ancient sites and monuments around the world. In 2013 he published a research paper on Göbekli Tepe based on precise computer simulations of changes in the sky brought about over long periods by precession[34] – a phenomenon that we have already explored. It is Magli's case that Sirius, the star the Ancient Egyptians identified with the goddess Isis, was an object of particular interest to the builders of Göbekli Tepe:

Simulating the sky in the tenth millennium BC, it is possible to see that a quite spectacular phenomenon occurred at Göbekli Tepe in that period: the 'birth' of a 'new' star, and certainly not of an ordinary one, as it is the brightest star and the fourth most brilliant object of the sky: Sirius. Indeed precession, at the latitude of Göbekli Tepe, brought Sirius under the horizon in the years around 15,000 BC. After reaching the minimum, Sirius started to come closer to the horizon and it became visible again, very low and close to due south, towards 9300 BC.[35]

Thereafter, Magli goes on to demonstrate, the rising points of Sirius along the horizon, which also change very slowly as a result of precession, appear to have been 'tracked' at Göbekli Tepe by Enclosure D, Enclosure C and Enclosure B. The extrapolated mean azimuths of these enclosures, taken as the mid-lines between the two central monoliths in each case, align with the rising azimuth of Sirius in respectively 9100 BC, 8750 BC and 8300 BC.[36] 'The structures of Göbekli Tepe,' Magli concludes, 'were conceived to celebrate, and then follow in the course of the centuries, the appearance of a brilliant 'guest' star in the sky: Sirius.'[37]

Professor Robert Schoch of Boston University, though not an astronomer, also detected astronomical alignments at Göbekli Tepe, and in the same region of the sky highlighted by Magli. However, Schoch came to a different conclusion about what stellar objects might have interested the builders. 'This is a difficult question to answer,' he wrote, before going on to offer the following hypothesis:

On the morning of the Vernal Equinox of circa 10,000 BCE, before the sun rose due east at Göbekli Tepe, the Pleiades, Taurus, and the top of Orion were in view in the direction indicated by the central stones of Enclosure D, with Orion's belt not far above the horizon as dawn broke (as seen from the best vantage points in the area). A similar scenario played out for the orientation of the central stones of Enclosure C in circa 9500 BCE and for Enclosure B in circa 9000 BCE. Enclosure A is oriented toward the Pleiades, Taurus, and Orion on the morning of the Vernal Equinox circa 8500 BCE, but due to precessional changes, the entire belt of Orion no longer rose above the horizon before dawn broke. By about 8150 BCE the belt of Orion remained below the horizon at dawn on the morning of the Vernal Equinox. These dates fit well the timeframe established for Göbekli Tepe on the basis of radiocarbon dating.[38]

Other non-astronomers, author Andrew Collins and chartered engineer Rodney Hale, looked in the opposite direction to Schoch and Magli, i.e. north instead of south, and found strong alignments with the setting of Deneb, the brightest star in the constellation of Cygnus. Again the alignments turn out to track the changes in the position of the star caused by precession.[39] The growing impression that the builders of Göbekli Tepe paid close attention to the stars and were fully aware of the effects of precessional motion on the celestial landscape, was confirmed in January 2015 in an article in the journal *Archaeological Discovery*, by Alessandro De Lorenzis and Vincenzo Orofino, both of the Department of Mathematics and Physics at the University of Salento, Italy. They concluded that Collins and Hale were correct and that, on the northern side of their orientations, 'the central pillars of the studied enclosures are in fact turned to face the setting of Deneb.'[40] Lorentis and Orofino refined the dates given by Collins and Hale, pushing them back by about 200 years, but agreed that subtle changes in the orientation of the enclosures were evidence of the tracking of precession.[41]

Astrophysicist Juan Antonio Belmonte also looked at the astronomical characteristics of Göbekli Tepe. He noted that amongst the circular enclosures, 'there is one with nearly rectangular walls, which were almost perfectly aligned to the cardinal points.'[42] Needless to say such exact alignments, as at the Great Pyramid of Giza in Egypt, cannot have been achieved without the use of equally exact astronomical observations.

Belmonte also paid attention to the 'profuse decoration' of the T-pillars at Göbekli Tepe, concluding that these may represent:

> yet other astronomical observations, such as the crescent and the star, so common in later cultures of the Middle East . . . Then there are what could be interpreted as totemic representations of animals, which, if we may continue to speculate, could symbolise constellations such as Leo, Taurus and Scorpio.

This is the right moment to deal with Klaus Schmidt's argument (see Chapter One) that there couldn't possibly be any 'astronomical figures' at Göbekli Tepi, because 'the zodiac constellations were not recognised until Babylonian times, nine thousand years after Göbekli Tepe'. I didn't challenge him on this point when I interviewed him, because I was more interested in hearing his own views on Göbekli Tepe, rather than engaging him in a possibly acrimonious debate. Clearly, however, Belmonte, who knows his stuff, does not agree with the position taken by Schmidt.

Neither, for that matter does the Russian astronomer and historian of science Alexander Gurshtein, who traces the first recognition and naming of constellations – notably the Great Bear – to 20,000 BC,[43] and more detailed knowledge of the zodiac to the epoch of 5600 BC.[44]

German archaeoastronomer Michael Rappengluck pushes the origins of the zodiac even further back than that, however. He has identified an accurate depiction of the zodiacal constellation of Taurus painted more than 17,000 years ago in the Hall of Bulls in Lascaux cave in France.[45]

Rappengluck points out that there are four key moments of the year, the spring equinox, the autumn equinox, the winter solstice and the summer solstice. We've seen already how the 'character' of a world age has long been thought to be governed by the zodiacal constellation that 'houses' the sun on the spring equinox, but other constellations also 'house' the other three prominent 'stations of the sun' at the autumn equinox, and at the summer and winter solstices, and when a shift of age takes place with one constellation giving way to another on the spring equinox, so the constellations governing the other three 'stations' also shift.

There is not space to go into the evidence in detail here, but the essence of Rappengluck's argument concerning Lascaux is that depicted there is the whole constellation of Taurus (in one of the aurochs or 'bull' figures in the Hall of Bulls) and also above its shoulder, in a distinctive pattern of six dots, the six visible stars of the Pleiades, which form a highly recognizable element of Taurus. Moreover a date can be put on this depiction:

> The Pleiades in 15,300 BC were very near the point of the autumn
> equinox . . . The six stars in the 'Salle des Taureaux' therefore

represent a striking and excellent heavenly marker for the beginning of autumn . . . The epoch calculated astronomically lies extraordinarily close to the . . . carbon-14 dating [for human activity in this part of the cave] corresponding to 15,300 BC.[46]

In other work Rappengluck provides further compelling evidence that our ancestors, at least as early as the epoch between 16,000 BC and 10,000 BC:

recognised single and very complex star patterns, including the Milky Way, the Northern Crown in the cave of El Castillo (Spain), the Pleiades in the cave of Lascaux (France) and the main constellations of the sky at the same location.[47]

He also documents a rock panel in the cave of La Tete du Lion (France) that:

shows the combination of a star pattern – Aldebaran in the Bull and the Pleiades – with a drawing of the moon's cycle above. This picture comes from the Solutrean epoch [ca 19,000 to 20,000 BC]. It shows not only a remarkable similarity with the representation in the Lascaux cave, but clearly connects the star pattern with part of the lunar cycle.[48]

Rappengluck's conclusion, and again I must cut a long story short, is that:

hunter-gatherers of Palaeolithic epochs looked up to the starry sky and saw the open cluster of the Pleiades with the wandering moon and sun near or between the Golden Gate of the ecliptic, 21,000 years ago.[49]

The 'Golden Gate of the ecliptic' that Rappengluck refers to here was traditionally conceived of as that area of the heavens bounded by the Hyades and the Pleiades (both of which are star groups within the constellation of Taurus), between which, as though through a great celestial 'gate', the ecliptic passes.[50] The 'ecliptic' is the technical term for the sun's perceived 'path' through the heavens. The implication, therefore, is that the path of the sun (and the moon[51]) against the background of the constellations of the zodiac was observed, depicted and understood in the Palaeolithic, perhaps as much as 10,000 years *before* Göbekli Tepe was built. For this reason Belmonte makes a point of citing Rappengluck's work, and indeed of showing a photo provided by Rappengluck of the Taurus figure in the Hall of Bulls at Lascaux,[52] when he makes his seemingly off the cuff remark that zodiacal constellations 'such as Leo, Taurus and Scorpio' might be the inspiration for the 'totemic' animals depicted at Göbekli Tepe.

For Belmonte, in summary, Göbekli Tepe offers evidence that:

> a completely unknown hunter-gatherer society more than 11,000 years ago sought to create monumental structures linked to the heavens. This series of sanctuaries, built presumably one after the other and even one upon another, may have been used for centuries, perhaps millennia, to chart the heavens. However, for reasons which are unknown, the constructors deliberately buried the structures, creating conditions which contributed to their excellent state of preservation despite their great antiquity.[53]

Certainly the indigenous inhabitants of the Göbekli Tepe area were hunter-gatherers – and completely unknown hunter-gatherers at that! But it has been my thesis throughout this book that their sudden venture into spectacular monumental architecture, closely followed by their equally spectacular 'invention' of agriculture, is very strange. Indeed it amounts to an almost inexplicable 'great leap forward' that cries out for a coherent explanation which archaeology has yet to provide. The hypothesis we are exploring here, and that I believe might explain these anomalies, is that the survivors of a lost civilization, who had already mastered agriculture and knew everything there was to know about building with megaliths, had settled amongst the hunter-gatherers of Göbekli Tepe following the Younger Dryas cataclysm and transferred some of their skills to them.

Now, in addition to megalithic architecture and agriculture we must take the evidence of astronomy into account. At first sight, while the work of Belmonte, Collins, Hale, Schoch, Magli and others confirms that competent astronomers must have been at work at Göbekli Tepe, we cannot say that the level of knowledge manifested in the alignments of the pillars and enclosures was necessarily that of a sophisticated 'civilization'. We've seen from the research done by Gurshtein and Rappengluck that careful observations of the sky, and identification of constellations we can still recognise today, can be traced back into the Neolithic and beyond that into the art of the painted caves of the Palaeolithic 20,000 or more years ago. So expressions of such knowledge at Göbekli Tepe need not surprise us unduly.

But suppose there was something else – something that hunter-gatherers, no matter how savvy, could not be expected to have known under any circumstances?

It is that elusive 'something else' that Paul Burley's work brought home to me, like a shot of adrenaline, when I re-read his paper in my hotel room in Şanlıurfa in July 2014.

Neolithic puzzle

Burley's paper is entitled 'Göbekli Tepe: Temples Communicating an Ancient Cosmic Geography'. He wrote it originally in June 2011, I met him at the Conference of Precession and Ancient Knowledge in Sedona, Arizona, in September that year, we exchanged a couple of emails during 2012, and in February 2013 he asked me to read his paper, which he said concerned 'evidence of a zodiac on one of the pillars at Göbekli Tepe'. I read it, replied that I found it 'very persuasive and interesting, with significant implications' and told him I'd like to publish it on the Articles page of my website. Paul agreed and the article went live on 8 March 2013.[54] It's still there, accessible through the URL provided in the note.

'Significant implications', I now realise as I read through the paper again in my hotel room in Şanlıurfa, was a huge understatement. But I didn't make my first visit to Göbekli Tepe until September 2013 and by then, clearly, I'd forgotten the gist of Burley's argument, which focuses almost exclusively on Enclosure D and on the very pillar, Pillar 43, that

I'd been most interested in when I was there. My interest in it had been sparked by Belmonte's suggestion that the relief carving of a scorpion near its base (which the reader will recall was hidden by rubble that Schmidt refused to allow me to move) might be a representation of the zodiacal constellation of Scorpio. So it was a lapse on my part not to have re-read Burley's paper documenting 'a zodiac' on the same pillar before I travelled to the site. But we're all human, we all make mistakes, we all forget things and despite acknowledging its 'significant implications' in our correspondence six months earlier, what Burley had discovered had slipped my mind entirely on my September 2013 visit.

Here's where he gets to his point:

One of the limestone pillars [in Enclosure D] includes a scene in bas relief on the upper portion of one of its sides. There is a bird with outstretched wings, two smaller birds, a scorpion, a snake, a circle, and a number of wavy lines and cord-like features. At first glance this lithified menagerie appears to be simply a hodgepodge of animals and geometrical designs randomly placed to fill in the broad side of the pillar.

The key to unlocking this early Neolithic puzzle is the circle situated at the centre of the scene. I am immediately reminded of the cosmic Father – the Sun. The next clues are the scorpion facing up toward the sun, and the large bird seemingly holding the sun upon its outstretched wing. In fact the sun figure appears to be located accurately on the ecliptic with respect to the familiar constellation of Scorpio, although the scorpion on the pillar occupies only the left portion, or head, of our modern conception of that constellation. As such the sun symbol is located as close to the galactic centre as it can be on the ecliptic as it crosses the galactic plane.

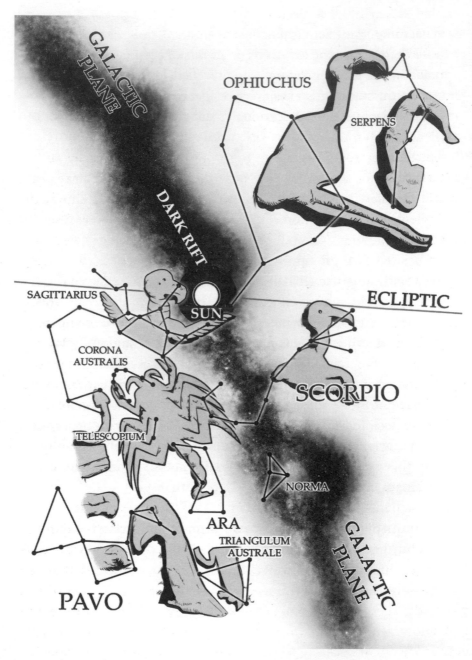

Figure 46: The celestial imagery of Pillar 43.

Bear with me, and I'll explain all this. Meanwhile, let's continue with Burley's article because it's his next statement that really has me sitting up and paying attention:

> What's important here is *for some unknown reason the builders of Göbekli Tepe constructed a temple apparently highlighting a time 11,600 years in their future.* Yet this scene is intentional. The symbolism is clear and in keeping with many mythologies describing this very same event – occurring at the very time we live in today!

Burley then presents a graphic that 'illustrates the crossing of the galactic plane of the Milky Way near the centre of the galaxy, with several familiar constellations nearby'. A second graphic shows the same view with the addition of the ancient constellations represented on the pillar:

> Note that the outstretched wings, sun, bird legs and snake all appear to be oriented to emphasise the sun's path along the ecliptic . . . The similarity of the bas relief to the crossing of the ecliptic and galactic equator at the centre of the Milky Way is difficult to reject, supporting the possibility that humans recognised and documented the precession of the equinoxes thousands of years earlier than is generally accepted by scholars . . . Göbekli Tepe was built as a symbolic sphere communicating a very ancient understanding of world and cosmic geography. Why this knowledge was intentionally buried soon afterward remains a mystery.

I don't immediately understand everything that Burley is saying in all this, but I understand enough to get started on it and fortunately I have astronomy software – Stellarium – on my computer that can simulate the ancient skies taking account of precession. More importantly, the program can show me the sky of our own time and will allow me to scroll through it day by day, month by month, going forward or back as I wish, enlarging and inspecting any specific elements that I'm interested in. Most often I study ancient skies, not modern ones, but tonight it's our own time I need to take a look at.

Or, rather, not exactly our own time, July 2014 as I sit in front of my computer in Şanlıurfa, but a year and a half earlier, the winter solstice, 21 December 2012 – the much hyped 'end date' (that passed with not so much as a whimper, let alone a bang) of the famous Mayan calendar.

Message on a pillar?

Here's what I'm aware of already as I open Stellarium on my computer. When Paul Burley talks about the sun depicted on the Göbekli Tepe pillar being located 'as close to the galactic centre as it can be on the ecliptic', and when he also makes a point of telling me that Scorpio is involved, I know he can only be referring to one epoch – the epoch of the year 2000, give or take a maximum of about 40 years on either side (i.e. from 1960 to 2040). The great band of stars and clouds of interstellar dust arching across the sky that we call the Milky Way, and that is in fact our own home galaxy viewed edge on, is crossed by the ecliptic – i.e. the sun's apparent path through the heavens – twice a year. One of these gigantic interchanges is in the North between the constellations of Gemini and Taurus; in our epoch the sun stands here at the northern hemisphere's summer solstice, i.e. around 21 June. The second interchange is in the South between the constellations of Sagittarius and Scorpio, and in our epoch the sun stands here at the northern hemisphere's winter solstice, i.e. around 21 December.

The reader will recall that precession has the visual effect, as viewed from earth, of causing the constellations that 'house' the sun at the four key moments of the year – the two equinoxes and the two solstices – to shift very slowly around the belt of the zodiac, with the sun spending 2,160 years 'in' each zodiacal constellation at each key moment, before the whole system slips round far enough for the sun to have passed completely from one constellation into another. When this happens at the equinox, it happens at the other three 'stations' as well. Indeed, it is a good mental exercise to imagine a circle – which repre-

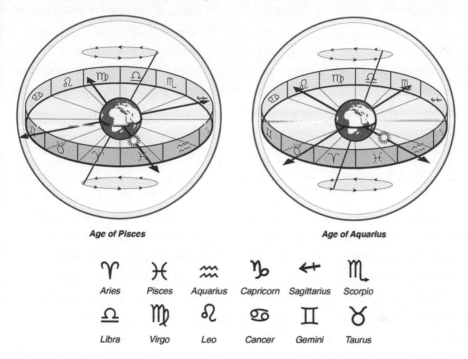

Age of Pisces **Age of Aquarius**

♈	♓	♒	♑	↤	♏
Aries	Pisces	Aquarius	Capricorn	Sagittarius	Scorpio

♎	♍	♌	♋	♊	♉
Libra	Virgo	Leo	Cancer	Gemini	Taurus

Figure 47: The precessional shift from the Age of Pisces into the Age of Aquarius. As the position of the sun against the background zodiacal constellations on the spring equinox shifts from Pisces into Aquarius, so the summer solstice will shift from Gemini into Taurus, the autumn equinox from Virgo into Leo, and the winter solstice from Sagittarius into Scorpio.

sents the ecliptic, i.e. the annual path of the sun – and to mark out at equal intervals around the circumference of this circle the twelve constellations of the zodiac. Now place four spokes arranged in the form of a cross inside the circle. Where each of the four ends of the cross touch the edge of the circle, you have one of the key stations of the sun – the northern hemisphere's spring equinox (21 March), summer solstice (21 June), autumn equinox (21 September), and winter solstice (21 December). In our epoch, the zodiacal constellations housing the sun at these four stations are Pisces on the March equinox, Gemini on the June solstice, Virgo on the September equinox, and Sagittarius on the December solstice.

However, precession has the effect of very slowly rotating the spokes of the cross. We are nearing the end of the 'Age of Pisces' now (i.e. of the 2,160 years when Pisces houses the sun on the March equinox)

313

and the end of the spoke that was in Pisces will soon rotate into Aquarius (hence the song, 'we live in the dawning of the Age of Aquarius'). But because the cross is, if you like, welded together to form a single fixed unit, all its spokes must move together with the result that as the March equinox shifts from Pisces into Aquarius, so the June solstice will shift from Gemini into Taurus, the September equinox from Virgo into Leo, and the December solstice from Sagittarius into Scorpio.

I want to avoid undue complications as far as possible here, but let us now return to the Milky Way which, as we've seen, is crossed by the path of the sun twice a year. Remember that at each crossing point a pair of zodiacal constellations sits on either side of the Milky Way, effectively forming the pillars of two celestial gates through which the 'road' of the Milky Way passes – Gemini and Taurus in the North (with the sun presently housed by Gemini at the June solstice) and Sagittarius and Scorpio in the South (with the sun presently housed by Sagittarius at the December solstice). *The relationship of these two pairs of zodiacal constellations to the Milky Way is not affected by precession and NEVER CHANGES.* Gemini and Taurus will always mark the northern 'gate' of the Milky Way and Sagittarius and Scorpio will always mark the southern 'gate' of the Milky Way.

Of the two, however, it is the Sagittarius–Scorpio gate that is the most important, because it so happens that the part of the Milky Way seen through this gate as we look up at the night sky forms the very centre and heart of our galaxy. Not only that, but because it is the galactic centre, in the midst of which, astronomers now believe, sits an immense black hole – 'a hyperdense object from which even light cannot escape'[55] – there is a notable bulge in precisely this area. Last but not least, in the midst of this so-called 'nuclear bulge' is another absolutely distinctive feature that astronomers call the 'dark rift', which figures prominently in many ancient mythologies,[56] and which is created by a series of overlapping, non-luminous molecular dust clouds.

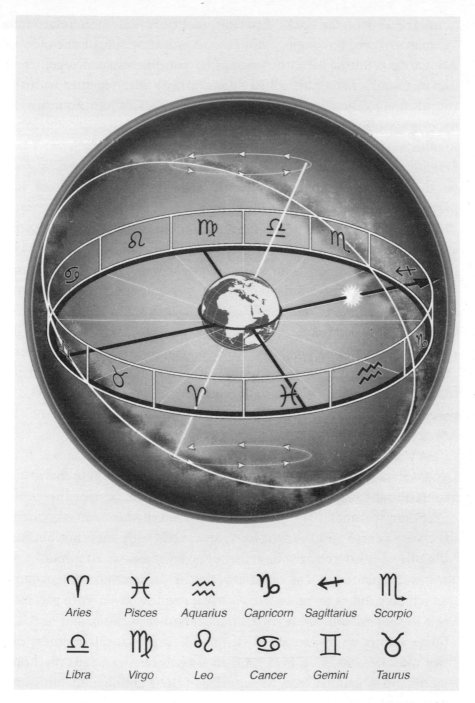

Figure 48: The celestial gateways: Sagittarius/Scorpio at right, with the sun presently housed by Sagittarius at the winter solstice; and Gemini/Taurus at left, with the sun presently housed by Gemini at the summer solstice.

As a result of precession, the December solstice sun is presently housed by Sagittarius and thus, as viewed from earth, 'targets' the galactic centre like the bead on the barrel of a rifle. The last time this grand celestial line-up of earth, December-solstice sun and the galactic centre occurred was a full precessional cycle of 25,920 years ago and the next time it will happen is a full precessional cycle of 25,920 years in the future. We live, in other words, in a very special, indeed rather unique, moment in terms of cosmic and astronomical symbolism. I will elaborate in the next chapter on the symbolic aspect, and why the December solstice matters in particular, but first it is important to make something else clear.

If, hypothetically, some ancient civilization wished to deploy its knowledge of the regular movements and changes in the heavens in order to draw attention to a particular moment in the flow of time, a possibility that we have considered with the monuments of Giza, then the precessional world ages, while useful, are not really precise enough to spell out an exact date. After all, the broad configurations of each precessional age hold good for 2,160 years. If we want to be more specific than that, then we are going to need to find a celestial event in the period we wish to draw attention to which is (a) an artefact of precession and (b) occurs in a much narrower window than that of a full precessional world age of 2,160 years.

Such an event occurs in our time. It is the arrival of the sun at the December solstice in the southern gate of the Milky Way between Sagittarius and Scorpio, where it targets the galactic centre. There are certain imprecisions, mainly to do with the width of the sun's disc and over what period we can say it lines up exactly with the centre of the Milky Way when viewed from earth, but nonetheless, we are not talking about 2,160 years here. The exact targeting of the galactic centre occurs in a window that is no more than 80-years wide and we will continue to be in that window for approximately another 25 years.

This creates an interesting situation with regard to the message of Pillar 43 at Göbekli Tepe, because if Paul Burley is right, the reliefs on that pillar use symbolic language to depict the December solstice sun at the southern gate of the Milky Way between Sagittarius and Scorpio.

In other words, those reliefs are speaking to our time.

They are speaking to us.

Chapter 15
The Place of Creation

—◆—

As I sit in my hotel room in Şanlıurfa in July 2014 spinning the skies on my computer screen, I'm coming more and more to the conclusion that Paul Burley has had a genius insight about the scene on Pillar 43 at Göbekli Tepe. Burley's language in his paper is careful – almost diffident. As we saw in Chapter Fourteen, he says that 'the sun figure appears to be located accurately on the ecliptic with respect to the familiar constellation of Scorpio'. He speaks of other 'familiar constellations' nearby. And he draws our attention to the large bird – the vulture – 'seemingly holding the sun upon an outstretched wing'. He does not say which constellation he believes the vulture represents, but the graphics he includes to reinforce his argument leave no room for doubt that he regards it as an ancient representation of the constellation of Sagittarius.[1]

We've already seen that there is evidence for the identification of constellations going far back into the Ice Age, some of which were portrayed in those remote times in forms that are recognizable to us today. From the last chapter the reader will recall Michael Rappengluck's work on the zodiacal constellation of Taurus, depicted at Lascaux some 17,000 years ago as an aurochs (ancient species of wild cattle) with the six visible stars of the Pleiades on its shoulder.

Acknowledging such surprising continuities in the ways that some constellations are depicted does not mean that all the constellations we are familiar with now have always been depicted in the same way by all cultures at all periods of history. This is very far from being the case. Constellations are subject to sometimes radical change depending on which imaginary figures different cultures choose to project upon

317

the sky. For example, the Mesopotamian constellation of the Bull of Heaven and the modern constellation of Taurus share the Hyades cluster as the head, but in other respects are very different.[2] Likewise the Mesopotamian constellation of the Bow and Arrow is built from stars in the constellations that we call Argo and Canis Major, with the star Sirius as the tip of the arrow. The Chinese also have a Bow and Arrow constellation built from pretty much the same stars but the arrow is shorter, with Sirius forming not the tip but the target.[3]

Even when constellation boundaries remain the same from culture to culture, the ways in which those constellations are seen can be very different. Thus the Ancient Egyptians knew the constellation that we call the Great Bear, but represented it as the foreleg of a bull. They saw the Little Bear (Ursa Minor) as a jackal. They depicted the zodiacal constellation of Cancer as a scarab beetle. The constellation of Draco, which we see as a dragon, was figured by the Ancient Egyptians as a hippopotamus with a crocodile on its back.[4]

There can therefore be no objection in principle to the suggestion that the constellation we call Sagittarius, 'the Archer' – and depict as a centaur man-horse hybrid holding a bow with arrow drawn – could have been seen by the builders of Göbekli Tepe as a vulture with outstretched wings.

I spend hours on Stellarium toggling back and forth between the sky of 9600 BC and the sky of our own epoch, focusing on the region between Sagittarius and Scorpio – the region Burley believes is depicted on Pillar 43 – and looking at the relationship of the sun to these background constellations.

The first thing that becomes clear to me is that a vulture with outstretched wings makes a *very good* figure of Sagittarius; indeed it's a much better, more intuitive and more obvious way to represent the central part of this constellation than the centaur/archer that we have inherited from the Mesopotamians and the Greeks. This central part of Sagittarius (minus the centaur's legs and tail) happens to contain its brightest stars and forms an easily recognised asterism often called the 'Teapot' by astronomers today – because it does resemble a modern teapot with a handle, a pointed lid and a spout. The handle and spout elements, however, could equally effectively be drawn as the outstretched

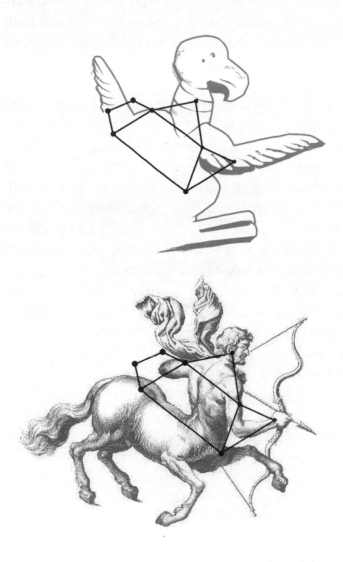

Figure 49: A vulture with outstretched wings makes a much better, more intuitive and more obvious way than an archer to represent the bright, central 'Teapot' asterism within the constellation of Sagittarius.

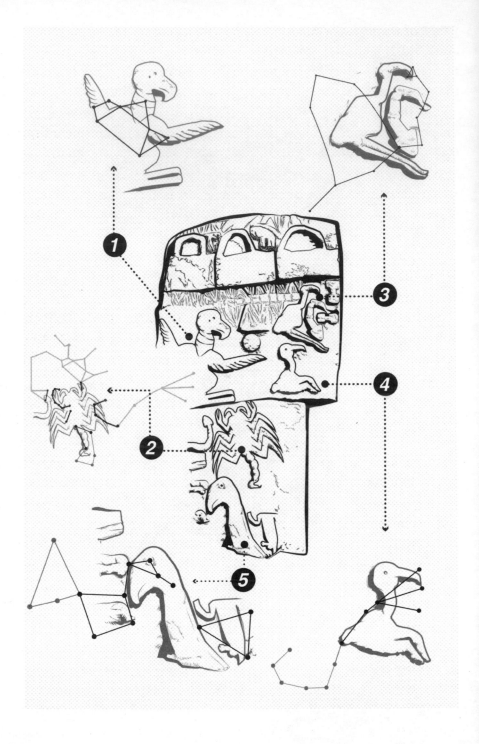

Figure 50: Sagittarius and neighbouring constellations as interpreted on Pillar 43.

wings of a vulture, while the pointed 'lid' becomes the vulture's neck and head. It is the outstretched wing in front of the vulture – the spout of the teapot – that Burley sees as 'holding the sun', represented by the prominent disc in the middle of the scene on Pillar 43.

But the vulture and the sun are only two aspects of the complex imagery of the pillar. Below and just a little to the right of the vulture is a scorpion. Above and to the right of the vulture is a second large bird with a long sickle-shaped beak, and nestled close to this bird is a serpent with a large triangular head and its body coiled into a curve. A third bird, again with a hooked beak, but smaller, with the look of a chick, is placed below these two figures – again to the right of the vulture, indeed immediately to the right of its extended front wing. Below the scorpion is the head and long neck of a fourth bird. Beside the scorpion, rearing up, is another serpent.

Part of the reason for my growing confidence in Burley's conclusion, though he makes little of it in his paper, is that these figures, with only minor adjustments, compare intriguingly with other constellations around the alleged Sagittarius/vulture figure.

First and foremost, there is the scorpion below and a little to the right of the vulture, which we've seen already has an obvious resemblance to Scorpio, the next constellation along the zodiac from Sagittarius. Its posture and positioning are wrong – we'll look more closely into the implications of this in a moment – but it's there and it is overlapped by the tail end of the constellation that we recognise as Scorpio today.

Secondly, there's the large bird above and to the right of the vulture with the curved body of a serpent nestled close to it. These two figures are in the correct position and the correct relationship to one another to match the constellation we call Ophiuchus, the serpent holder, and the serpent constellation, Serpens, that Ophiuchus holds.

Thirdly, immediately to the right of the extended front wing of the vulture there's that other bird, smaller, like a chick, with a hooked beak. I email Burley about this, and about the different position and orientation of the scorpion on the pillar and the modern constellation of Scorpio, and we arrive, after some back and forth, at a solution. Constellation boundaries, as the reader will recall, are not necessarily drawn in the same place by all cultures at all periods and it's clear that there's been a shift over time in the constellation boundaries here. The chick on Pillar 43 appears to have formed a small constellation of its own in the minds of the Göbekli Tepe astronomers – a constellation that utilized some of the important stars today considered to be part of Scorpio. The chick's hooked beak is correctly positioned, and its body is the correct shape, to match the head and claws of Scorpio.[5]

Fourthly, beside the scorpion on Pillar 43 is a serpent and beneath the scorpion are the head and long neck of yet another bird, with a headless anthropomorphic figure positioned to its right. The serpent matches the tail of Sagittarius (as we've seen, the vulture appears to be composed from the central part of Sagittarius only – the Teapot – so this leaves the remainder of the constellation available to the ancients for other uses). The best contenders for the bird, and for the peculiar little anthromorphic figure to its right are parts of the constellations we know today as Pavo and Triangulum Australe. The remainder of Pavo may be involved with further figures present on the pillar to the left of the bird.

As is the case with Sagittarius, elements of the modern constellation of Scorpio have been redeployed in the ancient constellations depicted on Pillar 43. Only the tail of our Scorpio is in the correct location to match the scorpion on Pillar 43 and its head faces to the right, whereas the head of the scorpion on the pillar faces to the left. The scorpion on the pillar is also below the vulture, whereas modern Scorpio is a very large constellation lying parallel and to the right of Sagittarius. I suggest the solution to this problem is that the scorpion on Pillar 43 is conjured from a combination of the tail of the modern constellation of Scorpio (right legs of the Pillar 43 scorpion), an unused part of the 'Teapot' asterism of Sagittarius (right claw of the Pillar 43 scorpion) and the constellations that we know as Ara, Telescopium and Corona Australis (respectively the tail, left legs and left claw of the Pillar 43 scorpion). Meanwhile, as noted above, the claws and head of the modern constellation of Scorpio have been co-opted to form the chick with the hooked beak on Pillar 43.

This whole issue of the relationship between the modern constellations of Scorpio and Sagittarius and the scorpion and vulture figures

Figure 51: Man-scorpion Sagittarius figures from Bablylonian Kudurru stones (left) are frequently depicted with the legs and feet of birds, further strengthening the identification of the vulture figure on Pillar 43 with Sagittarius. In other Mesopotamian representations (right) we see a second scorpion beneath the body of Sagittarius occupying a similar position to the scorpion on Pillar 43.

depicted on Pillar 43 takes on a new level of significance when we remember that in some ancient astronomical figures Sagittarius is depicted not only as a centaur – a man-horse – but also as a man-horse hybrid with the tail of a scorpion, and sometimes simply as a man-scorpion hybrid.[6] On Babylonian *Kudurru* stones (often referred to as boundary stones, although it is likely that their function has been misunderstood[7]) a figure of a man-scorpion drawing a bow frequently appears that 'is universally identified with the archer Sagittarius'.[8] What further cements the identification of Sagittarius with the vulture on Pillar 43 is that these man-scorpion figures from the Babylonian *Kudurru* stones are very often depicted with the legs and feet of birds.[9] Moreover, in some representations a second scorpion appears beneath the body – i.e. beneath the Teapot asterism – of Sagittarius,[10] reminiscent of the position of the scorpion on Pillar 43 (see Figures 50 and 51).

When all this is taken together it goes, in my opinion, far beyond anything that can be explained away as mere 'coincidence'. The implication is that ideas of how certain constellations should be depicted that were expressed at Göbekli Tepe almost 12,000 years ago, including the notion that there should be a scorpion in this region of the heavens, were passed down, undergoing some changes in the process, but nonetheless surviving in recognizable form for millennia to find related expression in much later Babylonian astronomical iconography. But given the close connections with ancient Mesopotamia, its antediluvian cities, its Seven Sages and its flood survivors washed up in their Ark near Göbekli Tepe, we should perhaps not be too surprised.

Last but not least, there's the mystery of the three 'bags' or 'buckets' in the upper register of Pillar 43, which caught my eye on my first visit to Göbekli Tepe and which are discussed in Chapter One. As astronomer Giulio Magli has noticed, these:

> three 'bags' are pretty similar to the three 'houses in the sky' occurring in the much (very much!) later Babylonian *Kudurru* traditions.[11]

Figure 52: Astronomer Giulio Magli notes of Pillar 43 at Göbekli Tepe (right) that the 'bags' in the top register are similar to the 'houses in the sky' occurring on much later Babylonian pillars (left).

What Magli calls the 'houses in the sky' (again see accompanying illustrations) are the symbols of Mesopotamian deities, notably Enlil, who sent the Deluge to destroy mankind, and Enki, the god of wisdom who intervened to save us.[12] The reader will recall from Chapter Eight that it was Enki who warned the patriarch Zisudra of the coming cataclysm and urged him to build the great Ark that would ultimately bring the flood survivors to the region of Ararat so close to Göbekli Tepe. It's hard to avoid the conclusion that all these shared themes in the iconography of Mesopotamia as late as the first millennium BC, and of Göbekli Tepe as early as the tenth millennium BC, have much older antediluvian origins in a lost civilization that was the progenitor of both – and perhaps of many other cultures around the world – and that took pains, through deliberately engineered myths and wisdom traditions, and through carefully structured teachings passed on from generation to generation by initiated Sages, to ensure that its memory would not be lost forever from the earth.

The Maya

Late into the night, as I work through the whole scenario in my hotel room in Şanlıurfa, my confidence in Burley's case continues to grow. Once all the surrounding context is taken into account, the vulture 'holding the sun' on its front wing really does look like the figure of an ancient constellation representing the Teapot asterism of the constellation of Sagittarius.

This then raises the next part of the puzzle: *when* does the vulture/ Sagittarius 'hold the sun'? Burley makes clear that he believes the moment represented on Pillar 43 still lay far in the future when Göbekli Tepe was built – indeed 11,600 years in the future, i.e. in our own time, the epoch of 2012. And he comes to this conclusion because it is only in our epoch, specifically in the 80-year window from 1960 to 2040, that the sun on 21 December, the winter solstice, not only sits over the outstretched front wing of the bird (i.e. over the spout of the 'teapot' in the modern conception of this asterism) but also targets the 'nuclear bulge' and the dark rift at the centre of the Milky Way galaxy. So, arguably, this is a very significant astronomical moment that is symbolised on Pillar 43.

Very significant indeed, as it turns out, because it is also this exact same 80-year window (where the year 2012 falls just a little after the midpoint) that is signalled in the famous – or perhaps it would now be better to say infamous – Mayan calendar. A great deal of nonsense was talked about that calendar, and particularly about the 21 December 2012 date, which many wrongly took to be something absolute and precise, when in reality it was always an 'indication date' and nothing more.

In getting to grips with this mystery, it is only the astronomy that counts – and naked-eye astronomy at that. We are not talking about radio telescopes or astrophysics here. With regard to the naked-eye astronomy of the ancient Maya, the real scholars of this subject, amongst whom there is none more pre-eminent than John Major Jenkins, made valiant efforts – for a long while before 2012 – to teach us that what the end-date of the Mayan calendar was based on was in fact the once-in-26,000-years conjunction of the winter solstice sun with the centre of the galaxy, i.e. with the dark rift and nuclear bulge of the Milky Way. Because of the diameter of the sun and the limitations of naked-eye astronomy this conjunction cannot be pinned down to an exact year but is best considered, as I've indicated here, as a window 80-years wide spanning the period 1960-2040.

As an artefact of precession, the winter solstice sun was moving slowly and steadily towards its conjunction with the centre of the galaxy for thousands of years before 2012 – and in his books, going back at least as far as *Maya Cosmogenesis*, which he published in 1998, John Major Jenkins made this eminently clear. Diagrams that he offered to his readers showed the journey of the winter solstice sun from 3000 BC, when it was 70 degrees away from the dark-rift crossing point in Sagittarius, through the time of Christ when it had halved the distance that remained for it to travel, to the epoch of 2012 (that 80-year window between 1960 and 2040) when it most closely conjuncts the dark rift, and onwards to AD 5000 when it will have moved 70 degrees past the dark rift.[13]

More than this, Jenkins meticulously documented *why* the conjunction of the winter solstice sun with the dark rift in the central bulge of the Milky Way was important in Mayan cosmology – because this was the region of the heavens that the Maya thought of as 'the place

8. The author at Baalbek with the southernmost Trilithon block at his feet. The wall behind him, built on top of the Trilithon, is a later Arab fortification.

9. The three huge Trilithon blocks in the west side of the U-shaped megalithic wall flanking, but not touching, the platform of the Temple of Jupiter.

40. The author's right foot is placed in front of the fragment of a Roman column drum used as a block in the foundations beneath the Trilithon.

41. The Roman column drum was excavated and measured by the German Archaeological Institute who believe it could not be the result of later Arab repairs to the foundations and that the Trilithon must, therefore, be the work of the Romans.

42. A fortification wall built by the Arabs at Baalbek using recycled Roman materials. Note the column drum placed horizontally to the right of the arch.

43. Close-up of the recycled column drum in the Arab fortification wall. Note the drum is perfectly flattened at top and bottom exactly like the column drum in the foundations beneath the Trilithon. The argument that the Arabs lacked the technical expertise to cut and fit blocks so precisely therefore makes no sense.

44. Northern arm of the U-shaped megalithic wall surrounding the platform of the Temple of Jupiter. Note the smaller size of the blocks with which the platform itself (right side of picture) is built.

45. The author standing on the southern arm of the U-shaped megalithic wall with the six remaining columns of the Temple of Jupiter on the edge of the platform behind him.

6. The author, for scale, standing on the 970-ton 'Stone of the Pregnant Woman' still *in situ* in the quarries at Baalbek. The block visible beneath it, to the left, was newly excavated in 2014 and is estimated to weigh 1,650 tons.

7. A third block in the quarries weighing 1,250 tons.

48. Above: The tips of buried megalithic pillars jut out from a hillside at Karahan Tepe, sister site to Gobekli Tepe.

49. Left: The 'Astronomical Tower" at Harran. In its present form it dates from the Islamic period but it occupies the site of an earlier tower that stood within a temple dedicated to the Moon God of the Sabians.

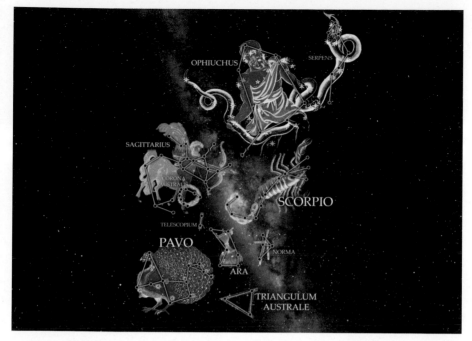

50. The constellations, as we envisage them today, of the area of the sky depicted on Pillar 43 at Gobekli Tepe.

51. The same constellations overlaid on the figures of Pillar 43 at Gobekli Tepe. See discussion in chapter 15 and fig no. 50.

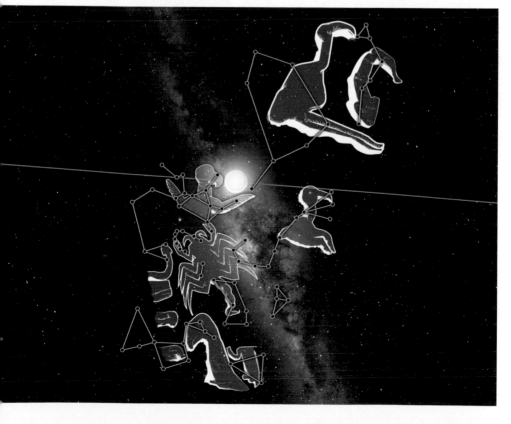

52. Left: The eerie limestone 'Totem Pole' of Gobekli Tepe – a complex, hybrid entity.

53. Above: 'Urfa Man', the oldest three-dimensional sculpture of a human figure to have survived anywhere in the world. It dates to the same period as Gobekli Tepe and was found nearby. Note that the position of the hands matches the hand positions of the T-shaped anthropomorphic pillars of Gobekli Tepe (see, for example, plate 4).

of creation' with the central bulge viewed as 'the womb or birthplace of the sky':

> The Maya understood this dense, bright bulge as a Cosmic Centre and Creation Place, a conclusion based solely on naked-eye observation that is, in fact, very true: the centre of our saucer-shaped galaxy lies within this bright and wide part of the Milky Way . . . that hyperdense region out of which the Milky Way and everything in it, including us, has poured.[14]

It is not my purpose here to go in depth into the whole enigma of the Mayan calendar, not least since I wrote about this subject at some length in *Fingerprints of the Gods*.[15] However, my understanding since the publication of *Fingerprints* in 1995 has moved on, and it is important to be clear that in signalling the decades around 2012 as the end of a great cycle, the Maya were not speaking of the end of the world, as such, but rather of the end of an age – 'a time of great transformation and world rebirth'[16] – that would be followed by the beginning of a new great cycle or world age. This, in the Mayan scheme of things, is the turbulent and dangerous time of transition we live in today. It is therefore strange, and indeed somewhat eerie, to find the solar and astronomical coordinates of the exact same 80-year window between 1960 and 2040 prophesied by the Maya to mark a turning point in human history, carved in high relief on a 12,000-year-old pillar in Göbekli Tepe in far-off Turkey.

Eliminating the impossible

I want to be sure that I could be right to read some kind of prediction or prophecy for our age, some sort of notification, some sort of message sent specifically to us, in the reliefs on Pillar 43. Before even beginning to consider what that message might speak of, the first step is to confirm that Paul Burley's discovery is a solid one.

I'm already persuaded by his identification of Sagittarius with the vulture and of the disc held up by its wing with the sun. The general context of the surrounding constellations is also an excellent fit. Could it be, however, that the reliefs on the pillar do indeed depict the sun's conjunction with Sagittarius and the centre of the Milky Way, but at some time other than the winter solstice in the years between 1960 and 2040?

Of course, the winter solstice alignment recurs once every 26,000 years, so in 24,000 BC the sun would have been seen in Sagittarius, targeting the centre of the galaxy exactly as it does today, and this rare alignment will happen again 26,000 years from now, i.e. in AD 28,000. It's not impossible that any hypothetical message could be to do with these remote dates.

It's intriguing, however, that there's another 'message', from a completely different culture – the ancient Maya – that uses the same system of coordinates and that is indeed focused, very exactly, on the years between 1960 and 2040.

Meanwhile at Göbekli Tepe there are also the other three key moments of the year to consider – the summer solstice and the two equinoxes. Was there any alignment through Sagittarius with the centre of the galaxy at any of these three other 'stations of the sun' in the epoch of 9600 BC when Göbekli Tepe was built?

I know from my work on Ancient Egypt that the sun was in Leo

Figure 53 Spring equinox sunrise at Göbekli Tepe, 9600 BC

on the spring equinox in 10,800 BC. Now a few moments on the computer confirm that this remained the case 1,200 years later; in 9600 BC the equinox sun was still in Leo and was thus at a point on its ecliptic path that was very far from any alignment with the centre of the galaxy. I feel quite safe, therefore, in ruling out the spring equinox, at least in that epoch.

The same is also true for the autumn equinox in 9600 BC. Because the sun was then in the constellation of Aquarius, and again very far from alignment with the centre of the galaxy, I rule it out too.

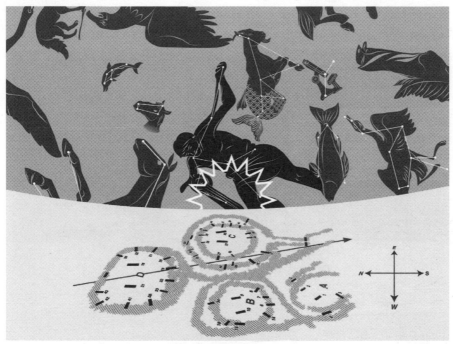

Figure 54: Autumn equinox sunrise at Göbekli Tepe, 9600 BC

Moreover, after reminding myself of the orientation of all the enclosures at Göbekli Tepe, it becomes clear that the equinoxes can be ruled out in *all* periods. This is the case because all of the four major enclosures, A, B, C and D – remember Pillar 43 is in Enclosure D – have a very definite *north-west to south-east* orientation.[17] None of them come anywhere near to due east where the equinox sun rises, or due west where the equinox sun sets. If the builders of Göbekli Tepe had wished to direct our attention to either of the equinoxes in a piece of symbolic art like Pillar 43, their very first step would have been to provide an obvious clue by aligning the site east to west. Since they did not do so, it is safe to assume that events at the equinoxes were not what they had in mind.

This leaves us with the solstices. The sun rises south of east and sets south of west on the winter solstice. On the summer solstice it rises north of east and sets north of west. In theory, therefore, sunrise alignments (south of east) on the winter solstice and sunset alignments (north of west) on the summer solstice can be considered as relevant to the north-west to south-east orientation of Göbekli Tepe.

As we've seen, a winter solstice alignment involving the sun, Sagittarius, and the centre of the galaxy can be ruled out for 9600 BC,

Figure 55: Winter solstice sunrise at Göbekli Tepe, 9600 BC

since that alignment only occurs in our own epoch, or in 24,000 BC or in AD 28,000. On the winter solstice in 9600 BC the sun was in Taurus and very far from alignment with the centre of the galaxy. A summer solstice sunrise alignment north of east can also be ruled out, not only in 9600 BC but in all epochs, given the site's distinct south-east to north-west orientation.

Figure 56: Summer solstice sunrise at Göbekli Tepe, 9600

By a process of deduction, therefore, we are left with only one possible alignment that might work in 9600 BC and this is to the summer solstice *sunset*, north of west, which presents no conflict to the general south-east to north-west orientation of Göbekli Tepe. Moreover, computer simulations show that on the summer solstice in the epoch of 9600 BC the sun was in the constellation of Scorpio and while it did not align with the centre of the galaxy (having moved past the dark rift and the nuclear bulge), it was still reasonably close to that target. As the reader will recall, Sagittarius and Scorpio straddle the dark rift and the nuclear bulge but it is in Sagittarius, not Scorpio, that the exact alignment with the centre of the galaxy occurs. Nonetheless, it seems reasonable to accept the summer solstice sunset, north of west, in the epoch of 9600 BC as a candidate for the scene depicted on Pillar 43. A relatively minor error of draughtsmanship by the sculptor who carved the figures would, in theory, be enough to explain the discrepancy.

There is, however, a difficulty which Andrew Collins, his colleague Rodney Hale, and the mathematicians Alessandro de Lorenzis and

Vincenzo Orofino all seem to have missed in their focus on possible alignments towards the north-west, specifically to the setting of the star Deneb in the constellation of Cygnus, reviewed in the last chapter. Deneb did indeed set north of west in the epoch of 9600 BC in alignment with the orientation of Enclosure D but this alignment, though accurate enough, was purely theoretical and could never in fact have been observed from Enclosure D, for the simple reason that Enclosure D is built into the side of the steep ridge of the Tepe that rises to the north of the main group of enclosures. No observation of the setting of Deneb would have been possible from Enclosure D and for the same reason no observation of the summer solstice sunset would have been possible. The sun would have dropped out of sight behind the ridge for approximately twenty minutes before it actually set and in order to observe its setting, it would have been necessary to leave Enclosure D and climb the ridge.

For this reason, therefore, combined with the fact that the sun in Scorpio, while close, does not target the centre of the galaxy, a summer solstice sunset alignment must also be ruled out.

'When you have eliminated the impossible,' Arthur Conan Doyle's character Sherlock Holmes famously pronounced, then 'whatever remains, *however improbable*, must be the truth.' By a process of elimination we have seen that Göbekli Tepe cannot be inviting us to consider the equinoxes, and nor can it be inviting us to consider the summer solstice, even at the favourable moment of sunset. This leaves us only with the winter solstice with the sun in Sagittarius targeting the centre of the Milky Way galaxy, the definitive astronomical signature of the years between 1960 and 2040 in our own epoch – a signature that recurs only at 26,000-year intervals. However improbable it may seem, therefore, we are obliged to consider the possibility that in 9600 BC the builders of Göbekli Tepe were already so advanced in their knowledge of the recondite phenomenon of precession that they were able to calculate its effects for thousands of years backward and forward in time in order to produce an accurate symbolic picture of the Sagittarius/winter solstice conjunction.

If this speculation is correct then it is appropriate to remind ourselves that two comparable scientific achievements of prehistoric antiquity have also survived the ages and come down to us in the same degree of completeness.

One is the Mayan calendar that envisaged a great cycle in the life of the world coming to an end in exactly the same 80-year period between 1960 and 2040. Moreover, it used exactly the same yardstick – the progress of the winter solstice sun towards alignment with the centre of our galaxy – to predict when the fateful conjunction would occur and to define the cusp between the end of the old age and the beginning of the new.

The other is the grand astronomical geoglyph of Egypt's Giza plateau, inscribed on the west bank of the Nile in the forms of the Great Pyramids and the Great Sphinx. The reader will recall that these master-pieces of megalithic architecture deploy a deep knowledge of preces-sion to offer us a picture of the sky on the spring equinox in 10,800 BC. Here, too, as we shall see in Chapter Nineteen, there are the distinc-tive characteristics of a message, a message sent across the ages and directed, quite specifically, at our time and at us.

In our search to discover what these messages might mean, perhaps the Sabians of Harran, those 'star-worshippers' whose city lies barely 25 miles from Göbekli Tepe, those followers of the wisdom god with their mysterious pilgrimages to the Pyramids of Giza, will be able to give us a clue.

Chapter 16
Written in the Stars

———◆———

In Chapters Eight to Eleven we explored the secret tradition of the Sages, maintained in Egypt for thousands of years, perpetuating itself through recruitment and initiation down the ages. And we considered the possibility that these 'mystery teachers of heaven', these 'Followers of Horus' – these 'Magicians of the Gods' – played a key role, not once but many times, at crucial moments in Egyptian history, in moving that remarkable culture forward.

In Chapter Twelve we looked into the connection between the incredible megalithic site of Baalbek and an enigmatic group of colonists from ancient Canaan who settled near Egypt's Giza plateau, where they made regular devotional offerings to the Great Sphinx, named by them variously as Hauron or Hurna after a Canaanite falcon deity.

In Chapter Fourteen we saw that another group, known as the Sabians and renowned as 'star-worshippers', came from even further away as pilgrims to the Pyramids of Giza. Their home city was Harran, located near Göbekli Tepe in what is now southeastern Turkey. There is no record of when these pilgrimages began but Harran had already been settled for thousands of years[1] when the earliest surviving written reference to it appears in an inscription dated to around 2000 BC.[2] What is remarkable is that Sabian pilgrimages to Giza were still taking place as late as AD 1228 when the Arab geographer Yakut el-Hamawi mentioned them in his *Mo'gam-el-Buldan* ('Dictionary of Countries'). As Egyptologist Selim Hassan notes in the passage quoted in Chapter Fourteen, Hamawi's account shows that the Sabians 'fully recognised the Pyramids of Khufu and Khafre as being monuments connected with the stellar cult.'[3]

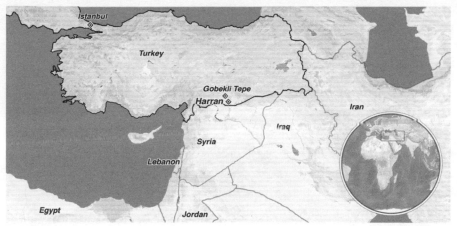

Figure 57

This may seem like a small point, and 'experts' on the Sabians have ignored it, but it proves the continuation of a hidden tradition. Ancient Egyptian religion and Ancient Egyptian culture ceased to exist hundreds of years before AD 1228 (the last known inscription in sacred hiero-glyphs dates to AD 394), while Egyptologists did not rediscover the evidence of the stellar nature of the Pyramid 'cult' until the early 1900s.[4] There is, therefore, no way other than a hidden tradition that the Sabian 'star-worshippers' could have known the Pyramids were connected to the stars or could have been motivated to make them objects of pilgrimage.

Ah but Harran . . . Harran – the fabled city of the Sabians. What a lowly mess it is today. Fashioned from mud-brick, a few of the traditional beehive-shaped houses still survive, grouped together into a centre retailing trinkets for the amusement of tourists. The ramshackle modern town is located in the midst of a vast, desolate plain with the ridges of the Taurus mountains, blue and hazy, looming 25 miles (40 kilometres) to the north. Göbekli Tepe stands on one of those ridges, and indeed the two sites are theoretically intervisible[5] – in other words, if your eyes were good enough, you could see Göbekli Tepe from Harran, and vice versa.

What would have made such a sighting easier, in antiquity, would have been a tall tower annexed to the temple that once stood here – a temple dedicated to *Su-En* (usually contracted to *Sin*), the Moon God of the Sabians.[6] After telling us that there were 'powerful images in this temple', the Greek Philosopher Libanius (AD 314-394), describes the tower, noting that 'from its top one could overlook the entire plain of Harran'.[7]

The Temple of the Moon God was already remotely ancient in the first millennium BC, when we know from inscriptions that several restorations were required. For example, repairs were carried out on it by the Assyrian King Shalamensar III (859-824 BC), and by Ashurbanipal (685-627 BC). Later, Nabonidus, who ruled the Neo-Babylonian Empire from 556-539 BC, rebuilt the temple.[8] Like Thutmosis IV of Egypt, who restored the Great Sphinx of Giza (see Chapter Ten), Nabonidus was inspired by a dream to undertake this work.[9]

It is a remarkable thing that the 'pagan' religion of Harran survived for several hundred years into the Islamic era. This owed much to the acceptance of the Sabians as a 'people of the book' (the reader will recall from Chapter Fourteen that they successfully claimed Hermes as their prophet and offered a compilation of the Hermetic texts as their Scriptures). Thus when the Arab general Ibn Ghanam conquered Harran in the seventh century AD, he co-opted the site where stood the Temple of the Moon God, with its fabulous tower, for the construction of a Grand Mosque. It seems that the temple was destroyed to make way for the mosque, but that Ghanam offered the Sabians an alternative site in the city where they were permitted to build a new temple.[10] They continued to practise their 'star-worship' there, without significant disruption, until the eleventh century AD, when either in 1032, or in 1081 – accounts are conflicting – a new generation of Muslim rulers turned against them, suppressed their faith and destroyed their last temple.[11]

Two centuries later the Mongol invasions began and Harran was frequently the scene of fierce conflicts. In a succession of episodes in 1259, 1262 and 1271, the city's Islamic places of worship were destroyed.[12] The Grand Mosque still lies in ruins today, but when we remember that the Temple of the Moon God once stood here under a lofty tower, it's curious that the one almost intact architectural remnant, with a square base measuring only 4 metres (13 feet) on each side, stands more than 50 metres (164 feet) tall and overlooks the Harran plain, just as its Sabian predecessor did. No doubt it is merely a surviving minaret of Ibn-Ghanam's Grand Mosque – the architecture is definitely Islamic. Still it is thought-provoking, to say the least, that local people refer to it to this day as the 'Astronomical Tower', as though preserving an ancient memory of the time when their Sabian ancestors climbed the long-vanished spire of the Temple of the Moon God to observe the heavens.

The few archaeological expeditions mounted in Harran from the 1950s onwards, while finding a number of inscriptions relating to the Moon God, have as yet revealed no physical traces of the pre-Islamic temples.[13] A team from the Chicago Oriental Institute was about to start a major dig around the ruins of the Grand Mosque in 1986, but it seems that the Turkish authorities insisted on such restrictive practices that the project had to be abandoned.[14] Current excavations by Harran University and the Şanlıurfa Museum Directorate show little interest in recovery of substantive remains from the city's pre-Islamic period.[15]

Thus far, based on the minimal archaeology done, datable artefacts from Harran itself go back to around 5000 BC,[16] though there is every possibility that older remains will be found with further excavations. At a settlement mound called Asagi Yarimca, a few kilometres north-west of the city, characteristic Halaf monochrome wares dating to 6000 BC have been collected.[17] And six kilometres south of Harran, excavations since 2006 by Turkish archaeologist Nurettin Yardimci have established the existence of an even older permanent settlement dated to 8000 BC.[18]

Since 8000 BC – 10,000 years ago – marks the approximate epoch in which Göbekli Tepe was abandoned and the last of its stone circles deliberately buried, I was intrigued to learn that the site of Yardimci's excavations has been known since time immemorial as *Tell Idris* – i.e. 'the settlement mound of Idris'. This is interesting, because Idris, in the Koran, is the name of the Biblical prophet Enoch, the seventh of the ten patriarchs who lived in the times before the Flood.[19] To be specific, Enoch is the son of Jared, the father of Methuselah, the grandfather of Lamech, and the great-grandfather of Noah himself.[20] Moreover, Muslim traditions associate Idris/Enoch with Hermes.[21] The Persian Islamic philosopher Abu Mashar (AD 787-886) expresses the matter as follows:

The name Hermes is a title. Its first bearer, who lived before the Flood, was . . . he whom the Hebrews call Enoch, whose name in Arabic is Idris. The Harranians declare his prophethood.[22]

This antediluvian Enoch/Idris/Hermes, was a master of the sciences, 'especially astronomy'. In addition:

He wrote many books, whose wisdom he preserved on the walls of Egyptian temples lest it be lost. It was he who constructed the pyramids.[23]

Abu Mashar's comments contain strong echoes of the Edfu Building Texts, also supposedly derived from lost antediluvian books and inscribed on the walls of the Temple of Horus to ensure that their message would not be lost. And the sense here that the pyramids are remotely ancient and were built by Hermes – that 'master of astronomy', the Egyptian Thoth, as the reader will recall – finds resonance with the tradition of the 'number of the secret chambers of the sanctuary of Thoth', reported in Chapter Eleven, which, in historic times, the Pharaoh Khufu wished to consult and copy in his own construction works at Giza.

Once again, confronted by such material, it doesn't seem unreasonable to suppose that we may have stumbled across the traces of a project, set in motion by the survivors of a global flood cataclysm, to bring about 'the resurrection of the former world of the gods'. Wherever this project took root, it seems to me, its essence was a *tradition*, passed down from generation to generation by initiated masters and thus theoretically capable of implementation in any place, and in any epoch, when the time was right.

With their ability to blend in and survive changing circumstances, with their knowledge of the astronomical qualities of the pyramids preserved until as least as late as the thirteenth century AD, and with their very name, as Selim Hassan rightly recognised, derived from *Sba*, the Ancient Egyptian word for 'star',[24] the Sabians of Harran have all the hallmarks of carriers of the secret tradition.

Mystery of the Watchers

Apart from his genealogy in the line of patriarchs before Noah, and the enigmatic statements that he 'walked with God' and was mysteriously 'taken up' by God without experiencing death,[25] the canonical Bible has nothing else to tell us about Enoch. Happily much more information is available in several ancient non-canonical works – i.e. works that Biblical redactors for one reason or another chose not to include within the officially sanctioned scriptures. Of these the most famous by far is the Book of Enoch. Prior to the eighteenth century, scholars had believed it to be irretrievably lost. Composed long before the birth of Christ,[26] and considered to be one of the most important pieces of Jewish mystical literature, it was only known from fragments and from references to it in other texts. All this changed, however, after polymath adventurer James Bruce of Kinnaird visited Ethiopia in the years 1770-72. Amongst other remarkable achievements there,[27] he procured and brought back to Britain several copies of the Book of Enoch that, in antiquity, had been translated into *Ge'ez*, the Ethiopic sacred language. These were the first complete copies ever to be seen in Europe.[28]

I note in passing that the Book of Enoch has always been of great significance to Freemasonry. Indeed, certain Masonic rituals – in curious resonance with Islamic traditions – identify Enoch with the Ancient Egyptian wisdom god Thoth and also with his Greek avatar Hermes.[29] An entry in the *Royal Masonic Cyclopaedia*, first published in 1877, tells us that Enoch was the inventor of writing, that 'he taught men the art of building', and that, before the Flood, he 'feared that the real secrets would be lost – to prevent which he concealed the Grand Secret, engraven on a white oriental porphyry stone, in the bowels of the earth.'[30] *The Cyclopaedia* contains its own hint of a secret tradition transmitted down the ages, when it further suggests that Enoch was himself a Freemason and that at the end of his days on earth 'he delivered up the Grand Master's office to Lamech.'[31]

The Book of Enoch is a very strange document, purporting, amongst many other elements, to be a vision of the future cataclysm of the Flood, and why it is to be unleashed upon the world. In a

339

series of dreams,[32] Enoch receives advance notice of the warning that God will give to his descendant Noah that 'a deluge is about to come upon the whole earth, and destroy all that is on it'.[33] This, of course, is familiar ground – merely a précis, or restatement, of what we can read in Genesis. So, too, is the passage that follows in which Enoch is given to understand that arrangements will be made for Noah to escape so that 'his seed may be preserved for all the generations of the world'.[34]

What comes next is intriguing. Regardless of the fact that the express purpose of God's Deluge is to kill off most of mankind – apart, of course, from Noah and his descendants – there is talk of the need to:

> heal the earth which the angels have corrupted . . . that all the children of men may not perish through all the secret things which the Watchers have disclosed and have taught their sons.[35]

This is only the second mention of these mysterious 'Watchers' in the Book of Enoch. The first, a few pages earlier, tells us nothing about them except that they 'shall quake' at the prospect of the coming events.[36] So far we have no real clue as to who or what they are except that they have transgressed some divine law by teaching 'secret things' – apparently *dangerous* things – to humanity, and that they (and most of the human race through the agency of the Deluge) are to be punished grievously because of this.

Certain names of the Watchers, or at any rate the leadership of the Watchers, are given – Azazel, Semjaza, Armen, Rumjal, Turel, Armaros, Danjal, Kokabel, and about a dozen more.[37] More specifically, we're told about the nature of the 'secret things' that they taught to mankind:

> And Azazel taught men to make swords and knives, and shields, and breastplates, and made known to them the metals of the earth, and the art of working them, and bracelets, and ornaments, and the use of antimony, and the beautifying of the eyelids, and all kinds of costly stones, and all colouring tinctures. And there arose much godlessness, and they committed fornication, and they were led astray, and became corrupt in all their ways. Semjaza

taught enchantments, and root-cuttings, Armaros the resolving of enchantments, Baraquijal taught astrology, Kokabel the constellations, Ezequeel the knowledge of the clouds, Araquiel the signs of the earth, Shamsiel the signs of the sun, and Sariel the course of the moon . . .[38]

Next we begin to understand that the Watchers are divided into two mutually opposed groups, because we read that the leaders of one group summon Enoch – remember this is all happening to him while he is in a dreamlike, visionary state – to deliver a message to the leaders of the other group, named as 'the Watchers of the heaven'.[39] It seems these 'Watchers of the heaven' (sometimes also referred to as 'the heavenly Watchers'[40]) have 'defiled themselves with women, and have done as the children of the earth do, and have taken unto themselves wives'.[41] They have also 'wrought great destruction upon the earth'.[42] For this they are going to be punished in various deeply unpleasant and terrifying ways.[43]

Obedient and dutiful, Enoch sets off, bearing his heavy message of murder and mayhem from the Watchers to . . . the Watchers.

So what's going on here?

A more careful scan of the pages reveals the backstory:

And it came to pass when the children of men had multiplied that in those days were born unto them beautiful and comely daughters. And the angels, the children of heaven, saw and lusted after them, and said to one another, 'Come, let us choose us wives from among the children of men and beget us children.' And Semjaza, who was their leader, said unto them: 'I fear ye will not indeed agree to do this deed, and I alone shall have to pay the penalty of a great sin.' And they all answered him and said: 'Let us all swear an oath, and all bind ourselves by mutual imprecations not to abandon this plan but to do this thing.' Then sware they all together and bound themselves by mutual imprecations upon it. And they were in all two hundred, who descended in the days of Jared on the summit of Mount Hermon . . .[44]

Now things are becoming clearer. 'Watchers' is a general term referring to angels. Amongst them are bad angels. They want to have sex and make babies with beautiful human women and while they're at it, as we can gather from passages quoted earlier, they're going to teach mankind a thing or two about metals, and the constellations and the course of the sun and the moon (or the ecliptic as this 'course' – this 'path' – is known to astronomers today). As the first step in implementing their plan these bad Watchers descend upon Mount Hermon, which happens to be in ancient Canaan, now the Lebanon, and only 45 miles (73 kilometres) from Baalbek.

Meanwhile there are good angels, 'the Holy Angels who watch'[45] – amongst them Uriel, Raphael, Raguel, Michael, Saraquel, Gabriel and Remiel.[46] And it's these good Watcher angels who appear to Enoch in a dream and give him that message of death and destruction to take to the bad Watcher angels on Mount Hermon. He tells us specifically where he received this dream:

I went off and sat down at the waters of Dan, to the south of the west of Hermon . . . I fell asleep and behold a dream came to me and visions fell down upon me and I saw visions of chastisement and a voice came bidding me to tell it to the sons of heaven and reprimand them. And when I awakened I came unto them . . .[47]

As I read these passages, set before the Flood, when the people of the Lebanon and ancient Turkey were still at the hunter-gatherer stage of development, it seems more and more obvious to me that Enoch is a shamanic figure. And like all shamans, everywhere, in all times and places, he sets great store by visions – which in his case come in the form of dreams received 'in sleep'. What's interesting, however, is that when he wakes up from this visionary state, he's able to go to a real physical place on Mount Hermon where the bad Watchers are and talk to them face to face:

'And I recounted before them all the visions which I had seen in sleep, and I began to speak the words of righteousness, and to reprimand the heavenly Watchers.'[48]

Does this not suggest, rather strongly, that the bad Watchers are physical beings? I don't know what the good Watchers are, because they only appear to Enoch in his dreams. Quite possibly they are real at some level. Readers of my book *Supernatural*, which is about shamanism, will know my view that in altered states of consciousness (including dream states) the 'receiver wavelength' of the brain may be retuned allowing us to make contact with other dimensions of reality.[49] But in Enoch's story the bad watchers must be real – real on the earthly plane of physical existence – because when he wakes up he's able to climb Mount Hermon and reprimand them.

We must also entertain the possibility that the bad Watchers – whoever or whatever they are – may not in fact be bad. All we can say is that they are judged to be bad and portrayed as bad in Enoch's dream-visions. One possibility that we should keep in mind, alongside the alternative possibility that the 'Book of Enoch' is just an ancient work of fantasy fiction, is that Enoch's encounters with the 'bad' Watchers really did happen and that he hated and resented them for changes they were seeking to introduce to the hunter-gatherer way of life of his people. In that case the reprimands he delivers to them, mediated through his subconscious as coming from the good Watchers, may simply express his own deeply entrenched views, the views of a bigoted old shaman who feels threatened by change – even though he himself will later be transformed by his contacts with the Watchers.

There isn't space here to review the entire, bizarre, impenetrable, wildly suggestive text of the Book of Enoch. What I'm interested in is the much more specific possibility that the two hundred Watchers who 'descended' on Mount Hermon were indeed real beings, not phantasms. I'd like to understand more about what kind of beings they could have been. And I want to look at the picture Enoch paints of them, laden with hatred and resentment though it is, as bringing skills and sciences to our ancestors – skills and sciences which, ultimately, will also be revealed to him by the good Watchers, and with which his own name will come to be associated in legend and tradition.[50]

Mystery of the Nephilim

The Watchers begin their development project in quite small ways, teaching 'charms and enchantments, and the cutting of roots' to humans, and making them 'acquainted with plants'.[51] This sounds fairly harmless; apart from a bit of 'enchantment', it's not really above and beyond basic hunter-gatherer level skills. But pretty soon, as we saw earlier, our ancestors are being initiated into the secrets of metals, and how to make swords and knives, and how to study the heavens – and also how to beautify themselves with eye-makeup and jewellery.

In return (a bit like the GIs who allegedly bought favours from British women with gifts of nylon stockings, cigarettes and chewing gum during World War II),[52] the Watchers are getting sex – lots of sex! – and it seems this is what annoys Enoch the most. He speaks reprovingly, again and again, of the 'fornication' of the Watchers,[53] of their 'lust' for 'beautiful and comely' human women[54] who they 'sleep with',[55] 'go into'[56] and 'defile themselves' with,[57] and to whom they reveal 'all kinds of sins'.[58]

From such admonishments we may reasonably deduce a number of things about the Watchers, most particularly that they must be about the right size and shape, and equipped, moreover, with the necessary organs and impulses to want, to have, and to enjoy sex with human women. To me, the obvious conclusion from this is the Watchers are in fact human, or at any rate extremely closely related at the genetic level to anatomically modern human beings – close enough, indeed, to make human women pregnant and to have 'children of fornication'[59] with them. These offspring are not sickly as one might expect from an even slightly mismatched genetic makeup. On the contrary, they thrive so vigorously that Enoch, or the 'good' angels speaking through him, want not only to destroy the Watchers but also to 'destroy the children of the Watchers'.[60]

But there is something very odd about the hybrid offspring, at least if we take Enoch's word for it, because he tells us that when human women 'became pregnant' by the Watchers they gave birth to:

great giants whose height was three thousand ells, who consumed all the acquisitions of men. And when men could no longer sustain them, the giants turned against them and devoured mankind.[61]

Three thousand ells is equivalent to 4,500 feet or 1,371 metres. Whatever the truth behind this account may be, therefore, it's obvious the angry old shaman is embellishing it fantastically here in his bid to discredit the Watchers. The prospect of human women giving birth to babies who would grow to more than a kilometre in height is patently absurd. Nonetheless, it brings us back to familiar Biblical territory again – indeed to one of the more notorious passages in the Book of Genesis which reads:

And it came to pass, when men began to multiply on the face of the earth, and daughters were born unto them, that the sons of God saw the daughters of men that they were fair; and they took them wives of all which they chose. And the Lord said, 'My spirit shall not always strive with man, for that he also is flesh: yet his days shall be an hundred and twenty years.' *There were giants in the earth in those days; and also after that, when the sons of God came in unto the daughters of men, and they bare children to them, the same became mighty men which were of old, men of renown.*[62]

That's the King James Version (I've added the emphasis in the final lines), but other translations give the original word *Nephilim*, that the KJV translates as 'giants', and we read:

The Nephilim were on the earth in those days – and also afterward – when the sons of God went to the daughters of humans, and had children by them. They were the heroes of old, men of renown.[63]

So now further clarity begins to emerge. A group of bad angels, 'Watchers of the heaven', have come to earth – 'descended', specifically, on Mount Hermon in Lebanon – transferred some technology, mated with human females, and produced offspring who are in some way gigantic and are called Nephilim. Here's what we're told in the very next verses:

> The Lord saw how great the wickedness of the human race had become on the earth, and that every inclination of the thoughts of the human heart was only evil all the time. The Lord regretted that he had made human beings on the earth, and his heart was deeply troubled. So the Lord said, 'I will wipe from the face of the earth the human race I have created—and with them the animals, the birds and the creatures that move along the ground—for I regret that I have made them.' But Noah found favour in the eyes of the Lord.[64]

An amazing amount of credulous nonsense has proliferated around these verses in recent years on the internet, much of it deriving from the late Zecharia Sitchin's science-fiction novels, notably the *Earth Chronicles* series, which he successfully passed off to the public as serious factual studies. I've already touched in Chapter Thirteen on Sitchin's misrepresentation of Baalbek and while I'm not saying that everything he wrote was fiction – he did throw in some quite valuable and interesting facts – his overall body of work is marred by enough blatant fabrications and fantasy to call for caution, rather than immediate, trusting acceptance, on the part of his readers.

His treatment of the subject of the Nephilim (he spells the word Nefilim, but this is not important) is a case in point. Claiming to be an expert in Biblical languages he asks:

> What then does the term *Nefilim* mean? Stemming from the Semitic root *NFL* ('to be cast down'), it means exactly what it says. It means *those who were cast down upon earth*![65]

The problem, however, as Michael S. Heiser, a genuine Biblical scholar and ancient Semitic languages expert, has conclusively demonstrated, is that:

Sitchin assumes 'nephilim' comes from the Hebrew word 'naphal' which usually means 'to fall'. He then forces the meaning 'to come down' onto the word, creating his 'to come down from above' translation. In the form we find it in the Hebrew Bible, if the word *nephilim* came from Hebrew *naphal*, it would not be spelled as we find it. The form *nephilim* cannot mean 'fallen ones' (the spelling would then be *nephulim*). Likewise nephilim does not mean 'those who fall' or 'those who fall away' (that would be*nophelim*). The only way in Hebrew to get *nephilim* from *naphal* by the rules of Hebrew morphology (word formation) would be to presume a noun spelled *naphil* and then pluralise it. I say 'presume' since this noun does not exist in biblical Hebrew – unless one counts Genesis 6:4 and Numbers 13:33, the two occurrences of *nephilim* – but that would then be assuming what one is trying to prove! However, in Aramaic the noun *naphil(a)* does exist. It means 'giant', making it easy to see why the Septuagint (the ancient Greek translation of the Hebrew Bible) translated *nephilim* as *gigantes* ('giant').[66]

Heiser is plainly right about this because, as he points out, there is a later passage in the Old Testament, in Numbers 13 where the word Nephilim appears again. This is thousands of years after the Deluge, indeed in the historical period, surely not later than 1200 BC, when the Israelites first entered Canaan after the Exodus from Egypt. Advance scouts report to Moses:

All the people we saw there are of great size. We saw the Nephilim there . . . We seemed like grasshoppers in our own eyes, and we looked the same to them.[67]

The context leaves no room for doubt that the Nephilim are people of 'great size', the references to them as 'giants' in the King James and other versions of the Bible therefore make complete sense, and the 'translation' that Sitchin gives is obviously bogus. Did he know it was bogus even as he retailed it in his books? There can be no certainty because, as Heiser goes on to prove, Sitchin's grasp of Biblical languages was so weak that he was unable to distinguish Aramaic from Hebrew.[68] The notion that the Nephilim were beings who were 'cast down from heaven', or who 'came down from heaven', was deployed by Sitchin, Heiser believes, simply because it served his argument and allowed him to 'make the *nephilim* sound like ancient astronauts'.[69]

Again the criticism is justified because Sitchin goes beyond what could be an innocent error to give further 'translations' of the word Nephilim that are even more self-serving and phoney. For example, he makes them 'Gods of Heaven upon Earth',[70] and, worse still, 'the People of the Rocket Ships'[71] – an interpretation for which there is no possible justification in any ancient text but that allows him to speak, amongst other egregious and deceptive fictions, of 'the Aeronautics and Space Administration of the Nefilim'.[72]

It is also important, while reviewing this material which has had such an impact on public perceptions of the past, to be clear that the Watchers, who are never mentioned at all in the Bible, but *are* said in the Book of Enoch to have descended from heaven, are quite distinct from the Nephilim. There is nothing in the Book of Enoch that says the Nephilim fell or were cast down or came down from heaven in any way. The most we may gather from the Book of Enoch is that the Nephilim are the progeny of the mating of Watchers and human women, but even this is complicated.

An authoritative English translation of the Ethiopic text brought back by Bruce was made by the Reverend R.H. Charles and first published in 1917.[73] It contains no mention of the Nephilim and describes the Watcher-human offspring simply as 'giants'.[74] Likewise the word Nephilim does not appear in the 1979 translation of Professor Michael A. Knibb which, as well as the Ethiopic text, takes account of newly discovered Aramaic fragments from the Dead Sea Scrolls.[75] However, a more recent translation, by George W. Nickelsburg and James C. VanderKam, published in 2012, draws on further fragments not considered by Knibb and here, in Chapter 7, Verse 2, the word Nephilim appears twice, as follows:

And they [human women] conceived from them [the Watchers] and bore to them great giants. And the giants begot Nephilim, and to the Nephilim were born Elioud. And they were growing in accordance with their greatness.[76]

The Nephilim do not appear again in the Nickelsburg and VanderKam translation. Nonetheless, the verse quoted above leaves no room for doubt: they are not to be considered as 'fallen' or 'cast down' or any such thing but as the progeny of Watcher-human mating. Nor is it the first generation, the 'great giants', who are named as Nephilim. It is the second generation, i.e. the offspring of the giants, who are the Nephilim, and they in turn will produce offspring of their own – the 'Elioud'.

If nothing else these 'Elioud', about whom very little is known outside Jewish mystical traditions, are further evidence of the close genetic relationship between Watchers and humans – so close that they must really be classified as the same species. Generally when two different species breed, even when they are close enough to produce offspring – such as horses and donkeys for example – those offspring are themselves sterile. But unlike the sterile mules that result from horse-donkey matings, the Nephilim are clearly not sterile, since they themselves are able to go on to produce offspring, i.e. the Elioud.

The only reasonable conclusion, as I have already indicated, is that the Watchers must have been human beings – no doubt surrounded by some aura or glamour to do with their mastery of technology and the sciences, but no more and no less human than the women they mated with – and that therefore their offspring were human too. Quite possibly they were of large stature. Quite possibly the epithet of 'giants' attached to them may also have had something to do with their intellectual abilities, which might have been seen to be superior. But they were human nonetheless and I see no good reason to conclude otherwise.

Meanwhile, because this is a subject around which much confusion swirls, it is necessary to reiterate that there is no suggestion either in Genesis or in Numbers – the only places they are mentioned in the Bible – that the Nephilim had 'fallen', even in the metaphorical sense of having sinned. On the contrary, far from being censured, they are described as 'mighty men of old', 'heroes', 'men of renown'. Genesis is unequivocal, as the reader can confirm from the passages cited earlier, that it is human wickedness, and the evil in human hearts, that causes God to send the Flood – a cataclysm that is survived not only by Noah's descendants, but by the Nephilim themselves who were still in Canaan, and still of great stature as the Book of Numbers attests, when the Israelites came to take possession of the Promised Land.

Emissaries

After this brief excursion into the foundations of the Sitchin Nephilim cult, let us return to the Watchers, and who and what they might be.

Enoch's condemnation of them for 'fornicating' with human women finds its counterpart in Genesis where, though not named, they are clearly 'the sons of God' who 'saw the daughters of men that they were fair; and they took them wives of all which they chose.' Thereafter the story of exactly what happened is only preserved in Enoch, where we're led to understand that the Watchers:

> taught all unrighteousness on earth and revealed the eternal secrets which were preserved in heaven, which men were striving to learn.[77]

Turning now to another of the non-canonical scriptures, the Book of Jubilees, which purports to be a revelation given by God to Moses, we read of the Watchers again and in a context that brings us back to the Sabians and Harran. According both to the Islamic historian Al-Masudi, and the Christian chronicler Gregory Bar Hebraeus, Harran was originally founded by Cainan,[78] the great-grandson of Noah.[79] By definition, therefore, though early, Harran is a post-diluvian city. Cainan (sometimes the name is spelled Kainam) was the son of Arpachsad:

> And the son grew, and his father taught him writing, and he went to seek for himself a place where he might seize for himself a city. And he found a writing, which former generations had

carved on the rock, and he read what was thereon, and he transcribed it and sinned owing to it, for it contained the teaching of the Watchers in accordance with which they used to observe the omens of the sun, moon and stars in all the signs of heaven.[80]

Here, then, is the origin of the star worship of the Sabians traced all the way back to the mysterious Watchers – whoever they were, whatever they were – who settled in the Near East in antediluvian times, taught our ancestors forbidden knowledge, broke some fundamental commandment by mating with human women and, as a result, were remembered as being responsible for the great global cataclysm of the Deluge.

Were these Watchers the emissaries of a lost civilization of the Ice Age? Perhaps a civilization as far ahead of the Upper Palaeolithic hunter-gatherers, who made up the majority of the population of the world at that time, as our own civilization is ahead of uncontacted tribes in the Amazon rainforest today? When I say 'ahead' I am, of course, not speaking of moral or spiritual values but simply of technology, skills and knowledge. Since such discrepancies still exist in the twenty-first century I see no reason in principle why they should not have existed in the remote epoch before the great cataclysms of the Younger Dryas set in between 10,800 BC and 9600 BC.

To continue with this line of speculation, could it be that there was some sort of outreach *before* those cataclysms?

A very careful, considered, structured outreach programme, to observe, to study – in other words to *watch* – hunter-gatherer populations, but not to intermingle with them, not to enter into the complicated entanglements of sexual and family relationships with them, and above all not to transfer any technology to them?

One could imagine that a group of anthropologists and scientists sent off to study a previously uncontacted Amazon tribe today might be bound by similar strictures. But suppose some of them disagreed? Suppose some of them 'went native' – as used to be said of colonialists in the days of the British Empire who allowed themselves to get too close to indigenous populations they interacted with.

Is that perhaps what happened to the troop of two hundred 'Watchers' on Mount Hermon? Somewhere around 10,900 BC, did they break the commandments of their own culture and 'go native' amongst the hunter-gatherers of the Near East? And were the first chance encounters with the fragments of a giant comet a century later in 10,800 BC – encounters that devastated the world – somehow blamed upon their moral lapse?

And some final thoughts. Did their civilization survive, albeit in truncated, damaged, reduced form through the rigours of the Younger Dryas, until the second fateful encounter with the comet's debris stream in 9600 BC that ended the 'long fatal winter', but also led to the final sinking and destruction of 'the Homeland of the Primeval Ones'?

That 'island' realm, far-off in the ocean, that bears such striking resemblances to Plato's description of Atlantis.

Was it then that the last survivors of the once advanced and prosperous civilization set out to wander the world in ships to initiate their great design intended ultimately, perhaps after thousands of years, to bring about the resurrection of the former world of the gods?

And were Egypt, Baalbek, and Göbekli Tepe amongst the places these 'Magicians of the Gods' chose to settle in order to set their plan in motion – perhaps precisely because there had been outreach in these areas before the cataclysms and therefore their potential and the character of their inhabitants were known?

Was Harran part of the second stage of this plan, when the work of the last initiates at Göbekli Tepe was done and the time-capsule they had created there was buried to be rediscovered in a future age?

Buried in the bowels of the earth like that 'white porphyry stone' spoken of in the Masonic tradition cited earlier?

Or like the 'writing carved on rock' containing the teachings of the Watchers which Cainan found and transcribed at the time he established Harran, bringing into his city knowledge of the omens of the sun, moon and stars and 'all the signs in heaven'?

Knowledge of exactly the type that would be central to the mysterious star religion of the Sabians in the millennia to come . . .

Astronomy and earth measuring

Archaeoastronomer James Q. Jacobs has noticed something rather odd about Harran. The city's latitude, 36.87 degrees north of the equator, appears to be non-random, since the figure is the same as that for the acute angle of a 3:4:5 right triangle[81] – i.e. a triangle which contains one 90 degree right angle and whose side lengths are in the ratio 3:4:5. In all such triangles – which form the basis for trigonometry and are thus fundamental to astronomy and geodesy – the other two angles are, with rounding, 53.13 degrees and 36.87 degrees.

Is it a coincidence that a 3:4:5 right triangle with the same internal angles exists inside the King's Chamber of the Great Pyramid of Egypt? The floor of this austere and uninscribed red granite room, in which no pharaoh was ever found entombed, forms a 2:1 rectangle, exactly 20 Egyptian royal cubits in length and 10 royal cubits in width (10.46 x 5.23 metres). The right triangle is formed with its shortest dimension (15 cubits) represented by the diagonal across the west wall from the lower south-west corner to the upper north-west corner; its median dimension (20 cubits) is drawn along the entire length of the floor on the south side of the chamber; its long dimension (25 cubits) is drawn from the upper north-west corner of the chamber to the lower south-east corner.[82]

These side lengths of 15 cubits, 20 cubits and 25 cubits can be expressed as the ratio 3:4:5 because if we allocate the value '3' to the length of 15 cubits then 20 cubits must naturally have a value of '4' and 25 cubits must have a value of '5'. All right-angled triangles with side lengths in this special 3:4:5 ratio are called 'Pythagorean' – after Pythagoras, the Greek philosopher and mathematician of the sixth century BC, who was supposedly the first to discover that they share a unique characteristic. This is that the square of the short side (3 units x 3 units = 9 units), added to the square of the median side (4 units x 4 units = 16 units), together result in a figure equal to the square of the long side (5 units x 5 units = 25 units, i.e. the sum of 9 plus 16).[83] The real 'secret magic' of the triangle, however, as the Icelandic mathematician Einar Palsson has pointed out, is only revealed when the numbers are cubed.[84] Then we get:

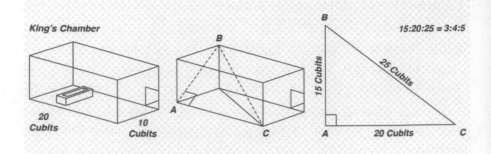

Figure 58: The 3:4:5 right triangle hidden within the King's Chamber of the Great Pyramid.

$$3 \times 3 \times 3 = 27$$
$$4 \times 4 \times 4 = 64$$
$$5 \times 5 \times 5 = 125$$

The total of 27 plus 64 plus 125 is 216, and as the reader will recall from earlier chapters, 216 is one of the sequence of numbers identified by historians of science Giorgio de Santillana and Hertha von Dechend as being derived from precise observations of the precession of the equinoxes, those long-term changes in the sky that unfold at the rate of one degree every 72 years. Numbers derived from this precessional sequence turn out to be encoded in ancient myths and monuments all around the world, tracing their origins back to what Santillana and von Dechend can only conclude was some 'almost unbelievable' ancestor civilization of prehistoric antiquity that 'first dared to understand the world as created according to number, measure and weight'.[85]

The heartbeat of the cycle, as we've seen, is 72 – the number of years required for the unfolding of one degree of precessional change. In observational terms a one degree shift over 72 years – effectively an entire human lifetime – is barely perceptible, being roughly equivalent to the width of a forefinger held up towards the horizon. A 30 degree shift – through one entire zodiacal constellation, requiring 30 x 72 = 2,160 years to complete – is impossible to miss, but its progression could only be precisely recorded and noted by many generations of conscientious and accurate observers. A 60 degree shift, i.e. through two zodiacal constellations, takes 4,320 years (2,160 x 2 = 4,320), which is why a 360 degree shift (all 12 zodiacal constellations – 'the Great Year') requires a grand total of 25,920 years.

Within the 'precessional code' as Santillana and von Dechend showed conclusively, it is permissible to divide and multiply the 'heartbeat number' of 72 (the number of years required for one degree of precessional change). This is done in myths and monuments all around the world (for example at Angkor, in Cambodia, as we saw in Chapter Twelve, and at Borobudur, in Indonesia, as we will see in Chapter Eighteen). Thus 216 is 3 x 72 (or 2,160 divided by 10). Its derivation from the 3:4:5 triangle inside the King's Chamber of the Great Pyramid is therefore most unlikely to be an accident and the relationship of all this to astronomy and geodesy – earth-measuring – is clear. This is further confirmed by the external dimensions of the Great Pyramid which, as I showed in *Fingerprints of the Gods*, encode the dimensions of our planet on the precessional scale of 1:43,200.[86]

Essentially, if you measure the height of the Great Pyramid and multiply it by 43,200 you get the polar radius of the earth and if you measure the base perimeter of the Great Pyramid and multiply by 43,200 you get the equatorial circumference of the earth. The fact that 43,200 is one of the sequence of precessional numbers identified by Santillana and von Dechend further reduces the likelihood of coincidence, and requires us to take seriously the proposition that we are indeed looking at part of the intellectual legacy of some 'almost unbelievable' ancestor civilization that had measured the earth and observed the changes in the stars with scientific accuracy, long before what we understand as 'history' began.

So, to return to Harran, James Q. Jacobs' discovery certainly suggests that the founders of this city made a deliberate geodetic choice when they set it at latitude 36.87 degrees north. What adds to this impression is that Jacobs has also found a geodetic relationship between Harran and the fabled Mesopotamian city of Ur with which it was known to have enjoyed a close relationship in antiquity:[87]

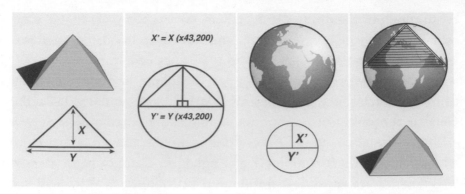

Figure 59: The Great Pyramid encodes the dimensions of our planet on the precessional scale of 1:43,200. The height of Great Pyramid multiplied by 43,200 gives us the polar radius of the earth and the base perimeter of the Great Pyramid multiplied by 43,200 give us the equatorial circumference of the earth with only minor errors in both cases.

The history/myth of Mesopotamia holds that Ur and Harran are two important, related Sumerian centres, both associated with the moon. I checked the [latitude of] the Ur ziggurat, at 30. 963 degrees. At first I did not notice colatitude equals 5/3 arctangent (atan). Colatitude is the distance to the nearest pole, a geodetic reference point. Latitude references the equator, the mid-poles plane perpendicular to the rotation axis. The local level plane at Harran intersects the rotation axis at a 4/3 atan angle, forming a 3:4:5 right triangle, as does latitude in relation to the equator and geodetic centre. Summarizing, colatitude at Harran equals 4/3 atan and at Ur 5/3 atan. Thus latitude at Harran equals 3/4 atan and at Ur 3/5 atan. Perhaps these 'idolators' were doing astronomy?[88]

I would go further and say *undoubtedly* the Sabian 'star-worshippers' of Harran were doing astronomy. And given the evidence we've reviewed in Chapters Fourteen and Fifteen for precise calculations of precession by the makers of Göbekli Tepe – so precise that they were able to create a symbolic picture of the winter solstice sky in our own epoch, 11,600 years in their future – I am not surprised by further evidence in this region of extremely ancient and extremely precise scientific astronomy and geodesy. This evidence goes far beyond the capabilities normally attributed to the historical civilization of Mesopotamia and because it draws back the veil, requiring us to look very deeply into prehistory, it again raises the spectre of a lost civilization.

Jacobs has noticed this and admits to being puzzled by it. His final discovery of relevance here concerns the geodetic relationship between Göbekli Tepe and Harran:

> The sites are apparently intervisible, just over 40 km apart. The difference in latitude from Harran to Göbekli Tepe equals precisely 1/1,000 of earth's circumference. This is where we enter a twilight zone in ancient astronomy. Of course the opposite metaphor – 'the dawn' of ancient astronomy – is the proper one regarding the implication. Göbekli Tepe features the oldest known room aligned north-south, evidence of astronomy in practice.
>
> Even non-archaeos understand stratification and deposition basics – deeper is older. Göbekli Tepe is 12,000 years old. Harran is equated . . . with Ur of Sumeria, the 'Civilised Land' and a 'cradle of civilization'. That cradle and astronomy is presumed to be 4,000 to 5,000 years old, not 12,000. Harran is located at 3/4 atan latitude, a fixed parameter, and Göbekli Tepe is at a specific latitude difference north. Because the fixed parameter must come first, the conundrum, of course, is that this precise 1/1,000 of circumference latitude difference is either a coincidence, or ancient astronomy just took a leap back to 12,000 years ago.[89]

My understanding is that Jacobs is no fan of alternative history and he has commented forthrightly on the amount of 'utterly unbelievable pseudo-science' that is presently in circulation on the internet and in the media concerning Göbekli Tepe.[90] Kudos to him, therefore, for going where the genuine science takes him and keeping an open mind to the possibility that ancient astronomy and precise earth-measuring may indeed go back much further into the 'twilight zone' than mainstream archaeology has hitherto supposed.

The Magi of Harran

As Harran was in its beginning – a centre of the 'exact sciences' as Jacobs proposes[91] – so it continued to be throughout the millennia when the Sabians practised their 'star worship' here. As late as the ninth century AD, Al-Battani, better known in the west as Albategnius, arguably the most distinguished astronomer and mathematician of the Middle Ages, was born in Harran and went on during a long and distinguished life[92] to record many remarkable scientific achievements.

Of particular note, combining both exact astronomy and exact geodesy, was his calculation of the greatest distance of the moon from the earth (since the moon's orbit is elliptical it has both a perigee, the point at which it is closest to the earth and an apogee, the point at which it is furthest away). Al-Battani's estimate of the moon's distance at apogee was within 0.6 per cent of the modern value.[93] He is also noted for his calculation of the length of the solar year at 365 days, 5 hours, 46 minutes and 24 seconds[94] – an error of only 2 minutes 22 seconds when compared with the figure produced by modern astronomers with the benefit of advanced technology.[95] Al-Battani catalogued 489 stars,[96] produced more accurate measurements of the sun's path than Copernicus would achieve 600 years later,[97] and gave important trigonometric formulae for right triangles,[98] a fact of the history of science that is perhaps noteworthy in view of the relationship of Harran's latitude to right 3:4:5 triangles discussed above.

Al-Battani's full name, which includes a number of revealing epithets, was Abu Abdallah al-Battani Ibn Jabir Ibn Sinan al-Raqqi al-Harrani al-Sabi. The origin of the epithet 'al-Battani' itself is unknown, but is conjectured to refer to a street or district of Harran, his birth city – from whence 'al-Harrani' is of course also derived. 'Al-Raqqi' refers to the city of al-Raqqa, on the Euphrates river in Syria, where al-Battani spent much of his working life. Most interesting, however, is the epithet 'al-Sabi' which, according to the authoritative *Dictionary of Scientific Biography*, indicates that al-Battani's ancestors, if not he himself:

had professed the religion of the Harranian Sabians in which a considerable amount of the ancient Mesopotamian astral theology and star lore appears to have been preserved and which, tolerated by the Muslim rulers, survived until the middle of the eleventh century. The fact that al-Battani's elder contemporary, the great mathematician and astronomer Thabit ibn Qurra hailed from the same region and still adhered to the Sabian religion, seems indicative of the keen interest in astronomy that characterised even this last phase of Mesopotamian star idolatry.[99]

Thabit ibn Qurra (AD 836-901, and also born in Harran), would have had little patience with loaded terms like 'star idolatry' which seek to place the 'paganism' of the Sabians on a lower level than the deadly, and often bigoted, narrow-minded and unscientific clerical monotheism of religions like Christianity, Judaism and Islam. Thabit was well aware that, underlying the ancient Sabian practices misunderstood by these young religions as 'star idolatry', were indeed exact sciences of great benefit to mankind, and thus he wrote:

> Who else have civilised the world, and built the cities, if not the nobles and kings of Paganism? Who else have set in order the harbours and rivers? And who else have taught the hidden wisdom? To whom else has the Deity revealed itself, given oracles, and told about the future, if not the famous men amongst the Pagans? The Pagans have made known all this. They have discovered the art of healing the soul; they have also made known the art of healing the body. They have filled the earth with settled forms of government, and with wisdom, which is the highest good. Without Paganism the world would be empty and miserable.[100]

To the above should be added that even this translation fails to do justice to what Thabit was attempting to convey here. The Syriac word *hanputho* that he used in his original text, and that is translated above as 'paganism' in fact means 'the pure religion'.[101] Its cognate in Arabic is the word *hanif*, which appears in the Koran referencing ancient pre-Islamic faiths that were regarded as pure and thus not to be persecuted.[102]

Indeed the Sabians were accorded recognition by many leading thinkers in the early centuries of Islam as the archytypal *hanifs*[103] and this, together with their famous claim to be a 'people of the book', was amongst the reasons why they were left free for so long to practise the old ways.

We've already seen how the Sabians were allowed to build a new Temple of the Moon God, and to continue their religious rites, after the Arab General Ibn Ghanam conquered Harran in the seventh century AD. This in itself is a sign of most unusual favour, since Islamic armies normally offered 'pagans' the choice of either conversion or death. Even more interesting, however, is the Sabians' encounter with the Abbasid Caliph Abu Jafar Abdullah al-Ma'mun, who passed through their city in AD 830 and reportedly quizzed them intensively on their religion.[104]

Remembering the Sabian pilgrimages to Giza, it is reasonable to wonder whether there is any connection with the fact that in AD 820, a decade before he visited Harran, it was Ma'mun who tunnelled into the Great Pyramid and opened its previously hidden passageways and chambers. Indeed, it is through 'Ma'mun's Hole' that visitors still enter the monument today.[105] Described by Gibbon as 'a prince of rare learning',[106] it seems Ma'mun's investigation was prompted by information he'd received about the Great Pyramid, specifically that it contained:

> a secret chamber with maps and tables of the celestial and terrestrial spheres. Although they were said to have been made in the remote past, they were supposed to be of great accuracy.[107]

Like his father Harun al-Rashid of Arabian nights fame, Ma'mun belonged to a line of learned and open-minded Caliphs. By the eleventh century, however, when the last Temple of the Moon God in Harran was finally destroyed, a new, more fundamentalist and far less tolerant faction had seized the reins of Islam and the suppression of 'the pure religion' of the Sabians began in earnest. We know they continued to make their pilgrimages to Giza until the thirteenth century, but after that they disappear from history and, while some scholars feel that elements of their faith survive amongst such sects as the Mandeans and the Yazidis of Iraq[108] (who themselves have been subjected to intense Islamic persecution in modern times), there seems to be no trace left of the Sabians today.

Except for one tantalizing and intriguing thought.

The sacred Book of the Sabians was the compilation of texts now known as the *Hermetica*,[109] a copy of which most mysteriously found its way into the hands of Leonardo de Pistoia, an agent of Cosimo de Medici, founder of the Medici political dynasty of Florence. It was 1460 and Pistoia was travelling in Macedonia at the time, but immediately returned to Florence with the treasure of ancient wisdom that he had acquired. With equal speed, Cosimo ordered his adopted son Marsilio Ficino to delay translation of the complete works of Plato, on which he had just begun, and to translate the Hermetica instead.[110] It was, as the late Dame Frances Yates, one of the world's leading experts on the Renaissance, has observed, 'an extraordinary situation'.[111]

Indeed so, particularly since there is much to suggest that it was this introduction of Hermetic ideas into fifteenth century Europe that kicked the Renaissance into high gear and gave birth to the modern world.[112]

Or was it, perhaps, not so much the birth of a new world as it was the rebirth – the 'resurrection' in the language of the Edfu texts – of the former world of the gods?

Signs of the hands

As we have seen, the Edfu texts speak of the Seven Sages, bringers of wisdom to mankind, teachers of science and magic. The Mesopotamian texts also speak of Seven Sages – the Apkallus – whose functions are identical to those of their Egyptian counterparts. We have explored all this in earlier chapters and need not repeat ourselves here. What I was unaware of, however, until I began to investigate the traditions of the Watchers in the Book of Enoch, the Book of Jubilees and elsewhere, is that scholars have discovered close links between the Watchers and the Apkallus.

For example, 'figurines of Apkallus were buried in boxes in the foundation deposits in Mesopotamian buildings in order to avert evil . . . The term *massare*, Watchers, is used of these sets'.[113] Likewise the

Apkallus were said to have taught antediluvian sciences to humanity and so, too, were the Watchers.[114] As one scholar concludes, however: 'The Jewish authors often inverted the Mesopotamian intellectual traditions with the intention of showing the superiority of their own cultural foundations. [Thus] . . . the antediluvian sages, the Mesopotamian Apkallus, were demonised as the "sons of God" and . . . appear as the Watchers . . . illegitimate teachers of humankind before the flood.'[115]

All in all, what this body of research reveals is a series of links between the Watchers and the Apkallus so close that they might reasonably be supposed to be two different names, or titles, for the same beings.[116] There is neither space nor need here to explore this material with all its multiple interconnections in any further detail, but I find it tempting to imagine that it might be these very beings – these Watchers, these Sages – who are depicted on the tall megalithic pillars at Göbekli Tepe.

Notwithstanding their resemblance to the symbols of Mesopotamian deities (see Chapter Fifteen), the presence of the bag-like objects on the upper register of Pillar 43 in Enclosure D that I first drew attention to in Chapter One continues to intrigue me, since these objects are also so similar to the bags held in the hands of the Apkallu figures in many ancient depictions. And that similarity, as the reader will recall, is not confined to the Near East. In a sculpture from the Olmec site of La Venta, overlooking the Gulf of Mexico, a relief of Quetzalcoatl, the Feathered Serpent, the legendary bringer of civilization to the peoples of Central America, carries an identical bag.

Before leaving Turkey in July 2014 we make one more trip back to Göbekli Tepe. I can hardly bear to see it under its horrible, heavy wooden roof, which plunges all four of the main enclosures into a looming sepulchral gloom. But there's a particular reason why I want to take a final look at Enclosure D, not this time at Pillar 43, but at the two central pillars with their crooked arms and their hands with long fingers that almost meet over their stone bellies.

When I'm satisfied I've seen enough we have our driver take us back in to Şanlıurfa, to the main museum, where numerous artefacts from Göbekli Tepe, thought too precious to leave at the site, are on display. I've been here before, too, but there are a number of details I want to remind myself of.

I spend a long time in front of a mesmerizing sculpture of a human figure. It wasn't found at Göbekli Tepe, but was an accidental discovery made in the 1980s in Şanlıurfa itself, in the heart of the old town where deep foundations were being dug for a car park. It has been dated to the Göbekli Tepe period – i.e. to around 9000 BC – and is 'on its way,' Klaus Schmidt has written, 'to become world famous as the oldest completely preserved life-sized statue of mankind.'[117]

Unlike the megalithic pillars at Göbekli Tepe where the 'heads' are stylised – resembling the upper crossbar of the letter 'T' – this figure has a fully formed human head and face with glittering black obsidian eyes, a pronounced chin that gives every impression of being bearded, a pectoral in the form of a large double 'V' carved in high relief across its chest, and its arms crooked in the manner of the Göbekli Tepe figures with the fingers almost meeting across the front of the belly.

I move on to the second piece I want to examine, the so-called 'Totem Pole'. It's even eerier than the first. Again it's about normal human height but it is by no means entirely human. Instead it's a complex hybrid with multiple different characteristics. The head is badly damaged, but the ears and eyes have been preserved and suggest a predator of some kind, perhaps a bear, or perhaps a lion or leopard. So it's a therianthrope. Then large serpents wind up along the outside of its legs. They have oversized heads which project forward at about the level of the figure's groin.

There are two sets of arms and hands that seem to belong to the figure itself. In the case of the upper pair, the arms are crooked in the usual Göbekli Tepe manner and the hands are brought together, with the fingers almost touching across the chest. Then there's a second pair of what seem to be forearms and hands only, with the fingers again coming together and almost touching across the belly roughly at the level of the navel.

Moving down, at about the level of the genitals, a small head and two further arms protrude outwards from the midline of the figure. Again there are those long-fingered hands almost meeting, but this time they appear to be playing a drum. Beside them, but just below them, there is the hint, much damaged, of a further pair of arms and hands.

Much about all this is familiar to me.

Very familiar.

Not from Göbekli Tepe, though, as we'll see in the next chapter, but from the far side of the world.

Part VII

Distance

Chapter 17
Mountain

———◆———

It's October 2013 and I'm on the slopes above the city of Cuzco, in the high Andes of Peru exploring the incredible megalithic site of Sacsayhuaman with Jesus Gamarra, a descendant of the Incas. Gamarra is in his mid-seventies, more than ten years older than me, but you'd never guess it from looking at him. He's as nimble as a mountain goat, fully acclimatised to the altitude of 3,701 metres (12,142 feet), and fit as an Olympic athlete after years of clambering around the passes and trails of his homeland during a lifetime of research into the origins of Inca culture.

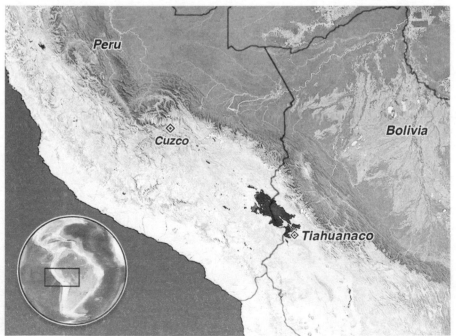

Figure 60

367

My first visit to Sacsayhuaman was in 1992, and I've been back many times since, always learning something new. In *Fingerprints of the Gods*, published in 1995, I expressed my scepticism of the orthodox theory that practically all of the great monuments of the Andes are the work of the Incas – whose empire was not much more than a century old at the start of the Spanish conquest of Peru in 1531. 'Since it was known that the Incas made extensive use of Sacsayhuaman,' I wrote in *Fingerprints*, 'I could easily understand why it had been assumed that they had built it. But there was no obvious or necessary connection between these two propositions. The Incas could just as well have found the structures already in place and moved into them.'[1] In *Heaven's Mirror* (1998) I further developed the argument that the gigantic megalithic and rock-hewn constructions of the Andes, which are by no means confined to Sacsayhuaman but are found all over the region, were *not* the work of the Incas but of a much earlier, predecessor civilization long lost to history:

> In such an event it is not necessary to imagine a complete break in continuity between the hypothesised 'elder culture' and the Incas; on the contrary, the latter could have inherited some of the traditions and knowledge of the former and attempted, on a smaller scale, to mimic their cyclopean world.[2]

I didn't know Gamarra or his work when I wrote the passages quoted above. Now, as he shows me around Sacsayhuaman, carefully and painstakingly explaining everything he wants me to see, taking me to hidden nooks and corners of the site that I was completely unaware of before, he opens my eyes to all sorts of details that support and reinforce my earlier intuitions. More than that, he presents a solid archaeological case, originally worked out by his father Alfredo Gamarra, and greatly refined and extended by himself, that would, I feel, be worthy of serious consideration by mainstream scholars – if, that is, the mainstream were not so locked in to the rigid preconception that all these monuments are just a few hundred years old and entirely the work of the Incas.[3]

It is notoriously difficult to know, with any useful level of certainty, the age of anonymous, uninscribed stone monuments. Carbon dating of associated organic materials is only useful when we can be absolutely certain that the materials being dated were deposited at the same time as the cutting and placing of the stone we are interested in. In the case of many megalithic structures this is impossible. Surface luminescence dating, which we saw in Chapter Ten has already produced some anomalous results at the Pyramid of Menkaure and at the Sphinx and Valley Temples of Giza, has not yet been widely taken up by the archaeological establishment and has never been applied to the monuments of the Andes. In the absence of useful objective tests, therefore, the next routine strategy is to look at architectural style and methods. Just as different styles of pottery can often provide reliable indications as to what culture in what period made a particular piece, so too with architecture. The rule of thumb is that very different styles and approaches to the construction or creation of stone monuments, even if they stand side by side, are indicative of the involvement of different cultures working at different periods in the past.

Unfortunately this logical and reasonable technique of stylistic dating is not popular with archaeologists studying the monuments of the Andes – perhaps because, if they were to deploy it here, as they do elsewhere, they would be forced to question the established theory that the Incas made everything. Archaeology is a deeply conservative discipline and I have found that archaeologists, no matter where they are working, have a horror of questioning anything their predecessors and peers have already announced to be true. They run a very real risk of jeopardizing their careers if they do. In consequence they focus – perhaps to a large extent subconsciously – on evidence and arguments that don't upset the applecart. There might be room for some tinkering around the edges, some refinement of orthodox ideas, but God forbid that anything should be discovered that might seriously undermine the established paradigm.

What Gamarra is showing me as we walk around Sacsayhuaman is that there are three distinctly different styles of architecture here – so different, indeed, that it is extremely difficult to understand why archaeologists insist they are all the work of the same Inca culture, and were all made during the century or so prior to the arrival of the

Spanish. It is unnecessary to repeat the detailed descriptions of this site that I have given in my earlier books. In brief, however, Sacsayhuaman stands on a hillside above and overlooking the city of Cuzco and consists of a series of three parallel rows of walls, all about 6 metres (20 feet) high, constructed entirely of gigantic megaliths, some weighing in excess of 360 tons,[4] each wall offering a jagged, almost zig-zag profile, built into the side of a slope and arranged in step fashion one above the other. Past the uppermost wall the slope continues to rise towards the south and is littered with the ruins of a number of much smaller buildings; one of these, right at the top, consisting of three concentric circles of nicely-cut blocks, preserved at foundation level only, must have been impressive when it was intact. Beyond it, a valley overgrown with trees and dense bushes slopes steeply down to the south with Cuzco nestling in its floor.

Turning northwards, a grassy plateau perhaps 100 metres wide extends from the base of the lowest of the three megalithic walls along

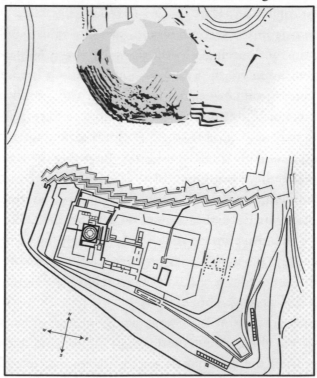

Figure 61: Plan of Sacsayhuaman, zigzag megalithic walls to the south, shaped rocky knoll to the north.

its full length of some 400 metres. On the north side of the plateau, a natural rocky knoll of volcanic diorite rises, but it has been cut and shaped into intricate terrace and step formations. This is where Gamarra and I are now standing and he launches into an explanation.

'This is "Hanan Pacha" work,' he says, indicating the beautifully cut diorite terraces at our feet. 'The first world. It was made thousands of years before the time of the Incas. They knew how to shape stone then.' A mischievous grin. 'They could do anything they wanted with it. Maybe it was easy for them.' He stoops, beckons for me to look closely at the surface of the rock. 'You see?'

I shrug. I'm puzzled. I'm not sure what he wants me to see.

'No tool marks,' he says. He gestures proudly at the whole carved, sculpted artefact, the whole gigantic work of art that the knoll has been transformed into. 'No tool marks anywhere.'

'So what did they do? Buff the tool marks off after they'd cut the stone?'

'No,' says Gamarra. 'They didn't need tools. They had another way. It was the same in the second world, too, which I call "Uran Pacha".' He points to the looming megalithic walls opposite. There is some disagreement amongst the experts about exactly what kind of stone they are made from and where it was quarried. The consensus, although some green diorite porphyry and some andesite are also present, is that a very hard and dense form of local limestone was used for the megaliths themselves. Quarries at 15 kilometres distance and at 3 kilometres distance have been identified as sources for the limestone.[5]

We scramble down the side of the knoll and across the grassy plaza until we stand beneath the courses of hulking megaliths that have become the definitive image that Sacsayhuaman now projects to the world. As always when I'm here, my first sensation is of wonder. I feel small, diminished, pint-sized. It's not just that the walls, and the blocks they're built of, are big. They seem to have – dare I say it? – a personality of their own, and it is the personality of a slumbering giant.

What's spectacular about these walls, quite apart from their size, quite apart from the fact that there are at least a thousand individual blocks, is the breathtaking virtuoso feat that has been performed in joining them together. I mean, let's be serious here. When you are building a wall in which the smallest block you plan to use weighs a ton, while the majority weigh over 20 tons, where many weigh 100 tons, some weigh 200 tons and a few weigh more than 300 tons, you have already set yourself a formidable logistical challenge.

But then suppose, just for the hell of it, you decide to up the ante a little more and insist that these walls must be constructed in the form of huge three-dimensional jigsaw puzzles. Every block has to be a polygon with anywhere between six and a dozen sides, every polygon has to be different – no two alike – and they must all fit together with one another so tightly that you won't be able to get a razor blade between the joints.

I can't speak for the *back* of the blocks where they lock into other blocks behind them – again, presumably, multi-dimensionally – but the patterns made along their weird cyclopean façades are already complicated enough without considering what's going on out of sight. It's obvious, gazing up in stupefied awe at the scale and complexity of the project, that this must have been an incredibly difficult thing to do! Whoever was responsible for Sacsayhuaman's megalithic phase can only have been top-class professionals with years of experience behind them and a very long tradition of distilled knowledge to draw upon. You can't conceive, and plan, and build something like this with only a century or two of trial and error behind you – as is supposed to be the case with the Incas. These megaliths of Sacsayhuaman are the mature work of grandmasters of stone.

Moreover, throughout the Andes, there is no evidence of apprentices learning how to do this, no early prototypes that are good but don't quite succeed. Other structures might not be on the scale of Sacsayhuaman (though many come close) but all of them, whether at Pisac, or Ollantaytambo or Machu Picchu, or at a score of other sites, share the same level of complexity while embracing different challenges – such as extremely difficult locations very far from the quarries – that Sacsayhuaman does not have to overcome. All of them are masterworks from the beginning. All of them are perfect. It's almost as if, as Gamarra says, 'it was easy for them'.

I know he has a theory to explain this. The theory is that gravity was lower during his first two 'worlds' – the *Hanan Pacha* stage and the *Uran Pacha* stage – and that this made stone lighter and easier to manipulate. The lowered gravity is linked in his mind with the notion that the earth once made much closer orbits around the sun – an orbit of 225 days and an orbit of 260 days – before settling in to its present 365 day path.[6] He could be right; new science suggests that the orbits of the planets are not fixed and stable but can be subject to radical changes that, amongst other things, are capable of increasing the flux of comets into the inner solar system.[7]

However, this isn't the part of his theory I'm interested in. Where I feel he is solidly persuasive is in his observations of the anomalous character of the monuments of the Andes – observations that are based on fifty years of his own field work and sixty years of fieldwork by his father. The Gamarras have walked the walk and earned the right to speak out on this matter, and when they speak, though they themselves are of Inca descent, their message is absolutely clear – many of the great architectural works that are attributed to the Incas were not made by the Incas. There are traces of a lost civilization here. Indeed not just one lost civilization, but – if Gamarra's time-frame is correct – two.

'All the big blocks of Sacsayhuaman are from the Uran Pacha period,' he says. We're standing in a corner at a junction of a dozen or so of these incredible blocks. Gamarra highlights again the precision of their joints that look as though some modern machine tool has been at work, and the daunting complexity of the patterns they form. Then he draws my attention to something else. Several of the blocks have weird circular hollows and shallow tracks with raised edges scalloped into their faces along with other peculiar, seemingly random, patterns. 'No tool marks,' he reiterates. 'No chisels. No hammers.'

'So how did they do it?'

'Doesn't it look,' Gamarra asks, 'like they worked with the stone when it was soft?' He runs his hand along the curves and angles of a polygonal joint. 'Like butter? So they could mould everything together?'

Suddenly all becomes clear. The strange shapes I'm seeing in the rock would be easy, indeed effortless, to create if these blocks were made of something of the consistency of room-temperature butter instead of cold, hard limestone. Then as well as moulding them together to create this massive jigsaw puzzle effect, the tip of a table-knife could be used to gouge out the shallow scallops and the back of a spoon would serve to make the hollows.

It's an attractive idea and I don't have to buy into Gamarra's theories about orbits and gravity in order to explore it further. There are other ways of explaining the patterns. For example, the technology of a lost civilization might have been up to the challenge of softening rock so that it could be worked like butter. Perhaps heat was involved? An intriguing study by the Institute of Tectonics and Geophysics of the Russian Academy of Sciences, working in cooperation with Peru's Ministry of Culture, produced evidence that the limestone of the Sacsayhuaman megaliths was at some point subjected to temperatures in excess of 900 degrees centigrade and possibly as high as 1100 degrees centigrade.

When the Russian researchers went to the quarries where the blocks are believed to have been cut, they found the natural limestone filled with tiny organic fossils. This is what you would expect, since limestone is a sedimentary rock that forms under ancient seas and consists largely of the remains of tiny shells and the micro-skeletons of other marine organisms. Strangely, when samples from the Sacsayhuaman megaliths were assayed by the researchers they confirmed that the rock was indeed limestone of 'high density'.[8] However there were:

no obvious fossils and organic remains in it, but only clearly visible fine-grained structure.[9]

Their conclusion was that the blocks had been subjected to intense heat between the time when they were quarried and the time when they were placed into the wall and that this heat was sufficient to reduce the fossils to indeterminate fine-grained structure:

Of course we need more detailed researches and analysis in order to estimate the real reason for the thermal effects on the studied limestone . . . But the fact remains the fact – recrystallization of biogenic siliceous limestone into microcrystalline siliceous limestone. The result of this process we can see in the material forming the wall polygonal blocks of Sacsayhuaman. In normal nature conditions this process is absolutely impossible.[10]

'Some magic presided over its construction . . .'

Jesus Gamarra and I continue our exploration by climbing the stairways through the lines of the megalithic walls until we reach the slope above and can approach the dilapidated ruins littering the hilltop. 'These,' says Gamarra, indicating the ruins, 'are examples of what was done in the Ukun Pacha period – the work of the Incas.' Some of it, he makes clear, for example the structure of three concentric circles of walls, was very nicely done. The Incas called it Muyuc Marca, he tells me. It was a tower that once rose to over 30 metres in height and was built as an imperial residence for the Emperor – whose title was 'the Inca'. Only later, and by extension, did the entire nation become 'the Incas'.

Gamarra's argument is that in buildings like Muyuc Marca we are looking at the finest results the Incas were capable of. Yet these results are so patently inferior to the megaliths – and so different – that they must obviously be accepted as the work of another culture.

Curiously, although such ideas are regarded as heresy by archaeologists today, this was not the case when the Andes first came under serious scientific scrutiny in the late nineteenth and early twentieth centuries. For example, the great geographer Sir Clements Markham, who travelled extensively in Peru and wrote the classic study *The Incas of Peru*, states that 'the Incas knew nothing' of the origins of Sacsayhuaman:

> Garcilaso refers to towers, walls, and gates built by the Incas, and even gives the names of the architects; but these were later defences built within the great cyclopean fortress. The outer lines must be attributed to the megalithic age. There is nothing of the kind which can be compared to them in any other part of the world.[11]

The 'Garcilaso' mentioned by Markham is the chronicler Garcilaso Inca de la Vega, the son of a Spanish conquistador and an Inca princess, a heritage that gave him unique access to genuine Inca traditions, particularly since he was born and brought up in Cuzco and spoke Quechua, the language of the Incas, as his mother tongue. Had the megalithic elements of Sacsayhuaman been recent work, done in the century before Garcilaso's birth, there should have been fresh and clear memories, even eye-witness accounts, of so magnificent an achievement. But Garcilaso reports nothing of the sort and instead can only offer magic as an explanation for what he describes as 'an even greater enigma than the seven wonders of the world'. Here is what he wrote about Sacsayhuaman in his *Royal Commentaries*:

> Its proportions are inconceivable when one has not actually seen it; and when one has looked at it closely and examined it attentively, they appear to be so extraordinary that it seems as though some magic had presided over its construction; that it must be the work of demons, instead of human beings . . . If we think, too, that this incredible work was accomplished without the help of a single machine, is it too much to say that it represents an even greater enigma than the seven wonders

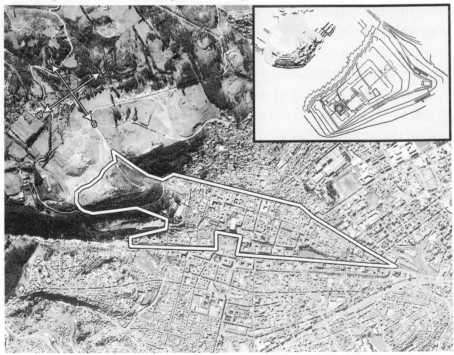

Figure 62: The Cuzco-Sacsayhuaman 'puma'.

of the world? How can we explain the fact that these Peruvian Indians were able to split, carve, lift, carry, hoist and lower such enormous blocks of stone, which are more like pieces of a mountain than building stones, and that they accomplished this, as I said before, without the help of a single machine or instrument? An enigma such as this one cannot be easily solved without the help of magic.[12]

Are we looking, yet again, at the handiwork of the Magicians of the Gods? Remembering that the great temple of Edfu in Upper Egypt was dedicated to the god Horus, who was sometimes depicted as a falcon and sometimes as a lion, it is intriguing to discover that the very name 'Sacsayhuaman' means Falcon (specifically 'Satisfied Falcon'). Furthermore, it has long been recognised that Sacsayhuaman forms part of a large geoglyph, once visible from surrounding mountain peaks, in which it combines with the oldest quarters of Cuzco to form the shape of an immense feline – a puma, the closest creature in the Americas to an old world lion. The river Tullumayo (now diverted underground where it passes through the city) used to serve as the spine of this ancient lion. The torso was the spit of land between the Tullamayo to the east and the river Huatnay (now also underground) to the west. Sacsayhuaman is still recognizable as the head of the lion. The zigzag walls, that Jesus Gamarra attributes to the second (*Uran Pacha*) episode of civilisation in the Andes, outline the upper side of its snout and muzzle, with the snout facing due west, the direction of the equinox sunset, just as the Great Sphinx of Giza faces due east, the direction of the equinox sunrise.[13]

There are traditions, supported by some modern excavations, of a network of tunnels under the Sphinx where mysterious treasures lie concealed.[14] There are virtually identical traditions – again supported by recent excavations – of a labyrinth of enormously long tunnels under the head of the Sacsayhuaman lion 'into which people descend to be lost forever, or to emerge, gibbering, mad, clutching items of treasure'.[15]

Before we leave Sacsayhuaman, Jesus Gamarra takes me to a very strange place a few hundred metres to the north-east of the megalithic walls, where a narrow stairway with a dozen steps appears to have been moulded – not cut – into the midst of a massive boulder 20 feet high and as many wide. The stairway would only have been visible from above when it was made, but the boulder has been split into two parts – by an earthquake, Gamarra thinks – with one side standing upright and the other leaning away from it at an angle of about 40 degrees, thus exposing the steps which we approach from ground level. At the point where the lowest of the steps would originally have touched the earth, Gamarra shows me the entrance to what looks like a deep, dark hole, now filled up with slabs of rock. 'It's a tunnel,' he tells me. 'It goes under the ground all the way to Cuzco, but the government blocked the entrance to stop people exploring it.'

Civilizing mission

Over the next few days Jesus Gamarra shows me more of the evidence behind his theory. Indeed now that I've understood his reasoning, I can see examples everywhere.

In downtown Cuzco – the name of the city means 'the navel of the earth' in the Quechua language of the Incas[16] – he takes me to the ancient temple known as the Coricancha, which was converted into a cathedral after the Spanish conquest. The temple was used by the Incas, indeed it was central to their sacred life, but Gamarra does not believe that the Incas built it. In his view, though they undertook some repairs and added some minor constructions of their own, the bulk of the polished, precise, sharply angled grey granite stonework is from the *Uran Pacha* ('second world') period and thus predates the Incas by thousands of years. He's reluctant to commit to a timescale, but suggests that the Coricancha was originally raised up 'more than 20,000 years ago' in order to venerate an even earlier *Hanan Pacha* ('first world') monolithic site – the original 'uncovered navel stone' from which the city derives its name.[17]

The Incas preserved a tradition, passed down to us by Garcilaso Inca de la Vega, concerning the foundation of Cuzco. It seems that some sort of cataclysm had affected the world, some sort of disaster, and the inhabitants of the Andes had fallen into a very lowly state. Garcilaso was told by his own uncle, an Inca nobleman, that the people of that far-off time 'lived like wild beasts, with neither order nor religion, neither villages nor houses, neither fields nor clothing . . . They lived in grottoes and caves and, like wild game, fed upon grass and roots, wild fruits, and even human flesh . . . Seeing the condition they were in, our father the Sun was ashamed for them, and he decided to send one of his sons and one of his daughters from heaven to earth' to bring them the gifts of civilization and to teach them – 'to obey his laws and precepts . . . to build houses and assemble together in villages.'[18]

This royal couple – for, like Isis and Osiris in Egypt they were brother and sister as well as husband and wife – travelled the land carrying a golden rod given to them by the Sun God, who instructed them to plunge it into the earth at various points until they found a place where it would disappear at one thrust and there they were to establish their court. Finally, 'the Inca and his bride entered into Cuzco valley. There [at a spot called *Cuzco Cara Urumi*, the Uncovered Navel Stone] they tried their rod and not only did it sink into the earth, but it disappeared entirely . . . Thus our imperial city came into existence.'[19]

There is an exact parallel here to the story of the Zoroastrian patriarch Yima, recounted in Chapter Seven, who was given a golden poniard by a god and who likewise plunged it into the earth as the founding act of a civilization.

And what a civilization it was that flowered in the Andes! Certainly the extraordinary accomplishment of the giant edifices of the Coricancha seems to suggest the application of more than ordinary skills and abilities. The huge granite blocks are so finely cut – Gamarra insists they were moulded into shape – that the towering inner chambers look more like the parts of some gigantic, sophisticated machine than of a temple. Adding to this impression are the complicated series of grooves, channels, holes and niches indented into several of the blocks, giving them the appearance of printed circuit boards from which the circuitry has been removed, leaving only empty tracks.

After spending some hours inside the Coricancha, Gamarra takes me outside into the neighbouring Loreto Street which he promises will provide a particularly graphic demonstration of his arguments. It's a narrow alley bounded by high walls and in these walls, surmounted by sections of modern plasterwork, four distinctly different styles of stone masonry are visible. Of these, Gamarra says, two are Inca, *Ukun Pacha,* one is from the colonial period around the seventeenth or eighteenth century, and one dates back to the *Uran Pacha* period.

Along a large part of one side of the street there are granite blocks that are every bit as fine and beautifully fitted as those inside the Coricancha. Indeed, this section of the wall is the exterior elevation of one of the Coricancha's large chambers, and therefore, according to Gamarra, is from the *Uran Pacha* period. The joints between the blocks are so thin, and yet so complex, with interlocking elements, that they do indeed seem moulded together. In addition – and he has previously shown me examples of this at Sacsayhuaman as well – there is a curious glassy sheen around the joints, which he believes is evidence of 'vitrification caused by exposure to intense heat'. He makes a convincing case that what we're looking at is different from the normal shine that passers-by might impart to the stone by rubbing and touching it over the centuries. Indeed the 'vitrified' elements – and I make no claim that this is what they are – form a clear skin over the underlying blocks that is particularly evident where areas have been damaged or broken.

Beside the courses of *Uran Pacha* blocks, though not rising to the same height, are others that look superficially similar but that, on closer examination, prove to be much more crudely made with obvious tool marks, no glassy sheen and yawning gaps between some of the joints. 'Good *Ukun Pacha* work,' comments Gamarra. 'Made by the Incas. They were doing their best to imitate the Uran Pacha style, but they couldn't quite succeed and their efforts got poorer and poorer.'

He indicates four courses of irregular cobbles higher up with wide spaces between the joints filled by adobe. 'Colonial period,' he says.

Finally he takes me to the other side of the street to show me a long section of dry-stone wall. The cobbles have been subjected to a certain amount of shaping, but are clumsily and unevenly fitted together. There's no adobe in the gaping joints. 'Made by the Incas,' says Gamarra.

'And what's the opinion of the archaeologists?' I ask.

A grin. 'They recognise the colonial work, but they've fooled themselves into believing that everything else was done by the Incas. They are so convinced there was no earlier, more advanced civilization here, that they're blind to the huge differences between the *Uran Pacha* blocks and the Inca workmanship.'

'I suppose the fact that the Incas themselves sometimes attempted to imitate the *Uran Pacha* style – at least in that section over there – makes things more complicated?'

'More complicated, yes. But still they should be able to see. Such profound changes in the quality of workmanship, especially when examples like this are found all over the region, should give the hint that different cultures were involved.'

Sacred valley

If the focus around the Coricancha is the fine megalithic work that Gamarra associates with the *Uran Pacha* period, there are many other structures in the area that he sees as pure *Hanan Pacha* – the oldest phase of Andean civilization, where the work in stone is entirely monolithic. Several great outcrops of bedrock have been completely refashioned into bizarre complexes of steps, terraces and alcoves. At Qenko, one such outcrop a little way beyond Sacsayhuaman, there are multiple snake-like grooves and channels winding their way down the sides of a mystic dome filled with caves, ledges, passageways and hidden niches. On the very top, again carved – or moulded – from the raw stone, is an oval protrusion surmounted by a stubby double prong. There are also the outlines of various animals – a puma, a condor, a llama – and yet more terraces and steps leading nowhere.

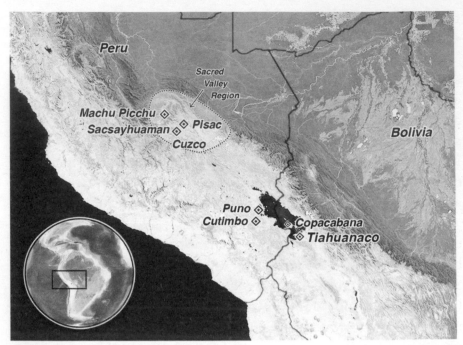

Figure 63

We go on to another sculpted outcrop a hundred metres tall known locally as the Temple of the Moon. At the base of the mound there's a dark, mysterious, folded slit that leads within, along the edge of which, at about shoulder height, emerges the sinuous sculpted form of a serpent with a strange bulbous head. To the right of the entrance the rock takes distinctive shape as the head of an elephant, complete with trunk, eyes and ears. About the serpent there's no doubt, but is the elephant an example of what psychologists call *pareidolia* – the human tendency to see meaningful shapes and patterns that don't really exist? Or did some cunning artist in ancient times deliberately set out to sculpt the appearance of an elephant emerging from the rock? If the latter, than we have a problem with history, since the last species related to elephants that could be portrayed here – *Cuvieronius* – became extinct in South America at least six thousand years ago, while the Incas who are supposed to have made the Temple of the Moon date back less than a thousand years.

I'll have more to say about the serpent, and the 'elephant', later. Meanwhile, as I stoop down through the slit in the rock to enter the temple I notice another carved stone animal – a puma, this time, and somewhat damaged – at my feet.

Now I'm inside what feels like the womb of the mountain, and a soft velvety gloom envelops me. The cave is five metres wide with an organic, meandering feel to it, but to my left a couple of deep alcoves have been cut into the wall, while twenty metres ahead a shaft of brilliant, golden light finds its way in through some aperture in the rocky mound above and illuminates a stone plinth about a metre and a half high with two large steps. I climb up onto the plinth and sit there, my back resting against the living rock, deep in thought.

Gamarra says this place is from the most ancient *Hanan Pacha* epoch, that it has nothing to do with the Incas, and that it long predates the *Uran Pacha* period that was responsible for the megaliths of Sacsayhuaman and the stunning, high-precision architecture of the Coricancha. Looking around, taking in the atmosphere, I'm more and more inclined to agree with him. The people who made this cave temple were not the same as those who made the Coricancha. It's not just different building styles that are involved in each of the different periods. It's a different ethic and a different spiritual heartbeat.

From the Temple of the Moon we go straight on to Pisac, a drive of eighteen kilometres along the edge of the Sacred Valley of the Vilcanota River. Its waters sparkle far below us, while all around the spectacular mountain country glows emerald, thanks to countless fertile terraces that the Incas undoubtedly did create and that provided their empire with vast agricultural wealth. The sheer magnitude of the task of organizing and building the thousands upon thousands of neat dry-stone walls that hem in these terraces – which are found in every viable spot throughout the length and breadth of the Andes – almost beggars belief. It's a comparable achievement to the architectural wonders. And so too are many other aspects of Inca civilization – which I do not mean to diminish in any way with the suggestion that there might have been earlier cultures. Quite the contrary, I suspect part of the reason the Incas were so remarkable is that they were the inheritors of an incredible legacy of wisdom and knowledge from the past.

So it's in a setting of great natural beauty overlooking the Sacred Valley that we explore Pisac, a site less famous, but in many ways more spectacular than Machu Picchu, which lies another seventy kilometres to the north-west.

As at Machu Picchu, the centrepiece at Pisac, around which everything else seems focused, is an *Intihuatana* (the word means 'hitching post of the sun') – a massive outcrop of rock, shaped by human hands in what Gamarra calls the *Hanan Pacha* style, with a gnomon sticking up from its summit. Surrounding it, and in some cases moulded to its surface, are walls of beautifully shaped polygonal blocks in the later *Uran Pacha* style, which seem to have been designed to cradle and protect the *Intihuatana*. And around them are *Ukun Pacha* – Inca – structures of simpler, cruder stonework.

'Each of these cultures,' Gamarra explains, 'venerated and respected the culture that went before. They expressed their feelings of respect by building over and around the work of their predecessors and by attempting to copy what they did. As I showed you in Loreto Street, the Incas sought to emulate the *Uran Pacha* style, but they didn't have the knowledge or the right conditions to do such a good job.'

By 'the right conditions' Gamarra means the lowered gravity and greater malleability of stone that he hypothesises in past epochs, but I don't need to embrace that to accept that his observations about the different building styles and their likely origination by different cultures make complete sense of what we're looking at.

I see many more examples of these three distinctive styles, sometimes with Gamarra to guide me, sometimes not. Machu Picchu itself, which I've written about at length in previous books, is, of course, the archetypal *Hanan Pacha* site adopted and overbuilt by later cultures. Then there's a mysterious little cave overlooking a remote valley, through the floor of which passes the rail track connecting Cuzco to Machu Picchu.[20] It's quite a clamber three hundred metres up the almost sheer valley side and along a narrow track, but the end result is worth the effort. At the front of the cave (see Plate 60) a black andesite boulder has been sculpted – or moulded? – into a curious-looking shrine with a step-pyramid motif engraved upon it.

Treasure hunters have been here and dynamited the shrine, but enough of it survived the explosion to get a sense of how beautiful it must have been before it was attacked. In the same *Hanan Pacha* style, one wall of the cave appears to have been planed smooth and an alcove with absolutely precise straight edges, as though milled by a machine tool, has been cut into it. But on the other side, on my right as I look out of the cave, an Inca wall of rough stone mortared together with adobe has been built, and into this wall – crudely done – six alcoves have been fashioned in an obvious attempt to mimic the high-precision rock-cut alcove on the left. The qualities and styles of workmanship are so completely different that it makes no sense, as is presently the case, to insist that both the rock-cut work and the crude wall were produced by the same culture. Gamarra's theory that a much older monument has been honoured and mimicked by the Incas better fits the evidence before my eyes.

Déjà vu

Heading out of Peru on our way to Bolivia, we stop in the town of Puno on the shores of Lake Titicaca, 3,812 metres (12,507 feet) above sea level and from there, the next day we drive 22 kilometres south to a dramatic mesa at an altitude of 4,023 metres (13,198 feet), on top of which is perched the archaeological site of Cutimbo. The main features of the site – several tall towers, some circular, some square, and known collectively as *chullapas* – are visible from the road. They are thought to have been built as tombs for the nobility of a local Indian culture, the Lupakas, who were made vassals of the Incas in the period between AD 1470 and AD 1532.[21] Undoubtedly there were burials within the *chullapas* in that period,[22] but the possibility must be considered that these were intrusive and that the towers, made from fine polygonal blocks that have all the hallmarks of Jesus Gamarra's *Uran Pacha* style, are much older than their latest use.

I'm getting accustomed to the thin air of the Andes by now, but it's a long hike through yellow pampas grass up the side of the mesa under a burning morning sun. Once we get to the top, however, my fatigue vanishes when I start finding, and Santha starts photographing, really interesting imagery carved in high relief on the sides of a number of the towers and on scattered blocks lying at random here and there, the result of more demolition efforts by treasure hunters.

It's this imagery, on the far side of the world, including that stone serpent in the Temple of the Moon, that a year later will suddenly come to mind in Şanlıurfa Museum, as I study the collection of reliefs from Göbekli Tepe. I leave readers to form their own views from Plates 61-72, but the obvious parallels include the following:

At Göbekli Tepe there is a creature, sculpted in high-relief, identified by Klaus Schmidt as a beast of prey with splayed claws and powerful shoulders, its tail bent to its left over its body. A very similar animal is seen at Cutimbo with the same splayed claws and the same powerful shoulders, while the tail instead of being bent to its left is bent to its right.

At both Göbekli Tepe and Cutimbo, reliefs of salamanders and of serpents are found. The style of execution in all cases is very similar.

At about the level of the genitals of the so-called 'Totem Pole' of Göbekli Tepe, a small head and two arms protrude. The head has a determined look, with prominent brows. The long fingers of the hands almost meet. The posture is that of a man leaning down through the stone and playing a drum. This is also the posture of two figures at Cutimbo, who emerge from a large convex block on one of the circular towers. They have the same determined features and prominent brow ridges as the figure on the 'Totem Pole'.

The two serpents on the side of the 'Totem Pole' have peculiarly large heads, making them look almost like sperm. So, too, does the serpent that emerges from the dark narrow entrance of the Temple of the Moon above Cuzco.

Lions feature in the reliefs at Göbekli Tepe, pumas feature in the reliefs at Cutimbo and again the manner of representation is similar.

I don't know what to make of these similarities. Just coincidences? Very likely. Even so they go on.

City of Viracocha

It's quite a trial crossing the land border from Peru into Bolivia through a series of bureaucratic hurdles and long queues, but close by is the charmingly-named town of Copacabana and a comfortable hotel overlooking Lake Titicaca. If we had more time we'd visit the Islands of the Sun and Moon by boat from here; but we've been to them often before and they're not our target on this trip. It's Tiahuanaco up on the Altiplano at 12,800 feet, near the south-eastern shore of the giant lake, that we're keen to get back to.

Orthodox archaeologists date Tiahuanaco to the period between 1580 BC and AD 724, but in both *Fingerprints of the Gods* and *Heaven's*

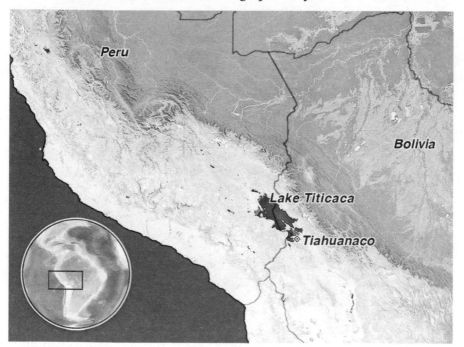

Figure 64

Mirror I argued that it might ultimately prove to be many thousands of years older than that. Up to now less than two per cent of the site has been excavated and I think it likely that further excavations will force a change of the archaeological paradigm. It is perhaps a sign of things to come that on 27 March 2015 Bolivia's Tiahuanaco Archeological Research Center reported that a survey with ground- penetrating radar had revealed the existence of a complete 'buried pyramid' in a previously unexcavated area of the site, together with 'a number of underground anomalies' that are thought to be monoliths. A five-year plan of excavation to learn more about these mysterious structures has now been launched.[23]

Since I've already described Tiahuanaco at length in my previous books, it seems superfluous to repeat those descriptions here. What's new for me on my October 2013 visit is a much closer look at the machine-age precision of the megaliths littered around the immense platform of the Puma Punku, and the truly intricate manner in which so much of the stone has been cut – moulded, I think Jesus Gamarra would say. As at the Coricancha, I come across several megaliths that resemble circuit boards stripped of their circuits. There are others with cross-shaped indentations that look as though they were part of some contraption – as though perhaps they were to receive the ends of metal axles, or connecting pieces that have long since oxidised or been carried off by looters.

Particularly striking, because I've missed them before on all

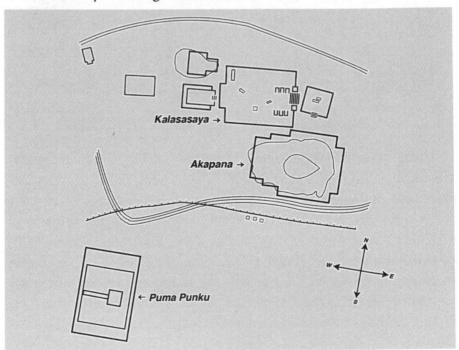

Figure 65: The principal structures of Tiahuanaco.

previous visits, are a couple of rows of massive andesite blocks all identical, as though stamped out of some mould, and all shaped like the letter 'H'. The comparison with the 'H' motif at Göbekli Tepe, on the belts of the pillars, for example, is irresistible even if it is just another coincidence (see Plates 75 and 76).

Figure 66: Above artist's impression of Toxodon. Below the imagery on the pillar in the semi-subterranean temple at Tiahuanaco (left, photograph; right, highlighted).

Then there's the pillar statue in the semi-subterranean temple at Tiahuanaco. Like the Totem Pole of Göbekli Tepe, it is anthropomorphic. Like the Totem Pole at Göbekli Tepe, it has serpents writhing up its side. Like the Totem Pole at Göbekli Tepe, the long fingers of its hands almost meet in front of its body. The face is human not animal, however, and it's heavily bearded. Nonetheless, the figure of an animal is carved on the side of its head and this animal resembles no known species more closely than it does Toxodon (see illustration above), a sort of New World rhino that went extinct during the cataclysms at the end of the Ice Age around 12,000 years ago. This isn't *pareidolia* – the figure is definitely there. So there's only one question

– and it's difficult to answer: is this a depiction of Toxodon, or is it some creature of the artist's imagination?

I move on into the Kalasasaya, the huge open rectangle, bounded by megalithic walls, that appears to have been the central ceremonial area of ancient Tiahuanaco. On the monolithic Gateway of the Sun is carved the image of another elephant with tusks and trunk, like the elephant sculpted into the living bedrock of the Temple of the Moon near Sacsayhuaman. This Tiahuanaco 'elephant' has been dismissed by critics as merely the heads of two condors side by side, but if that is the case, then the image on the matching – mirror – side of the Gateway is puzzling (see illustration below), since it definitely shows two condors side by side yet is different from the elephant relief.

If it was modelled from nature it doesn't have to be *that* old – *Cuvieronius*, as noted earlier, survived in South America until 6,000 years ago. On the other hand, most related mastodon species went extinct during the Younger Dryas between 12,800 and 11,600 years ago.

Figure 67: An elephant on the Gateway of the Sun? Or just two condors side by side?

The Kalaysasaya is a huge, largely empty, open space. But there are two statues here that I want to take another look at – the Ponce Monolith, named after Carlos Ponce Sanginés, the 'godfather' of Bolivian archaeology, and *El Fraile* ('the Friar') a smaller, slightly different version done in the same general style.

What's striking about both of them are the hand positions, with the fingers almost meeting across the belly – virtually identical to the hand positions on the Göbekli Tepi pillars or on the Totem Pole. However, the Tiahuanaco figures, like the Mesopotamian Apkallus, carry objects in their hands – not a cone and a bucket but, as archaeologist and ethnobotanist Constantino Manuel Torres has demonstrated, snuff trays for the consumption of hallucinogenic DMT powders from the Amazon.[24]

It's a reminder, even up here in the cold, austere highlands of the Altiplano, that the Amazon with its riotous, exuberant life is not far away. When we are looking for the remnants of a lost civilization that once perhaps spanned the globe, it might not be the first place we would think of, but its dense jungles hide so much and recent clearances have revealed the remains of ancient cities, megaliths, gigantic earthworks, and soils enriched by some mysterious process that keeps them fertile for thousands of years.[25]

What is also clear is that a legacy of high-level scientific skills, inherited from *somewhere*, was passed down through generation after generation of shamans. The making of a psychedelic, DMT-containing brew – Ayahuasca – from two jungle plants, neither of which is an orally active psychedelic in its own right, is an astonishing pharmacological achievement when we remember that there are 150,000 different species of plants and trees in the Amazon. Likewise a nerve poison like Curare, which has eleven different ingredients and which produces lethal fumes during preparation, is not something that can be dreamed up overnight, but requires the application of a thoroughly worked-out science.

Another point of interest about the Tiahuanaco monoliths is that their garments from the waist down are patterned in the form of fish scales. Here, too, is a parallel to the Apkallus – the bearded, 'fish-garbed figures' who brought high civilization to Mesopotamia and whose mysteries we explored in earlier chapters. Nor is it as though bearded figures are missing from the repertoire of Tiahuanaco. Two have survived, and one on the pillar in the semi-subterranean temple has been identified since time immemorial with the great civilizing deity Kon-Tiki Viracocha, who I wrote about at length in my previous books and who is described in multiple myths and traditions as being white skinned and bearded. Garcilaso Inca de La Vega, who lived through the last years of the conquest and grew up in Cuzco, wrote that Viracocha:

> wore a thick beard – whereas the Indians are clean shaven – and his robe came down to the ground, while that of the Incas came only to their knees; this is why the Peruvian people called the Spanish 'Viracochas' the minute they saw them . . . The Indians had no difficulty believing that the Spaniards were all the sons of God . . .[26]

In other words, with their white skins and beards the Spanish fitted an ancient tribal memory, passed down from generation to generation, of civilizing heroes who had come to the Andes in remote prehistory and taught the people there the skills of agriculture, architecture and engineering.

And what about Kon-Tiki Viracocha himself? What happened to him?

It seems after a civilizing mission across the Americas:

> His travels took him to Manta (Ecuador) from where he crossed the Pacific Ocean, walking on the water.[27]

I am not going to repeat here the stories and traditions of Viracocha that I reported in my previous books, but he is the Osiris and the Quetzalcoatl of the Andes who comes in a time of darkness, after a great flood, bringing the gifts of civilization.

That he should leave eventually, and that he should do so by some high-tech means, 'walking on the water' across the Pacific Ocean, is intriguing.

Let's follow him and see where he might have gone . . .

Chapter 18
Ocean

—◆—

According to the most ancient traditions of Mesopotamia, humanity was created at the 'navel of the earth', in *uzu* (flesh), *sar* (bond), *ki* (place, earth).[1] In the *Rig Veda*, the most ancient scripture of India, the universe was born and developed 'from a core, a central point'.[2] Bearing markings that Jesus Gamarra would instantly nominate as belonging to the oldest, *Hanan Pacha*, style of the Andes, the *Shetiyah* – Foundation Stone – of the Temple Mount in Jerusalem, now the 'rock' of the Dome of the Rock (see Chapter Twelve), is considered to be 'the centre of the earth'.[3] Indeed this notion that there are certain primordial centres of creation from which all else grows is a global theme of ancient religion and mythology:

> The Most Holy One created the world like an embryo. As the embryo grows from the navel, so God began to create the world by the navel and from there it spread out in all directions.[4]

In the Greek myth of the universal Deluge, sent by Zeus to punish mankind for wickedness, the only survivors are Deucalion and Pyrrha. Their Ark comes to rest on Mount Parnassus, high above Delphi, a site regarded throughout classical antiquity as the 'navel of the earth'.[5] Just as Heliopolis in Egypt possessed the sacred Benben, a *betyl* stone fallen from heaven (see Chapter Eleven), so too Delphi possessed a *betyl*, nominated as its omphalos, or 'navel stone'. It was specifically identified in Greek mythology as the stone which had been fed to the monstrous time-god Kronos – who devoured his own children – in place of the infant Zeus. When Zeus grew to manhood, he took revenge on Kronos, 'driving him from the sky to the very depths of the universe' after first – in imagery that calls to mind the debris stream of a comet – forcing him to vomit up the stone.[6] 'It landed in the exact centre of the world, in the shrine at Delphi.'[7]

We saw in the last chapter that the name of Cuzco, the megalithic city in the Peruvian Andes, means 'the navel of the earth'. More than 4,000 kilometres (2,500 miles) to the south-west, across the Pacific Ocean, the ancient name of Easter Island, *Te-Pito-O-Te-Henua* also means 'the navel of the earth'[8] – which in turn has affinities to the ancient name of Tiahuanaco, *Taypicala*, 'the stone at the centre'.[9] Indeed, on the edge of Easter Island's La Perouse Bay there is a mysterious spherical, carefully-tooled stone called *Te-Pito-Kura* – the 'golden navel stone' – which is regarded as the navel of the island itself.[10]

Traditions state that there was once a time when 'great magicians' used this stone to focus their *mana* power – literally 'sorcery' – to make the *Moai*, the famous megalithic statues of the island 'walk' from the quarry to the places where they were to be set up.[11] An almost identical notion is preserved amongst the indigenous Aymara of Bolivia, who have lived in the vicinity of Tiahuanaco since time immemorial. They state that the mysterious city with its own extraordinary megalithic statues was built by magic in a single night and that 'the stones came down of their own accord, or at the sound of a trumpet, from the mountain quarries and took up their proper positions at the site.'[12]

Nor do the parallels stop there. Since the late 1940s, when Thor Heyerdahl undertook his Kon-Tiki expedition (named after Kon-Tiki Viracocha, the civilizing deity of Tiahuanaco, whom we met at the end of the last chapter), it has been noticed that there are similarities between the statues of Tiahuanaco and the Moai of Easter Island. For example, as we've seen, the figures of Viracocha at Tiahuanaco display prominent and pronounced beards (a sharp contrast to the indigenous inhabitants of the Andes who are not able to grow strong beards) and there is no doubt that the prominent chins of the Easter Island figures are also meant to represent beards (Plates 78 and 79). As Heyerdahl commented:

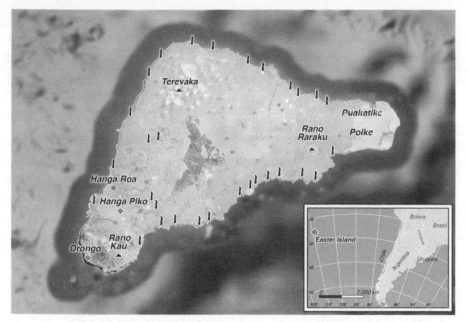

Figure 68: Easter Island and its region. (After Eric Gaba, Wikimedia Commons).

The statues on Easter Island . . . had their chins carved pointed and projecting, because the sculptors themselves grew beards.[13]

The Norwegian adventurer was likewise struck by the way that the Easter Island figures and the Tiahuanaco figures have 'their hands laid in position on their stomachs'.[14] Both also wear distinctive broad belts. 'The sole decoration of the Easter Island figures,' he wrote:

is a belt which was always carved round the figure's stomach. The same symbolic belt is to be found on every single statue in Kon-Tiki's ancient ruins by Lake Titicaca.[15]

Heyerdahl, who I had the privilege to know and who was a strong supporter of the lost civilization hypothesis,[16] did not have the opportunity to visit Göbekli Tepe before he passed away in 2002. Had he done so, however, I think he would have been struck by the resemblance between the hand positions depicted on the 'Totem Pole' figure from Göbekli Tepe and the hand positions on the Viracocha pillar statue and on the Ponce and *El Fraile* monoliths at Tiahuanaco. I pointed these resemblances out in the last chapter, but there's more.

For example, the larger anthropomorphic pillars at Göbekli Tepe feature thick sculpted belts very similar to those seen on the Tiahuanaco and Easter Island figures. Also noteworthy are the hand positions seen on the larger Göbekli Tepe pillars, with long fingers placed forward and almost meeting across the belly. Identical hand positions are seen on the Easter Island Moai. Last but not least, just as Easter Island, Tiahuanaco and Cuzco share the odd concept of being 'navels of the earth', so too does Göbekli Tepe; whether expressed in Turkish, or in the Armenian language as *Portasar*, its very name means 'the hill of the navel'.[17]

If all these are coincidences then their profusion is rather extraordinary – unless, of course, the same Magicians of the Gods who created and then buried the Göbekli Tepe time capsule at the end of the Younger Dryas some 11,600 years ago were also at work in Easter Island.

Unless, in other words, the Moai of Easter Island are older – much older – than archaeologists think they are . . .

A remnant of antediluvian lands?

Archaeologists believe that the oldest of the Easter Island Moai was made around AD 690 and the youngest about a thousand years later in AD 1650. This chronology is based on radiocarbon dating which also puts the earliest human settlement on the island at AD 318.[18] As we have seen, however, radiocarbon cannot date stone monuments directly. Inferences have to be made about the relationship between the organic materials that have been dated and the stone, and sometimes these inferences can be extremely misleading.

For example, it would be a mistake to conclude that the Ahu (platform) at Ahu Nau Nau on Anakena Bay is the same age as the seven Moai mounted on it. The platform is obviously the work of a later culture that must have re-erected the statues because, incorporated in the masonry of the platform itself, an ancient and heavily weathered Moai head has been reused as a construction block.

Likewise, if, for example, human beings had settled here during the Younger Dryas when sea level was much lower than it is today, and Easter Island was part of a chain of steep and narrow antediluvian islands as long as the Andes mountain range, then how much in the way of organic materials would they have left for archaeologists to carbon date? Perhaps the peak of the East Pacific Rise that we now know as Easter Island was not used for residential purposes at all, but kept exclusively for religious ceremonies in which the great monolithic statues played a part? Perhaps people came from other parts of the archipelago to attend those ceremonies and then returned to their home islands – islands that are all now underwater?

This is conjecture, of course, pure speculation, but it is temptingly suggested by a legend of the Easter Islanders themselves concerning a supernatural being called Uoke who in remote times:

> travelled around the Pacific with a gigantic lever with which he pried up whole islands and tossed them into the sea where they vanished forever under the waves. After thus destroying many islands he came at length to the coast of *Te-Pito-O-Te-Henua*, then a much larger land than it is today. He began to lever up parts of it and cast them into the sea. Eventually he reached a place called Puko Pihipuhi . . . in the vicinity of Hanga Hoonu [La Perouse Bay, site of the 'golden navel stone']. Here the rocks of the island were too sturdy for Uoke's lever, and it was broken against them. He was unable to dispose of the last fragment, and this remained as the island we know today. Thus *Te-Pito-O-Te-Henua* continues to exist only through the accident of Uoke's broken lever.[19]

Legends also speak of a primeval Pacific homeland called 'Hiva' from which the first inhabitants of Easter Island came – a homeland that also fell victim to the 'mischief of Uoke's lever' and was 'submerged under the sea'. What is particularly intriguing about all this, because of its resonance with the Seven Sages – the Apkallu – spoken of in Mesopotamian antediluvian traditions, and with the Seven Sages of the Edfu Building Texts, who sought out new lands in which to recreate the drowned and devastated world of the gods, is that Seven Sages – 'kings sons, all initiated men' – are also said to have been instrumental in the original settlement of Easter Island.[20] Exactly as was the case with the Apkallu, who laid the foundations of all the future temples of Mesopotamia, and with the Edfu Sages who travelled the length and breadth of Egypt establishing the sacred mounds on which all future pyramids and temples were to be built, the first task of the Seven Sages from Hiva after their arrival on Easter Island was 'the construction of stone mounds'.[21]

Could there be anything to this? Is it possible that the Moai statues of Easter Island are the work of the survivors of a lost civilization dating back to the Ice Age 12,000 or more years ago?

One possible hint comes from a discovery made by Dr Robert J. Menzies, Director of Ocean Research at the Duke University Marine Laboratory, Beaufort, North Carolina. In 1966 Menzies led a six-week oceanographic investigation of the Pacific off the coast of Peru and Ecuador in the waters of the Milne–Edwards Deep, a trench that drops off in places to almost 19,000 feet (5,791 metres). Dr Menzies' research vessel, the *Anton Bruun*, deployed underwater cameras that were state of the art at the time and about 55 miles west of Callao (the port of Lima, capital of Peru), at a depth of 6,000 feet in an area prone to marine subsidence, 'strange carved rock columns' were photographed on the sea bed:[22]

> Two upright columns, about two feet or more in diameter, were sighted extending five feet out of the mud. Two more had fallen down and were partially buried, and another angular squarish block was seen.[23]

'We did not find structures like these anywhere else,' commented Dr Menzies in an interview with *Science News*. 'I have never seen anything like this before.'[24] The later official report of the cruise of the research vessel added that one of the columns bore markings that appeared to be 'inscriptions'.[25]

So far as I have been able to establish Dr Menzies' discovery, which hints at a real basis to the submerged land of Hiva, was never followed up. Meanwhile what of Easter Island itself, where the survivors are said to have settled in order to reconstitute their lost world? The science of geology has some clues for us to consider.

What lies beneath . . .

Professor Robert Schoch of Boston University, renowned for his geological redating of the Great Sphinx of Giza, does not easily or quickly bestow greater antiquity on monuments than is allowed by mainstream archaeology. Most often he goes with the orthodox chronology but when he diverges, as he has with the Great Sphinx, and with Gunung Padang in Indonesia (see Chapter Two), it is only because he has first been persuaded by strong geological evidence that archaeology has overlooked.

This is the case with his analysis of the Moai statues of Easter Island. Here's his considered opinion after a research visit:

> I was particularly impressed by the varying degrees of weathering and erosion seen on the different moai, which could be telltale signs of major discrepancies in their ages. The levels of sedimentation around certain moai also impressed me. Some moai have been buried in up to an estimated six metres of sediment, or more, such that even though they are standing erect, only their chins and heads are above the current ground level. Such high levels of sedimentation could occur quickly, for instance if there were catastrophic landslides, mudflows, or possibly tsunamis washing over the island, but I could not find any such evidence (and landslides or tsunamis would tend to shift and knock over the tall statues). Rather, to my eye, the sedimentation around certain moai suggests a much more extreme antiquity than most conventional archaeologists and historians believe to be the case – or believe to be possible.[26]

Schoch adds that he has begun to collect evidence on typical weathering, erosion and sedimentation rates on Easter Island during the modern period since records began to be kept. 'So far it seems that sedimentation over the past century has been on the whole relatively modest.'[27]

As usual, Schoch understates his case, which is best illustrated at Rano Raraku crater, an extinct volcanic caldera that served as the principal quarry from which the Easter Island Moai were extracted. The inner slopes of the caldera, leading down to a small, reed-fringed lake, are lined with an estimated 270 statues in various stages of completion. Some lie on their backs or sides, many are perfectly upright, others jut at various crazy angles out of the ground, and the overall impression is one of some extraordinary Surrealist show interrupted in mid-preparation and abandoned forever by the artist.

What it was all about, what it was all *for*, no one can honestly say, though there are many theories. Nonetheless, the setting is unmistakably geological and the statues are themselves first and foremost geological artefacts separated from the natural bedrock, yet still sufficiently in place to have remained part of their original setting. Mostly what you see, as you wander in bemused wonderment amongst them, are their serene, contemplative bearded faces, their long-eared heads, their shoulders, and parts of their upper torsos.

You could be forgiven for imagining that this is all there is to them – that they are set just a metre or so into the ground, sufficient to anchor them and no more. But Thor Heyerdahl, that indefatigable adventurer and explorer, proved this was not the case when he excavated a number of the Rano Raraku Moai in 1956 and again in 1987, discovering that, like icebergs, the larger part of their mass lies beneath the surface. Photographs from those excavations show statues that go down more than 9 metres (30 feet) beneath the ground into a deep thick sediment of yellow clay.[28] Studying these images, it becomes immediately apparent that Schoch's argument has merit and that there is no way, in just a few hundred years (as noted earlier, archaeologists maintain that production of the Moai stopped as recently as 1650) that such a massive amount of sedimentation could have accumulated.

That would be the case even if Easter Island were part of a large, continuous landmass, where there was potential for wind and water to transport soils from one area and deposit them in another. But Easter Island as we know it today, though an enigma of giant proportions, is just a tiny dot on the map in the midst of the world's largest and deepest ocean. Not only is it situated more than 2,000 miles from the coast of South America, but it is also more than 2,000 miles from Tahiti, the next substantial group of islands.[29] With a total land area of just 63.2 square miles (163.6 square kilometres) it is therefore all the more inconceivable that Easter Island itself could have contributed the 30-foot-deep sediment load seen around the Moai in Rano Raraku crater. Such a volume of sedimentation might, however, have been possible more than 12,000 years ago when sea-level was lower and, as we've seen, Easter Island was part of an extensive archipelago.

Here, too, could be the answer to another mystery identified by Schoch, which is the existence of a small number of Moai carved from basalt. The problem is that there are no deposits of basalt on Easter Island itself. Schoch speculates that:

> the 'lost basalt quarries' might be under sea level now because they are of extreme antiquity, and thus the basalt moai carved from them are extremely ancient. Sea levels have risen dramatically since the end of the last Ice Age, some ten thousand or more years ago, and if the basalt moai were quarried along the coast of Easter Island from areas since inundated by the sea, this could help to date the basalt moai and is immediately suggestive that they are thousands of years older than conventionally believed to be the case.[30]

The same solution – that Easter Island was once part of a much larger landmass – would also explain another, very different puzzle, namely the so-called Rongo Rongo script.[31] It is unprecedented in human history for a sophisticated fully developed writing system to be invented and put into use by a small, isolated island community. Yet Easter Island does have its own script, examples of which, mostly incised on wooden boards, copies of copies of copies of much older lost originals, were collected in the nineteenth century and have found their way into a number of museums around the world. None remain on Easter

Island itself and even in the period when they were collected no native Easter Islanders were able to read them. To this day the script remains undeciphered – yet another of the many enigmas of this island of mystery.

The Sage of Bada Valley

It's 28 May 2014 and I'm thousands of miles from Easter Island in the middle of the Bada Valley of Central Sulawesi, in Indonesia, standing in front of a huge Moai-like figure carved from solid basalt and deeply embedded in a grassy field. What's striking about the statue, apart from its sheer size – the visible part, which slopes steeply over to its left, extends more than four metres (13 feet) out the ground – is the posture of its arms and hands. These are arranged in exactly the manner of the Easter Island Moai, and also of the Göbekli Tepe figures, with the arms crooked at the sides and the hands brought together across the front of the belly with the fingers almost meeting. The big difference is that this figure, known locally as *Watu Palindo*, 'The Wise Man',[32] shows off an erect penis and a pair of testicles between those extended fingers.

How old is the 'Wise Man'?

'Nobody knows,' admits Iksam Kailey, Curator of the Province Museum of Central Sulawesi, who has kindly accompanied me on this sector of a long research journey through Indonesia, 'archaeology is in its infancy in our island.' Kailey himself is inclined to the view that the statue, and a dozen others like it here in Bada Valley, are at least 4,000 years old.[33] Other estimates vary between 5,000 years and less than 1,000 years,[34] but none are of the slightest value since no definitive archaeological dating has been done or can be done; the intrusion of organic materials from the different cultures that have lived and farmed this valley for millennia, several of which have at different periods dug up *Watu Palindo* looking for treasure, mean that we will never get to the truth. Artefacts from the not too far distant Besoa Valley have been carbon dated to 2,890 years ago,[35] but so what? That tells us nothing at all about the age of the Wise Man.

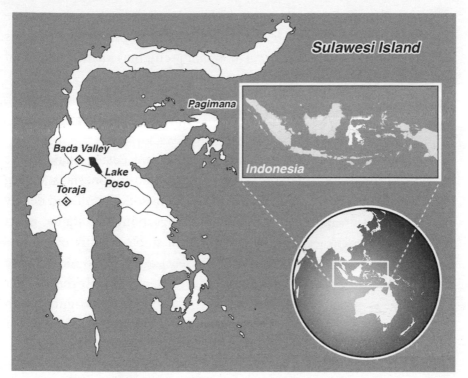

Figure 69: The island of Sulawesi in its regional context.

Getting to Bada Valley is quite a trek. Santha and I are travelling with Danny Hilman Natawidjaja, the geologist who has brought the mysterious pyramid of Gunung Padang in West Java (see Chapter Two) to the attention of the world. Also accompanying us is Danny's friend and colleague Wisnu Ariastika, who has kindly looked after the logistics of our journey. We start off in Jakarta on 26 May and fly to Palu, the capital of the province of Central Sulawesi, where Iksam Kailey joins us on the morning of 27 May. Then we drive all day on an awesomely bad road through spectacular mountain country, reaching the town of Tentana on giant Lake Poso the same evening. The following day, 28 May, we drive an additional fifty kilometres to the village of Bomba in the heart of the Bada Valley, which, like so much of Indonesia, is stunningly beautiful, a broad flat plateau, surrounded by green mountains plumed by silver clouds that reflect magically off gleaming rice fields. Reaching Bomba by mid-morning we check into a basic but comfortable guest house and go straight out megalith hunting.

There are, essentially, two kinds of megaliths in the valley, one being very large stone cisterns called *Kalamba*, precisely cut and hollowed out within and in some cases weighing more than a ton, the other being figures like *Watu Palindo* weighing up to twenty tons. For two days we tramp along the borders of waterlogged rice fields and on rough tracks through forests. At one point we come to a statue lying on its back in the midst of a clearing, staring up at the heavens, a little later we find another, also on its back, lying in the midst of a river. Both show the same hand and arm positions as *Watu Palindo*, the Sage. A third figure with weird, fish-like features is buried up to its neck in deep-water rice. A fourth stands lonely on a ridge gazing at a distant range of mountains.

The frustrating thing is that nothing – really nothing at all – is known about these megaliths. Who created them? When? Why? All is mystery.

Hobbits, dragons and the Flood

From the Bada Valley we make a long road journey to Toraja in South Sulawesi – all journeys are long here; Sulawesi is the eleventh largest island in the world. We spend a couple of days in the area. There is an eerie cult of the dead, which involves digging up the bodies of the deceased once a year, dressing them in new clothes, combing their mouldering hair, tidying their coffins and reinterring them. Lifelike effigies of the deceased are also placed in rock-cut shrines high up in cliff faces and there are caves full of bones.

What we've come here to see are not the dead but megaliths. This being Toraja, however, the megaliths are all about the dead and, unlike in other parts of the world – and indeed other parts of Indonesia – they aren't relics of a remote and forgotten past, but part of a living, active, fully functional cult. We visit Bori Parinding, a site dominated by a cluster of tall, needle-like menhirs that might be transplanted without difficulty to any one of a dozen locations in Europe and confidently dated to 5000 years old or more. Yet Bori Parinding is just two hundred years old.

The oldest megalith here was erected in 1817. Each one is a monument to a deceased Torajan notable and new menhirs are still quarried and put in place every year. Those cut from andesite are mined from a nearby deposit and shaped with hammers and metal chisels – a local elder shows me how it's done. Those cut from limestone, weighing in some cases an estimated 15 tons, are brought from a quarry five kilometres away by teams of hundreds of men working in shifts for more than a week, who haul the menhirs to the site on wooden rollers.

Indonesia, I'm beginning to realise, is a land where ancient traditions live on in fascinating ways and the connection to the remote past is ever present.

That's a realization that's brought home to me all the more strongly on our next stop, the island of Flores. We reach it by driving all day from Toraja to Makassar, where we catch a flight to Bali and thence, via Komodo, famous for its large predatory lizards known as 'Komodo Dragons', to Ende, the chief 'city' of Flores – a city with a population of just 60,000. In recent times, Flores has attracted fame for the discovery on the island of the remains of *Homo floresiensis*, an extinct

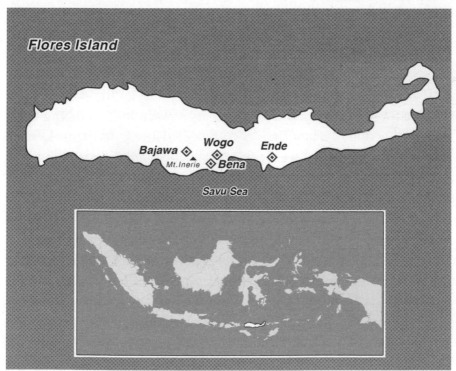

Figure 70: The island of Flores in its regional context.

405

species of human that stood, in adulthood, just 1.1 metres (3.5 feet tall) and has, accordingly, been dubbed 'the Hobbit'. I'll have more to say about these creatures later, but as I land at Ende after that stopover in Komodo I can't help reflecting that Indonesia is truly a mythical place – the only country in the world today where dragons and hobbits are not the stuff of fantasy but of science.

Flores is charming – far out on the edge of the world, simple, lacking in many modern conveniences, but with a sweet, gentle spirit. We base ourselves in the town of Bajawa, and in the couple of days we spend here, we visit a number of villages where the tidy bamboo and thatch houses are built upon and around extensive megalithic monuments.

In the village of Bena, about 16 kilometres from Bajawa, with distant glimpses of the Savu Sea and of Mount Inerie, we're shown around by Joseph, a venerable elder of 88 years. The village has two parallel rows of houses with the high, thatched roofs, triangular in cross section, that are characteristic of the area. The houses are separated by a long and wide public space filled with an incredible assortment of menhirs and dolmens which, as with the menhirs of Toraja, would not look out of place if they were excavated from Neolithic strata in Europe. Joseph tells us that the dolmens aren't tombs (as is usually the case in Europe), but altars used by members of each of the different clans resident in the village. From time to time buffalo sacrifices are carried out on the altars in honour of deceased notables, and the megaliths have a function in aiding communication with the departed and in connecting the supernatural and earthly realms.

Such ideas don't syncretise well with Christianity, which is also a part of daily life here; indeed, at the far end of the village there is a shrine to the Virgin Mary. Joseph tells us that dolmens and menhirs were still being erected when he was a young man, but that this is no longer done and the tradition is dying out. When I ask him about the origins of the megalithic cult, however, he tells me a remarkable story.

'Our ancestors,' he says, 'came here in a ship around 12,000 years ago during a great flood.' Indeed it seems that the whole village is laid out in commemoration of that ship, which was propelled not by sails but by an 'engine'. Joseph shows me a megalithic chamber, roughly in the middle of the village, that symbolises the place where the 'engine house' was located in the original ship. I ask him where all the megaliths come from and he tells me that they were brought from 20 kilometres away on the slopes of Mount Inerie and moved into position by special 'powers' possessed by the ancestors. He adds that 'an American scholar, a certain Professor Smith' has confirmed the story.

This mention of the name of a foreign researcher – whose identity and bona fides I was not subsequently able to establish – raises the nagging possibility in my mind that the whole tale might not be of indigenous origin at all, but might be an imported concoction, a fantasy even, which Joseph believes to be true. Certainly we were not told the same story in other megalithic villages of Flores. At Wogo Baru, for example, elders spoke of a 'giant' called Dhake, who was so huge that he had single-handedly carried the megaliths down from the slopes of Mount Inerie.

What all the accounts seem to have in common, however, is a whiff of wonder and magic.

Queen of the Southern Ocean

Leaving Flores, we fly from Ende via Denpasar in Bali to the city of Palembang in Sumatra, then make a two-day road journey from east to west across south Sumatra. Again our focus is megaliths, but most of what we see, in the form of large sculpted human and anthropo-morphic figures, shows the influence of Hindu and Buddhist art and thus is certainly not prehistoric. It's only when we come to a coffee plantation in the mountains near the city of Pagar Alam that we find something really interesting – a series of gigantic megalithic subter-ranean chambers (see Plate 81), several of which are painted with swirling designs in striking colours of red ochre and black charcoal, amidst which animal figures can be discerned.

No dating work has been done on them, but similar chambers such as West Kennet Long Barrow in England or Gavrinis in Carnac, Brittany, are more than 5,000 years old, while the painted caves of France and Spain are even older, going back 33,000 years in the case of Chauvet, for example. The Sumatran paintings have much in common with those of southern Europe, being profoundly visionary, with characteristic 'entoptic' patterns indicating that the artists were shamans, who had experienced and were depicting visions seen in deeply altered states of consciousness, likely induced by psychedelic plants or fungi.[36]

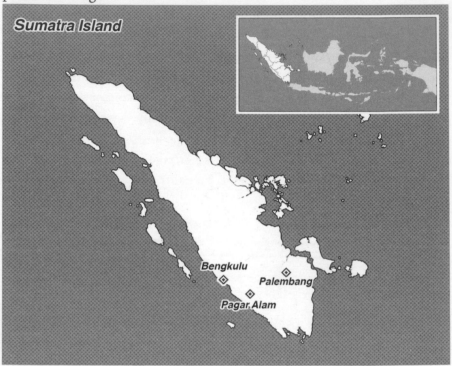

Figure 71: The island of Sumatra in its regional context.

We drive on to the city of Bengkulu and fly from there to Jakarta, the massive, sprawling Indonesian capital on the island of Java. Jakarta is like a giant octopus; once it has entangled you in the tentacles of its clogged roadways, it is extremely difficult to get free. Late the same evening, however, we eventually reach our next destination, Pelabuhan Ratu on the south-west coast of Java, facing the Indian Ocean. It's only an overnight stop – in the morning we'll be going to another megalithic site inland – but it turns out that Pelabuhan Ratu (which means 'Harbour of the Queen') is of interest in its own right. Indeed the Samudra Beach Hotel where we're staying has a room – room 308 – that no one is allowed to reserve because it's permanently set aside

408

for the Queen of the Southern Ocean, a kind of sea fairy or goddess, who rules over a submerged city and occasionally appears on land to interact with mortal humans.

Obviously I'm interested in submerged cities, particularly submerged cities around the islands of Indonesia, which were all part of a giant continent, known to geologists as Sundaland, that was above water and connected to the rest of Southeast Asia until about 11,600 years ago. When sea levels rose cataclysmically at the end of the Younger Dryas, this region lost more habitable land, including a massive, low-lying plain, than almost anywhere else on earth.[37] Although it's close to midnight, I therefore insist on paying a visit to Room 308, which is fully decorated and furnished as a royal boudoir, complete with imaginative paintings of Njai Lara Kidul, the Queen of the Southern Ocean.

It's a romantic story and, who knows, there may be something to it. Certainly, no attempt to uncover the mysterious origins of human civilization can afford to ignore the rapid drowning of Sundaland, which was fertile and well watered with four major river-systems before

Figure 72: The island of Java in its regional context.

it was flooded.[38] Indeed it's because of this, and because much of the flooding occurred around 11,600 years ago, precisely the date that Plato gives for the submergence of Atlantis, that our travelling companion, geologist Danny Natawidjaja, believes Indonesia *is* Atlantis[39] and has made such efforts to investigate the extraordinary megalithic pyramid of Gunung Padang.

Gunung Padang, which I first visited in December 2013 (described in Chapter Two) is 120 kilometres north of us, and we'll be going back there at the end of this trip. Before we do, however, there's one more site we want to see. It's called Tugu Gede, near the village of Cengkuk, 20 kilometres into the mountains north of Pelabuhan Ratu.

We set off in the morning on another of those precipitous and slightly alarming roads that Indonesia has so many of, but once again the trip is worth it. We go as far as the car can take us and then have a long walk, first through a village in the midst of banana plantations, and then into quite dense forest, coming eventually to a mystic glade where a massive central menhir, shaped at its sides, coming to a point like an obelisk, juts 3 metres straight up out of the earth. It is surrounded by a ring of smaller menhirs, some fallen, some still standing, and round about there are huge numbers of further worked stones, many with patterns of cupules carved into them very similar to the cupules at Karahan Tepe in Turkey.

Tugu Gede has been the subject of some cursory excavations, but there appears to be no clear consensus on its antiquity. The megaliths themselves are accepted as prehistoric – 'thousands of years old', although exactly how many thousands no one seems to know – but there are also later occupation layers that have yielded up pottery and artefacts that are only a few hundred years old, and of course the site stands close to (and is impacted by) human settlements to this day. One of the most anomalous finds is a small statue. On no very good grounds, archaeologists suppose it to be a representation of the Hindu god Shiva, but it bears no resemblance to any images of Shiva that I've seen and – to my eye at least – looks much more like a crudely worked Ancient Egyptian figure with its crossed hands and distinctive headdress.

Mainstream archaeology does not believe that the Ancient Egyptians could have reached Indonesia, so this possibility has never been considered. However, there is compelling evidence that long-distance oceanic voyages were undertaken from Egypt during Pharaonic times – for example, the presence in nine mummies dated between 1070 BC and AD 395 of cocaine and tobacco, both indigenous American plants not previously thought to have been present in the Old World before the time of Columbus.[40]

These findings by S. Balabanova, F. Parsche and W. Pirsig have been disputed by other scholars, who regard long-distance Ancient Egyptian sea voyages as *a priori* impossible. According to Egyptologist John Baines, for example: 'The idea that the Egyptians should have travelled to America is overall absurd . . . and I also don't know anyone who spends time doing research in these areas, because they're not perceived to be areas that have any real meaning for the subject.'[41] The way I see it, however, this comment by Baines is more indicative of a deep-seated problem within Egyptology itself, and within archaeology in general, than of a problem in the factual findings of Balabanova et al. Archaeology is too much constrained by a rigid reference frame of what is possible and what is not, and tends to ignore, sidestep, or ridicule evidence that challenges that reference frame. This is equally true when it comes to the case for a lost civilization of the Ice Age, which again is dismissed on no good grounds other than that it is considered to be *a priori* impossible.

Meanwhile, since the validity of Balabanova's findings has subsequently been vindicated,[42] and therefore – we must assume – the Ancient Egyptians did indeed make voyages as far as the Americas, I see no good reason to ignore the possibility that they also made voyages in the other direction, eastwards towards Indonesia and beyond. Indeed, Ancient Egyptian hieroglyphic inscriptions – though once again disputed – have been found at a wilderness site near the town of Gosford, to the north of Sydney in eastern Australia. I have had the opportunity to study these glyphs myself and do not agree with the mainstream view that they can easily be dismissed as twentieth-century hoaxes. On the contrary, a recent (October 2014) deciphering of the glyphs by hieroglyphics experts Mohamed Ibrahim and Yousef Abd'el Hakim Awyan concluded:

Not only are the Gosford Glyphs legitimate, the scribes accurately used several ancient hieroglyphs and grammatical variations which, crucially, were not even documented in Egyptian hieroglyphic texts until 2012, immediately disproving all long-standing 'hoax' theories. The specific style of hieroglyphs used also provides a linguistic time-frame that places an Egyptian presence in Australia *at least* 2,500 years ago, while the translated text is even so detailed as to identify the ancient scribes, by name and occupation.[43]

I'm not claiming that the case is settled yet; the Gosford Glyphs may or may not be a hoax; much more work needs to be done to settle the matter. My point, however, is that the use by orthodox archaeologists of *a priori* assumptions about what happened in the past as a reason not to conduct wide-ranging investigations into what actually did happen in the past is poor scholarship. In my view, therefore, rather than simply ruling out the possibility that the Ancient Egyptians might have reached not only the Americas, but also Indonesia and Australia, we should be asking ourselves why, and over what sort of time span, they might have made such voyages. In particular, I wonder if it is possible that the tradition of a drowned homeland of the gods somewhere in the east that is so strongly expressed in the Edfu Building Texts might be connected to this mystery.

To be specific, could Indonesia, once part of the mainland of Southeast Asia and broken up into more than 13,000 islands by cataclysmic sea-level rise at the end of the Ice Age – and perhaps particularly Java with its 45 active volcanoes – have been associated in the Ancient Egyptian mind with the 'Isle of Fire', which R.T. Rundle Clark describes as 'the mystic land of origin beyond the horizon[44]?'

The very same 'Isle of Fire', as we saw in Chapter Eleven, from which *Hike*, the vital, magical essence was brought by the Phoenix to Heliopolis, the symbolic centre and navel of the earth?[45]

The Isle of Fire with which Horus of Edfu was directly associated[46] and where Thoth, the Sage, the Lord of Wisdom, 'made shrines for the gods and goddesses'?[47]

The dead hand of orthodox archaeology

The final leg of our 2014 Indonesia journey takes us back to Gunung Padang, the mysterious pyramid, for so long thought to be a natural hill, that geologist Danny Natawidjaja, through determined efforts, has brought to the attention of the world. I won't describe it again, since I have already introduced it to the reader in Chapter Two.

We've seen how the megalithic site of columnar basalt visible on the uppermost terraces of Gunung Padang is simply the latest episode in its long story and how Danny and his team used seismic tomography, ground-penetrating radar and other remote-sensing technologies to show that the man-made structures go down tens of metres beneath the surface. Core drilling into these buried structures was undertaken producing organic materials with impeccable provenance that yielded ever more ancient carbon dates extending back, ultimately to more than 22,000 years ago – before the end of the last Ice Age, when our ancestors are supposed (according to the orthodox archaeological model) to be have been nothing more than primitive hunter-gatherers, incapable of large-scale construction and engineering feats. Intriguingly, as I also reported in Chapter Two, the remote sensing equipment flagged up the presence deep within the pyramid of what appear to be three hidden chambers, so rectilinear in form that they are most unlikely to be natural. The largest of these lies at a depth of between 21.3 and 27.4 metres (70 to 90 feet) and measures approximately 5.5 metres (18 feet) high, 13.7 metres (45 feet) long and 9.1 metres (30 feet) wide.[48]

On our visit to Gunung Padang in early June 2014, excavations were still being held up by objections from archaeologists but by August, following a decisive intervention by Indonesia's then President Susilo Bambang Yudhoyono, Danny and his team were finally able to proceed for a first short season. Unfortunately, however, the work was halted very soon afterwards, in October 2014, when President Yudhoyono completed his second term of office and stepped down. His successor, President Joko Widodo, has thus far not shown the same level of interest in and enthusiasm for the project, perhaps because of objections from Bandung Archaeological Center Chief Desril Shanti, who launched a public attack on the Gunung Padang excavations in late September 2014, complaining that they did not follow the standard methods that are usually applied in archaeological projects. 'I've yet to go to the site,' she said, 'but I can judge it from photographs. An archaeological excavation method shouldn't have been carried out in that way.'[49] She also objected that funding had been allocated to the work. This funding, she felt, should have gone to her own department.[50]

At the beginning of October 2014, as the reader will recall from Chapter Two, Danny had written to me enthusiastically as follows:

> The research progress has been being great. We have excavated three more spots right on top of the megalithic site in the past couple of weeks, which give more evidence and details about the buried structures. We have uncovered lots more stone arte-facts from the excavations. The existence of the pyramid-like structure beneath the megalithic site is now loud and clear; even for non-specialists, it is not too difficult to understand if they come and see for themselves. We have found some kind of open hall buried by soil five to seven metres thick; however we have not yet got into the main chamber. We are now drilling to the suspected location of the chamber (based on subsurface geophysic) in the middle of the megalithic site.[51]

It was only a few days after Danny sent me that mail that the Presidency changed hands and the drilling and excavations were stopped. Nonetheless, the first, short, interrupted season did produce important results. As Danny confirmed in his correspondence with me, even the relatively young layer that was all they had time to excavate – the second artificial columnar rock-layer beneath the megalithic site visible on the surface – yielded a radiocarbon date of 5200 BC (i.e. 7,200 years ago, nearly 3,000 years older than the orthodox dating for the Pyramids of Giza in Egypt) and there are firm indications from the original remote sensing and core drilling work of much older layers below.[52] In short, it is now evident to all that Gunung Padang is vastly older than the 3,000 years that archaeologists had insisted upon for decades. Even the most hostile amongst them, therefore, have begun to reframe their assessment of the site and to refer to it as 'a gigantic terraced tomb, which was part of the biggest megalithic culture in the archipelago'.[53]

I stayed in touch with Danny during the writing of this book. On 14 January 2015 he emailed me to tell me the disappointing news that further fieldwork had not yet been authorised. 'We are still waiting for the new government to take action on the continuity of the national team for Gunung Padang,' he wrote. He was concerned, he added, about construction activities that had been undertaken at Gunung Padang in the interim 'by Public Works, Tourism Department and others . . . They are conducted without a clear plan/design and consultation with us, so they are destroying the site.' He remained optimistic, however, that he and his team would be allowed to continue with their excavations shortly. If so, he said, 'by the end of 2015 I hope to know more about the second layer (the 7000 years-old constructions) and begin to understand about the third layer (pre-10,000 years ago).'[54]

On 10 March 2015, I heard from Danny again. Most unfortunately, he could only report that there had been no progress at all since his mail of 14 January:

> The new Ministry of Culture has not activated the national team yet. We are still waiting and hoping the new Ministry will have a good attitude toward Gunung Padang research.[55]

Time will tell, but the auspices do not look good, and as *Magicians of the Gods* goes to press I fear that the dead hand of orthodox archaeology may once again have prevailed, in what almost appears to be a deliberate strategy to prevent us from learning the truth about our past. Below the layers dated to approximately 7,000 and 10,000 years ago are the even older strata of man-made constructions at Gunung Padang. These strata, as yet unexcavated, as yet unexplored, identified only by core-drilling and remote sensing equipment, go back before the cataclysmic episode of the Younger Dryas (12,800 years ago to 11,600 years ago) and deep into the last Ice Age, when the lost civilization still thrived – the lost civilization that we know only through myths and traditions, and through the works of its survivors as they sought to recreate 'the former world of the gods'.

Indonesia must rank amongst the most plausible candidates anywhere on earth for the heartland in which that civilization could have evolved and grown to maturity. In recognition of this, a number of serious researchers, including Danny Natawidjaja and Professor Arysio Santos, have presented evidence that Plato has been misunderstood over the location of Atlantis in the Atlantic Ocean.[56] All the clues, they say, really point east and place the lost civilization between the Indian and the Pacific Oceans – i.e. on the exact spot once occupied by the flooded Ice Age continent of Sundaland, of which the Indonesian islands are the surviving remnant. Mainstream archaeology remains strongly opposed to the notion of *any* lost civilization by *any* name, regardless of whether it is said to be located in the west or in the east. In my opinion, however, there's already enough ancient 'high strangeness' around Indonesia to raise question-marks over such thinking. A few examples:

- I've already mentioned *Homo floresiensis*, the 'Hobbit', quite possibly a completely different human species from our own[57] that survived for tens of thousands of years after our other evolutionary cousins the Neanderthals and the Denisovans had vanished from the earth. It's intriguing that the date of extinction of *Homo floresiensis* appears to have been around 12,000 years ago[58] – exactly in the apocalyptic Younger Dryas window.
- In its issue of 8 October 2014, the prestigious academic journal *Nature* reported, in a tone of astonishment, that elaborate, sophisticated cave paintings had been found on the Indonesian island of Sulawesi with a minimum age of 39,900 years, making this art as old, or older, than anything comparable ever found in Europe – previously considered to be the exclusive home of such early, advanced symbolic behaviour.[59]
- And it was *Nature* again, in its issue of 12 February 2015, that reported the discovery on Java of geometric engravings 'generally interpreted as indicative of modern cognition and behaviour' yet dated to half a million years ago – which is 300,000 years older than the supposed first appearance of anatomically modern humans on our planet.[60]

If evidence like this that rewrites the human story has remained undiscovered in Indonesia until so recently, how much else is still to be found and why shouldn't the next turn of the archaeologists' spade reveal a hitherto unrecognised civilization? Given the vast loss of terrain suffered across this entire region as a result of more than 100 metres of sea-level rise at the end of the Ice Age, anything is possible. This is why Gunung Padang is so important. And most important of all, perhaps, is that huge chamber identified by ground-penetrating radar and other remote sensing technologies lying deep within the pyramid between 70 and 90 feet beneath its apex.

Is it the Hall of Records of the lost civilization?

Once again, only time will tell . . .

Mountains of fire and ash

Gunung Padang wasn't quite the end of our June 2014 research trip. After re-exploring that amazing site, absorbing its ancient, mellow, slightly perplexing atmosphere and understanding again, even more clearly than before, why it is still to this day known as the Mountain of Light by local people who love and revere it, Santha and I travel back to Bandung, the regional capital. From there the following morning we catch a train for the seven hour journey to Yogyakarta in Central Java, where we mean to spend a few days around the fabled Buddhist temple of Borobudur.

The train journey is . . . charming, and the endless vistas it affords of rice fields and mountains and green trees everywhere bursting with life, and the friendly, busy people, are a delight. It's nightfall by the time we arrive in Yogyakarta, but the next morning we're up at 4 a.m. to drive to Punthuk Setumbu, a hillside looking down into the valley where Borobudur stands. The air's not cold – it's never seriously cold here – but it's fresh and there's a wide pool of darkness beneath us . . . expectant darkness, because that's where Borobudur is and will soon be lit up by the sun.

But the sun rises slowly, light seeping into the sky, gradually illuminating the thickly forested mountainside and the valley below, showing us the distant slopes of the towering twin volcanoes that also overlook Borobudur – Mount Merapi (literally 'Fire Mountain'), which is still active, and Mount Merbabu ('Mountain of Ash'), which is dormant. By around 5 a.m. the dense trees that carpet the valley floor begin to become visible, though shrouded in low-lying cloud, and soon afterwards a breath of wind stirs the mist, giving us our first glimpse of the massive, jagged pyramidal form of Borobodur, crowned with a towering stupa that seems to reach for the heavens, a cosmic axis piercing the navel of the earth to connect sky and underworld. As the sun rises higher the mist swirls and expands, winding and curling amongst the trees, pooling in the deeper parts of the valley, but above it all Borobodur stands out clear, like some mythical island from the dawn of time.

We're impatient to visit it after this tantalizing invitation, but we have another plan for today and drive east out of Yogyakarta heading first for Surakata City (usually referred to by its residents as Solo) and then onwards further east to Mount Lawu, another massive, dormant volcano. The whole of Java, it seems, is straddled by these slumbering giants, whose outpourings in the past have blessed the island with essential nutrients, making its soils incredibly verdant, fertile and productive.

We wind our way up Lawu's precipitous slopes through green glittering tea plantations until at an altitude of 910 metres (2,990 feet), with the peak of the volcano still towering more than 2,000 metres above us, we reach the little hamlet where Danny Natawidjaja has recommended we take a look at Candi Sukuh, a rather odd and mysterious little temple. 'It seems out of place in Indonesia,' he told us. 'It looks more like a Mayan step pyramid.'

This, it turns out, is absolutely correct. Sukuh, though smaller, is astonishingly similar in general appearance to the step-pyramid of Kukulkan/Quetzalcoatl at Chichen Itza in the Yucatan. Sukuh was built in the fifteenth century, just before the conversion of Indonesia from Hinduism and Buddhism to Islam. Why it was built, however, or why its style is so distinctive and unusual for Indonesia, remains a mystery to scholarship. The Kukulkan Pyramid, in its present incarnation – though it encloses an older structure – is thought to have been built between the ninth and twelfth centuries. Thousands of miles and hundreds of years therefore separate the two structures and the likelihood of any direct influence of one upon the other is slim. As I explore Sukuh, however – and it has a mystical air about it enhanced by a late afternoon mist that wreathes the whole mountainside – I find myself wondering whether the similarities are pure accident, or whether they might not be better explained by the influence in both regions of the same remotely ancient common source.

The signal

Certainly such an influence is present at Borobudur, a pyramid-temple consisting of 1.6 million blocks of volcanic andesite,[61] constructed over a period of fifty years from the last quarter of the eighth to the first quarter of the ninth century AD.[62] There is no dedication inscription, indeed almost no inscriptions of any kind. [63] This is, however, undoubtedly a Buddhist monument – a fact of which one could hardly be in any doubt since its acres of exquisitely beautiful reliefs are devoted for the most part to stories from the life of Buddha. Within Buddhist thought it is to be regarded as:

> a cosmic mountain, a sacred replica of the universe designed to lead the pilgrim to the realization of full enlightenment, *sambodhi*, by which a Bodhisattva becomes a Buddha – the ultimate goal of Buddhism . . . The devotee follows a path to the top of this mountain, keeping his right shoulder to the monument. Subsequently his path brings him along the . . . many galleries that show panels with scenes in stone relief of which the Buddhist character has become clear and which have been recognised to represent the ancient Buddhist texts.[64]

On this clockwise perambulation of the monument, gradually working your way up from earth to sky, you pass 504 life-sized statues of the Buddha, of which 432 are found on the square stepped terraces with the remaining 72 on the three circular terraces at the summit surrounding the great central stupa. In addition, calculations of the correct pilgrim route through the four bas-relief galleries have shown that the direction of the path:

as well as the number of times that each gallery must be walked, is determined by the bas-reliefs on each side of the gallery walkway. In order to 'read' the entire collection in the correct order, worshippers are compelled to complete a total of ten circuits around the galleries in the clockwise direction. In so doing, each worshipper passes by a Buddha image an additional 2,160 times before reaching the summit entranceway . . .[65]

The reader will realise immediately, as I did when I undertook my own perambulations of Borobudur, that with these numbers we are back once again in the mysteriously insistent and universal numerical code described in previous chapters. This code, as we've seen, is based on the hard to observe phenomenon of the precession of the equinoxes that unfolds at the rate of one degree every 72 years, that sees the equinoctial sun housed in turn by each constellation of the zodiac for 2,160 years and that is deployed to make the Great Pyramid of Giza a model of our planet on a scale of 1 to 43,200.

Its presence also at Baalbek, and at Göbekli Tepe, and now here at Borobudur, as well as in myths and traditions from all around the world, can only be explained by a remote common influence manifesting in all these places and forms – that 'almost unbelievable' ancestor civilization identified by Giorgio de Santillana and Hertha von Dechend, that 'first dared to understand the world as created according to number, weight and measure'.[66]

It's my intuition, as I've suggested at several points throughout this book, that the lost civilization sought to send a signal to the future – indeed to us, today, in the twenty-first century – and that the carrier wave of this signal is the precessional code.

Two different means were used to ensure the signal's survival through time.

First, it was embedded in myths and legends and in mathematical and architectural precepts that would be passed on and renewed again and again by the different cultures that received them, thus boosting the signal and allowing it to remain intact for thousands of years. Even if those through whose hands and minds the signal passed no longer understood its meaning, the weight of sacred tradition, hoary with age, would ensure that they continued to transmit it and would do their utmost to keep it free from interference.

Secondly, the signal was hard-wired into certain megalithic sites. Some were hidden in plain view like the Giza complex, which successive cultures continued to work on and perfect for thousands of years according to the 'divine' canon. Others were buried in the ground – timc-capsules like Göbekli Tepe, and perhaps like that mysterious chamber deep beneath Gunung Padang – and primed for rediscovery when the time was right.

'There shall be memorials mighty of their handiworks upon the earth,' the Sacred Sermon of Hermes tells us, 'leaving dim trace behind when cycles are renewed.'[67]

According to G.R.S. Mead, the pioneer scholar in the field of Gnostic and Hermetic Studies, these lines are meant to turn our attention back towards the past:

> to a time when a mighty race, devoted to growth in wisdom, lived on earth and left great monuments of their wisdom in the work of their hands, dim traces of which were to be seen in the 'renewal of the times' . . .[68]

Mead finds in this an echo of the ancient conviction 'that there were alternate periods of destruction by fire and water, and of renewal':[69]

> In Egypt, the common belief . . . was that the last destruction had been by water and flood. Before this Flood . . . there had been a mighty race of Egyptians, the race of the first Hermes . . . Some dim traces of the mighty works of this bygone, wisdom loving civilization were still to be seen . . .[70]

And Mead adds, as few modern scholars would dare:

> I am, myself, strongly inclined to believe this tradition; and I have sometimes speculated on the possibility of there being buried beneath one or more of the pyramids the remains of some prehistoric buildings that have survived the Flood.[71]

There is more in the *Hermetica* that touches on this theme, and quite specifically a reminder of the 'Books of Thoth', of their creation by Thoth-Hermes himself, and of their purpose:

> For what he knew, he graved on stone; yet though he graved them onto stone he hid them mostly, keeping sure silence though in speech, that every younger generation of cosmic time might seek for them.[72]

Depositing his books, the wisdom god uttered the following words, admitting in the process his own 'perishability' – and thus, perhaps, that he was no god but a mortal human being:

> Ye Holy Books, which have been written by my perishable hands, but have been anointed with the drug of imperishability . . . remain ye unseen and undiscovered by all men who shall go to and fro on the plains of this land, until the time when Heaven, grown old, shall beget organisms worthy of you . . .[73]

Mead provides no explanation of this strange word 'organisms' – sometimes also translated as 'instruments' – but in his own edition of the *Hermetica*, Sir Walter Scott does. 'After long ages,' he says, it means that 'there will be born men that are worthy to read the books of Hermes.'[74]

Has that time come?

Are we worthy, at last, to read those 'books' of lost wisdom hidden away before the Flood?

And, if so, what might they say?

4. Giant 'jigsaw-puzzle' walls at Sacsayhuaman, built thousands of years before the Incas according to Jesus Gamarra.

5. Below left: Loretto Street, Cuzco. Different styles of architecture suggest the work of different cultures.

6. Below right: Inferior architecture of the Temple of the Virgins, known to have been built by the Incas.

57. Near Cuzco, Peru.

58. Alaca Hoyuk, Turkey. Is it possible that the same prehistoric megalithic culture was at work in both places?

9. The author with Jesus Gamarra at Pisac.

o. Cave shrine. The different architectural styles evident here and at Pisac are indicative of the work of different cultures. In Gamarra's view it is absurd to attribute everything to the Incas.

is page: 69. Above left: The author studying serpent with peculiarly large head carved in
gh relief at the 'Temple of the Moon' near Cuzco. Compare 70. Above right: Serpent with
culiarly large head carved in high relief at Gobekli Tepe.

. Above: Cutimbo. Compare with 72. Right:
obekli Tepe.

73. Above: Easter Island.
74. Top right: 'Urfa Man', Turkey.
75. Middle right: 'H' Blocks, Tiahuanaco.
76. Bottom right: Gobekli Tepe pillar figure. Note similar hand positions in 73, 74, and 76. Note 'H' motif in 75 and 76.

The recycling of an ancient Easter Island head as a construction block suggests the wall is much younger than the figures.

Below left: The bearded face of Viracocha, at Tiahuanaco.

Below right: Bearded Easter Island head, Rano Raraku quarry. The bodies of the figures in the quarry are buried in up to 30 feet of sediment, suggesting great antiquity.

80. *Watu Palindo*, the 'Sage of Bada Valley', Sulawesi, Indonesia.

81. Painted megalithic chamber near Pagar Alam, Sumatra.

Part VIII

Closure

Chapter 19
The Next Lost Civilization?

———◆———

More than two thousand flood myths that have come down to us from the remote past are eerily consistent on many points, and on one in particular: the cataclysm was not a random accident, we are told; we brought it upon ourselves by our own behaviour.

Our arrogance and our cruelty towards one another, our noise and strife and the wickedness of our hearts, angered the gods. We ceased to nurture spirit. We ceased to love and tend the earth and no longer regarded the universe with reverent awe and wonder. Dazzled by our own success, we forgot how to carry our prosperity with moderation.

So it was, Plato tells us, with the once generous and good citizens of Atlantis, who in former times possessed 'a certain greatness of mind, and treated the vagaries of fortune and one another with wisdom and forbearance', but who became swollen with overweening pride in their own achievements and fell into crass materialism, greed and violence:

> To the perceptive eye the depth of their degeneration was clear enough, but to those whose judgement of true happiness is defective they seemed, in their pursuit of unbridled ambition and power, to be at the height of their fame and fortune.[1]

If ever a society could be said to meet all the mythological criteria of the next lost civilization – a society that ticks *all* the boxes – is it not obvious that it is our own? Our pollution and neglect of the majestic garden of the earth, our rape of its resources, our abuse of the oceans and the rainforests, our fear, hatred and suspicion of one another multiplied by a hundred bitter regional and sectarian conflicts, our consistent track record of standing by and doing nothing while millions suffer, our ignorant, narrow-minded racism, our exclusivist religions, our forgetfulness that we are all brothers and sisters, our bellicose chauvinism, the dreadful cruelties that we indulge in, in the name of nation, or faith, or simple greed, our obsessive, competitive, ego-driven production and consumption of material goods and the growing conviction of many, fuelled by the triumphs of materialist science, that matter is all there is – that there is no such thing as spirit, that we are just accidents of chemistry and biology – all these things, and many more, in mythological terms at least, do not look good for us.

Meanwhile, we have made ourselves the possessors of a technology so advanced that it seems almost like magic, even while we use it constantly in our daily lives. Computer science, the internet, aviation, television, telecommunications, space exploration, genetic engineering, nuclear weapons, nanotechnology, transplant surgery . . . The list goes on and on, yet very few of us are able to understand how more than a tiny fraction of it works, and as it proliferates the human spirit withers and we engage in 'all manner of reckless crimes, wars and robberies and frauds, and all things hostile to the nature of the soul'.[2]

Suppose for a moment that a cataclysm besets us, a cataclysm so vast that our complex, networked, highly specialised technological civilization collapses – collapses utterly beyond any hope of redemption. If such a scenario were to unfold it is likely that the meekest and most marginalised of the peoples who inhabit our world today – the hunter-gatherers of the Amazon jungle and the Kalahari desert, for example, who are used to making do with very little and whose survival skills are exemplary – would be the very ones most likely to make it through and therefore carry on the story of humanity in post-cataclysmic times.

How would their descendants remember us a thousand or ten thousand years from now? How, for example, might something that we regard as routine, like our ability to receive 24-hour rolling television news and hear sound and view images from all parts of the world, and even from outer space, be recollected in myth and tradition? Might it not be said wonderingly of us, as it was of 'the Forefathers' recalled in the *Popol Vuh*, the sacred book of the ancient Quiche Maya:

They were endowed with intelligence; they saw and instantly they could see far, they succeeded in seeing, they succeeded in knowing all that there is in the world. When they looked, instantly they saw all around them, and they contemplated in turn the arch of heaven and the round face of the earth. The things hidden in the distance they saw all without first having to move; at once they saw the world, and so, too, from where they were, they saw it. Great was their wisdom; their sight reached to the forests, the lakes, the seas, the mountains and the valleys.[3]

Yet, in common with so many other memories that seem to hark back to an advanced lost civilization of prehistoric antiquity, we learn that in due course the 'Forefathers' became arrogant and proud and over-stepped their bounds so that the gods asked: 'Must they perchance be the equals of ourselves, their Makers? Let us check a little their desires, because it is not well what we see.'[4] Punishment swiftly followed:

The Heart of Heaven blew mist into their eyes, which clouded their sight as when a mirror is breathed on. Their eyes were covered and they could see only what was close, only that was clear to them. In this way all the wisdom and all the knowledge of [the Forefathers] were destroyed.[5]

It is interesting to note the mechanisms used by the gods to keep our ancestors in their place, as described in the *Popol Vuh*:

A flood was brought about by the Heart of Heaven . . . A heavy resin fell from the sky . . . The face of the earth was darkened and a black rain began to fall by day and by night . . .[6] The faces of the sun and the moon were covered . . .[7] There was much hail, black rain and mist and indescribable cold . . .[8]

All these phenomena very accurately reflect the complex nature of the cataclysm that afflicted the earth 12,800 years ago at the beginning of the Younger Dryas cold epoch when, as we saw from the mass of evidence presented in Part II, many scientists are now certain that the earth was struck by several large fragments of a disintegrating giant comet.

It is my opinion, indeed it is the reason I have written this book, that we need to pay attention to such accounts, and the universal details that unite them, whether they come down to us from Mexico, from Peru, from Easter Island, from Mesopotamia, from Ancient Egypt, from ancient Canaan or from Turkey. It is intriguing, for example, against the background of flood and cataclysm it describes, that the *Popol Vuh* makes mention of 'fish-men',[9] exactly like the Apkallu Sages of Mesopotamia ('who had the whole body of a fish, but underneath and attached to the head of the fish there was another head, human, and joined to the tail of the fish, feet like those of a man').[10] Exactly like the Apkallu, too, these fish men reported in the traditions of the ancient Maya possessed magical powers and 'worked many miracles'.[11]

It is perhaps not surprising, therefore, that Quetzalcoatl, the Feathered Serpent, the civilization bringer who appears in the *Popol Vuh* under the name of Gucumatz,[12] should be represented, as we saw in Chapter One, by an ancient image from La Venta on the Gulf of Mexico in which he holds the exact same sort of bag or bucket that the Apkallu hold in the Mesopotamian reliefs and that is also figured on Pillar 43 at Göbekli Tepe in Turkey. La Venta was one of the centres of the mysterious early civilization of the Olmecs, who left behind sculptures of bearded men with features that do not look at all like those of native Americans, but resemble the bearded figures shown in the Mesopotamian Apkallu reliefs and in the statues of Kon-Tiki Viracocha at Tiahuanaco in Bolivia – again hinting at universal symbolism associated with a group of individuals who sought to disseminate the gifts of civilization all around the world. Moreover, it is widely recognised that the extraordinary astronomical science for which the Maya are famed was part of a wider body of advanced knowledge that had been passed down to them by the Olmecs and that the Mayan calendar itself is probably best understood as one of these Olmec legacies.

As we saw in Chapter Fifteen, a great cycle of the Mayan calendar came to an end on 21 December 2012. It is an end date that was calculated to mark the once-in-26,000-year conjunction of the winter

428

solstice sun and the centre of the Milky Way galaxy – a conjunction that is itself, because of the diameter of the sun and the limitations of naked-eye astronomy, not so much a precise moment in time as a window 80-years wide spanning the period 1960-2040. We saw, too, how Pillar 43 at Göbekli Tepe uses solar and constellation symbolism to depict the exact same window through which, as any astronomical software program will confirm, the winter solstice sun is still trans-iting today.

My intuition is that these devices, both the Mayan calendar and the Göbekli Tepe pillar, are an attempt, using the precessional code, to send a message to the future. I see the lineaments of that message also in the huge astronomical geoglyph formed by the Pyramids and the Great Sphinx of Giza. Using the same code, and their relationship to the constellations of Orion and Leo, these monuments draw our attention to the epoch of the Younger Dryas between 12,800 and 11,600 years ago and, through the symbolism of the return of the Phoenix, to the epoch that falls half a precessional cycle later, i.e. once again our own epoch (see Chapter Eleven).

The targeting here is not so precise as that afforded by the Göbekli Tepe pillar and the Mayan calendar, but then neither is the science by which the impacts that set off the Younger Dryas are dated to 12,800 years ago. The resolution of the carbon-14 evidence upon which scien-tists base this chronology means that a tolerance of plus or minus 150 years must be allowed. In other words, the Younger Dryas comet – let us, for convenience, refer to it as 'the Phoenix' – could have struck the earth as late as 12,650 years ago (i.e. in 10,635 BC, since I am writing in AD 2015) or as early as 12,950 years ago (i.e. in 10,935 BC).

Bearing in mind that half a precessional cycle is 12,960 years (or 12,954 years in the peculiarly exact calculations of the return of the Phoenix reported by Solinus[13]), we are therefore being invited to consider a period that begins in just ten years from the time of writing, i.e. around AD 2025, and that cannot be considered to have passed safely until AD 2325 – i.e. until the full 12,960 years have elapsed after the latest possible date for 'the Phoenix' impacts. The Mayan calendar and Pillar 43 at Göbekli Tepe, however, refine the calculation, as we've seen. If I understand the message correctly, we're in the danger zone now and will be until 2040. I'm reminded of the Ojibwa tradition cited in Chapter Three:

> The star with the long, wide tail is going to destroy the world some day when it comes low again. That's the comet called Long-Tailed Heavenly Climbing Star. It came down here once, thousands of years ago. Just like the sun. It had radiation and burning heat in its tail.
>
> The comet burnt everything to the ground. There wasn't a thing left. Indian people were here before that happened, living on the earth. But things were wrong; a lot of people had abandoned the spiritual path. The holy spirit warned them a long time before the comet came. Medicine men told everyone to prepare.
>
> Things were wrong with nature on the earth . . . Then that comet went through here. It had a long, wide tail and it burnt up everything. It flew so low the tail scorched the earth . . . The comet made a different world. After that survival was hard work. The weather was colder than before . . .[14]

Does it sound like scaremongering to suggest that the comet remembered in this, and in so many other myths and traditions from all parts of the globe, might be about to stage its 'Great Return'.

Am I reading too much into recondite ancient monuments and calendars and into the fact that everywhere, universally, across all cultures, comets have always been regarded with fear and loathing and as omens of impending doom and destruction?[15]

I'm not sure what the right answer to these questions is. From a personal point of view, as a loving father and grandfather I would greatly prefer it if there was no such danger, yet at the same time, if there is danger, we would be foolish to bury our heads in the sand and pretend that there's nothing to worry about and no action we need to take. I'm therefore obliged to point out that the most recent science on this subject is in complete agreement with the ancient wisdom.

There is danger.

The house of history is built on sand

We are in the midst of a profound paradigm shift regarding how we view the evolution of human civilization. As noted at the end of Chapter Five, archaeologists have been in the habit of regarding cosmic impacts, supposedly only occurring at multi-million year intervals, as largely irrelevant to the 200,000-year story of anatomically modern humans. When we believed that the last big impact had been the dinosaur-killing asteroid of 65 million years ago, there was obviously little point in trying to relate cosmic accidents on such an almost unimaginable scale in any way to the much shorter time-frame of 'history'. But the nightmare scenario raised by the group of scientists behind the Younger Dryas impact hypothesis, and supported by the mass of compelling evidence reviewed in Part II – namely that a huge, earthshaking, extinction-level event occurred just 12,800 years ago, in our historical backyard – changes everything . . .

First and foremost, it means the historical timeline taught as 'fact' in all our schools and institutions of higher learning, the slow painful steps from Palaeolithic to Neolithic, the development of agriculture, the rise of the first cities, and so on and so forth – in short, all the conclusions archaeology has come to about the origins of civilization – rest on false foundations. For by what word other than 'false' can the underpinnings of the existing historical paradigm be described, when we now know that they were put in place without taking account of the single biggest cataclysm to hit the earth since the extinction of the dinosaurs? This cataclysm, moreover, unfolded in a very specific and very recent period, the Younger Dryas between 12,800 and 11,600 years ago, and was immediately followed by the first signs of the emergence of civilization at Göbekli Tepe in Turkey, and soon afterwards at many other points around the globe.

To recognise, as archaeologists now do, that these early experiments in civilised living all took place right *after* the Younger Dryas 'punctuation mark', yet to take no account of the massive worldwide trauma and destruction unleashed by the cosmic impacts that *caused* the Younger Dryas, is a real lapse of scholarship. What is worse, however, is the parallel failure to devote even a moment's consideration to the possibility that crucial chapters of the human story – perhaps even a great civilization of prehistoric antiquity – might have been erased from the historical record by those impacts and by the floods, the black bituminous rain, the time of darkness and the indescribable cold that followed.

If our own civilization were to pass through a comparable cascade of giant impacts would we survive?

All the indications are that we would not and this is why, in my view, the growing recognition of the reality of the Younger Dryas comet lays a duty upon archaeologists to desist – *at the very least* – from pouring further scorn upon 'Atlantis', and other rumours of a lost Ice Age civilization that have come down to us from the past. Rather than doing everything in their power to dismiss, minimise, and ridicule the myths, the anomalous monuments, and the other tantalizing hints, traces and clues of a great forgotten episode of human history, the evidence of the comet impacts 12,800 years ago requires that a thorough investigation of these mysteries, drawing on the full resources of science, should be undertaken for the first time.

Agenda?

Great resistance will have to be overcome before such an investigation can be mounted – and for the same reasons that James Kennett, Allen West, Richard Firestone and the other leading researchers of the Younger Dryas impacts have faced resistance from their gradualist, 'uniformitarian' colleagues. As Kennett has observed, the Younger Dryas impact hypothesis challenges existing paradigms across a broad range of disciplines – not just archaeology, but also paleontology, paleocean-ography, paleoclimatology and impact dynamics.[16]

Inevitably when one presents new evidence that treads on so many different toes, there is going to be opposition. Academic turf wars, however, are one thing; keeping us all in the dark about a real and present danger that threatens the human future, simply because recognizing the existence of that danger requires some scholars to abandon long-cherished positions, is quite another.

Yet this is precisely what seems to be involved in the ideological attacks, masquerading as genuine criticism, that have been made on the work of Kennett, West, Firestone and others – attacks, as we saw in Part II, that they have repeatedly and amply refuted, but that can be expected to continue so long as myopic territorialism prevails in science over the rational appraisal of disturbing and, in the case of the Younger Dryas comet, utterly convincing new evidence.

And there may be more to this than just an academic turf war – indeed something that much more closely resembles a conspiracy to hide unpalatable truths. As I was researching *Magicians of the Gods*, I exchanged a number of emails with Allen West, since I wanted to check facts and he's the team member listed as the corresponding author on most of the academic papers about the Younger Dryas impact. Our discussions became quite wide-ranging and at one point he wrote:

> I think your new book will open up the comet hypothesis to a much larger audience and that is very good for our planet, because this impact topic is not just interesting past history. The Younger Dryas impact was devastating, but much smaller ones could devastate a city, region, or country today, and they are much more frequent than publicly admitted by NASA and the ESA [European Space Agency], though there seems to be growing awareness.[17]

Picking up on this issue of the apparently deliberate suppression of information about impacts, and about the Younger Dryas impacts in particular, I emailed West as follows:

> Having seen the shoddy way catastrophist ideas have been treated again and again down the years, I suppose I should not be surprised by the concerted hostility of your critics, how they spin things, and their constant crowing about the latest 'requiem' for the comet theory – which turns out to be not a requiem at all but just propaganda basically! But still, I can't help feeling there is something odd about the way your critics seem almost deliberately to ignore crucial evidence that you have presented in order to generate headlines like 'study casts doubt on

433

mammoth-killing impact' or to say things like 'for the Syria site the impact theory is out', when it isn't 'out' at all!

Is it just that they desperately want the world to be a safe, predictable place and seek to fulfil their own wish by fudging the facts in their papers? Or is there some other agenda at work?[18]

West's reply was intriguing:

> That certainly is one aspect. One critic complained to me that 'Well, if you are right, we will have to rewrite the textbooks!' As if that were a bad thing . . . [But], curiously, some of our most virulent critics are associated with NASA and the government. A NASA employee tells me that this attitude of opposition to impact threats is entrenched in NASA and is only now slowly beginning to change. When it became obvious to NASA decades ago that asteroids and comets are a serious threat, their employees were instructed by top government officials to downplay the risk. The government was concerned that the populace would 'panic' over space rocks and demand action, when NASA couldn't do anything about them and didn't want to admit it. Plus, trying to mitigate any impact hazards would have used up funding they wanted to put elsewhere.[19]

The dark traveller

As long ago as 1990, before any of the physical, geological evidence for the Younger Dryas comet impacts had been discovered, astrophysicist Victor Clube and astronomer Bill Napier warned of the view:

> that treats the cosmos as a harmless backdrop to human affairs, a view which Academe now often regards as its business to uphold and to which Church and State are only too glad to subscribe.[20]

Such a view, in Clube and Napier's prescient 1990 opinion, was dangerous in that its effect was to 'place the human species a little higher than the ostrich, awaiting the fate of the dinosaur.'[21]

As can be seen from the reactions of some members of 'Academe' to the Younger Dryas impact hypothesis, this view, and what Clube and Napier call the 'great illusion of cosmic security'[22] that it engenders, are still powerful forces in the world today. Much more than the truth about our own past is at stake, however, for there is a chilling convergence between Clube and Napier's findings on the one hand, and the findings of Kennett, West and Firestone on the other, as to what the Younger Dryas comet really means for humanity.

To understand the implications of this convergence properly it will be necessary to review some of the discoveries made by Clube, Napier and others in the 1980s and 1990s – discoveries, remember, that are completely independent of the later work of the Kennett/West/Firestone team on the Younger Dryas impacts. To cut a long story short, as I've already indicated in Chapter Eleven, the burden of these discoveries is that it is possible – indeed highly probable – that we are not yet done with the comet that changed the face of the earth between 12,800 years ago and 11,600 years ago. Clube and Napier's work, with important contributions also from the late Sir Fred Hoyle, and from mathematician and astronomer Professor Chandra Wickramasinghe, has raised the chilling possibility that the Younger Dryas comet was itself only a fragment of a much larger, giant comet – once perhaps as much as 100 kilometres in diameter – which entered the inner solar system about 30,000 years ago and was captured by the sun and flung into an earth-crossing orbit. It remained relatively intact for the next 10,000 years. Then around 20,000 years ago it underwent a massive 'fragmentation event' somewhere along its orbit that transformed it from a single deadly and potentially world-killing object into multiple objects grading down from 5 kilometres to 1 kilometre or less in diameter, each and every one of which would still, in its own right, be capable of causing a global cataclysm.[23]

The evidence is that it was several fragments on this scale that hit the earth 12,800 years ago, causing the Younger Dryas,[24] that we crossed the debris stream of the comet again 11,600 years ago with equally dramatic effects that ended the Younger Dryas,[25] and – finally – that *we can expect further encounters with the remaining fragments in the future.*[26] 'This unique complex of debris,' write Clube and Napier, 'is undoubtedly the greatest collision hazard facing the earth at the present time.'[27]

The Taurid meteor stream, so called because it produces showers of 'shooting stars' that look to observers on the ground as though they originate in the constellation of Taurus, is the most familiar and best-known product of the ongoing fragmentation of the original giant comet. The stream sprawls completely across the earth's orbit – a distance of more than 300 million kilometres – cutting it in two places so that the planet must pass through it twice a year: in late June and early July (when the 'shooting stars' are not visible because they are encountered in daylight) and again from late October into November when a spectacular 'Halloween firework' display is put on.[28] Since the earth travels more than 2.5 million kilometres along its orbital path every day, and since each passage takes approximately twelve days, it is obvious that the Taurid stream is at least 30 million kilometres 'wide' or 'thick'. Indeed, what the earth encounters during these two periods is best envisaged as a sort of 'tube' or 'pipe' of fragmented debris – a bit like a huge doughnut. The geometrical term for such a shape is a 'torus'.

'Shooting stars' are harmless – nothing more than tiny meteors burning up in the atmosphere – so why should we be in the least bit concerned about a meteor stream? In the case of the fifty or so distinct and separate meteor streams that have now been discovered by astronomers – the Leonids, the Perseids, the Andromedids, etc – the answer to this question is that in most cases there is probably no danger and nothing to fear. Since most of the particles that they contain are indeed tiny, they represent no threat to the earth.

But it is quite a different matter with the Taurids. As Clube, Napier, Hoyle and Wickramasinghe have demonstrated, the Taurid stream is filled to overflowing with other much more massive material, sometimes visible, sometimes shrouded in clouds of dust, and all of it flying through space at tremendous velocities and intersecting the earth's orbit twice a year, regular as clockwork, year in year out. Amongst the massive, deadly members of the Taurid family are Comet Encke, which is estimated to have a diameter of around five kilometres. But Comet Encke is not alone. According to Clube and Napier there are also:

between one and two hundred asteroids of more than a kilometre diameter orbiting within the Taurid meteor stream. It seems clear that we are looking at the debris from the breakup of an extremely large object. The disintegration, or sequence of disintegrations, must have taken place within the last twenty or thirty thousand years, as otherwise the asteroids would have spread around the inner planetary system and be no longer recognizable as a stream.[29]

In addition to Comet Encke, there are at least two other comets in the stream – Rudnicki, also thought to be about five kilometres in diameter, and a mysterious object named Oljiato, which has a diameter of about 1.5 kilometres.[30] Initially believed to be an asteroid, this extremely dark, earth-crossing projectile sometimes shows signs, visible in the telescope, of volatility and outgassing and most astronomers now regard it as an inert comet that is in the process of waking up.[31] Comet Encke itself is known to have been inert for a long period, until it suddenly flared into life and was first seen by astronomers in 1876.[32] It is now understood to alternate regularly, in extended cycles, between its inert and volatile states.

Clube and Napier's research had convinced them that an *as yet undetected companion* to Comet Encke is orbiting at the very heart of the Taurid meteor stream.[33] They believe that this object is of exceptional size, that it is a comet, and that like Encke and Oljiato it sometimes – for very long periods – shuts itself down. This happens when pitch-like tars that seethe up continuously from its interior during episodes of outgassing become so copious that they coat the entire outer surface of the nucleus in a thick, hardening shell and seal it off completely – perhaps for millennia.[34] On the outside all falls silent after the incandescent 'coma' and tail have faded away and the seemingly inert object tears silently through space at a speed of tens of kilometres per second. But, at the centre of the nucleus, activity continues, gradually building up pressure. Like an overheated boiler with no release valve, the comet eventually explodes from within, breaking up into fragments that can become individual comets every one of which threatens the earth.

Calculations indicate that this presently invisible object at the heart of the Taurid stream might be as much as 30 kilometres in diameter.[35] Moreover, it is thought likely that other large fragments accompany it. According to Professor Emilio Spedicato of the University of Bergamo:

> Tentative orbital parameters which could lead to its observation are estimated. It is predicted that in the near future (around the year 2030) the earth will cross again that part of the torus that contains the fragments, an encounter that in the past has dramatically affected mankind.[36]

Rebirth

The year 2030 is, of course, exactly in the window of danger indicated by the Mayan calendar and Pillar 43 at Göbekli Tepe. The dinosaur-killing asteroid 65 million years ago was only 10 kilometres in diameter, yet it set off a global firestorm and changed the world forever. A collision with an object 30 kilometres in diameter would – at the very least – mean the end of civilization as we know it, and perhaps even the end of all human life on this planet. Its consequences, as noted in Chapter 11, would certainly be orders of magnitude greater than the Younger Dryas impacts 12,800 years ago that had a thousand times the combined explosive power of all the nuclear devices stockpiled in the world today and that left us as a species with amnesia, obliged to begin again like children with no memory of what went before.

However, it doesn't have to be like that. First and foremost, the universe might spare us. Imagine crossing that torus is a bit like crossing a six-lane freeway, on foot, wearing a blindfold. Luckily for you, however, there's not much heavy traffic on the road, so though you have to cross the freeway twice a year you usually don't bump into much. What makes some crossings more risky than others, however, is the fact that the big trucks and other heavy traffic do have a tendency to cluster and bunch in places. Effectively what Clube and Napier have done with their calculations, backtracking the orbits of known objects in the Taurid 'freeway', is to issue a warning that now and for the coming decades, our crossings carry a greatly enhanced risk of a series of collisions with some very menacing 'heavy traffic'.

The evidence that just such a series of collisions occurred between 12,800 years ago and 11,600 years ago and that fragmentation of the progenitor giant comet that gave rise to all the Taurid objects was the cause, should, at the very least, focus our minds. No longer are we dealing with something that only happens at intervals of multiple millions of years, but rather with what appears to be *a cataclysmic process that is still unfolding* within the framework of historical time.

Even so, we need not give up hope, nor waste a single moment of our precious lives embracing gloom and doom. While I am convinced a civilization flourished during the Ice Age and had mastered advanced sciences that seemed like magic to more primitive cultures, I do not believe that it followed our own particular path of technological development. That path has many negative consequences, but it equips us with abilities that the lost civilization clearly lacked – in particular, the ability to intervene in our immediate cosmic environment and to deflect or destroy asteroids and comets that threaten the very survival of humanity.

What it will take is the recognition that we are, after all, one species, one people, one family, and that rather than waste our energies on murderous feuds in the name of 'God', or 'country', or political ideology, or selfish greed, the time has come for love and harmony to displace fear and turmoil in every aspect of our lives, so that that we can secure the human future. If we are to do this, we will have to stop seeking out our own reflections in the mirror and learn to look up into the cosmos instead, we will have to banish hatred and suspicion and learn to pool our resources, our intelligence and our talents in a grand effort for the redemption of mankind.

We will, in short, have to awaken to the full mystery of the magnificent gift of consciousness and realise we must not squander it an instant longer.

For this, too, was the promise of the Mayan calendar – that we who are alive today will find ourselves at the threshold of a new age of human consciousness. If we can bring that age to birth, with all it implies, then preventing the remaining fragments of the Younger Dryas comet from devastating the earth will be child's play and in the process we will have discovered, perhaps for the first time in more than 12,000 years, who we really are.

It is our choice.

It always has been.

Nothing stands in our way but ourselves.

Appendices

Figure 73: The Orion Correlation is not 'upside down'. If we look at it simply as an artistic project – make a painting (or three-dimensional model) of the three stars of Orion's belt and then lay that painting (or model) down in the most natural way in front of us – we will find that it does match/correlate exactly with the positions of the three pyramids on the ground.

Appendix I

The Orion correlation is not upside down

Modern astronomers view the sky as a curved dome overhead. So the painter in the graphic opposite is looking south at Orion, and the Orion correlation says that the three stars of Orion's belt are represented by the three pyramids on the ground. The lowest star is represented by the Great Pyramid, the middle star by the Pyramid of Khafre (second pyramid) and the highest star is represented by the Pyramid of Menkaure (the third and smallest of the pyramids, just as the highest star is visually the smallest – least bright – of the three stars).

Now, the Great Pyramid on the ground is the northernmost of the three, the second pyramid is in the middle, of course, and the third pyramid is the southernmost of the three. The objection of astronomers such as Ed Krupp of the Griffiths Observatory in Los Angeles is based on their modern convention that the sky is a curved dome overhead. If you view the sky that way then the highest star – which is represented by Mankaure's Pyramid, according to the Orion correlation – is in fact the northernmost star (remember we are looking south, the sky is imagined to be curving overhead – so the higher you go, the closer you get to the north pole of the sky which is behind the painter in the diagram), and the lowest star, which is represented by the Great Pyramid, according to the Orion correlation, is in fact the southern-most star. But on the ground, the Great Pyramid is the northernmost pyramid and the Pyramid of Menkaure is the southernmost pyramid. Hence Dr Krupp argues that the correlation is 'upside down'.

What the diagram demonstrates is that this is only correct according to the astronomical convention of the sky being the inside of a sphere that curves overhead. If we look at it simply as an artistic project – make a painting of the three stars of Orion's belt and then lay that painting down in the most natural way on the ground in front of us – we will find that it does match/correlate exactly with the positions of the three pyramids on the ground.

References

Chapter 1

1. 'The Turkish word *Göbek* means navel or belly.' Klaus Schmidt, *Göbekli Tepe, A Stone-Age Sanctuary in South-Eastern Anatolia*, Ex Oriente, Berlin, 2012, p. 88. See also http://www.ancient.eu/article/234/and http://archive. archaeology.org/0811/abstracts/turkey.html.
2. Or 'Belly Mountain'. See Klaus Schmidt, *Göbekli Tepe, A Stone-Age Sanctuary in South-Eastern Anatolia*, op. cit., p. 88.
3. Interview with Professor Dr Klaus Schmidt conducted by Graham Hancock at Göbekli Tepe, 7 and 8 September 2013. All subsequent statements by Dr Schmidt quoted in this chapter are from the same interview.
4. John Anthony West, *Serpent in the Sky*, Harper and Row, New York, 1979, p. 13.
5. Interview with Klaus Schmidt, op. cit., and see also Klaus Schmidt, *Göbekli Tepe – the Stone Age Sanctuaries: New Results of Ongoing Excavations with a Special Focus on Sculptures and High Reliefs*, in Documenta Praehistorica XXXVII, 2010, p. 243.
6. Klaus Schmidt, *Göbekli Tepe – the Stone Age Sanctuaries*, op. cit., p. 245.
7. Juan Antonio Belmonte, *Journal of Cosmology*, Vol 9 (2010), pp. 2052-2062.
8. See Chapter Fourteen.
9. My friend Andrew Collins elaborates on these human-like characteristics of the vulture figure on p. 99 of his *Göbekli Tepe: Genesis of the Gods*, Bear & Co., Vermont, 2014, for which I wrote the Introduction.
10. For further details of the excavations in Enclosure H see *Göbekli Tepe Newsletter 2014*, German Archaeological Institute, pp. 5-7. Available as a pdf here: http://www.dainst.org/documents/10180/123677/Newsletter+G% C3%B6bekli+Tepe+Ausgabe+1-2014.
11. Klaus Schmidt, *Göbekli Tepe – the Stone Age Sanctuaries*, op. cit., p. 242.
12. Schmidt elaborates on these ideas in *Göbekli Tepe – the Stone Age Sanctuaries*, op. cit., p. 243.
13. Neil Baldwin, *Legends of the Plumed Serpent: Biography of a Mexican God*, Public Affairs, New York, 1998, p. 17.

445

14. Graham Hancock, *Fingerprints of the Gods*, William Heinemann Ltd., London, 1995, p. 130.
15. Neil Baldwin, *Legends of the Plumed Serpent*, op. cit., p. 17.
16. Gerald P. Verbrugghe and John M. Wickersham (Eds.), *Berossos and Manetho: Native Traditions in Ancient Mesopotamia and Egypt*, University of Michigan Press, 1999, p. 44.
17. Benno Lansberger, 'Three Essays on the Sumerians II: The Beginnings of Civilisation in Mesopotamia', in Benno Lansberger, *Three Essays on the Sumerians*, Udena Publications, Los Angeles, p. 174; *Berossos and Manetho*, op. cit., pp. 17 and 44; Stephanie Dalley, *Myths from Mesopotamia*, Oxford University Press, 1990, pp. 182-3, 328; Jeremy Black and Anthony Green (Eds.), *Gods, Demons and Symbols of Mesopotamia*, British Museum Press, London, 1992, pp. 41, 82-3, 163-4.
18. John Biershorst, *The Mythology of Mexico and Central America*, William Morrow, New York, 1990, p. 161.
19. North America of Antiquity, p. 268, cited in Ignatius Donnelly, *Atlantis: The Antediluvian World*, Dover Publications Inc. Reprint, 1976, p. 165.
20. Sylvanus Griswold Morley, *An Introduction to the Study of Maya Hieroglyphs*, Dover Publications Inc., New York, 1975, pp. 16-17.
21. John Biershorst, *The Mythology of Mexico and Central America*, op. cit., p. 161.
22. Sylvanus Griswold Morley, *An Introduction to the Study of Maya Hieroglyphs*, op. cit., pp. 16-17.
23. See Graham Hancock, *Fingerprints of the Gods*, op. cit., note 16, p. 517.
24. Plato, *Timaeus and Critias*, Penguin Classics, London, 1977, p. 36.

Chapter 2

1. See *New Scientist Magazine*, cover story on Göbekli Tepe, 5 October 2013, 'The True Dawn: Civilization is Older and More Mysterious than we Thought.'
2. Plato, *Timaeus and Critias*, op. cit., p. 36.
3. Email from Danny Hilman Natawidjaja to Graham Hancock, 2 October 2014.
4. Danny Hilman Natawidjaja, *Plato Never Lied: Atlantis in Indonesia*, Booknesia, Jakarta, 2013.
5. Schoch and I, who have known each other for many years, were both invited to present papers at the Gotrasawala Festival and Cultural Conference (devoted largely to discussions of Gunung Padang) that was held in Bandung on 5, 6 and 7 December 2013. A professional fieldtrip to Gunung Padang, at which Dr Natawidjaja shared his findings, was organised as part of the Conference.
6. Reported in *Fingerprints of the Gods*, op. cit., p. 420ff.

7. Robert M. Schoch Ph.D., 'The Case for a Lost Ice Age Civilization in Indonesia', *Atlantis Rising Magazine*, March–April 2014, p. 41ff.
8. 'I frequently receive communications from people who wish to consult me concerning their unpublished ideas,' Einstein wrote. 'It goes without saying that these ideas are very seldom possessed of scientific validity. The very first communication, however, that I received from Mr Hapgood electrified me. His idea is original, of great simplicity, and – if it continues to prove itself – of great importance to everything that is related to the history of the earth's surface.' From the Foreword by Albert Einstein to Charles H. Hapgood, *Earth's Shifting Crust: A key to some Basic Problems of Earth Science*, Pantheon Books, New York, 1958, pp. 1-2.

Chapter 3

1. *Archaeoastronomy: The Journal of the Center for Archaeoastronomy*, Vol. VIII, Nos. 1–4, January–December 1985, p. 99.
2. Thor Conway in Ray A. Williamson and Claire R. Farrer, Eds., *Earth and Sky: Visions of the Cosmos in Native American Folklore*, University of New Mexico Press, Albuquerque, 1992, pp. 243-4.
3. Reported in W. Woelfi and W. Blatensperger, 'Traditions connected with the Pole Shift Model of the Pleistocene', in *arXiv: 1009.578vl*, 26 September 2010, p. 24.
4. Thor Conway in Ray A. Williamson and Claire R. Farrer, Eds., *Earth and Sky*, op. cit., p. 246.
5. Cited in Richard Firestone, Allen West and Simon Warwick-Smith, *The Cycle of Cosmic Catastrophes: Flood, Fire and Famine in the History of Civilization*, Bear & Co., Rochester, Vermont, 2006, pp. 152-3.
6. Ibid.
7. Castoroides. Its average length was approximately 1.9 metres (six feet) and it could grow as large as 2.2 metres (seven feet). It was the largest-known rodent in North America during the Pleistocene and the largest known beaver.
8. Richard Erdoes and Alfonso Ortiz, *American Indian Myths and Legends*, Pantheon Books, New York, 1984, p. 181.
9. Martha Douglas Harris, *History and Folklore of the Cowichan Indians*, The Colonialist Printing and Publishing Company, Victoria, British Columbia, 1901, pp. 11-12.
10. Ibid.
11. Ella E. Clark, *Indian Legends of the Pacific Northwest*, University of California Press, Berkeley, 1953, pp. 161-2.
12. Richard Erdoes and Alfonso Ortiz, *American Indian Myths and Legends*, op. cit., p. 474.

13. *New Larousse Encyclopedia of Mythology*, Paul Hamlyn, London, 1989, p. 426.
14. Sir J.G. Frazer, *Folklore in the Old Testament: Studies in Comparative Religion, Legend and Law*, Macmillan, London, 1923, pp. 111-12.
15. *New Larousse Encyclopedia of Mythology*, op. cit., p. 431.
16. http://www.firstpeople.us/FP-Html-Legends/AlgonquinFloodMyth-Algonquin.html.
17. From Lynd's History of the Dakotas, cited in *Atlantis: The Antediluvian World*, op. cit., p. 117.
18. For further discussion see Gail J. Woodside, *Comparing Native Oral History and Scientific Research to Produce Historical Evidence of Native Occupation During and After the Missoula Floods: A Project submitted to Oregon State University, University Honors College, in partial fulfillment of the requirements for the degree of Honors Baccalaureate in Natural Resources*, 28 May 2008. Woodside concludes that 'oral histories shared by Native people located in the area of the flood regions, when compared with actual geologic information give evidence of occupation and survivability of Native populations in flood regions.'
19. Carlson's website is www.sacredgeometryinternational.com.
20. J Harlen Bretz, *The Channeled Scabland of Eastern Washington*, Geographical Review, Vol. 18, No. 3, July 1928, p. 446.
21. John Soennichesen, *Bretz's Flood: The Remarkable Story of a Rebel Geologist and the World's Greatest Flood*, Sasquatch Books, Seattle, 2008, p. 17.
22. Ibid., p. 33.
23. Ibid., p. 39.
24. Ibid., p. 43.
25. Ibid., p. 79-90.
26. Ibid., p. 110.
27. Ibid., p. 126.
28. Ibid.
29. J Harlen Bretz, The Channeled Scablands of the Columbia Plateau, *The Journal of Geology*, Vol. 31, No. 8, Nov-Dec 1923, p. 621-2.
30. Ibid., p. 649.
31. John Soennichesen, *Bretz's Flood*, op. cit., p. 131.
32. David Alt, *Glacial Lake Missoula and its Humongous Floods*, Mountain Press Publishing Company, Missoula, Montana, 2001, p. 17.
33. Ibid., p. 17.
34. Ibid.
35. J Harlen Bretz, The Spokane Flood beyond the Channeled Scablands, *The Journal of Geology*, Vol. 33, No. 2, Feb-March 1925, p. 98.
36. Cited in Stephen Jay Gould, 'The Great Scablands Debate', *Natural History*, August/September 1978, pp. 12-18.

37. Cited in Victor R. Baker, 'The Spokane Flood Controversy and the Martian Outflow Channels, *Science*, New Series, Vol. 202, No. 4734, 22 December 1978, p. 1252.
38. Cited in Stephen Jay Gould, 'The Great Scablands Debate', op. cit.
39. Cited in John Soennichsen, *Bretz's Flood*, op. cit., p. 192.
40. Ibid.
41. Ibid.
42. Ibid.
43. Ibid.
44. Bretz, cited in Victor R. Baker, 'The Spokane Flood Controversy', op. cit, pp. 1252-3.
45. Bretz, cited in ibid., pp. 1252-3.
46. Victor R. Baker, ibid., p. 1253.
47. Bretz, writing in the Bulletin of the Geological Society of America, No. 39, 1928, p. 643, cited in Victor R. Baker, 'The Spokane Flood Debates: Historical Background and Philosophical Perspective, Geological Society, London, Special Publications 2008, Vol. 301, p. 47.'
48. Bretz et al writing in the Bulletin of the Geological Society of America, 67, 957, 1956, cited in Victor R. Baker, 'The Spokane Flood Controversy', op. cit., p. 1249.
49. J Harlen Bretz, 'The Spokane Flood beyond the Channeled Scablands, II', *The Journal of Geology*, Vol. 33, No. 3, April–May, 1925, p. 259.
50. Bretz, Outline for a Presentation before the Geological Society of Washington, January 1927, p. 5, cited in John Soennichsen, *Bretz's Flood*, op. cit., p. 185.
51. John Soennichsen, *Bretz's Flood*, op. cit., p. 206.
52. Lake Missoula and the Spokane flood [abstracts], Geological Society of America Bulletin, 1 March 1930, Vol. 41, No. 1, pp. 92-3, cited in John Soennichsen, *Bretz's Flood*, op. cit., p. 185.
53. The Grand Coulee, by J Harlen Bretz, New York, American Geographical Society, 1932, cited in John Soennichsen, *Bretz's Flood*, op. cit., p. 210.
54. Cited in John Soennichsen, *Bretz's Flood*, op. cit., p. 222.
55. Ibid., pp. 222-3.
56. Bretz, 'Washington's Channeled Scabland', p. 53, cited in John Soennichsen, *Bretz's Flood*, op. cit., p. 227.
57. John Soennichsen, *Bretz's Flood*, op. cit., p. 229.
58. Stephen Jay Gould, 'The Great Scablands Debate', op. cit.
59. John Soennichsen, *Bretz's Flood*, op. cit., p. 231.
60. http://en.wikipedia.org/wiki/J_Harlen_Bretz.
61. J Harlen Bretz, 'The Lake Missoula Floods and the Channeled Scabland', *The Journal of Geology*, Vol. 77, No. 5, September 1969, pp. 510-11.
62. Victor R. Baker, 'The Spokane Flood Debates', op. cit., p. 46.

63. J Harlen Bretz, 'The Channeled Scablands of the Columbia Plateau', op. cit., p. 649.
64. J Harlen Bretz, Presentation of the Penrose Medal to J Harlen Bretz: Response, *Bulletin of the Geological Society of America*, Part II, 91, 1095, cited in Victor R. Baker, 'The Spokane Flood Debates', op. cit., p. 48.
65. See, for example, discussion in James E. O'Connor, David A. Johnson, et al, 'Beyond the Channeled Scabland', *Oregon Geology*, Vol. 57, No. 3, May 1995, pp. 51-60. See also Gerardo Benito and Jim E. O'Connor, 'Number and Size of last-glacial Missoula floods in the Columbia River Valley', *Geological Society of America Bulletin*, 115, 2003, pp. 624-38; Richard B. Waitt Jr., 'About Forty Last-Glacial Lake Missoula Jökulhlaups through Southern Washington', *The Journal of Geology*, Vol. 88, No. 6, November 1980, pp. 653-79; E.P. Kiver and D.F. Stradling, 'Comments on Periodic Jökulhlaups from Pleistocene Lake Missoula', Letter to the Editor, *Quaternary Research* 24, 1985, pp. 354-6; John J. Clague et al, 'Palaeomagnetic and tephra evidence for tens of Missoula floods in Southern Washington', *Geology*, 31, 2003, pp. 247-50; Richard B. Waitt Jr., 'Case for periodic colossal jökulhlaups from Pleistocene Glacial Lake Missoula', *Geological Society of America Bulletin*, Vol. 96, October 1985, pp. 121-128; Keenan Lee, *The Missoula Flood*, Department of Geology and Geological Engineering School of Mines, Golden, Colorado, 2009.
66. Vic Baker, in an interview with John Soennichsen, *Bretz's Flood*, op. cit., pp. 251-2.
67. David Alt, *Glacial Lake Missoula and its Humongous Floods*, op. cit., p. 25.
68. Thomas J. Crowley and Gerald R. North, *Palaeoclimatology*, Oxford University Press, 1991, p. 62.
69. Lawrence Guy Strauss et al, *Humans at the End of the Ice Age*, Plenum Press, New York and London 1996, pp. 66 and 86. The Younger Dryas is explicitly a term for a European cold phase, although the phase itself was global. The same phase is thus sometimes referred to by different names in other places; but it is also a generic term and it is used as such here.
70. Crowley and North, op. cit., p. 63.
71. Adams and Otte give date of start of Younger Dryas cold period as 12,800 and the end as 11,400 calendar years ago, *Current Anthropology*, 1999, vol. 40, pp. 73-7, see 73.
72. Strauss et al, *Humans at the End of the Ice Age*, op. cit., p. 86.
73. Graham Hancock, *Underworld: Flooded Kingdoms of the Ice Age*, Penguin, London, 2002, pp. 194-5.

Chapter 4

1. See, for example, US Geological Survey, 'Columbia River Basalt Stratigraphy in the Pacific North West': http://or.water.usgs.gov/projs_dir/crbg/.
2. J Harlen Bretz, 'The Channeled Scablands of the Columbia Plateau', *The Journal of Geology*, Vol. 31 No. 8 op. cit., pp. 637-8.
3. Ibid., p. 622.
4. Randall Carlson: My Journey to Catastrophism, www.sacredgeometry international.com/journey-catastrophism.
5. Ibid.
6. All subsequent quotations from Randall Carlson in this chapter are from the interviews I conducted with him on our research trip in September–October 2014.
7. These figures are confirmed by the New York State Geological Survey. See: http://www.nysm.nysed.gov/nysgs/experience/sites/niagara/.
8. Ella E. Clark, *Indian Legends of the Pacific Northwest*, University of California Press, Berkeley, 2003, p. 71.
9. Wikipedia: http://en.wikipedia.org/wiki/Lake_Chelan.
10. See Eric Cheney, *Floods, Flows, Faults, Glaciers, Gold and Gneisses, From Quincy to Chelan to Wenatchee*, Northwest Geological Society, Fieldtrip Guidebook No. 24, 13-14 June 2009, p. 18. (http://www.nwgs.org/field_ trip_guides/floods,_flows_faults.pdf). 'Note the huge erratic of CRBG on the hillside above a house'. CRBG is an abbreviation for The Columbia River Basalt Group, a thick sequence of Miocene flood basalt that covered northern Oregon, eastern Washington, and western Idaho between 17 and 6 million years ago (http://or.water.usgs.gov/projs_dir/crbg/).
11. http://www.wvc.edu/directory/departments/earthsciences/2014NAGT-PNWFieldTrips.pdf.
12. Randall's figure of 1,200 feet is confirmed in David K. Norman and Jaretta M. Roloff, A Self-Guided Tour of the Geology of the Columbia River Gorge, Washington Division of Geology and Earth Resources, Open File Report 2004-7, March 2004, p. 3: 'The flood crest at Wallula Gap on the Columbia River at the Washington-Oregon border was about 1,200 ft (365 m) as evidenced by glacial erratics that were left stranded on the hillside. The water poured down the Columbia Gorge and widened the valley by cleaning off all the soil and talus up to 1,000 ft (300 m) elevation as far as The Dalles, Oregon. By the time it reached Crown Point, the surface of the last flood had dropped to about 600 ft (180 m) elevation.'
13. See discussion in Graham Hancock, *Fingerprints of the Gods*, op. cit., p. 46ff.

Chapter 5

1. Keenan Lee, 'Catastrophic Flood Features at Camas Prairie, Montana', Department of Geology and Geological Engineering, Colorado School of Mines, Golden, Colorado, 2009, pp. 4 and 5.
2. Ibid., p. 5.
3. Charles R. Kinzie, et al, 'Nanodiamond-Rich Layer across Three Continents Consistent with Major Cosmic Impact at 12,800 Cal BP', *The Journal of Geology*, Vol. 122, No. 5 (September 2014), pp. 475-505.
4. See for example, http://phys.org/news/2014-08-year-old-nanodiamonds-multiple-continents.html, and 'Wittke et al, Nanodiamonds and Carbon Spherules from Tunguska, the K/T Boundary, and the Younger Dryas Boundary Layer', paper presented at the American Geophysical Union, Fall Meeting, 2009 (http://adsabs.harvard.edu/abs/2009AGUFMPP 31D1392W).
5. Heather Pringle, *New Scientist*, 22 May 2007: http://www.newscientist.com/article/dn11909-did-a-comet-wipe-out-prehistoric-americans.html#.VJqZ88AgA.
6. Ibid.
7. Ibid.
8. Ibid.
9. Ibid.
10. Ibid.
11. R.B. Firestone, A. West, J.P. Kennett, et al, 'Evidence for an extraterrestrial impact 12,900 years ago that contributed to the megafaunal extinctions and the Younger Dryas cooling', *PNAS*, Vol. 104, No. 41, 9 October 2007, p. 16016.
12. Ibid., p. 16016.
13. Ibid., p. 16020.
14. The parallel is Comet Shoemaker-Levy 9 which broke up into multiple fragments that hit the planet Jupiter with spectacular effect in 1994.
15. R.B. Firestone, A. West, J.P. Kennett, et al, 'Evidence for an extraterrestrial impact 12,900 years ago that contributed to the megafaunal extinctions and the Younger Dryas cooling', op. cit, p. 16020.
16. Ibid., p. 16020.
17. Ibid.
18. Ibid.
19. Ibid., p. 16020-1.
20. Ibid., p. 16021.
21. Ibid., p. 16020.
22. http://en.wikipedia.org/wiki/Tsar_Bomba.
23. http://www.edwardmuller.com/right17.htm.

24. D.J. Kennett, J.P. Kennett, G.J. West, J.M. Erlandson, et al, in *Quaternary Science Reviews*, Vol. 27, Issues 27-28, December 2008, pp. 2530-45.

25. Douglas J. Kennett, James P. Kennett, Allen West, James H. Wittke, Wendy S. Wolback, et al, in *PNAS*, 4 August 2009, Vol. 106, No. 31, pp. 12623-8.

26. Andrei Kurbatov, Paul A. Mayewski, Jorgen P. Steffenson et al, in *Journal of Glaciology*, Vol. 56, No. 199, 2010, pp. 749-59.

27. W.M. Napier in *Monthly Notices of the Royal Astronomical Society*, Vol. 405, Issue 3, 1 July 2010, pp. 1901-6. The complete paper can be read online here: http://mnras.oxfordjournals.org/content/405/3/1901.full.pdf+html?sid =19fd6cae-61a0-45bd-827b-9f4eb877fd39, and downloaded as a pdf here: http://arxiv.org/pdf/1003.0744.pdf.

28. William C. Mahaney, David Krinsley, Volli Kalm in *Sedimentary Geology* 231 (2010), pp. 31-40.

29. Mostafa Fayek, Lawrence M. Anovitz, et al, in Earth and Planetary Science Letters 319-20, accepted 22 November 2011, available online 21 January 2012, pp. 251-8.

30. Isabel Israde-Alcantara, James L. Bischoff, Gabriela Dominguez-Vasquez et al, in *PNAS*, 27 March 2012, Vol. 109, No. 13, pp E738-47.

31. Ted E. Bunch, Robert E. Hermes, Andrew T. Moore et al, in *PNAS*, June 2012, 109 (28), pp. E1903-12.

32. Michail I. Petaev, Shichun Huang, Stein B. Jacobsen and Alan Zindler, in *PNAS*, 6 Aug 2013, Vol. 110, No. 32, pp. 12917-20.

33. William C. Mahaney, Leslie Keiser, David Krinsley, et al, in *The Journal of Geology*, Vol. 121, No. 4 (July 2013), pp. 309-25.

34. Charles R. Kinzie, et al, 'Nanodiamond-Rich Layer across Three Continents Consistent with Major Cosmic Impact at 12,800 Cal BP', op. cit., p. 475.

35. Boslough, Daulton, Pinter et al, 'Arguments and Evidence against a Younger Dryas Impact Event', *Climates, Landscapes and Civilizations*, Geophysical Monograph Series 198, American Geophysical Union, 2012, p. 21.

36. Nicholas Pinter, Andrew Scott, Tyrone Daulton et al, 'The Younger Dryas Impact Hypothesis: A Requiem', *Earth-Science Reviews*, Vol. 106, Issues 3-4, June 2011, pp. 247-64.

37. Boslough, Daulton, Pinter et al, 'Arguments and Evidence against a Younger Dryas Impact Event', p. 21.

38. James H. Wittke, James P. Kennett, Allen West, Richard Firestone et al, 'Evidence for Deposition of 10 million tons of impact spherules across four continents 12,800 years ago', *PNAS*, 4 June 2013, p. 2089.

39. Ibid., p. 2089.

40. Malcolm A. Le Compte, Albert C. Goodyear, et al, 'Independent Evaluation of Conflicting Microspherule Results from Different Investigations of the Younger Dryas Impact Hypothesis', *PNAS*, 30 October 2012, 109 (44), pp. E2960-9.

41. Ibid., pp. E2960 and E2969.
42. James H. Wittke, James P. Kennett, Allen West, Richard Firestone et al, 'Evidence for Deposition of 10 million tons of impact spherules across four continents 12,800 years ago', op. cit., p. 2089.
43. Ibid., p. 2089.
44. Ibid., p. 2088-9.
45. Ibid., p. 2096.
46. Ibid.
47. Cited in Robert Kunzig, 'Did a Comet Really Kill the Mammoths 12,900 years ago?' *National Geographic*, 10 September 2013 (http://news.nation algeographic.com/news/2013/09/130910-comet-impact-mammoths-climate-younger-dryas-quebec-science/).
48. Ibid.
49. Ibid.
50. Cosmic Tusk, 'In desperate hole, Pinter grabs a shovel': http://cosmictusk. com/nicholas-pinter-southern-illinois/comment-page-2/.
51. P. Thy, G. Willcox, G.H. Barfod, D.Q. Fuller, 'Anthropogenic origin of siliceous scoria droplets from Pleistocene and Holocene archaeological sites in northern Syria', *Journal of Archaeological Science*, 54 (2015), pp. 193-209.
52. Ibid., p. 193.
53. 'Study casts doubt on Mammoth-Killing Cosmic Impact', *UC Davis News and Information*, 6 January 2015: http://news.ucdavis.edu/search/news_ detail.lasso?id=11117.
54. Personal correspondence between Graham Hancock and Allen West. Email West to Hancock dated 18 March 2015.
55. Charles R. Kinzie et al, 'Nanodiamond-Rich Layer across Three Continents Consistent with Major Cosmic Impact at 12,800 Cal BP', op. cit.
56. Ibid. See in particular pp. 477-8.
57. Cited in Robert Kunzig, 'Did a Comet Really Kill the Mammoths 12,900 years ago?', *National Geographic*, 10 September 2013, op. cit.
58. E.g. see Mark Boslough et al, 'Faulty Protocols Yield Contaminated Samples, Unconfirmed Results', *PNAS*, Vol. 110, No. 18, 30 April 2013, and response in the same issue by Malcolm A. LeCompte et al, 'Reply to Boslough: Prior studies validating research are ignored'. See also Annelies van Hoesel et al, 'Cosmic Impact or natural fires at the Allerod-Younger Dryas Boundary: A Matter of Dating and Calibration', *PNAS* Vol. 110, No. 41, 8 October 2013, and response in the same issue by James H. Wittke, et al, 'Reply to van Hoesel et al: Impact related Younger Dryas Boundary Nanodiamonds from The Netherlands'. See also David L. Meltzer et al, 'Chronological evidence fails to support claim on an isochronous widespread layer of cosmic impact indicators dated to 12,800 years ago', in *PNAS*, 12 May 2014. I am informed by Allen West (email from Allen West to Graham Hancock, dated 18 March

2015) that a response paper to Meltzer et al is under preparation by 27 co-authors, is provisionally entitled 'Bayesian chronological analyses consistent with synchronous age of 12,820-12,740 cal BP for Younger Dryas Boundary on Four Continents' and will be submitted shortly. In the same email West notes that there is one point to add about the dating that is already in print (at 18 March 2015): 'In the YDB layer, we have found high-temperature proxies, including nanodiamonds, one of a group of proxies that are found in *all* impact events. The evidence is widespread – our YDB sites extend across more than a dozen countries on four continents (N. America, S. America, Europe, and Asia). In two papers, Wittke et al and Kinzie et al reported about a dozen high-resolution radiocarbon dates, averaging 12,800 ± 100 calendar years ago for the YDB layer. This means that, statistically, the YDB layer at all those sites *could* have been deposited on the same day – it doesn›t prove it did, but shows it is possible. Yet, even though those dates were *directly on* the YDB layer and are statistically identical, Meltzer et al rejected them as not being the same. Such a rejection is simply indefensible.'

59. Charles R. Kinzie et al, 'Nanodiamond-Rich Layer across Three Continents,' op. cit., p. 501.

60. Cited by Jim Barlow-Oregon, in 'Did Exploding Comet Leave Trail of Nanodiamonds?' *Futurity: Research News from Top Universities*: http://www.futurity.org/comet-nanodiamonds-climate-change-755662/. See also Charles R. Kinzie et al, 'Nanodiamond-Rich Layer across Three Continents Consistent with Major Cosmic Impact at 12,800 Cal BP', op. cit., p. 476.

61. Quoted in Julie Cohen, 'Nanodiamonds Are Forever: A UCSB professor's research examines 13,000-year-old nanodiamonds from multiple locations across three continents', *The Current*, UC Santa Barbara, 28 August 2014. http://www.news.ucsb.edu/2014/014368/nanodiamonds-are-forever

62. Charles R. Kinzie et al, 'Nanodiamond-Rich Layer across Three Continents Consistent with Major Cosmic Impact at 12,800 Cal BP', op. cit., pp. 498-9.

63. Quoted in Julie Cohen, 'Nanodiamonds Are Forever: A UCSB professor's research examines 13,000-year-old nanodiamonds from multiple locations across three continents', op. cit.

64. Ibid.

Chapter 6

1. Troy Holcombe, John Warren, et al, 'Small Rimmed Depression in Lake Ontario: An Impact Crater?', *Journal of the Great Lakes Research*, 27 (4), 2001, pp. 510-17.

2. Ian Spooner, George Stevens, et al, 'Identification of the Bloody Creek Structure, a possible impact crater in southwestern Nova Scotia, Canada', *Meteoritics and Planetary Science* 44, No. 8 (2009), pp. 1193-1202.

3. http://en.wikipedia.org/wiki/Corossol_crater.

4. Higgins M.D., Lajeunesse P., et al, 'Bathymetric and Petrological Evidence for a Young (Pleistocene?) 4-km Diameter Impact Crater in the Gulf of Saint Lawrence, Canada', 42nd Lunar and Planetary Science Conference, held 7-11 March 2011 at The Woodlands, Texas. LPI Contribution No. 1608, p. 1504.

5. Charles R. Kinzie et al, 'Nanodiamond-Rich Layer across Three Continents Consistent with Major Cosmic Impact at 12,800 Cal BP', *The Journal of Geology*, Vol. 122, No. 5 (September 2014), op. cit., p. 475.

6. Yingzhe Wu, Mukul Sharma, et al, 'Origin and provenance of spherules and magnetic grains at the Younger Dryas boundary', *PNAS*, 17 September 2013, p. E3557. Available to read online here: http://www.pnas.org/content/110/38/E3557.full.pdf+html.

7. Mukul Sharma cited in Becky Oskin, 'Did ancient Earth-chilling meteor crash near Canada?' http://www.livescience.com/39362-younger-dryas-meteor-quebec.html.

8. See for example W.C. Mahaney, V. Kalm, et al, 'Evidence from the Northwestern Venezuelan Andes for extraterrestrial impact: The Black Mat Enigma, *Geomorphology* 116 (2010), p. 54.

9. John Shaw, Mandy Munro-Stasiuk, et al, 'The Channeled Scabland: Back to Bretz', *Geology*, July 1999, Vol. 27, No. 7, pp. 605-8. E.g. p. 605: 'We present evidence that suggests that only one major late Wisconsin flood is recorded in the sedimentary record, and that sedimentation within the Glacial Lake Missoula basin was independent of sedimentation in the channeled scabland.' For further discussion and elaboration of the implications of Professor Shaw's work, and of the key evidence he presents, see Graham Hancock, *Underworld*, op. cit., Chapter Three.

10. G. Komatsu, H. Miyamoto, et al, 'The Channeled Scabland: Back to Bretz?': Comment and Reply, *Geology*, June 2000, Vol. 28, pp. 573-4.

11. Jim E. O'Connor and Victor R. Baker, 'Magnitudes and implications of peak discharges from Glacial Lake Missoula', *Geological Society of America Bulletin 1992*, 104, No. 3, p. 278.

12. US Geological Survey, 'The Channeled Scablands of Eastern Washington', section on Lake Missoula: http://www.cr.nps.gov/history/online_books/geology/publications/inf/72-2/sec3.htm.

13. C. Warren Hunt, 'Inundation Topography of the Columbia River System', *Bulletin of Canadian Petroleum Geology*, Vol. 25, No. 3, p. 472.

14. See Fiona Tweed, Andrew Russell, 'Controls on the formation and sudden drainage of glacier-impounded lakes: implications for jökulhlaup characteristics', *Progress in Physical Geography*, March 1999, Vol. 23, No. 1, p. 91. Reservations about the integrity of an ice dam more than 2,000 miles long and seven miles high are also expressed by Consulting

Engineering Geologist Peter James in 'The Massive Missoula Floods: An Alternative Rationale', *New Concepts in Global Tectonics Newsletter*, No. 48, September 2008, pp. 5-23.

15. C. Warren Hunt, 'Inundation Topography of the Columbia River System', *Bulletin of Canadian Petroleum Geology*, op. cit., p. 468 and p. 472.

16. Ibid., p. 473.

17. Ibid.

18. Ibid., and see also C. Warren Hunt, 'Catastrophic Termination of the Last Wisconsin Ice Advance: Observations in Alberta and Idaho, *Bulletin of Canadian Petroleum Geology*, Vol. 25, No. 3, pp. 456-67. Peter James, in 'The Massive Missoula Floods' op. cit, also invokes massive incursions of seawater, in his case linked to putative polar wandering. See, for example, p. 17.

19. C. Warren Hunt, *Environment of Violence: Readings of Cataclysm Cast in Stone*, Polar Publishing, Alberta, 1990, p. 137.

20. Ibid., pp. 118-19.

21. Ibid., p. 119.

22. Ibid.

23. Ibid.

24. Ibid., pp. 119-20.

25. Ibid., p. 120.

26. Firestone, West, Kennett, et al, 'Evidence for an Extraterrestrial Impact 12,900 years ago that contributed to the megafaunal extinctions and the Younger Dryas Cooling,' op. cit., p. 16020.

27. Henry T. Mullins and Edward T. Hinchley, 'Erosion and Infill of New York Finger Lakes: Implications for Laurentide Ice Sheet Deglaciation', *Geology*, Vol. 17, Issue 7, July 1989, pp. 622-5.

28. Julian B. Murton, Mark D. Bateman, et al, 'Identification of Younger Dryas outburst flood path from Lake Agassiz to the Arctic Ocean', *Nature* 464 (7289), April 2010, p. 740.

29. Alan Condron and Peter Winsor, 'Meltwater Routing and the Younger Dryas', *PNAS*, 4 December 2012, Vol. 109, No. 49, p. 19930.

30. James T. Teller, 'Importance of Freshwater Injections into the Arctic Ocean in triggering the Younger Dryas Cooling', *PNAS*, Vol. 109, No. 49, 4 December 2012, p. 19880. See also Claude Hillaire-Marcel, Jenny Maccali, et al, 'Geochemical and isotopic tracers of Arctic sea ice sources and export with special attention to the Younger Dryas interval', *Quaternary Science Reviews* (2013), p. 6.

31. S.J. Fiedel, 'The mysterious onset of the Younger Dryas', *Quaternary International* 242 (2011), p. 263.

32. Andreas Schmittner, John C.H. Chiang and Sydney R. Hemming, 'Introduction: The Ocean's Meridional Overturning Circulation', in Andreas

Schmittner et al, *Ocean Circulation: Mechanisms and Impacts – Past and Future Changes of Meridional Overturning*, Geophysical Monograph Series 173, 2007, p. 1 (published online 19 March 2013).

33. Ibid.

34. S.J. Fiedel, 'The mysterious onset of the Younger Dryas', op. cit., p. 264.

35. R.B. Firestone, A. West, Z. Revay, et al, 'Analysis of the Younger Dryas Impact Layer', Journal of Siberian Federal University, Engineering and Technologies, Vol. 3 (1), 2010, pp. 30-62 (page 23 of pdf: http://www.osti.gov/scitech/servlets/purl/1023385/).

36. Ibid.

37. J. Tyler Faith and Todd A. Surovell, 'Synchronous extinction of North America's Pleistocene mammals', *PNAS*, Vol. 106, No. 49, 8 December 2009, p. 20641. The last appearance dates of 16n of the 35 genera fall securely between 13,800 and 11,400 years ago – i.e. clustered very closely around the Younger Dryas. 'Analysis of the chronology of extinctions suggests that sampling error can explain the absence of terminal Pleistocene last appearance dates for the remaining nineteen genera.' In other words the extinction of North American Pleistocene mammals is 'a synchronous event'.

38. Ibid., p. 20641.

39. S.J. Fiedel, 'The mysterious onset of the Younger Dryas', op. cit., p. 264.

40. D.G. Anderson, A.C. Goodyear, J. Kennett, A. West, 'Multiple Lines of Evidence for a possible Human Population Decline during the Early Younger Dryas', *Quaternary International*, Vol. 242, Issue 2, 15 October 2011, pp. 570-83.

41. Sanjeev Gupta, Jenny S. Collier, Andy Palmer-Felgate, Graham Potter, 'Catastrophic Flooding Origin of the Shelf Valley Systems in the English Channel'. *Nature*, Vol. 448, 19 July 2007, pp. 342-5.

42. Don J. Easterbrook, John Gosse, et al, 'Evidence for Synchronous Global Climatic Events: Cosmogenic Exposure Ages of Glaciations', in Don Easterbrook, *Evidence-Based Climatic Science*, Elsevier, August 2011, Chapter 2, p. 54.

43. For further discussion of these possibilities, see W.C. Mahaney, V. Kalm, et al, 'Evidence from the Northwestern Venezuelan Andes for extraterrestrial impact', op. cit, p. 54, and William C. Mahaney, Leslie Keiser, et al, 'New Evidence from a Black Mat site in the Northern Andes Supporting a Cosmic Impact 12,800 Years Ago', *The Journal of Geology*, Vol. 121, No. 4 (July 2013) p. 317.

44. See in particular, Sir Fred Hoyle, *The Origin of the Universe and the Origin of Religion*, Moyer Bell, Wakefield Rhode Island and London, 1993, pp. 28-9. See also Fred Hoyle and Chandra Wickramsinghe, *Life on Mars? The Case for a Cosmic Heritage?*, Clinical Press Ltd., Bristol, 1997, pp. 176-7.

45. Sir Fred Hoyle, *The Origin of the Universe and the Origin of Religion*, op. cit., p. 29.
46. Jeffrey P. Severinghaus et al, 'Timing of abrupt climate change at the end of the Younger Dryas interval from thermally fractionated gases in polar ice', *Nature* 391 (8 January 1998), p. 141.
47. W. Dansgaard et al, 'The Abrupt Termination of the Younger Dryas Event', *Nature*, Vol. 339, 15 June 1989, p. 532.
48. Oliver Blarquez et al, 'Trees in the subalpine belt since 11,700 cal BP, origin, expansion and alteration of the modern forest', *The Holocene* (2009), p. 143.
49. Paul E. Carrara et al, 'Deglaciation of the Mountainous Region of Northwestern Montana, USA, as Indicated by Late Pleistocene Ashes', *Arctic and Alpine Research*, Vol. 18, No. 3, 1986, p. 317.
50. Walter Scott, Trans. and Ed., *Hermetica: The Ancient Greek and Latin writings which contain Religious of Philosophic Teachings Ascribed to Hermes Trismegistus*, Shambhala, Boston 1993, *Asclepius III*, pp. 345-7.

Chapter 7

1. The late Professor Cesar Emiliani of Miami University, a winner of the Vega Medal from Sweden and the Agassiz medal from the National Academy of Sciences of the United States, whose studies focused extensively on sea-level rise, did put a figure on it: 'As a result of the flood that formed the Scabland, the sea level rose very rapidly from minus 100 metres to minus 80 metres. By 12,000 years ago more than fifty per cent of the ice had returned to the ocean, and the sea level had risen to minus 60 metres.' The references to minus 100 metres, minus 80 metres and minus 60 metres are by comparison with today's sea-level. So, before the flood that formed the Scabland of the Columbia Plateau, sea level was 100 metres lower than it is today, after the flood it was 60 metres lower than it is today, i.e. a staggering rise of 40 metres or 131 feet. See Cesare Emiliani, *Planet Earth: Cosmology, Geology and the Evolution of Life and Environment*, Cambridge University Press, 1995, p. 543.
2. Ted E. Bunch, Richard B. Firestone, Allen West, James P. Kennett, et al, 'Very high temperature impact melt products as evidence for cosmic airbursts and impacts 12,900 years ago', *PNAS*, June 2012, 109 (28), op. cit., pp. E1903, 1909-10 and 1912. See also Kinzie et al, 'Nanodiamond-Rich Layer across Three Continents Consistent With Major Cosmic Impact 12,800 years ago', *The Journal of Geology*, Vol. 122, No. 5 (September 2014) op. cit., p. 476 and Appendix B 'Site descriptions and dating'.
3. Ted E. Bunch, Richard B. Firestone, Allen West, James P. Kennett, et al, 'Very high temperature impact melt products . . .' op. cit., p. E1912.

4. *Encyclopaedia Iranica*, 'Zoroaster ii. General Survey', http://www.iranicaon line.org/articles/zoroaster-ii-general-survey.
5. Ibid.
6. Ibid.
7. Ibid.
8. R.C. Zaehner, *The Dawn and Twilight of Zoroastrianism*, Weidenfeld and Nicolson, London, 1961, e.g. see page 135: 'The whole story of Yima's golden age, his excavation of the Vara, or underground retreat, and his re-emergence to re-people the earth (the last episode occurs only in the Pahlavi books) must belong to a very old stratum of Iranian folklore wholly untouched by the teachings of Zoroaster.'
9. J. Darmetester and H.L. Mills, Trans., F. Max Muller, Ed., *The Zend Avesta*, Reprint edition by Atlantic Publishers and Distributors, New Delhi, 1990, Part I, p. 5.
10. Ibid., p. 11.
11. Ibid.
12. Ibid., p. 13.
13. Ibid.
14. Reported by Frank Brown and John Fleagle in *Nature*, 17 February, 2005. And see *Scientific American*, 17 Feb 2005, http://www.scientificamerican. com/article/fossil-reanalysis-pushes/.
15. A golden age in which 'fields would bear plenty of grass for cattle: now with floods that stream, with snows that melt, it will seem a happy land in the world . . .' J. Darmetester and H.L. Mills, Trans., F. Max Muller, Ed., *The Zend Avesta*, op. cit., p. 16. See also the following passage from the Yasna, cited in R.C. Zaehner, *The Dawn and Twilight of Zoroastrianism*, op. cit., pp. 92-3: 'Kingly Yima, of goodly pastures, the most glorious of all men born on earth, like the sun to behold among men, for during his reign he made beasts and men imperishable, he brought it about that the waters and plants never dried up, and that there should be an inexhaustible stock of food to eat. In the reign of Yima the valiant there was neither heat nor cold, neither old age, nor death, nor disease . . .' 'Yima's golden reign, in which all men were immortal and enjoyed perpetual youth, lasted a full thousand years.'
16. J. Darmetester and H.L. Mills, Trans., F. Max Muller, Ed., *The Zend Avesta*, op. cit., pp. 15-18.
17. E.W. West, Trans., F. Max Muller, Ed., *Pahlavi Texts*, Part I, Reprint Edition, Atlantic Publishers and Distributors, New Delhi, 1990, p. 17.
18. J. Darmetester and H.L. Mills, Trans., F. Max Muller, Ed., *The Zend Avesta*, op. cit., p. 5.
19. Cited in Lokmanya Bal Gangadhar Tilak, *The Arctic Home in the Vedas*, Reprint edition by Arktos Media, 2011, p. 254.

20. E.W. West, Trans., F. Max Muller, Ed., *Pahlavi Texts*, op. cit., p. 17, note 5.
21. J. Darmetester and H.L. Mills, Trans., F. Max Muller, Ed., *The Zend Avesta*, op. cit., p. 18.
22. Ibid.
23. Ibid., p. 20. See also the US (1898) edition of Darmetester's translation of the Vendidad, reprinted 1995, edited by Joseph H. Peterson, p. 14, note 87.
24. R.C. Zaehner, *The Dawn and Twilight of Zoroastrianism*, op. cit., p. 135.
25. J. Darmetester and H.L. Mills, Trans., F. Max Muller, Ed., *The Zend Avesta*, op. cit., p. 17.
26. Ibid.
27. Ibid., p. 20.
28. Ibid., note 5.
29. Ibid., note 4.
30. *Encyclopaedia Iranica*, op. cit. 'Jamshid i' (http://www.iranicaonline.org/articles/jamsid-i) and 'Jamshid ii' (http://www.iranicaonline.org/articles/jamsid-ii).
31. E.W. West, Trans., F. Max Muller, Ed., *Pahlavi Texts*, op. cit., p. 26.
32. Delia Goetz, Sylvanus G. Morley, Adrian Reconis, Trans., *Popol Vuh: The Sacred Book of the Ancient Quiche Maya*, University of Oklahoma Press, 1991, p. 178.
33. Ibid., p. 93.
34. John Bierhorst, *The Mythology of Mexico and Central America*, Quill/William Morrow, New York, 1990, p. 41.
35. J. Eric Thompson, *Maya History and Religion*, University of Oklahoma Press, 1990, p. 333.
36. Genesis 6: 19-20.
37. Genesis 6: 16.
38. Louis Ginzberg, *The Legends of the Jews*, The Jewish Publication Society of America, Philadelphia, 1988, Vol. I, p. 162.
39. Ibid.
40. Omer Demir, *Cappadocia: Cradle of History*, 12th Revised Edition, p. 70.
41. http://en.wikipedia.org/wiki/Derinkuyu_%28underground_city%29.
42. *Hurriyet Daily News*, 28 December 2014 (http://www.hurriyetdailynews.com/massive-ancient-underground-city-discovered-in-turkeys-nevsehir-aspx?PageID=238&NID=76196&NewsCatID=375), *The Independent*, 31 December 2014 (http://www.independent.co.uk/news/world/middle-east/vast-5000-yearold-underground-city-discovered-in-turkeys-cappadocia-region-9951911.html).
43. E.g. see report in *The Independent*, 31 December 2014, op. cit.
44. *Turkey*, Lonely Planet, 2013, p. 478.
45. http://en.wikipedia.org/wiki/Derinkuyu_%28underground_city%29.

46. Omer Demir, *Cappadocia: Cradle of History*, 9th Revised Edition, p. 61.
47. For example in Proto-Hittite times up to 2,000 years earlier. See Omer Demir, op. cit., p. 70.
48. Ibid., p. 60.
49. Ibid.
50. Ibid., p. 59.
51. Ibid., p. 61.
52. R.C. Zaehner, *The Dawn and Twilight of Zoroastrianism*, op. cit., p. 135.

Chapter 8

1. Genesis 6: 7.
2. Genesis 6: 8-21.
3. Genesis 6: 19-20.
4. Genesis 8: 3.
5. Genesis 8: 4.
6. Genesis 8: 13-17.
7. Genesis 8: 20-1.
8. Genesis 9: 1-7.
9. For example see Jeremiah 51: 27; also Isaiah 37: 38; 2 Kings 19: 37.
10. Armen Asher and Teryl Minasian Asher, *The Peoples of Ararat*, Booksurge, 2009, p. 241.
11. Charles Burney and David Marshall Lang, *The Peoples of the Hills: Ancient Ararat and the Caucasus*, Phoenix Press, London, 1971, p. 127. See also Amelie Kurht, *The Ancient Near East*, Routledge, London and New York, 1995, Vol. II, p. 550: 'Archaeologically, the second millennium of the region is something of a blank at present.'
12. Ibid., p.17.
13. Armen Asher and Teryl Minasian Asher, *The Peoples of Ararat*, op. cit.
14. Moses Khorenatsi, *History of the Armenians*, Caravan Books, Ann Arbor, 2006, pp. 72 and 82ff. Haik, also spelled Hayk, is said to be the son of Torgomah [T'orgom], who was the son of Tiras [T'iras], who was the son of Gomer [Gamer], who was the son of Noah's son Japheth [Yapeth].
15. Arra S. Avakian and Ara John Movsesian, *Armenia: A Journey Through History*, The Electric Press, California, 1998-2008, p. 47. See also Armen Asher and Teryl Minasian Asher, *The Peoples of Ararat*, op. cit., p. 284-5.
16. http://www.armenian-genocide.org/genocidefaq.html.
17. https://www.youtube.com/watch?v=ahoFlLh2Y3E.
18. https://www.youtube.com/all_comments?v=ahoFlLh2Y3E.
19. The quotation is from William Faulkner's *Requiem for a Nun*, 1951.
20. This was the flood that formed the channeled scablands of the Columbia Plateau. Cesare Emiliani, *Planet Earth: Cosmology, Geology and the*

Evolution of Life and Environment, Cambridge University Press, 1995, p. 543, researched the extent of the sea level rise involved: 'As a result of the flood that formed the Scabland, the sea level rose very rapidly from minus 100 metres to minus 80 metres. By 12,000 years ago more than fifty per cent of the ice had returned to the ocean, and the sea level had risen to minus 60 metres.' The references to minus 100 metres, minus 80 metres and minus 60 metres are by comparison with today's sea-level. So, before the flood that formed the scablands, sea level was 100 metres lower than it is today, after the flood it was 60 metres lower than it is today, i.e. a staggering rise of 40 metres or 131 feet.

21. Cesare Emiliani held a Ph.D from the University of Chicago where he pioneered the isotopic analysis of deep-sea sediments as a way to study the Earth's past climates. He then moved to the University of Miami where he continued his isotopic studies and led several expeditions at sea. He was the recipient of the Vega Medal from Sweden and the Agassiz medal from the National Academy of Sciences of the United States.

22. Emiliani, *Earth and Planetary Science Letters*, 41 (1978), p. 159, Elsevier Scientific Publishing Company, Amsterdam.

23. E.g. see Karl W. Luckert, *Stone Age Religion at Göbekli Tepe*, Triplehood, 2013, p. 101.

24. Joris Peters and Klaus Schmidt, 'Animals in the symbolic world of Pre-Pottery Neolithic Göbekli Tepe, south-eastern Turkey: a preliminary assessment', *Anthropozoologica*, 2004, 39 (1), pp. 204-5.

25. Karl W. Luckert, *Stone Age Religion at Göbekli Tepe*, op. cit., pp. 100-2.

26. Genesis 9: 1.

27. Joris Peters and Klaus Schmidt, 'Animals in the symbolic world of Pre-Pottery Neolithic Göbekli Tepe', op. cit., pp. 206-8.

28. Samuel Noah Kramer, *The Sumerians: Their History, Culture and Character*, The University Press of Chicago, 1963, p. 33.

29. http://www.penn.museum/collections/object/97591.

30. http://www.schoyencollection.com/literature-collection/sumerian-litera ture-collection/sumerian-flood-story-ms-3026.

31. Samuel Noah Kramer, *History Begins at Sumer*, University of Pennsylvania Press, 1991, p. 148ff.

32. Kramer, *History Begins at Sumer*, op. cit., p. 148.

33. http://www.penn.museum/collections/object/97591.

34. http://www.schoyencollection.com/literature-collection/sumerian-literature-collection/sumerian-flood-story-ms-3026.

35. Ibid., and see Irving Finkel, *The Ark Before Noah*, Hodder and Stoughton, London, 2014, p. 91.

36. Kramer, *History Begins at Sumer*, op. cit., p. 149.

37. Ibid., p. 149.

38. Ibid.; William Hallow, *Journal of Cuneiform Studies,* Vol. 23, 61, 1970.

39. Cited in Kramer, *History Begins at Sumer,* op. cit., pp. 149-51.

40. Ibid., p. 151.

41. Ibid.

42. http://www.schoyencollection.com/literature-collection/sumerian-litera ture-collection/sumerian-flood-story-ms-3026. And again see Irving Finkel, *The Ark Before Noah,* op. cit., p. 91.

43. Kramer, *History Begins at Sumer,* op. cit., p. 151.

44. Ibid., p. 152.

45. Ibid.

46. Ibid.

47. Ibid., pp. 152-3.

48. Ibid., p. 153.

49. Ibid., p. 148.

50. See discussion in Gerald P. Verbrugghe and John M. Wickersham (Eds.), *Berossos and Manetho,* University of Michigan Press, 1999, p. 15ff.

51. Benno Lansberger, 'Three Essays on the Sumerians II: The Beginnings of Civilisation in Mesopotamia', in Benno Lansberger, *Three Essays on the Sumerians,* Udena Publications, Los Angeles, p. 174; Berossos and Manetho, op. cit., pp. 17, 44; Stephanie Dalley, Myths from Mesopotamia, op. cit., pp. 182-3, 328; Jeremy Black and Anthony Green (Eds.), *Gods, Demons and Symbols of Mesopotamia,* British Museum Press, London, 1992, pp. 41, 82-83, 163-4.

52. Berossos and Manetho, op. cit., p. 43.

53. Ibid., p. 44.

54. George Smith, with A.H. Sayce, *The Chaldean Account of the Genesis,* Sampson Low, London, 1880, p. 33.

55. Berossos and Manetho, op. cit., pp. 26 and 34. See also George Smith, with A.H. Sayce, *The Chaldean Account of the Genesis,* op. cit p. 32.

56. Amar Annus, 'On the Origin of the Watchers: A comparative Study of the Antediluvian Wisdom in Mesopotamian and Jewish Traditions', *Journal of the Study of Pseudepigrapha,* Vol. 19.4 (2010), p. 285.

57. Ibid.

58. Ibid.

59. Ibid., e.g. pp. 282, 290, 297, 301, 306. See also Jonas C. Greenfield, 'The Seven Pillars of Wisdom (Prov 9:1): A Mistranslation', *The Jewish Quarterly Review,* New Series, Vol. 76, No. 1, Essays in Memory of Moshe Held (Jul., 1985), p. 16.

60. Ibid., p. 281: 'Many kinds of Mesopotamian sciences and technologies were ideologically conceived as originating with antediluvian apkallus'.

61. Erica Reiner, 'The Etiological Myth of the Seven Sages', *Orientalia* NS 30 (1961), p. 10.

62. Jonas C. Greenfield, 'The Seven Pillars of Wisdom' op. cit., p. 15.
63. Amar Annus, 'On the Origin of the Watchers', op. cit., p. 289.
64. Jonas C. Greenfield, 'The Seven Pillars of Wisdom', op. cit., p. 16.
65. Amar Annus, 'On the Origin of the Watchers', op. cit., p. 289.
66. Ibid., p. 283, See also: W.G. Lambert, 'Ancestors, Authors and Canonicity', *Journal of Cuneiform Studies*, Vol. 11, No. 1, 1957, pp. 8-9: 'The sum of revealed knowledge was given once and for all by the antediluvian sages.'
67. Jeremy Black and Anthony Green (Eds.), *Gods, Demons and Symbols of Mesopotamia*, op. cit., p. 46.
68. Amar Annus, 'On the Origin of the Watchers', op. cit., p. 293.
69. Jeremy Black and Anthony Green (Eds.), *Gods, Demons and Symbols of Mesopotamia*, op. cit., p. 46.
70. Ibid., p. 170.
71. Amar Annus, 'On the Origin of the Watchers', op. cit., p. 293.
72. Jeremy Black and Anthony Green (Eds.), *Gods, Demons and Symbols of Mesopotamia*, op. cit., p. 171.
73. Amar Annus, 'On the Origin of the Watchers', op. cit., p. 293.
74. Anne Draffkorn Kilmer, 'The Mesopotamian Counterparts of the Biblical Nepilim', in E.W Conrad and E.G. Newing (Eds.), *Perspectives on Language and Text: Essays and Poems in Honour of Francis I. Andersen's Sixtieth Birthday, July 28, 1985*, Winona Lake, IN, Eisenbrauns, p. 41. For Enki/Ea and the Abzu see Jeremy Black and Anthony Green (Eds.), *Gods, Demons and Symbols of Mesopotamia*, op. cit., pp. 75 and 27: 'It was anciently believed that the springs, wells, streams, rivers and lakes drew their water from and were replenished from a freshwater ocean which lay beneath the earth in the abzu (apsu) . . . The salt sea, on the other hand, surrounded the earth. The abzu was the particular realm and home of the wise god Enki . . . Enki was thought to have occupied the abzu since before the creation of mankind. According to the Babylonian Epic of Creation, Apsu was the name of a primal creature, the lover of Tiamat, and when Ea killed Apsu he set up his home on the dead creature's body, whose name was henceforth transferred to Ea's residence . . .'
75. Jeremy Black and Anthony Green (Eds.), *Gods, Demons and Symbols of Mesopotamia*, op. cit., p. 75.
76. S. Denning-Bolle, cites in Amar Annus, 'On the Origin of the Watchers', op. cit., p. 314.
77. Amar Annus, 'On the Origin of the Watchers', op. cit., p. 287.
78. Jeremy Black and Anthony Green (Eds.), *Gods, Demons and Symbols of Mesopotamia*, op. cit., p. 76.
79. Ibid., pp. 76 and 75: see also Gwendolyn Leick, *A Dictionary of Near Eastern Mythology*, Routledge, London and New York, 1998, pp. 4-6.

80. *The Epic of Gilgamesh*, Penguin Classics, London, 1988, p. 108.
81. E.g. see Jeremy Black and Anthony Green, *Gods, Demons and Symbols of Ancient Mesopotamia*, op. cit., p. 84.
82. Berossos and Manetho, op. cit., pp. 49-50. NB. In this fragment Berossos, preserved by Syncellus, Enki is rendered as 'Kronos'. The translators explain in footnote 17 that: 'Kronos was the father of Zeus, as Enki was the father of Marduk. Berossos or Syncellus here has used the Greek equivalent for the Babylonian god.'
83. In the Epic of Gilgamesh the flood survivor, though manifestly the same figure as Zisudra/Xithoutros, is known by the name of Utnapishti. As Irving Finkel, Assistant Keeper in the Department of the Middle East at the British Museum explains: 'The name Zisudra is very suitable for an immortal flood hero, since in Sumerian it means something like He-of-Long-Life. The name of the corresponding flood hero in the Gilgamesh epic is Utnapishti, of roughly similar meaning. In fact, we are not sure whether the Babylonian name is a translation of the Sumerian or vice versa.' Irving Finkel, *The Ark Before Noah*, op. cit., p. 92.
84. *The Epic of Gilgamesh*, op. cit., p. 111.
85. *Berossos and Manetho*, op. cit., p. 50.
86. Amar Annus, 'On the Origin of the Watchers', op. cit., p. 282; Anne Draffkorn Kilmer, 'The Mesopotamian Counterparts of the Biblical Nepilim', op. cit., p. 43.
87. Anne Draffkorn Kilmer, 'The Mesopotamian Counterparts of the Biblical Nepilim', op. cit., pp. 39-40.
88. Amar Annus, 'On the Origin of the Watchers', op. cit., p. 295.
89. Jeanette C. Fincke, The Babylonian Texts of Nineveh: Report on the British Museum's Library Project, *Archiv fur Orientforschung* 50 (2003/2004), p. 111.

Chapter 9

1. John Baines and Jaromir Malek, *Atlas of Ancient Egypt*, Time-Life Books, 1990, p. 76.
2. Ibid. The inner and outer enclosure walls date from the Old Kingdom, and a later wall running outside the outer one dates from the First Intermediate Period (2134-2040 BC). There are remains of other structures that have been dated to the Second Intermediate Period (1640-1532 BC) and to the New Kingdom (1550-1070 BC).
3. E.A.E. Reymond, *The Mythical Origin of the Egyptian Temple*, Manchester University Press, 1969, p. 8.
4. Ibid., p. 151: 'The mythological situation which we have been analyzing discloses a tradition which originated in another place . . .'

5. Ibid., pp. 55, 90, 105, 274.
6. Ibid., p. 55.
7. Ibid., pp. 109, 113-14, 127.
8. E.g. See p. 19 'the crew of the Falcon'. See also pp. 27, 177, 180, 181, 187, 202. There are repeated references throughout the Edfu texts to the crews of ships and to sailing. Thus, p. 180: 'The Shebtiw sailed . . .' p. 187: 'They were believed to have sailed to another part of the primeval world'.
9. Ibid., p. 190.
10. Ibid., p. 274: 'They journeyed through the unoccupied lands of the primeval age and founded other sacred domains'.
11. Ibid., p. 122.
12. Ibid., p. 134.
13. Ibid., pp. 106-7.
14. E.g. Ibid., pp. 44, 258: 'At Edfu we have only fragments. A selected number of accounts, from a great and important history of the Egyptian temples.'
15. The last known inscription in the sacred hieroglyphs of Ancient Egypt was made at the Temple of Isis at Philae in AD 394 and the last known example of demotic graffiti was also found there, dated to AD 425. 'If knowledge of the hieroglyphs persisted beyond this time, no record of it has been found.' John Anthony West, *The Traveller's Key to Ancient Egypt*, Harrap Columbus, London, 1987, p. 426.
16. Howard Vyse, *Operations Carried on at the Pyramids of Gizeh in 1837, with an Account of a Voyage into Upper Egypt*, James Fraser, Regent Street, London, 1840, Vol. I, pp. 67-8.
17. The Mesopotamian and Egyptian chronologies are well known. For Peru see Ruth Shady Solis et al, *Caral: The Oldest Civilization in the Americas*, Proyecto Especial Arqueologico Caral-Supe/INC, 2009.
18. Plato, *Timaeus and Critias*, Penguin Classics, 1977, p. 36.
19. Ibid., pp 34-8.
20. J. Gwynn Griffiths, *Atlantis and Egypt With Other Selected Essays*, Cardiff, University of Wales Press, 1991, pp. 3-30.
21. Miriam Lichtheim, *Ancient Egyptian Literature, Vol. I: the Old and Middle Kingdoms*, University of California Press, 1975, p. 211.
22. Ibid., pp. 212-13.
23. Ibid., p. 215, note 3.
24. Margaret Buson, *The Encyclopedia of Ancient Egypt*, Facts on File, New York, Oxford, 1991, p. 130.
25. Ibid.
26. Ibid.
27. Miriam Lichtheim, *Ancient Egyptian Literature*, op. cit., p. 213.
28. Ibid., p. 214.
29. Ibid.

30. Plato, Critias Benjamin Jowett Translation, Internet Classics Archive, http://classics.mit.edu/Plato/critias.html.

31. Plato, *Timaeus and Critias*, Penguin Classics Edition, op. cit., p. 38.

32. J. Gwynn Griffiths, *Atlantis and Egypt*, op. cit., p. 23.

33. https://egyptsites.wordpress.com/2009/03/03/sa-el-hagar/.

34. Ibid.

35. E.A.E. Reymond, *The Mythical Origin of the Egyptian Temple*, op. cit., p. 324.

36. Ibid., p. 213.

37. Ibid., p. 31.

38. Ibid., p. 111.

39. Ibid., p. 142.

40. Plato, *Timaeus and Critias*, op. cit., Critias, p. 136.

41. E.A.E. Reymond, *The Mythical Origin of the Egyptian Temple*, op. cit., p. 113.

42. Ibid., p. 109.

43. Ibid., p. 127.

44. Plato, *Timaeus and Critias*, op. cit., Timaeus, p. 38.

45. Ibid.

46. Ibid., p. 35.

47. E.A.E. Reymond, *The Mythical Origin of the Egyptian Temple*, op. cit., p. 19.

48. E.W. West, Trans., F. Max Muller, Ed., *Pahlavi Texts*, Part I, Reprint Edition, Atlantic Publishers and Distributors, New Delhi, 1990, p. 17.

49. E.A.E. Reymond, *The Mythical Origin of the Egyptian Temple*, op. cit., p. 113.

50. Ibid., p. 279.

51. Ibid., p. 113.

52. Ibid.

53. *Archaeoastronomy: The Journal of the Center for Archaeoastronomy*, Vol. VIII, Nos. 1-4, January-December 1985, p. 99.

54. Thor Conway in Ray A. Williamson and Claire R. Farrer, Eds., *Earth and Sky*, op. cit, p. 246.

55. Plato, *Timaeus and Critias*, op. cit., Timaeus, p. 38.

56. Ignatius Donnelly, *Atlantis: The Antediluvian World*, Dover Publications Inc., New York, 1976, p. 23.

57. Plato, *Timaeus and Critias*, op. cit., Timaeus, p. 37.

58. Plato, Critias Benjamin Jowett Translation, Internet Classics Archive, http://classics.mit.edu/Plato/critias.html.

59. Plato, *Timaeus and Critias*, op. cit., Critias, p. 138.

60. E.A.E. Reymond, *The Mythical Origin of the Egyptian Temple*, op. cit., p. 37.

61. Ibid., p. 220.

62. Ibid., p. 240.
63. Ibid., p. 198.
64. Ibid., p. 108.
65. Ibid.
66. Ibid., p. 109.
67. Ibid., pp. 202, 323-4.
68. Plato, *Timaeus and Critias*, op. cit., Timaeus, p. 38.
69. E.A.E. Reymond, *The Mythical Origin of the Egyptian Temple*, op. cit., p. 171: 'A *pāy*-land is said to have originated after the Creator dried up the water around his place of origin.' See also p. 172: 'The word *pāy*-land describes a land that emerged from the water . . .'
70. Ibid., p. 162.
71. Ibid., p. 173.
72. Ibid., p. 324.
73. Ibid., p. 194.
74. Ibid., p. 274.
75. Ibid., p. 187.
76. Ibid., p. 274.
77. Ibid., p. 190.
78. Ibid., p. 274.
79. Ibid., p. 190. See also p. 33.
80. Ibid., p. 33.
81. Ibid., p. 24: 'the *Shebtiw* whose function is described as *din iht*, to name (= create) the things'. See also p. 180.
82. Ibid., p. 41.
83. Ibid., p. 28.
84. Ibid., pp. 95, 96, 108, 110-11.
85. Ibid., p. 96.
86. Ibid., p. 91.
87. Ibid., p. 92.
88. Ibid.
89. Ibid., p. 25, 41, 289.
90. Ibid., p. 159.
91. Ibid., e.g. pp. 28, 66, 236.
92. Ibid., pp. 310-11.
93. Ibid., p. 9.
94. Ibid., p. 48.
95. Ibid., p. 273.
96. Plato, *Timaeus and Critias*, Penguin Classics, op. cit., Timaeus, p. 36.
97. Ibid.

1. Plato, *Laws* II, in John M. Cooper, Ed., *Plato: Complete Works*, Hackett Publishing Company, Indianapolis/Cambridge, 1997, p. 1348.
2. Graham Hancock, *Fingerprints of the Gods*, William Heinemann Ltd., London, 1995, e.g. p. 446 ff., pp. 456-8.
3. Robert Bauval and Adrian Gilbert, *The Orion Mystery*, William Heinemann Ltd., London, 1994.
4. Robert Bauval and Graham Hancock, *Keeper of Genesis*, William Heinemann Ltd., London, 1996.
5. Giorgio de Santillana and Hertha von Dechend, *Hamlet's Mill: An Essay Investigating the Origins of Human Knowledge and its Transmission through Myth*, Nonpareil Books, 1977, reprinted 1999, p. 59.
6. Graham Hancock and Santha Faiia, *Heaven's Mirror: Quest for the Lost Civilization*, Michael Joseph, London, 1998.
7. See ibid for an extensive discussion.
8. Paolo Debertolis, Goran Marjanovic, et al, *Archaeoacoustic analysis of the ancient site of Kanda (Macedonia)*, Proceedings in the Congress 'The 3rd Virtual International Conference on Advanced Research in Scientific Areas' (ARSA-2014) Slovakia, 1-5 December 2014: 237-251. Published by: EDIS-Publishing Institution of the University of Zilina, Univerzitná 1, 01026 Žilina, Slovak Republic. Paper available online here: https://www.academia.edu/9818666/Archaeoacoustic_analysis_of_the_ancient_site_of_Kanda_Macedonia_._Preliminary_results.
9. http://www.usbr.gov/lc/hooverdam/History/essays/artwork.html.
10. Ibid.
11. Ibid.
12. Richard Guy Wilson, 'American Modernism in the West: Hoover Dam.' *Images of an American Land*, ed., Thomas Carter. Albuquerque: University of New Mexico Press, 1997. P. 10, cited in, *The Hoover Dam: Lonely Lands Made Fruitful*, http://xroads.virginia.edu/~1930s/display/hoover/modern.html.
13. E.g. see: https://www.wisdomuniversity.org/ChartresOverview.htm: 'This is the magic and mystery of Chartres, site of the "queen of the cathedrals". This is also the power of "Astronomica", as it was known among the ancients, which marks the last and highest of the seven liberal arts, the oldest continuously developed learning system known to humanity, which emanated out of Ancient Egypt and was taken to its highest refinement by the Chartrian masters. Sacred astronomy is embedded in the stones and stained glass of Chartres cathedral. It was considered the highest of the liberal arts because it alone contemplates the entire cosmos and seeks to discern ultimate meaning and purpose to all of creation.'

14. See discussion in Graham Hancock, *Fingerprints of the Gods*, op. cit., Chapter 49, p. 443ff.
15. E.A.E. Reymond, *The Mythical Origin of the Egyptian Temple*, op. cit., p. 134, cited in Chapter Nine.
16. Michael A. Hoffman, *Egypt Before the Pharaohs*, Michael O'Mara Books Ltd., 1991, pp. 89-90. See also Karl W. Butzer, *Early Hydraulic Civilization in Egypt*, The University of Chicago Press, 1876, p. 9.
17. Graham Hancock, *Fingerprints of the Gods*, op. cit., Chapter 52, p. 497.
18. For a discussion of the geological dating of the Sphinx by Professor Robert Schoch of Boston University see ibid., Chapter 46, p. 420ff.
19. L. Liritzis, A. Vafiadou, 'Surface Luminescence Dating of Some Egyptian Monuments', *Journal of Cultural Heritage* 16 (2015), Table 1, p. 137.
20. Ibid., pp. 134-50.
21. Ibid., p. 134.
22. Ibid., pp. 134-50.
23. Ibid., Table 1, p. 137.
24. Ibid.
25. Personal communication from Professor Robert Schoch by email dated 20 January 2015.
26. L. Liritzis, A. Vafiadou, 'Surface Luminescence Dating of Some Egyptian Monuments', *Journal of Cultural Heritage*, op. cit., Table 1, p. 137.
27. Personal communication from Professor Robert Schoch by email dated 20 January 2015.
28. L. Liritzis, A. Vafiadou, 'Surface Luminescence Dating of Some Egyptian Monuments', *Journal of Cultural Heritage*, op. cit., Table 1, p. 137.
29. Ibid.
30. For example see John Baines and Jaromir Malek, *Atlas of Ancient Egypt*, Time-Life Books, 1990, p. 36.
31. L. Liritzis, A. Vafiadou, 'Surface Luminescence Dating of Some Egyptian Monuments', *Journal of Cultural Heritage*, op.cit., p. 147.
32. Ibid.
33. E.A.E. Reymond, *The Mythical Origin of the Egyptian Temple*, op. cit., p. 187.
34. Toby A.H. Wilkinson, *Early Dynastic Egypt*, Routledge, London and New York, 1999, p. 325.
35. E.A.E. Reymond, *The Mythical Origin of the Egyptian Temple*, op. cit. p. 262
36. Ibid., p. 263.
37. Ibid.
38. Ibid.
39. Ibid., p. 262.
40. Reymond (*The Mythical Origin of the Egyptian Temple*, op. cit., p. 263) eventually opts for Saqqara as her favoured candidate for 'the place to

the north of Memphis' where the book was believed to have descended from the sky. Her logic escapes me. Henen-nesut stands at latitude 29.08, Memphis at latitude 29.84, Saqqara at latitude 29.87, the Great Pyramid of Giza at latitude 29.98, and Dhashur at latitude 29.80. Since the higher the number the further north you are, it is obvious we must rule Henen-nesut and Dhashur out: the former is located 0.76 of a degree south of Memphis and the latter is located 0.04 of a degree south of Memphis. Saqqara is north of Memphis but by just 0.03 of a degree – so close as to be on almost exactly the same latitude. By contrast Giza is 0.14 of a degree north of Memphis and much more obviously fits the bill.

41. E.A. Wallace Budge, *The Gods of the Egyptians*, Methuen and Company, Chicago and London, 1904, reprinted by Dover Books, 1969, Vol. I, pp. 467, 468, 473, etc.
42. Selim Hassan, *The Sphinx: Its History in the Light of Recent Excavations*, Government Press, Cairo, 1949, p. 80.
43. See discussion in Robert Bauval and Graham Hancock, *Keeper of Genesis*, op. cit., pp. 5, 156ff, 160ff, etc.
44. Rainer Stadelman, 'The Great Sphinx of Giza', in Zahi Hawass (Ed), *Egyptology at the Dawn of the Twenty-first Century* (Proceedings of the Eighth International Congress of Egyptologists, Cairo, 2000; Vol. I: Archaeology), The American University in Cairo Press, Cairo, New York, 2002, pp. 464-9.
45. Ibid., p. 465.
46. Selim Hassan, *The Sphinx*, op. cit., p. 75.
47. Ibid., p. 75.
48. Ibid., p. 76.
49. Ibid., pp. 76, 185.
50. Ibid., p. 76.
51. James Henry Breasted, *Ancient Records Of Egypt*, University of Illinois Press, Urbana and Chicago, 2001, Vol. 2, p. 323.
52. Ibid.
53. Ibid., pp. 320, 324.
54. Selim Hassan, *The Sphinx*, op. cit., p. 76.
55. Gaston Maspero, *The Dawn of Civilization*, SPCK, London, 1894, p. 366.
56. Gaston Maspero, *A Manual of Egyptian Archaeology*, Putnam's Sons, New York, 1914, p. 74.
57. Selim Hassan, *The Sphinx*, op. cit., p. 222.
58. For a translation of the full text of the Inventory Stela see James Henry Breasted, *Ancient Records of Egypt*, op. cit., Vol. I, pp. 83-5. See also Selim Hassan, *The Sphinx*, op. cit., pp. 222-7.

59. Selim Hassan, *The Sphinx*, op. cit., p. 225.
60. http://www.guardians.net/hawass/khafre.htm.
61. http://en.wikipedia.org/wiki/Khafra#Valley_Temple.
62. The so-called 'Mortuary Temple' attributed to Khafre. Email from Professor Stephen Quirke to Graham Hancock dated 2 April 2015.
63. I.E.S. Edwards, *The Pyramids of Egypt*, Pelican Books, 1947, reprinted 1949, p. 107ff.
64. Ibid., p.109.
65. I.E.S. Edwards, *The Pyramids of Egypt*, Penguin, 1993, p. 124. Emphasis added.
66. Kathryn A. Bard (Ed.), *Encylopaedia of The Archaeology of Ancient Egypt*, Routledge, 1999, pp. 342-5.
67. Breasted, *Ancient Records of Egypt*, op. cit., Vol. II, pp. 320-1, note b.
68. Henri Frankfort, *Kingship and the Gods*, The University of Chicago Press, Chicago and London, 1948, 1978, p. 148.
69. William Matthew Flinders Petrie, *Memphis I, The Palace of Apries (Memphis II), Meydum and Memphis III*, Cambridge University Press, 2013, p. 43.
70. Selim Hassan, *The Sphinx*, op. cit., pp. 222-4.
71. Ibid., pp. 224-5.
72. Ibid., p. 223.
73. Ibid.
74. For example, Tibet. Tibetan *Thotchkas* are made from meteoritic iron: 'The word thokcha is composed of two words, *thog* meaning above, first or thunderbolt and *lcags* meaning iron or metal. The meaning of thokcha can thus be given as "first or original iron" or "thunderbolt iron"': http://en.wikipedia.org/wiki/Thokcha.
75. E.A.E. Reymond, *The Mythical Origin of the Egyptian Temple*, op. cit., p. 10.
76. Ibid., pp. 8-10, 18.

Chapter 11

1. Plato, *Timaeus and Critias*, Penguin Classics, op. cit., pp. 35-6.
2. E.A.E. Reymond, *The Mythical Origin of the Egyptian Temple*, op. cit., p. 285.
3. This notion is already accepted by some Egyptologists who have 'proposed that Predynastic and/or early dynastic material was cleared away in creating the pyramid platforms.' See Serena Love, 'Stones, ancestors and pyramids: investigating the pre-pyramid landscape of Memphis,' in Miroslav Barta (Ed), *The Old Kingdom Art and Archaeology, Proceedings of the Conference held in Prague, 31 May–4 June 2004*, Czech Institute of Egyptology, Prague, 2006, p. 216.

4. E.A.E. Reymond, *The Mythical Origin of the Egyptian Temple*, op. cit., p. 327.
5. Letter to Robert Bauval dated 27 January 1993, cited in Robert Bauval and Graham Hancock, *Keeper of Genesis*, op. cit., p. 200 and note 11, p. 333.
6. E.A.E. Reymond, *The Mythical Origin of the Egyptian Temple*, op. cit., p. 59.
7. Ibid., p. 9.
8. E.A. Wallis Budge, *Egyptian Magic*, Kegan Paul, Trench, Trubner and Co., London, 1901, reprinted by Dover Publications Inc., New York, 1971, p. 143.
9. Cited in John Greaves, *Pyramidographia: Or a Description of the Pyramids in Egypt*, George Badger, London, 1646, reprinted by Robert Lienhardt, Baltimore, p. 96.
10. Ibid.
11. Ibid.
12. Ibid.
13. I.E.S. Edwards, *The Pyramids of Egypt*, 1947 edition op. cit., p. 134.
14. Miriam Lichtheim, *Ancient Egyptian Literature*, Vol. I, op. cit., pp. 218-19.
15. I.E.S. Edwards, *The Pyramids of Egypt*, 1993 edition, op. cit., p. 286.
16. F.W. Green, *Journal of Egyptian Archaeology*, Vol. XVI, 1930, p. 33.
17. Alan H. Gardiner, *Journal of Egyptian Archaeology*, Vol. XI, 1925, pp. 2-5.
18. E.A.E. Reymond, *The Mythical Origin of the Egyptian Temple*, op. cit., p. 77.
19. Ibid., p. 112.
20. See discussion in Robert Bauval and Graham Hancock, *Keeper of Genesis*, op. cit., pp 13, 108, 192, 193-6.
21. R.A. Schwaller de Lubicz, *Sacred Science, Inner Traditions*, Rochester, Vermont, 1988, p. 104.
22. Ibid., p. 111.
23. Sir Walter Scott (Ed. and Trans.), *Hermetica*, Shabbhala, Boston, 1993, p. 343.
24. See discussion in Sylvia Cranston (Ed.), *Reincarnation: The Phoenix Fire Mystery*,Theosophical University Press, Pasadena, 1998, p. 114ff.
25. R.T. Rundle Clark, *The Origin of the Phoenix*, University of Birmingham Historical Journal (1949-1950), p. 17: 'The Benben stone and the Bennu bird must have names derived from the same root bn or wbn. Both words are derivative, so we cannot say that one is an attribute of the other. The bird and the stone – if stone it is – are linked together.'
26. Henri Frankfort, *Kingship and the Gods*, The University of Chicago Press, 1978, pp. 153-4.

27. See, for example, E.A. Wallis Budge, *An Egyptian Hieroglyphic Dictionary*, John Murray, London, 1920, reprinted by Dover Publications Inc., New York, 1978, Vol. I, p. 217.

28. Robert Bauval, *Discussions in Egyptology*, Vol. 14, 1989.

29. PT 1652, cited in R.T. Rundle Clark, *The Origin of the Phoenix*, op. cit., p. 14.

30. E.A. Wallis Budge, *An Egyptian Hieroglyphic Dictionary*, op. cit., Vol. I, p. 217.

31. R.T. Rundle Clark, *The Origin of the Phoenix*, op. cit., p. 15.

32. Ibid., p. 18.

33. Graham Hancock, *The Sign and the Seal: A Quest for the Lost Ark of the Covenant*, William Heinemann Ltd., London, 1992, pp. 67-9.

34. Menahem Haran, *Temples and Temple Service in Ancient Israel*, Clarendon Press, Oxford, Reprinted by Eisenbrauns, Winona Lake, Indiana, 1985, p. 246.

35. For a discussion see Emma Jung and Marie-Louise von Franz, *The Grail Legend*, Coventure, London, 1986, p. 148, footnote 28.

36. Jennifer Westwood (Ed.), *The Atlas of Mysterious Places*, Guild Publishing, London, 1987, p. 74.

37. Ibid.

38. W.H. Roscher, *Lexicon der griechischen und romischen Mythologie*, 1884, cited in Emma Jung and Marie-Louise von Franz, *The Grail Legend*, op. cit., p. 148.

39. See ibid., p. 14-16.

40. R. T. Rundle Clark, *Myth and Symbol in Ancient Egypt*, Thames and Hudson, London, 1991, pp 246-7.

41. Ibid.

42. Summary of Lactantius from Elmer G. Suhr, 'The Phoenix', *Folklore*, Vol. 87, No. 1 (1976), p. 30.

43. E.V.H. Kenealy cited in Sylvia Cranston (Ed.), *The Phoenix Fire Mystery*, op. cit., p. 18.

44. R.T. Rundle Clark, *The Origin of the Phoenix*, op. cit., p. 1; Elmer G. Suhr, 'The Phoenix', op. cit., p. 31; R. Van den Broek, *The Myth of the Phoenix According to Classical and Early Christian Traditions*, E.J. Brill, 1972, pp. 68-72.

45. R.T. Rundle Clark, *The Origin of the Phoenix*, op. cit., p. 1; Gerald Massey, *The Natural Genesis*, Vol. 2, Black Classic Press, Baltimore, 1998 (Reprint Edition) p. 340.

46. M.R. Niehoff, 'The Phoenix in Rabbinic Literature', *The Harvard Theological Review*, Vol. 89, No. 3 (Jul 1996), p. 252.

47. R. Van den Broek, *The Myth of the Phoenix According to Classical and Early Christian Traditions*, op. cit., p. 73.

48. See Graham Hancock, *Fingerprints of the Gods*, op. cit., Chapters 28 to 32.
49. Giorgio de Santillana and Hertha von Dechend, *Hamlet's Mill*, op. cit., p. 132.
50. R. Van den Broek, *The Myth of the Phoenix*, op. cit., pp. 73-4.

Chapter 12

1. Exactly who was responsible for the murders has still not, at time of writing, been satisfactorily established. Five senior members of Hezbollah, the Shia militant and political group, have been indicted by a UN tribunal. Hezbollah itself blames Israel for the assassination. In addition there are suspicions that President Bashar al-Assad of Syria was directly involved. See for example http://www.bbc.co.uk/news/world-middle-east-13972350 and http://www.bbc.co.uk/news/world-middle-east-25749185 and http://www.jpost.com/Middle-East/Special-Lebanon-Court-permits-prosecutor-to-bring-evidence-against-Assad-in-Hariri-case-381986 and http://www.thenational.ae/world/lebanon/probe-into-hariris-assassination-to-focus-on-al-assad.

2. Including a raid by Israeli commandos in 2006 – see: http://www.foxnews.com/story/2006/08/02/israeli-commandos-raid-hezbollah-hideout-in-baalbek-hospital/. And see also: http://www.reuters.com/article/2013/04/26/us-syria-crisis-hezbollah-idUSBRE93P09720130426. For the missile strike on Baalbek in June 2013 see: http://www.ynetnews.com/articles/0,7340, L-4386949,00.html and http://www.arabtoday.net/home/also-in-the-news/syrian-missiles-reach-lebanons-baalbek.html.

3. For the history of Solomon's Temple and subsequent constructions on the Temple Mount see Graham Hancock, *The Sign and the Seal*, op. cit., Chapter 14.

4. Andreas J.M. Kropp and Daniel Lohmann, "'Master, look at the size of those stones! Look at the size of those buildings." Analogies in Construction Techniques between the Temples of Heliopolis (Baalbek) and Jerusalem', in *Levant*, Vol. 43, No. 1 (2011), Council for British Research in the Levant, 2011, p. 42-3.

5. Dan Bahat, *Carta's Historical Atlas of Jerusalem*, Carta, Jerusalem, 1989, p. 30.

6. For a discussion see Graham Hancock, *The Sign and the Seal*, op. cit., Chapter Five, pp. 91-2.

7. Ibid., p. 95.

8. For video see: https://www.youtube.com/watch?v=LCFGjSgTz00 (from about 1 minute 30 seconds forward). For photographs, see: http://survincity.com/2012/07/megaliths-of-israel-the-foundation-of-the-temple/ and http://earthbeforeflood.com/megalithic_blocks_on_the_temple_mount_in_jerusalem.html.

9. Andreas J.M. Kropp and Daniel Lohmann, 'Master, look at the size of those stones!', op. cit.

10. Selim Hassan, *The Great Sphinx and its Secrets: Historical Studies in the Light of Recent Excavations* (*Excavations at Giza 1936-1937*, Vol. VIII), Government Press, Cairo, p. 267.

11. See, for example, ibid., pp. 264-6.

12. Ibid. p. 49.

13. Ibid.

14. Ibid., p. 256.

15. Ibid.

16. Christiane Zivie-Coche, 'Foreign Deities in Egypt', in Jacco Dielman, Willeke Wendrich (Eds.), *UCLA Encyclopedia of Egyptology*, Los Angeles, 2011, p. 5. NB: In the quotes passage Zivie-Coche uses Harmachis, the Graecianised form of the Ancient Egyptian Hor-em-Akhet but I have taken the liberty of rendering it simply as Hor-em-Akhet to avoid further confusing multiplication of names!

17. Ibid., p. 6.

18. N. Wyatt, *Religious Texts from Ugarit*, Sheffield Academic Press, 1998, p. 378 ff.

19. Jacobus Van Dijk, 'The Canaanite God Hauron and his Cult in Egypt', *GM* 107 (1989), p. 61. Paper presented at the Fourth International Congress of Egyptology, Munich, 26 Aug-1 Sept 1985. Pdf available here: http://www.jacobusvandijk.nl/docs/GM_107.pdf.

20. N. Wyatt, *Religious Texts from Ugarit*, op. cit., p. 385.

21. Ibid., p. 386.

22. Nina Jidejian, *Baalbek: Heliopolis, City of the Sun*, Dar el-Machreq Publishers, Beirut, 1975, p. 5. See also Michael M. Alouf, *History of Baalbek*, American Press, Beirut, 1951, p. 38, and Friedrich Ragette, *Baalbek*, Chatto & Windus, London, 1980, p. 16.

23. Christiane Zivie-Coche, 'Foreign Deities in Egypt', op. cit., pp. 2-4, and Figure 4. See also Selim Hassan, *The Great Sphinx and its Secrets: Historical Studies in the Light of Recent Excavations* (*Excavations at Giza 1936-1937*, Vol. VIII), op. cit., p. 278.

24. Friedrich Ragette, *Baalbek*, op. cit., p. 16.

25. See David Grene (Trans.), Herodotus, *The History*, Book 2, The University of Chicago Press, Chicago and London, 1987, p. 132 ff.

26. Friedrich Ragette, *Baalbek*, op. cit., p. 20.

27. Ibid.

28. Ibid., pp. 16-17, 72.

29. Cited in Michael M. Alouf, *History of Baalbek*, op. cit., p. 65.

30. Ibid.

31. Cited in Ibid., p. 66.

32. Friedrich Ragette, Baalbek, op. cit., p. 27.
33. Michael M. Alouf, *History of Baalbek*, op. cit., pp. 69-70.
34. Ibid., p. 71.
35. Ibid.
36. Ibid., pp. 71-2.
37. Ibid., p. 73.
38. Ibid., p. 74.
39. Dell Upton, 'Starting from Baalbek: Noah, Solomon, Saladin, and the Fluidity of Architectural History', *Journal of the American Society of Architectural Historians*, Vol. 68, No. 4 (December 2009), p. 458.
40. Michael M. Alouf, *History of Baalbek*, op. cit., p. 86.
41. See Dell Upton, 'Starting from Baalbek', op. cit., pp. 459-60: 'The sense that Baalbek was profoundly European, a product of the Roman culture upon which "the West" was grounded, moved into the scholarly literature when the German archaeological excavations of the first years of the twentieth century gave us the Baalbek we know today.'
42. See, for example, Margarete van Ess and Llaus Rheidt (Eds.), *Baalbek-Heliopolis 10.000 Jahre Stadtgeschichte* [*Baalbek-Heliopolis: 10,000 Year History of The City*], Zabern Philipp Von GmbH, 2014.
43. Margaret van Ess, 'First Results of the Archaeological Cleaning of the Deep Trench in the Great Courtyard of the Jupiter Sanctuary', in 'Baalbek/Heliopolis: Results of Archaeological and Architectural Research 2002-5', in *Bulletin d'Archaeoligie et d'Architecture Libanaises* (BAAL), Hors-Serie IV, Beirut, 2008, p. 113. See also Daniel Lohmann, 'Giant Strides Towards Monumentality: The Architecture of the Jupiter Sanctuary in Baalbek/Heliopolis', *Bolletino Di Archeologia On Line*, 2010, Volume special/Poster Session 2, p. 29: 'Tell Balbek . . . was continuously inhabited since the pre-pottery Neolithic period.'
44. Timothy Hogan, *Entering the Chain of Union: An Exploration of Esoteric Traditions and What Unites Them*, 2012, pp. 238-9, 242-5.
45. For the cult of Mercury at Baalbek, see Nina Jidejian, *Baalbek Heliopolis*, op. cit., pp. 28, 29, 30, 33, 36, 37, 45, 54-5. For the Thoth-Hermes connection see Garth Fowden, *The Egyptian Hermes*, Cambridge University Press, 1987, and Patrick Boylan, *Thoth: Hermes of Egypt*, Ares Publishers, Chicago, 1987.
46. Nina Jidejian, *Baalbek Heliopolis*, op. cit., p. 54.
47. Hartoune Kalayan, 'Notes on the Heritage of Baalbek and the Beka'a', op. cit., p. 53.
48. Nina Jidejian, *Baalbek Heliopolis*, p. 30.
49. A piece identified as a fragment from the north corner of the pediment of the Temple of Jupiter. I have seen the piece and do not dispute the weight of 360 tons given in Christian and Barbara Joy O'Brien, *The Shining Ones*, Dianthus Publishing Ltd., Cirencester, 2001, p. 272.

50. Michael M. Alouf, *History of Baalbek*, op. cit., pp. 85-6.
51. Ibid., p. 85.
52. Giorgio de Santillana and Hertha von Dechend, *Hamlet's Mill*, op. cit., p. 162.
53. Dimensions for length and height given by Daniel Lohmann in our later personal correspondence (email dated 8 Feb 2015) and see also Michael M. Alouf, *History of Baalbek*, op. cit., pp. 86-7 who gives the width and very slightly different dimensions for length and height.
54. I am grateful to architect and archaeologist Daniel Lohmann for explaining these details to me in our later personal correspondence (email dated 8 February 2015).
55. Dell Upton, 'Starting from Baalbek,' op. cit: 'Ancient written documentation is almost non-existent, and most of what has survived was written centuries after the construction of these buildings. There is absolutely no evidence, for example, to tell us who commissioned, paid for, or designed any portion of the complex.'
56. Daniel Lohmann describes the design and construction of the wall as 'megalomaniac' in 'Giant strides towards Monumentality,' op. cit., p. 28.
57. Andreas J.M. Kropp and Daniel Lohmann, 'Master look at the size of those stones!' op. cit., p. 38.
58. Ibid., p. 39.
59. Ibid.
60. Ibid, p. 38.
61. Ibid, p. 44.
62. Daniel Lohmann, 'Giant Strides Towards Monumentality', op.cit., p. 29.
63. Daniel Lohmann, 'Master look at the size of those stones', op.cit., p. 39.
64. Personal correspondence with Daniel Lohmann, email of 8 February 2015.
65. Jean-Pierre Adam, 'A propos du trilithon de Baalbek: Le transport et le mise en oeuvre des megaliths', *Syria*, T. 54 Fasc 1.2 (1977) p. 52.

Chapter 13

1. H. Kalayan, 'The Engraved Drawing on the Trilithon and the Related Problems About the Constructional History of the Baalbek Temples', *Bulletin du Musee de Beyrouth*, XXII (1969), p. 151.
2. Daniel Lohmann, 'Drafting and Designing: Roman Architectural Drawings and their Meaning for the Construction of Heliopolis/Baalbek, Lebanon', Proceedings of the Third International Congress on Construction History, Cottbus, May 2009.
3. Daniel Lohmann, 'Giant Strides Towards Monumentality: The Architecture of the Jupiter Sanctuary in Baalbek/Heliopolis', *Bolletino Di Archeologia On Line*, 2010, Volume special/Poster Session 2, p. 28.

4. http://dictionary.reference.com/browse/podium?s=t.

5. Ibid.

6. http://dictionary.reference.com/browse/stereobate?s=t.

7. Ibid.

8. http://en.wikipedia.org/wiki/Crepidoma.

9. Personal correspondence with Daniel Lohmann, email of 9 February 2015: 'the Romans were rather pragmatic . . .'

10. H. Kalayan, 'The Engraved Drawing on the Trilithon and the Related Problems', op. cit., pp. 151-2.

11. http://www.jasoncolavito.com/blog/ancient-astronauts-at-baalbek. For his claim to be a debunker of fringe science and revisionist history see Jason Colavito's biography, here: http://www.jasoncolavito.com/biography.html.

12. https://gilgamesh42.wordpress.com/about/.

13. https://gilgamesh42.wordpress.com/2013/04/25/moving-the-stones-of-baalbek-the-wonders-of-roman-engineering/. Adair's whole argument is that below the three great stones of the Trilithon: 'are other impressive stones that act as a base for the Trilithon. While not as massive as the Trilithon stones these base structures each have a considerable mass. However below them was discovered a part of a drum to a column. The size of the drum corresponds to the columns used for the Jupiter temple, so this was likely a leftover or no longer useful piece of one of those columns. Because it is underneath the base stones, this drum must have been placed there before the Trilithon was put into place. Also, on top of one of the Trilithon stones there is a drawing of the plans for the Temple of Jupiter, which was built over by the Romans when it was no longer needed. By having pieces of the Jupiter temple below the Trilithon and these drawings on top we can be reasonably certain that the Trilithon stones were put into place contemporaneously with the construction of the Temple of Jupiter. So already, by having the Trilithon stones contemporaneous with the temple we have established the Roman provenance of the structure.'

14. Michael Alouf, refers to this exact section of wall in his *History of Baalbek*, op. cit., originally published in July 1890, and reprinted multiple times through until 1951. On p. 98 where he describes the Trilithon ('No description will give an exact idea of the bewildering and stupefying effect of these tremendous blocks on the spectator') and then notes: 'Above these blocks are the Arab fortifications built, as has already been said, of bases of columns, sculptured friezes and fallen fragments, still bearing an inscription dating to the time of Bahram Shah.'

15. Friedrich Ragette, Baalbek, Chatto & Windus, London, 1980, pp. 32-3.

16. E.g. as well as the above detailed in note 8, see Michael Alouf, *History of Baalbek*, op. cit., p. 85, and Nine Jidejian, *Baalbek Heliopolis*, p. 36.

17. Michael Alouf, *History of Baalbek*, op. cit., p. 86.
18. For the close identification of the Phoenicians with the Canaanites see Gerard Herm, *The Phoenicians*, Victor Gollancz Ltd., 1975 (Book Club Associates edition), p. 25.
19. Ibid., p. 83.
20. Before the Trojan war. See Harold W. Attridge and Robert A. Oden Jr., *Philo of Byblos: The Phoenician History*, The Catholic Biblical Quarterly Monograph Series 9, Washington DC, 1981, p. 4.
21. Ibid., pp. 1-3.
22. Ibid., p. 53.
23. Sabatino Moscati, *The World of the Phoenicians*, Cardinal/Sphere Books, 1973, p. 66.
24. E. Richmond Hodges (Ed.), *Cory's Ancient Fragments of the Phoenician, Carthaginian, Babylonian, Egyptian and other Authors*, Reeves and Turner, London, 1876, p. 13. Emphasis added.
25. Miriam Lichtheim, *Ancient Egyptian Literature*, Vol. III, University of California Press, Berkeley, Los Angeles, London, 1980, p. 148.
26. David Urquhart, *The Lebanon (Mount Souria): A History and a Diary*, Vol. 2, Thomas Cautley Newby, London, 1860, p. 369.
27. Dell Upton, 'Starting from Baalbek: Noah, Solomon, Saladin and the Fluidity of Architectural History,' *Journal of the Society of Archaeological Historians*, Vol. 68, No. 4 (December 2009), p. 461.
28. David Urquhart, *History and a Diary*, op. cit., p. 382.
29. Ibid., p. 371.
30. Ibid.
31. Ibid., pp. 370-3.
32. Ibid., p. 373.
33. Ibid., pp. 374-5.
34. Ibid., p. 377.
35. Ibid., pp. 376, 377, 378.
36. Ibid., p. 376.
37. The alleged 'tomb of Noah', Karak Nuh, can be seen within a mosque in the town of Zahle on the edge of the Bekaa Valley. The 'tomb' is 31.9 metres (105 feet) long, 2.7 metres (8.7 feet) wide and 0.98 metres (3.2 feet) high.
38. Cited in Michael Alouf, *History of Baalbek*, op. cit., pp. 39-40.
39. Ibid., p. 40.
40. Ibid., p. 41. The Arabic manuscript was 'found at Baalbek'.
41. Jean-Pierre Adam, 'A propos du trilithon de Baalbek: Le transport et la mise en oeuvre des mégaliths,' *Syria*, T. 54, Fase 1-2 (1977), p. 52.
42. Ibid., pp. 31-63.
43. Ibid., p. 54.
44. Ibid., p. 56.

45. Ibid., p. 61.
46. Ibid.
47. Ibid.
48. Friedrich Ragette, *Baalbek*, op. cit., pp. 114-19.
49. Ibid., p. 119.
50. See Christian and Barbara Joy O'Brien, *The Shining Ones*, Dianthus Publishing Ltd., London, Cirencester, 2001, p. 275.
51. Jean-Pierre Adam, '*A propos du trilithon*', op. cit., p. 62.
52. The upper surface of the southernmost block, where I sat in the shade as described at the beginning of this chapter, and on which the architectural drawing of the Temple of Jupiter pediment was found, is sufficiently clear of masonry to be sure of this. It is this upper surface, over the centre of mass, in which any hypothetical Lewis holes would have had to be made. Since there are no Lewis holes here, on the largest and heaviest of the three blocks, it is a reasonable assumption that there are none on the other two either.
53. See discussion in Graham Hancock and Robert Bauval, *Talisman: Sacred Cities, Secret Faith*, Penguin Books, London, 2005, pp. 302-5.
54. The weight of 1,250 tons for the Saint Petersburg megalith is given in Adam, *A propos du trilithon*, op. cit., p. 42. See also Ragette, *Baalbek*, op. cit., pp. 118-19.
55. Zecharia Sitchin, *The Stairway to Heaven*, Harper, London, 2007 (reprint edition), p. 241.
56. Ibid., pp. 235, 241.
57. Ibid., p. 310.
58. Elif Batuman, 'The Myth of the Megalith', *New Yorker*, 18 December 2004, http://www.newyorker.com/tech/elements/baalbek-myth-megalith.
59. Jean-Pierre Adam, '*A propos du trilithon*', op. cit., p. 52.
60. Erwin M. Ruprechtsberger, 'Von Steinbruch zum Jupitertempel von Heliopolis/Baalbek', *Linzer Archaeologische Forschungen* (1999) 30, 7-56.
61. German Archaeological Institute figures, http://www.dainst.org/pressemit teilung/-/asset_publisher/nZcCAiLqg1db/content/libanesisch-deutsches-forscherteam-entdeckt-weltweit-gro%C3%9Ften-antiken-steinblock-in-baalbek.
62. Personal correspondence with Daniel Lohmann, email sent from Daniel Lohmann to Graham Hancock, 8 February 2015.
63. Personal correspondence with Daniel Lohmann, email sent from Graham Hancock to Daniel Lohmann, 8 February 2015.
64. Personal correspondence with Daniel Lohmann, email sent from Daniel Lohmann to Graham Hancock, 9 February 2015.

65. http://www.panoramio.com/photo/46982253 and (back view): http://www.bc.edu/bc_org/avp/cas/fnart/arch/roman/carree02.jpg and a detailed view: http://www.maisoncarree.eu/wp-content/uploads/2012/07/1_1_1_5_DSCN 0047-650x487.jpg.
66. https://www.flickr.com/photos/97924400@N00/7421596468/.
67. Ibid.
68. Personal correspondence with Daniel Lohmann, email sent from Graham Hancock to Daniel Lohmann, 9 February 2015.
69. Ibid.
70. Personal correspondence with Daniel Lohmann, email sent from Daniel Lohmann to Graham Hancock, 13 February 2015.
71. Lohmann provided the following link to illustrate the point: http://www.unicaen.fr/cireve/rome/pdr_virtuel.php?virtuel=ultor&numero_image=0.
72. Personal correspondence with Daniel Lohmann, email sent from Daniel Lohmann to Graham Hancock, 13 February 2015.
73. Ibid.
74. Ibid.
75. The drawing, captioned 'Hossn Niha Tempelpodium, Profil', is from Daniel Krencker, Willy Zschietzschmann (Hrsg.), *Römische Tempel in Syrien nach Aufnahmen und Untersuchungen von Mitgliedern der deutschen Baalbekexpedition 1901–1904*, De Gruyter, Berlin/Leipzig, 1938, S. 122–34.
76. Personal correspondence with Daniel Lohmann, email sent from Daniel Lohmann to Graham Hancock, 13 February 2015.

Chapter 14

1. See Yosef Garfinkel, 'Neolithic and Eneolithic Byblos in Southern Levantine Context', in E.J. Peltenburg and Alexander Wasse, *Neolithic Revolution: New Perspectives on Southwest Asia in Light of Recent Discoveries on Cyprus (Levant Supplementary)*, Oxbow Books, 2004, p. 182.
2. The reader will recall from Chapter One that Professor Klaus Schmidt put the final abandonment and deliberate burying of Göbekli Tepe at 8200 BC.
3. Michael Dumper, Bruce E. Stanley (Eds.), *Cities of the Middle East and North Africa: A Historical Encyclopedia*, ABC-CLIO, 2006, p. 104.
4. Ibid.
5. Nina Jidejian, *Byblos Through the Ages*, Del El-Machreq Publishers, Beirut, 1971, p. 2.
6. Dell Upton, 'Starting from Baalbek: Noah, Solomon, Saladin, and the Fluidity

of Architectural History', *Journal of the American Society of Architectural Historians*, Vol. 68, No. 4 (December 2009), p. 457.

7. Ibid.

8. Nina Jidejian, *Baalbek: Heliopolis, City of the Sun*, Dar el-Machreq Publishers, Beirut, 1975, p. 17.

9. Dell Upton, 'Starting from Baalbek', op. cit., p. 458.

10. Ibid.

11. Daniel Lohmann, 'Giant Strides Towards Monumentality: The Architecture of the Jupiter Sanctuary in Baalbek/Heliopolis', *Bolletino Di Archeologia On Line*, 2010, p. 28.

12. See, for example, the discussion in James Bailey, *The God Kings and the Titans: The New World Ascendancy in Ancient Times*, Hodder & Stoughton, London, 1973, p. 36ff.

13. See discussion in E.A. Wallis Budge, *Osiris and the Egyptian Resurrection*, Dover Publications Inc., New York, 1973 (reprint edition), Vol. I,.

14. Ibid.

15. Ibid., p. 3.

16. Ibid., pp. 4-5.

17. Ibid., pp. 5-8.

18. Ibid., p. 93.

19. Selim Hassan, *Excavations at Giza*, Vol. VI, Part I, Government Press, Cairo, 1946, p. 11.

20. R.O. Faulkner (Trans. and Ed.), *The Ancient Egyptian Pyramid Texts*, Oxford University Press, 1969, Aris & Phillips reprint edition, Utterance 442, p. 147.

21. Ibid., Utterance 412, p. 135.

22. Ibid., Utterance 442, p. 147.

23. Selim Hassan, *Excavations at Giza*, Vol. VI, Part I, Government Press, Cairo, 1946, p. 45.

24. Ibid.

25. Francis Yates, *Giordano Bruno and the Hermetic Tradition*, The University of Chicago Press, Chicago and London, 1979, p. 49ff.

26. Tamara Green, *The City of the Moon God: Religious Traditions of Harran*, E.J. Brill, Leiden, New York, 1992, p. 3. The Sabians are mentioned three times in the Koran as a 'people of the book' – Koran 5:69 (http://www.usc.edu/org/cmje/religious-texts/quran/verses/005-qmt.php#005.069) is particularly clear, but see also Koran 2:62 (http://www.usc.edu/org/cmje/religious-texts/quran/verses/002-qmt.php#002.062), and Koran 22:17 (http://www.usc.edu/org/cmje/religious-texts/quran/verses/022-qmt.php#022.017).

27. Brian P. Copenhaver, *Hermetica: The Greek Corpus Hermeticum and the Latin Asclepius in a new English Translation with notes and introduction*,

Cambridge University Press, 1992. See also Sir Walter Scott (Ed. and Trans.), *Hermetica: The Ancient Greek and Latin Writings which contain Religious or Philosophic Teachings attributed to Hermes Trismegistus*, Shambhala, Boston, 1993.

28. Manfred Lurker, *An Illustrated Dictionary of The Gods and Symbols of Ancient Egypt*, Thames and Hudson, London, 1995, p. 121. See also Margaret Bunson, *The Encyclopedia of Ancient Egypt*, Facts on File, New York, Oxford, 1991, p. 264.

29. Michael Baigent, *From the Omens of Babylon: Astrology and Ancient Mesopotamia*, Arkana Penguin Books, London, 1994, p. 186.

30. Harold W. Attridge and Robert A. Oden Jr., *Philo of Byblos: The Phoenician History*, The Catholic Biblical Quarterly Monograph Series 9, Washington DC, 198, p. 29.

31. Nina Jidejian, *Byblos*, op. cit., p. 10.

32. Bahattin Celik, 'Karahan Tepe: A New Cultural Centre in the Urfa area of Turkey', *Documenta Praehistorica*, XXXVIII (2011), pp. 241-53.

33. Ibid., p. 242.

34. Giulio Magli, 'Sirius and the Project of the Megalithic Enclosures at Göbekli Tepe', http://arxiv.org/pdf/1307.8397.pdf, 2013. Magli's paper attracted considerable attention and was discussed in an article in *New Scientist* magazine, 'World's Oldest Temple Built to Worship the Dog Star', *New Scientist*, 16 August 2013, http://www.newscientist.com/article/mg21929303. 400-worlds-oldest-temple-built-to-worship-the-dog-star.html#.VOID7b CsXG8, and elsewhere, e.g. http://www.science20.com/science_20/gobekli_tepe_was_no_laughing_matter-120278.

35. Giulio Magli, 'Sirius and the Project of the Megalithic Enclosures at Göbekli Tepe', op. cit., p. 2.

36. Ibid.

37. Ibid.

38. Robert M. Schoch, *Forgotten Civilization*, Inner Traditions, Rochester, Vermont, 2012, pp. 54-5.

39. Andrew Collins, *Göbekli Tepe: Genesis of the Gods*, Bear & Co., Rochester, Vermont, 2014, p. 81ff.

40. De Lorenzis, A. and Orofino, V. (2015) 'New Possible Astronomic Alignments at the Megalithic Site of Göbekli Tepe, Turkey', *Archaeological Discovery*, 3, p. 40. doi: 10.4236/ad.2015.31005.

41. Ibid., pp. 40-50.

42. Juan Antonio Belmonte, 'Finding our Place in the Cosmos: The Role of Astronomy in Ancient Cultures,' *Journal of Cosmology*, Vol. 9, 2010, p. 2055.

43. Alexander A. Gurshtein, 'The Evolution of the Zodiac in the Context

of Ancient Oriental History', *Vistas in Astronomy*, Vol. 41, No. 4, 1998, p. 521.

44. Ibid. See also Alexander A. Gurshtein, 'The Origins of the Constellations', *American Scientist*, Vol. 85, No. 3 (May–June 1997), p. 268.

45. Michael A. Rappengluck, 'The Pleiades in the "Salle des Taureaux", Grotte de Lascaux. Does a Rock Picture in the Cave of Lascaux show the Open Star Cluster of the Pleiades at the Magdalenian Era (ca 15,300 BC)?' in C. Jashek and F. Atrio Barendela (Eds.), *Actas del IV Congresso de la SEAC*, Universidad de Salamanca, 1997, pp. 217-25.

46. Ibid.

47. Michael A. Rappengluck, 'Palaeolithic Timekeepers Looking at the Golden Gate of the Ecliptic', *Earth, Moon and Planets*, 85-86, 2001, p. 391.

48. Ibid.

49. Ibid., pp. 401-2.

50. http://freebook.fernglas-astronomie.de/?page_id=879. See also: http://www.analemma.de/jupisat.html. I emailed Michael Rappengluck on 17 February 2015 and received his confirmation on 18 February 2015 that he was indeed referring to the Hyades and the Pleiades when he wrote of the 'Golden Gate of the Ecliptic'. He added: 'In the case of the Pleiades and Hyades it is important to keep in mind that the moon can pass through both open clusters during his 18.36 draconic period: They are just ca. 5° away from the ecliptic indicating the lunar orbit with its extreme positions. That is why both open clusters had been recognised as very important and why this "gate" is unique.'

51. The moon's orbital plane is inclined to the ecliptic plane by only about 5.1 degrees. Its movements are therefore are confined quite closely to the plane of the ecliptic, and always within the zodiacal constellations.

52. Juan Antonio Belmonte, 'Finding our Place in the Cosmos', op. cit., p. 2054.

53. Ibid.

54. http://www.grahamhancock.com/forum/BurleyP1.php.

55. John Major Jenkins, *Maya Cosmogenesis*, 2012, Bear & Company, Rochester, Vermont, 1998, p. 113.

56. In Mayan mythology, for example – see ibid., p. 51ff and also, John Major Jenkins, *The 2012 Story*, Tarcher/Penguin, New York, 2009, p. 138ff. And in Inca mythology – see for example William Sullivan, *The Secret of the Incas*, Crown, New York, 1996, p. 30ff. And in for Germanic mythology: http://www.germanicmythology.com/ASTRONOMY/MilkyWay2.html.

Chapter 15

1. See Figures 4 and 5 here: http://www.grahamhancock.com/forum/BurleyP1. php.
2. Nick Kollerstrom, 'The Star Zodiac of Antiquity', *Culture and Cosmos*, Vol. 1, No. 2, Autumn/Winter 1997.
3. Giorgio de Santillana and Hertha von Dechend, *Hamlet's Mill*, Nonpareil, Boston, 1969, pp. 216-17.
4. E.C. Krupp, *In Search of Ancient Astronomies*, Chatto & Windus, London, 1979, pp. 199-200.
5. Email exchange with Paul Burley, 14 February to 17 February 2015.
6. Rupert Gleadow, *The Origin of the Zodiac*, Dover Publications Inc., 2001, p. 167.
7. See discussion by Kathryn Slanski, 'Classification, Historiography and Monumental Authority: The Babylonian Entitlement Narus (Kudurrus),' *Journal of Cuneiform Studies* 52 (2000), pp. 95-114. E.g. p. 114: 'Recategorizing the *Kudurrus* as monuments standing in association with the temple, rather than as boundary markers out in the fields, provides a context that makes these objects and their material, textual and iconographic aspects intelligible in relation to their function.'
8. Rupert Gleadow, *The Origin of the Zodiac*, op. cit., p. 167.
9. See here, for example: http://en.wikipedia.org/wiki/Nebuchadnezzar_ I#mediaviewer/File:Nabu-Kudurri-Usur.jpg.
10. Rupert Gleadow, *The Origin of the Zodiac*, op. cit, p. 167.
11. Giulio Magli, 'Sirius and the Project of the Megalithic Enclosures at Göbekli Tepe', http://arxiv.org/pdf/1307.8397.pdf, 2013.
12. Some photographs and further description can be found here: http://travel toeat.com/babylonian-kudurru-at-the-louvre-2/. See also Jeremy Black and Anthony Green, *Gods, Demons and Symbols of Ancient Mesopotamia: An Illustrated Dictionary*, British Museum Press, London, 1992, pp. 16-17, 113-14.
13. John Major Jenkins, *Maya Cosmogenesis*, 2012, Bear & Company, Rochester, Vermont, 1998, p. 111; John Major Jenkins, *Galactic Alignment*, Bear & Company, Rochester, Vermont, 2002, p. 19.
14. John Major Jenkins, *Maya Cosmogenesis*, op. cit., p. 107.
15. Graham Hancock, *Fingerprints of the Gods*, op. cit. See, in particular, Chapter 21, 'A Computer For Calculating The End of the World'.
16. Ibid., p. 105.
17. The most accurate figures are in Andrew Collins, *Göbekli Tepe, Genesis of the Gods*, Bear & Co., Rochester, Vermont, 2014, pp. 78-9. These figures are also used by A. De Lorenzis and V. Orofino (2015) 'New Possible Astronomic Alignments at the Megalithic Site of Göbekli Tepe, Turkey', *Archaeological Discovery*, 3, p. 40. doi: 10.4236/ad.2015.31005.

1. Kay Prag, 'The 1959 Deep Sounding at Harran in Turkey', *Levant* 2 (1970), pp. 71-2. 'That the site was occupied at an early date is certain.' Limited archaeology, however, so far supports this with only one item, a piece of Samarra Ware style pottery, circa 5000 BC found in a deep sounding of the ancient Tell of Harran.

2. Seton Lloyd and William Brice, 'Harran', *Anatolian Studies*, Vol. I (1951), p. 87.

3. Selim Hassan, *Excavations at Giza*, Vol. VI, Part I, Government Press, Cairo, 1946, p. 45.

4. The hieroglyphic inscription dated to AD 394 is in the Temple of Isis at Philae. The last known example of demotic graffiti is dated 425 AD. 'If knowledge of the hieroglyphs persisted beyond this time, no record of it has been found.' John Anthony West, *The Traveller's Key to Ancient Egypt*, Harrap Columbus, London, 1987, p. 426. Kurt Sethe's translation of the Pyramid Texts, in which the stellar cult around the Pyramids is made clear, was published in 1910; Breasted incorporated many quotations from Sethe's text in his *Development of Religion and Thought in Ancient Egypt*; R.O. Faulkner's definitive edition of the Pyramid Texts was not published until 1969. See discussion in R.O. Faulkner, *The Ancient Egyptian Pyramid Texts*, Oxford University Press, 1969, p. v.

5. http://jqjacobs.net/blog/gobekli_tepe.html.

6. Tamara Green, *The City of the Moon God: Religious Traditions of Harran*, E.J. Brill, Leiden, New York, 1992, p. 25.

7. Ibid., p. 52.

8. Ibid., p. 21.

9. Ibid.

10. Ibid., pp. 97, 121.

11. Ibid., pp. 95-7.

12. Ibid., p. 100.

13. Archaeologists excavating the Hoyuk – mound or tumulus – of Harran in 1985 felt confident they were 'near the temple of the god Sin' but I have been unable to find any subsequent reports of actual discoveries of its remains. See M. Olus Arik et al, 'Recent Archaeological Research in Turkey', *Anatolian Studies*, Vol. 36 (1986), p. 194.

14. See Michael Baigent, *From the Omens of Babylon: Astrology and Ancient Mesopotamia*, Arkana, London, 1994, p. 189. See also Lawrence E. Stager, 'The Harran Project' (University of Chicago): http://oi.uchicago.edu/sites/oi.uchicago.edu/files/uploads/shared/docs/ar/81-90/82-83/82-83_Harran.pdf.

15. See, for example, *Hurriyet Daily News*, 26 July 2012: http://www.hurriyetdailynews.com/harran-rises-once-more-with-dig.aspx?pageID=238&nID=

26318; and 4 September 2012: http://www.hurriyetdailynews.com/ancient-bath-remains-found-in-harran.aspx?pageID=238&nID=71288&NewsCatID=375; and: 7 December 2012: http://www.hurriyetdailynews.com/roman-traces-found-in-harran.aspx?pageID=238&nID=36271&NewsCatID=375.

16. Kay Prag, 'The 1959 Deep Sounding at Harran in Turkey', op. cit., pp. 71-2.

17. Seton Lloyd and William Brice, 'Harran', op. cit., p. 110.

18. *City of Civilizations, Harran*, T.C. Harran Kaymakamligi (official publication of the Government of Harran), p. 5.

19. Tamara Green, *The City of the Moon God*, op. cit., p. 183-4. See also Sir Walter Scott (Ed. and Trans.), *Hermetica: The Ancient Greek and Latin Writings which contain Religious or Philosophic Teachings attributed to Hermes Trismegistus*, Shambhala, Boston, 1993, p. 101. The description of Enoch as 'the seventh from Adam' is found in Jude 1:14. And see Genesis 5: 1-32, 'The Book of the Generations of Adam'. The ten patriarchs listed are Adam, Seth, Enos, Cainan, Mahalaleel, Jared, Enoch, Methusaleh, Lamech, Noah (https://www.biblegateway.com/passage/?search=Genesis+5&version=KJV). There is frequently confusion between Enos, the third patriarch and Enoch the seventh patriarch. However no special intelligence, skills or qualities are attributed to Enos whereas, by contrast, Enoch 'walked with God' (Genesis 5: 24) and mysteriously vanished from the Earth 'for God took him' (Genesis 5: 24). The Book of Hebrews elaborates (Hebrews 11: 5): 'By faith Enoch was taken away so that he did not see death, "and was not found, because God had taken him"; for before he was taken he had this testimony, that he pleased God.'

20. Genesis 5: 19-30.

21. E.g. see Tamara Green, *The City of the Moon God*, op. cit., p. 170.

22. Cited in ibid., p. 137.

23. Cited in ibid., p. 138.

24. Selim Hassan, *Excavations at Giza*, Vol. VI, Part I, op. cit., p. 45. It is noteworthy that while much learned speculation is reported by Tamara Green in her authoritative monograph, *The City of the Moon God*, op. cit., pp. 106, 117, etc, etc, concerning the origin of the name Sabian she seems unaware of the elegant solution proposed by Selim Hassan.

25. Genesis 5: 24. See also Hebrews 11: 5: 'By faith Enoch was taken away so that he did not see death, "and was not found, because God had taken him"; for before he was taken he had this testimony, that he pleased God.'

26. Around the third to second centuries BC. See R.H. Charles (Trans.), *The Book of Enoch*, SPCK, London, 1987, Introduction, p. xiii.

27. I write extensively about James Bruce, and about his travels and adventures in Ethiopia, in my book *The Sign and the Seal: A Quest for the Lost Ark of the Covenant*, Heinemann, London, 1992.

28. H.F.D. Sparks (Ed.), *The Apocryphal Old Testament*, Clarendon Paperbacks, Oxford, 1989, p. 170: 'Among the Ethiopia manuscripts that Bruce brought back were three containing what is now known as "1 Enoch" or "Ethiopian Enoch". One of these manuscripts (now in the Bodleian Library at Oxford) contained "1 Enoch" only; the second (also in the Bodleian) contained "1 Enoch" followed by Job, Isaiah, "The Twelve", Proverbs, Wisdom, Ecclesiastes, Canticles and Daniel; the third (now in the Bibliotheque Nationale in Paris) is a transcript of the second.'

29. Kenneth Mackenzie, *The Royal Masonic Cyclopaedia*, first published 1877, Aquarian Press reprint edition, 1987, p. 201.

30. Ibid.

31. Ibid., p. 202.

32. Ibid., e.g. pp. 40, 114, etc.

33. R.H. Charles (Trans.), *The Book of Enoch*, op. cit., p. 37.

34. Ibid.

35. Ibid.

36. Ibid., p. 31.

37. Ibid., pp. 35, 37, 89, etc.

38. Ibid., pp. 35-6.

39. Ibid., p. 39.

40. Ibid., p. 40.

41. Ibid., p. 39.

42. Ibid.

43. Ibid.

44. Ibid., pp. 34-5.

45. Ibid., p. 46.

46. Ibid.

47. Ibid., p. 40.

48. Ibid.

49. Graham Hancock, *Supernatural: Meetings with the Ancient Teachers of Mankind*, Century, London, 2005.

50. It is notable in later chapters of the Book of Enoch, after the bad Watchers have been admonished and received their punishment, that the good Watchers reveal to Enoch a great many of the secrets, notably astronomical lore, that the bad Watchers were condemned for revealing. See, for example, R.H. Charles (Trans.), *The Book of Enoch*, op. cit., Chapter 41, p. 60ff, Chapter 71, p. 93ff, Chapter 72, p. 95 ff, etc, etc. Perhaps it is because he comes into possession of this restricted knowledge himself that Enoch ultimately vanishes from the earth – 'taken away by God' as the Bible has it in Genesis 5: 24.

51. R.H. Charles (Trans.), *The Book of Enoch*, op. cit., p. 35.

52. E.g. see closing paragraphs of this article: http://www.dailymail.co.uk/news/

article-2513866/A-GI-Christmas-How-American-soldiers-bearing-gifts-extra-rations-proved-festive-hit-British-families-WWII.html.

53. R.H. Charles (Trans.), *The Book of Enoch*, op. cit., p. 37.
54. Ibid., p. 34.
55. Ibid., p. 36.
56. Ibid., p. 35.
57. Ibid.
58. Ibid., p. 36.
59. Ibid., p. 37.
60. Ibid.
61. Ibid.
62. Genesis 6: 4, King James Version.
63. Genesis 6: 4, New International Version.
64. Genesis 6: 5-8, New International Version. The King James Version reads as follows: 'And God saw that the wickedness of man was great in the earth, and that every imagination of the thoughts of his heart was only evil continually. And it repented the Lord that he had made man on the earth, and it grieved him at his heart. And the Lord said, I will destroy man whom I have created from the face of the earth; both man, and beast, and the creeping thing, and the fowls of the air; for it repenteth me that I have made them. But Noah found grace in the eyes of the Lord.'
65. Zecharia Sitchin, *The 12th Planet*, Harper, New York, 1976, reprinted 2007, p. 171. To be fair, Sitchin is not alone in making this mistake. A number of genuine Biblical scholars make it also. Writing in The *Jewish Quarterly Review* in 1985, for example, Jonas C. Greenfield describes the Nephilim as 'fallen angels' (Jonas C. Greenfield, 'The Seven Pillars of Wisdom', *The Jewish Quarterly Review*, New Series, Vol. 26, No. 1, p. 19). Likewise in a paper in the *Journal of Biblical Literature* published in 1987, Ronald S. Hendel tells us: 'Nephilim literally means "the fallen ones" . . . It is a . . . passive adjectival formation of the root *npl* ("to fall") . . . Similar uses of the verb *napal* and its derivatives are found elsewhere in the Hebrew Bible' (Ronald S. Hendel, 'Of Demigods and the Deluge: Toward an Interpretation of Genesis 6: 1-4', *Journal of Biblical Literature*, Vol. 106, No. 1, March 1987, p. 22).
66. http://www.sitchiniswrong.com/nephilim/nephilim.htm.
67. Numbers 13: 32-3.
68. http://www.sitchiniswrong.com/nephilim/nephilim.htm.
69. Ibid.
70. Zecharia Sitchin, *The 12th Planet*, op. cit., p. 257.
71. Ibid., p. 172.
72. Ibid., p. 267.
73. R.H. Charles (Trans.), *The Book of Enoch*, op. cit.

74. Ibid., for example, 7: 2 and 7: 4, p. 35; 9:9, p. 36; 15:3, p. 42.

75. Michael A. Knibb (Ed.), *The Book of Enoch: A New Edition in the Light of the Aramaic Dead Sea Fragments*, Oxford University Press, 1979.

76. George W.E. Nickelsburg and James C. VanderKamm, *1 Enoch: The Hermenia Translation*, Augusburg Fortress, Minneapolis, 2012.

77. R.H. Charles (Trans.), *The Book of Enoch*, op. cit., p. 36.

78. http://clavisjournal.com/the-shadow-of-harran/.

79. Luke 3: 36.

80. R.H. Charles, *The Book of Jubilees*, SPCK, London, 1927, pp. 71-2.

81. http://jqjacobs.net/blog/gobekli_tepe.html.

82. As demonstrated in Peter Tompkins, *Secrets of the Great Pyramid*, Harper & Row, New York and London, 1978, pp. 101-3.

83. Einar Palsson, *The Sacred Triangle of Pagan Iceland*, Mimir, Reykjavik, 1993, p. 32.

84. Ibid.

85. Giorgio de Santillana and Hertha von Dechend, *Hamlet's Mill: An Essay Investigating the Origins of Human Knowledge and its Transmission through Myth*, Nonpareil Books, 1977, reprinted 1999, p. 132.

86. The detailed workings can be found in Graham Hancock, *Fingerprints of the Gods*, William Heinemann & Co., London, 1995, pp. 434-6.

87. Tamara Green, *The City of the Moon God*, op. cit., p. 19.

88. http://jqjacobs.net/blog/gobekli_tepe.html.

89. Ibid.

90. Ibid.

91. Ibid.

92. AD 850 to AD 929 – http://www-history.mcs.st-andrews.ac.uk/Biographies/Al-Battani.html.

93. Nicholas Kollerstrom, 'The Star Temples of Harran', in Annabella Kitson (Ed.), *History and Astrology: Clio and Urania Confer*, Unwin, London, 1989, p. 57.

94. http://www-history.mcs.st-andrews.ac.uk/Biographies/Al-Battani.html.

95. http://www.physics.csbsju.edu/astro/newcomb/II.6.html.

96. http://www-history.mcs.st-andrews.ac.uk/Biographies/Al-Battani.html.

97. Ibid. citing Y. Maeyama, 'Determination of the Sun's orbit (Hipparchus, Ptolemy, al-Battani, Copernicus, Tycho Brahe)', *Arch. Hist. Exact Sci.* 53 (1) (1998), 1-49.

98. http://www-history.mcs.st-andrews.ac.uk/Biographies/Al-Battani.html.

99. *Complete Dictionary of Scientific Biography* (2008), cited in http://www.encyclopedia.com/doc/1G2-2830900300.html.

100. Cited in Walter Scott, *Hermetica*, op. cit., p. 105.

101. Tamara Green, *The City of the Moon God*, op. cit., p. 114.

102. Ibid., p. 12.

103. Ibid., p. 114.

104. Walter Scott, *Hermetica*, op. cit., pp. 97-9.

105. I describe Ma'mun's exploration of the Great Pyramid at some length in *Fingerprints of the Gods*, op. cit., pp. 296-9.

106. Peter Tompkins, *Secrets of the Great Pyramid*, op. cit., p. 5.

107. Ibid., p. 6.

108. For possible Mandean connections with the Sabians see, for example, Tamara Green, *The Temple of the Moon God*, op. cit., pp. 103, 119, 194-5, 205 ff.

109. 'The fact that the Harranian Pagans, when required to name a Scripture, chose the Hermetica, proves that in AD 830 a collection of Hermetica was known and read in Syria . . . It may be inferred from the occurrence of the names Tat, Asclepius, and Ammon in conjunction with that of Hermes in Arabic writings, that these Harranians had in their possession Hermetic *libelli* in which the pupils were so named; and among these were presumably some that are now lost, as well as those which have come down to us. In the ninth century, Hermetic documents were most likely known to some scholars at Harran in the original Greek; but the Hermetica had probably been translated into Syriac long before that time, and were doubtless usually read in Syriac by Harranians . . .' Walter Scott, *Hermetica*, op. cit., pp. 101-2.

110. Frances A. Yates, *Giordano Bruno and the Hermetic Tradition*, University of Chicago Press, Chicago and London, 1964, reprinted 1979, pp. 12-13.

111. Ibid., p. 13.

112. This is the primary thesis of my book *Talisman*, co-authored with Robert Bauval. See Graham Hancock and Robert Bauval, *Talisman: Sacred Cities, Secret Faith*, Penguin Books, London, 2005.

113. Amar Annus, 'On the Origin of Watchers: A Comparative Study of the Antediluvian Wisdom in Mesopotamian and Jewish Traditions', *Journal for the Study of Pseudoepigrapha*, Vol. 19. 4 (2010), p. 283.

114. Ibid., p. 291.

115. Ibid., p. 280-1.

116. See, for example, ibid., pp. 277-320, and Anne Draffkorn Kilmer, 'The Mesopotamian Counterparts of the Biblical Nepilim,' in E.W. Conrad and E.G. Newing (Eds.), *Perspectives on Language and Text: Essays and Poems on Honor of Francis I Andersen's Sixtieth Birthday*, Eisenbrauns, Winina Lake Indiana, 28 July 1985, pp. 39-44. Likewise there are references to the Watchers in the Ancient Egyptian Pyramid Texts. See for example, R.O. Faulkner (Ed. and Trans.) *The Ancient Egyptian Pyramid Texts*, Oxford University Press, 1969, Reprinted by Aris & Phillips Ltd. See, for example Utterance 373, p. 124 and Utterance 667A, p. 281.

117. Klaus Schmidt, *Göbekli Tepe: A Stone Age Sanctuary in South-Eastern Anatolia*, Ex Orient e.V., Berlin, Germany, 2012, p. 191.

Chapter 17

1. Graham Hancock, *Fingerprints of the Gods*, William Heinemann Ltd., London, 1995, p. 51.
2. Graham Hancock and Santha Faiia, *Heaven's Mirror*, Michael Joseph, London, 1998, p. 288.
3. J. Alden Mason, *The Ancient Civilizations of Peru*, Penguin Books, London, 1991, p. 163: 'It was formerly believed that the megalithic masonry, employing immense stones of irregular size and shape was pre-Inca in age . . . while masonry of stone blocks of relatively uniform size, laid in courses, was typical of the Inca. But it is now generally agreed that both types were built by the Inca, and that all the great masonry edifices and structures in the Cuzco region, including Sacsayhuaman, Ollantaytambo, Machu Picchu and Cuzco'.
4. John Hemming, *The Conquest of the Incas*, Macmillan London Ltd., 1993, p. 191.
5. J. Alden Mason, *The Ancient Civilizations of Peru*, Penguin Books, London, 1991, p. 163. See also http://www.roughguides.com/destinations/south-america/peru/Cuzco-and-around/inca-sites-near-Cuzco/sacsayhuaman/ and http://www.andeantravelweb.com/peru/destinations/Cuzco/sacsay huaman.html and http://www.world-mysteries.com/mpl_9.htm and http:// gosouthamerica.about.com/od/perucuzco/ig/Sacsayhuaman-/ Sacsayhuaman-Rock-Wall.htm#step-heading.
6. For full details see Jesus Gamarra's documentary *The Cosmogony of the Three Worlds*, http://www.ancient-mysteries-explained.com/archaeology-proofs.html#dvd.
7. http://www.bbc.co.uk/news/science-environment-31664162.
8. A. Kruzer, 'The Question of the Material Origin of the Walls of the Saqsaywaman Fortress', http://isida-project.ucoz.com/publ/my_articles/ peru/the_question_of_the_material_origin_of_the_saqsaywaman_. fortress/2-1-0-2.
9. Ibid.
10. Ibid.
11. Sir Clements Markham, *The Incas of Peru*, Smith, Elder & Co., London, 1911, p. 33.
12. Garcilaso de La Vega, *The Royal Commentaries of the Inca Garcilaso de La Vega, 1539-1616*, The Orion Press, 1961, pp. 233, 235.
13. Graham Hancock and Santha Faiia, *Heaven's Mirror*, op. cit., pp. 285-6.

14. See Graham Hancock and Robert Bauval, *Keeper of Genesis*, William Heinemann Ltd., London, 1996.
15. Peter Frost, *Exploring Cuzco*, Nuevas Imagenes, Lima, Peru, 1989, p. 63.
16. William Sullivan, *The Secret of the Incas*, Crown, New York, 1996, p. 118.
17. Ibid., p. 119.
18. Garcilaso de La Vega, *The Royal Commentaries*, op. cit., pp. 4-5.
19. Ibid., pp. 5-6.
20. The cave is known locally as *Naupa Iglesia*. In Quechua, the Inca language, *Naupa* means ancient while *Iglesia* is Spanish for church – thus 'ancient church'. Of course there is nothing of a church about it, but that it is an ancient sacred place, an ancient shrine, is not in doubt. See here for a mainstream interpretation: http://elcomercio.pe/peru/lima/naupa-iglesia-merece-revalorizado-segun-especialistas-noticia-1519677.
21. http://casadelcorregidor.pe/colaboraciones/_biblio_Tantalean.php.
22. Ibid.
23. Bolivia Detects Buries Pyramid at Tiahuanaco Site, http://barbaricum.net/news/23346892542865578 40 and http://latino.foxnews.com/latino/enter tainment/2015/03/27/bolivia-detects-buried-pyramid-at-tiahuanaco-site/.
24. Constantino Manuel Torres, David B. Repke, *Anadanenthera: Visionary Plant of Ancient South America*, The Haworth Herbal Press, New York, London, 2006, p. 35 ff.
25. See, for example, Martti Pärssinen, Denise Schaan and Alceu Ranzi (2009). 'Pre-Columbian geometric earthworks in the upper Purús: a complex society in western Amazonia', *Antiquity*, 83, pp. 1084-95; and Ranzi et al, 'Internet software programs aid in search for Amazonian geoglyphs', *Eos*, Vol. 88, No. 21, 22 May 2007, pp. 226, 229; and Carson et al, 'Environmental impact of geometric earthwork construction in pre-Columbian Amazonia', *PNAS*, 22 July 2014, Vol. 111, No. 29, pp. 10497-502; and 'Ancient Earthmovers of the Amazon', *Science*, Vol. 321, 29 August 2008, p.1148 ff; and Denise Schaan, et al, 'New radiometric dates (2000–700 BP) for pre-Columbian earthworks in western Amazonia, Brazil, *Journal of Field Archaeology*, 2012, Vol. 37, No. 2, p. 132ff; and Anjos et al, 'A New Diagnostic Horizon in WRB for Anthropic Topsoils in Amazonian Dark Earths (South America)', The 20th World Congress of Soil Science, 8-13 June 2014, Jeju, Korea; Michael Heckenberger and Eduardo Goes Neves, 'Amazonian Archaeology', *The Annual Review of Antiquity*, 2009, 38, pp. 251-66; and Heckenberger et al, 'Pre-Columbian Urbanism, Anthropogenic Landscapes, and the Future of the Amazon', *Science*, Vol. 321, 29 August 2008, p. 1214ff.
26. Garcilaso de La Vega, *The Royal Commentaries*, op. cit., pp. 132-3.
27. Ibid., p. 384.

Chapter 18

1. Mircea Eliade, *The Myth of the Eternal Return*, Princeton University Press, p. 16.
2. Micrea Eliade, *The Sacred and the Profane: The Nature of Religion*, Harcourt Inc., New York, 1987, p. 44.
3. Lewis Ginzberg (Ed.), *The Legends of the Jews*, Jewish Publication Society of America, Philadelphia, 1988, Vol. I, p. 12.
4. Cited in Micrea Eliade, *The Sacred and the Profane*, op. cit., p. 44.
5. Giorgio de Santillana and Hertha von Dechend, *Hamlet's Mill: An Essay Investigating the Origins of Human Knowledge and its Transmission through Myth*, Nonpareil Books, 1977, reprinted 1999, p. 57.
6. *New Larousse Encyclopedia of Mythology*, Paul Hamlyn, London, 1989, p. 91.
7. Kenneth McCleish, *Myth*, Bloomsbury, London, 1996, p. 684.
8. Thor Heyerdahl, *Easter Island: The Mystery Solved*, Souvenir Press, London, p. 77; Thor Heyerdahl, *The Kon-Tiki Expedition*, Unwin Paperbacks, London, 1982, pp. 140, 142; Father Sebastian Englert, *Island at the Center of the World*, Robert Hale and Company, London, 1972, p. 30; Francis Maziere, *Mysteries of Easter Island*, Tower Publications, New York, 1968, p. 16.
9. William Sullivan, *The Secret of the Incas*, Crown, New York, 1996, p. 119.
10. Thor Heyerdahl, *The Kon-Tiki Expedition*, op. cit., p.141.
11. Reported by David Hatcher Childress in *Lost Cities of Ancient Lemuria and the Pacific*, Adventures Unlimited Press 1988, p. 313.
12. Reported by Harold Osborne in *Indians of the Andes: Aymaras and Quechuas*, Routledge and Keegan Paul, 1952, p. 64.
13. Thor Heyerdahl, *The Kon-Tiki Expedition*, op. cit., p. 140.
14. Ibid.
15. Ibid., p. 140.
16. See my interview with Heyerdahl in Graham Hancock, *Underworld*, Michael Joseph, London, 2002, pp. 35-6.
17. *Tepe* means hill in the Turkish language and 'the Turkish word *Göbek* means navel or belly,' Klaus Schmidt, *Göbekli Tepe, A Stone-Age Sanctuary in South-Eastern Anatolia*, Ex Oriente, Berlin, 2012, p. 88. See also https://narinnamkn.wordpress.com/2013/12/04/portasar-or-gobekli-tepe-portasar is-the-old-name-of-what-is-now-called-gobekle-tepe-which-is-a-direct-translation-of-armenian-portasar/ andhttp://www.ancient.eu/article/234/ and http://archive.archaeology.org/0811/abstracts/turkey.html.
18. For a more detailed discussion of the archaeological dating of the Moai of Easter Island see Graham Hancock and Santha Faiia, *Heaven's Mirror*, Michael Joseph, London, 1998, pp. 227-8.

19. Father Sebastian Englert, *Island at the Centre of the World: New Light on Easter Island*, Robert Hale & Co., London, 1970, p. 45.
20. Francis Maziere, *Mysteries of Easter Island*, op. cit., p. 40.
21. Ibid., p. 41.
22. *Science News*, Vol. 89, No. 15, 9 April 1966, p. 239.
23. Ibid.
24. Ibid.
25. R. Menzies, Duke University Marine Laboratory and Edward Chin, Marine Laboratory of Texas A&M University, *Cruise Report, Research Vessel Anton Bruun, Cruise 11*, cited here: http://huttoncommentaries.com/article.php?a_id=59 and http://huttoncommentaries.com/article.php?a_id=59#Footnotes.
26. Robert M. Schoch, PhD., *Forgotten Civilization: The Role of Solar Outbursts in Our Past and Future*, Inner Traditions, Rochester, Vermont, 2012, p. 77.
27. Ibid.
28. See Thor Heyerdahl, *Easter Island: The Mystery Solved*, Souvenir Press, London, 1989, pp. 234-5.
29. Pitcairn Island (area 47 square kilometres) and Mangareva (area 15.4 square kilometres) are closer, the former standing at a distance of 2,075 kilometres and the latter at a distance of 2,606 kilometres, but this is still too far for these tiny islands to have contributed to the sedimentation load received by Easter Island.
30. Robert M. Schoch, PhD, *Forgotten Civilization*, op. cit., pp. 78-9.
31. For a discussion see Thor Heyerdahl, *Easter Island: The Mystery Solved*, op. cit., p.8off.
32. Translations of Watu Palindo's name as 'The Entertainer' given on a number of internet sources, are spurious. 'The Wise Man' is the correct translation. See Iksam, 'The Spread of Megalithic Remains in Central Sulawesi as Part of Austronesian Heritage', Presentation at National Museum of Prehistory, Taitung, Taiwan, 12 March 2012.
33. Personal communications during research trip with Iksam Kailey.
34. http://www.megalithic.co.uk/article.php?sid=26496.
35. Iksam, 'The Spread of Megalithic Remains . . .' op. cit.
36. For supporting arguments concerning the connection of this type of art to psychedelic experiences see Graham Hancock, *Supernatural: Meetings with the Ancient Teachers of Mankind*, Century, London, 2005.
37. Tubagus Solihuddin, 'A Drowning Sunda Shelf Model during Last Glacial Maximum and Holocene: A Review', *Indonesian Journal of Geoscience*, Vol. I, No. 2, August 2014, pp. 99-107.
38. Ibid., p. 102.
39. See Danny Hilman Natawidjaja, *Plato Never Lied: Atlantis in Indonesia*, Booknesia, Jakarta, 2013.

40. http://www.faculty.ucr.edu/~legneref/ethnic/mummy.htm.
41. Cited in http://www.faculty.ucr.edu/~legneref/ethnic/mummy.htm.
42. http://www.faculty.ucr.edu/~legneref/ethnic/mummy.htm.
43. http://wakeup-world.com/2014/10/14/hieroglyphics-experts-declare-ancient-egyptian-carvings-in-australia-authentic/.
44. R.T. Rundle Clark, *Myth and Symbol in Ancient Egypt*, Thames & Hudson, London, 1959, p. 222.
45. Ibid., pp. 246-7.
46. Ibid., p. 140.
47. Patrick Boylan, *Thoth: The Hermes of Egypt*, London, 1922, reprint edition by Ares Publishers, Chicago, 1987, p. 155.
48. Personal communication from Danny Natawidjaja PhD.
49. 'Archaeologists slam excavation of Gunung Padang Site', *Jakarta Post*, 24 September 2014: http://www.thejakartapost.com/news/2014/09/24/archae ologists-slam-excavation-gunung-padang-site.html.
50. Ibid.
51. Email from Danny Hilman Natawidjaja to Graham Hancock, 2 October 2014.
52. Ibid.
53. 'Archaeologists slam excavation of Gunung Padang Site', *Jakarta Post*, 24 September 2014: http://www.thejakartapost.com/news/2014/09/24/archae-ologists-slam-excavation-gunung-padang-site.html.
54. Email from Danny Hilman Natawidjaja to Graham Hancock, 14 January 2015.
55. Email from Danny Hilman Natawidjaja to Graham Hancock, 10 March 2015.
56. Danny Hilman Natawidjaja, *Plato Never Lied*, op. cit. and Professor Arysio Nunes dos Santos, *Atlantis: The Lost Continent Finally Found*, Lynwood, WA, USA, 2011.
57. Michael Carrington Westaway, Arthur C. Durband et al, 'Mandubular Evidence supports Homo floresiensis as a distinct species', *PNAS*, Vol. 112, No 7, 17 February 2015, pp. E604-5.
58. M.J. Morwood, R.P. Soejono, et al, 'Archaeology and age of a new hominin from Flores in eastern Indonesia', *Nature* (431) 28 October 2004, pp. 1087-91.
59. M. Aubert, A. Brumm, et al, 'Pleistocene Cave Art from Sulawesi, Indonesia', *Nature* (514), 9 October 2014, pp. 223-77.
60. Josephine C.A. Joordens, Francisco d'Errico et al, 'Homo erectus at Trinil on Java used shells for tool production and engraving', *Nature* (518), 12 February 2015, pp. 228-31.
61. Phil Grabsky, *The Lost Temple of Java*, Orion, London, 1999, p. 16.

62. Luis Gómez and Hiram W. Woodward Jr., *Barabudur: History and Significance of a Buddhist Monument*, Berkeley Buddhist Studies Series, 1981, p. 21.
63. Phil Grabsky, *The Lost Temple of Java*, op. cit., p. 17.
64. Jan J. Boeles, *The Secret of Borobudur*, J.J.B Press, Bangkok, 1985, p. 1 and XIX.
65. Caesar Voute, Mark Long, Fitra Jaya Burnama, *Borobudur: Pyramid of the Cosmic Buddha*, D.K. Printworld Ltd., Delhi, 2008, p. 198.
66. Giorgio de Santillana and Hertha von Dechend, *Hamlet's Mill: An Essay Investigating the Origins of Human Knowledge and its Transmission through Myth*, Nonpareil Books, 1977, reprinted 1999, p. 132.
67. G.R.S. Mead, *Thrice Greatest Hermes: Studies in Hellenistic Theosophy and Gnosis*, Samuel Weiser Inc., York Beach, Maine, 1992 (Reprint Edition in One Volume), *Book II: A Translation of the Extant Sermons and Fragments of the Trismegistic Literature*, p. 55.
68. Ibid.
69. Ibid.
70. Ibid.
71. Ibid.
72. Ibid., *Book III: Excerpts and Fragments*, p. 60.
73. Ibid., p. 61. Mead translates this passage as follows: 'O holy books, who have been made by my immortal hands, by incorruption's magic spells free from decay throughout eternity remain and incorrupt from time! Become unseeable, unfindable, for everyone whose foot shall tread the plains of this our land, until old Heaven shall bring forth meet instruments for you . . .' I have chosen, here, to use the same passage from the Sir Walter Scott translation – Sir Walter Scott (Ed. and Trans.), *Hermetica: The Ancient Greek and Latin Writings which contain Religious or Philosophic Teachings attributed to Hermes Trismegistus*, Shamhala, Boston, 1993, p. 461.
74. Ibid., p. 461, footnote 4.

Chapter 19

1. Plato, *Timaeus and Critias*, Penguin Books, London, 1977, *Critias*, p. 145.
2. Sir Walter Scott (Trans. and Ed.) *Hermetica*, Shambhala, Boston, 1993, p. 345.
3. Delia Goetz and Sylvanus G. Morley, Eds., from the translation of Adrian Recinos, *Popol Vuh: The Sacred Book of the Ancient Quiche Maya*, University of Oklahoma Press, 1991, p. 168.
4. Ibid., p. 169.
5. Ibid.

6. Ibid., p. 90.
7. Ibid., p. 93.
8. Ibid., p. 178.
9. Ibid., p. 155.
10. Gerald P. Verbrugghe and John M. Wickersham (Eds.), *Berossos and Manetho*, University of Michigan Press, 1999, p. 44.
11. Delia Goetz and Sylvanus G. Morley, Eds., *Popol Vuh*, op. cit., p. 156.
12. Ibid., p. 78, note 3.
13. R.T. Rundle Clark, *The Origin of the Phoenix*, op. cit., p. 1; Gerald Massey, *The Natural Genesis*, Vol. 2, Black Classic Press, Baltimore, 1998 (Reprint Edition) p. 340.
14. *Archaeoastronomy: The Journal of the Center for Archaeoastronomy*, Vol. VIII, Nos. 1-4, January-December 1985, p. 99.
15. See, for example, Gerrit L. Verschuur, *Impact: The Threat of Comets and Asteroids*, Oxford University Press, New York and Oxford, 1996, p. 55. See also Duncan Steel, *Rogue Asteroids and Doomsday Comets*, John Wiley and Sons, New York, 1995, p. 15ff.
16. Quoted in Julie Cohen, 'Nanodiamonds Are Forever: A UCSB professor's research examines 13,000-year-old nanodiamonds from multiple locations across three continents', *The Current*, UC Santa Barbara, 28 August 2014. See http://www.news.ucsb.edu/2014/014368/nanodiamonds-are-forever.
17. Personal correspondence with Allen West. Email from West to Hancock dated 19 December 2014.
18. Ibid., email from Hancock to West dated 8 January 2015.
19. Ibid., email from West to Hancock dated 8 January 2015.
20. Victor Clube and Bill Napier, *The Cosmic Winter*, Basil Blackwell, London, 1990, p. 12.
21. Ibid., pp. 12-13.
22. Ibid.
23. W.M. Napier, 'Palaeolithic Extinctions and the Taurid Complex', *Monthly Notices of the Royal Astronomical Society*, Vol. 405, Issue 3, 1 July 2010 pp. 1901-6. The complete paper can be read online here: http://mnras.oxfordjournals.org/content/405/3/1901.full.pdf+html?sid=19fd6cae-61a0-45bd-827b-9f4eb877fd39, and downloaded as a pdf here: http://arxiv.org/pdf/1003.0744.pdf. Victor Clube and Bill Napier, *The Cosmic Winter*, op. cit., pp. 150-3. See also Gerrit L. Verschuur, *Impact*, op. cit., p. 136.
24. See W.M. Napier, 'Palaeolithic Extinctions and the Taurid Complex', op. cit. See also William C. Mahaney, David Krinsley, Volli Kalm, 'Evidence for a Cosmogenic Origin of Fired Glaciofluvial Beds in the Northwestern Andes: Correlation with Experimentally Heated Quartz and Feldspar', *Sedimentary Geology* 231 (2010), pp. 31-40.
25. For the high probability that both the beginning and the end of the Younger

Dryas were caused by impacts of different fragments from the same giant comet see Fred Hoyle and Chandra Wickramsinghe, *Life on Mars? The Case for a Cosmic Heritage*, Clinical Press Ltd., Bristol, 1997, pp. 176-7. See also Gerrit Verschuur, *Impact*, op. cit., p. 139.

26. Victor Clube and Bill Napier, *The Cosmic Winter*, op. cit., pp. 244, 275-7. See also Duncan Steel, *Rogue Asteroids and Doomsday Comets*, op. cit., pp. 132-3.
27. Victor Clube and Bill Napier, *The Cosmic Winter*, op. cit., p. 153.
28. Ibid., p. 147.
29. Ibid., pp. 150-1.
30. Ibid., pp. 149-50.
31. Ibid., p. 149.
32. Jacqueline Mitton, *Penguin Dictionary of Astronomy*, Penguin Books, London, 1993, pp. 84-5; Duncan Steel, *Rogue Asteroids and Doomsday Comets*, John Wiley and Sons, 1995, p. 133.
33. Victor Clube and Bill Napier, *The Cosmic Serpent*, Faber and Faber, London, 1982, p. 151; Bailey, Clube, Napier, *The Origin of Comets*, Butterworth-Heinemann Ltd., 1990, p. 398; Clube and Napier, *The Cosmic Winter*, op. cit., p. 150.
34. Sir Fred Hoyle, *Lifecloud: Origin of the Universe*, Dent, 1978, pp. 32-3.
35. Emilio Spedicato, *Apollo Objects, Atlantis and other Tales*, Università degli studi di Bergamo, 1997, p. 12.
36. Ibid., pp. 12-13.

Index